THE CHURCH UNDER THE CROSS

THE HISTORICAL SERIES OF THE REFORMED CHURCH IN AMERICA
NO. 67
Missionary Memoir Series

THE CHURCH UNDER THE CROSS

Mission in Asia in Times of Turmoil

A Missionary Memoir: Volume One

Wendell P. Karsen

WILLIAM B. EERDMANS PUBLISHING COMPANY
Grand Rapids, Michigan / Cambridge, U.K.

Wm. B. Eerdmans Publishing Co.
2140 Oak Industrial Drive S.E., Grand Rapids, Michigan 49503 /
P.O. Box 163, Cambridge CB3 9PU U.K.
www.eerdmans.com

Printed in the United States of America

Library of Congress Cataloging-in-Publication Data

Karsen, Wendell P., 1936-
  The church under the Cross : mission in Asia in times of turmoil : a
missionary memoir / Wendell P. Karsen.
     p. cm. -- (The historical series of the Reformed Church in America ; no.
67-)
  Includes bibliographical references and index.
  ISBN 978-0-8028-6614-1 (pbk. : alk. paper) 1. Karsen, Wendell P., 1936- 2.
Missionaries--Taiwan--Biography. 3. Missionaries--China--Hong Kong--
Biography. 4. Missionaries--United States--Biography. I. Title.
  BV3431.2.K27A3 2010
  266'.02373051249--dc22
  [B]
                                    2010015136

*This book is dedicated
to the memory
of Joyce Hughes Karsen,
my loving and gifted mate
for twenty-nine years,
and to my wife,
Renske Greve Karsen,
who at the darkest hour in my journey
came into my life like a ray of sunshine
and has been my treasured companion
and colleague in life and in mission ever since.*

The Historical Series of the Reformed Church in America

The series was inaugurated in 1968 by the General Synod of the Reformed Church in America acting through the Commission on History to communicate the church's heritage and collective memory and to reflect on our identity and mission, encouraging historical scholarship which informs both church and academy.

The publication of a memoir creates a readily available primary source. It is important to let the voice of this source speak with all of its conviction, passion, and understanding of the events, dynamics, and the people of its time.

www.rca.org/series

General Editor
    Rev. Donald J. Bruggink, Ph.D., D.D.
    Western Theological Seminary
    Van Raalte Institute, Hope College

Associate Editor
    George Brown, Jr., Ph.D.
    Western Theological Seminary

Copy Editor
    Laurie Baron

Production Editor
    Russell L. Gasero

Commission on History
    Douglas Carlson, Ph.D., Northwestern College, Orange City, Iowa
    Mary L. Kansfield, M.A., East Stroudsburg, Pennsylvania
    Hartmut Kramer-Mills, M.Div., Dr.Theol., New Brunswick, New Jersey
    Jeffery Tyler, Ph.D., Hope College, Holland, Michigan
    Audrey Vermilyea, Bloomington, Minnesota
    Lori Witt, Ph.D., Central College, Pella, Iowa

Contents

Illustrations

All photographs are by or of the author, with the exception of the following:

Foreword

Missionaries never work in a vacuum. Sometimes, especially among "primitive" tribes, it is the culture itself that constitutes the most powerful force with which the missionary must deal. At other times, commercial interests may find the message of the missionaries "inconvenient," indeed antithetical to their interests. In the twentieth century it has perhaps been most often that governments, in whatever form, hold the ultimate secular power.

In all of these cases, the missionary faces the choice of compromise, with attendant distortion of the gospel, or confrontation, with the possibility of rejection and ejection. Where the powers that be are tolerant of Christian evangelization, missionaries often see their primary duty to be that of evangelization, preaching the gospel, and letting such needed transformation of societal structures rest in the hands of the converts. Even where injustice and exploitation were rampant, many missionaries saw their essential task as that of conversion. In many cases, meeting the needs of the sick and education also became means of ministry. However, confrontation with societal structures of injustice and exploitation, whether culturally embedded, commercial, or governmental, were all too infrequent.

An exception to this all too frequent omission was the ministry of Wendell Karsen. His memoirs are an exciting story of confrontation with injustice and oppression, governmental in Taiwan and commercial in Hong Kong.

All of this is not to say that Karsen neglected evangelization. The many who found new life in Christ as the result of his witness are evidence of his faithfulness. However, along with this witness to new life in Christ was also his keen sense of the need for righteousness in the political and moral order. Karsen's fearlessness and dogged determination in seeking liberation for the oppressed stood him in good stead in his struggle to put gospel precepts into action.

Karsen's telling, in this volume, of the struggle during his ministry in Taiwan and Hong Kong makes compelling reading.

Donald J. Bruggink
General Editor
Historical Series of the
Reformed Church in America

Preface

This work has been six years in the making. It began with an invitation in September 2003 by the Taiwan Foundation for Democracy to participate in a December conference on human rights and to receive an award for my involvement in the democracy and human rights struggle of the Taiwanese people during my missionary days there in the early 1970s. In preparation for this conference, I was asked to write a memoir of my experiences during what had become known as the "White Terror" period in Taiwan's history. A number of people who read that memoir encouraged me to write about my subsequent experiences in Hong Kong, China, and Indonesia as well. It happened that I was called to minister in those places at critical times in their histories—times of turmoil that proved to be times of testing for the churches there. Thus the common thread that runs throughout the book—the church under the cross. Although this memoir includes my story, it focuses as well on the wider church I served as my colleagues and the Christians for whom they were responsible struggled to come to terms with the sometimes terrible challenges they faced.

My goal in setting down my experiences, observations, and conclusions was to produce an account that was informative, interesting, and inspirational. Even today, I find that many people do not know much about many of the events recorded in this work. My hope is that this account will help fill those gaps. I also hope that readers will not fall asleep while plodding through the abundant pages of these two volumes, but will find them interesting, stimulating, and at times even humorous. My further hope is that readers will be as inspired as I was when I encountered the courageous Christians described in these pages as they faithfully practiced their faith and prophetically challenged "the powers."

No work is ever the result of one person's efforts. I am indebted to many friends and colleagues, without whom this account would never have seen the light of day. The general editor of the Reformed Church in America's Historical Series, Donald Bruggink, proved to be a wise counselor and a great source of encouragement. The cheerful and careful copy editor, Laurie Baron, spent many days pouring over the manuscript and making it better. The RCA's archivist, Russell Gasero, diligently formatted the rough manuscript into a polished printable document. Willem Mineur, at Eerdmans Publishing Company, gave invaluable assistance in cover design and in the oversight of the publication process.

Additional thanks go to overseas colleagues Lim Chhiong-hwa, Tso Man-king, Richard Daulay, and I. Wayan Mastra, who read the parts of the manuscript that pertain to their respective countries and offered invaluable corrections and comments. U.S. colleagues Charles Van Engen, Eugene Heideman, Roger Greenway, George Hunsberger, Charles Weber, Daniel Bays, and Kurt Selles were kind enough to read and comment on the entire manuscript. Long-time friend and supporter, Patrick Chen, provided a generous grant to the RCA Commission on History to make the publication of this work financially feasible. And finally, my wife Renske was a constant source of encouragement and support.

I am also indebted to the Reformed Church in America for giving me the opportunity to serve overseas as a cross-cultural missionary for so many years. Asian secretaries Glenn Bruggers, Elaine Tanis, Ken Zorgdragger, and Bruce Menning were invariably supportive and encouraging during the vicissitudes of missionary life and work. I also thank the forty-two RCA congregations that faithfully prayed for and financially supported our ministry over the years. Ultimate thanks go, of course, to God Almighty, whose grace, patience, challenge, forgiveness, and strength made possible whatever may have been accomplished.

Wendell P. Karsen
Holland, Michigan
December 2009

Missionary in the Making

It was the year 2000, a year that marked the end of a millennium and the end of a missionary career in Asia that had begun more than three decades earlier. My wife, Renske, and I were flying from Indonesia to New York City, where we would be retired at a meeting of the General Synod of the Reformed Church in America. As our plane touched down at JFK Airport, my thoughts went back to the day in December 1969 when, with three small children in tow, my then wife Joyce and I had taken off from that very same airport for a long journey to the unknown. We were headed half way around the world to Asia, a rather mysterious region that we had only heard about through missionary tales and "seen" through books, photos, and maps. Our specific destination was the island of Taiwan, with its sixteen million people, whom we had been called to serve and with whom we hoped to share the good news of the Christian faith.

Roots

The story had begun in Chicago, Illinois, where I was born in 1936. From childhood, my parents, Siebert and Margaret Karen, encouraged me to think about using my life in Christ's service and modeled that

The Karsen family in 1946, l-r: Margaret, Nancy, Wendell and Siebert

by the way they lived. They sent us to the Christian Reformed Church-sponsored Timothy Christian Grammar School and Chicago Christian High School. They often took my sister, Nancy, and me with them when they sang at the Christian Reformed Church's Helping Hand Mission, or when they helped lead services at the Pacific Garden Mission, on Chicago's "skid row." One Sunday afternoon a month, we accompanied them to a local radio studio where they participated in an evangelistic outreach broadcast to the area. For a number of years, my mother worked at the Christian Reformed Church's Chicago Jewish mission, the Nathanael Institute. During the summer, I sometimes accompanied her there on the streetcar and spent a half day among the Jewish ladies who came for Bible study and fellowship. My parents also sang for periodic outreach programs there in the evening, and my sister and I accompanied them and mixed with the Jewish families that came. Through these experiences, I was made aware at an early age of the need to reach out to others with the good news and to mix happily with people who were unlike me.

My parents also helped found the Missions Committee of the First Christian Reformed Church of Cicero. As a result, we had many missionary guests in our home—Bena Kok from Nigeria, John and Clarence Van Ens from Ceylon, Rolf Veenstra from Nigeria, Everett and Rose Van Reeken from China, and others. My sister and I used to listen wide eyed to the stories they had to tell of faraway lands with strange and wonderful customs, animals, events, and scenery; lands that were filled with people who had never heard the Christian gospel. Our parents also encouraged us to read children's books that were replete with missionary tales and accounts of missionary sacrifice. As a result, there were some early stirrings deep within me. Maybe I would like to become a missionary some day.

My more pious introduction to the notion of an eventual missionary career was augmented by a radio program that had kids' ears glued to their radios during the 1940s. The program was called "Terry and the Pirates," and the scene for the daily dramas was Hong Kong—a place that conjured up mental images of exotic smells, mysterious customs, fantastic scenes, exciting adventures, and Chinese people who sounded very strange to me. My name, Wendell, means "wanderer" or "adventurer." True to that name, I could see myself going off to some fantastic place like Hong Kong and having an adventure or two while serving the Lord.[1] At any rate, as I began to develop into a teenager, my interest in cross-cultural mission began to develop as well.

Trauma

My life changed suddenly in September of 1954 after my first day of classes at Wheaton College in Wheaton, Illinois. I was walking the mile back to my home alone in the dark, having just attended a Big Brother/Big Sister party, when disaster struck. The city of Wheaton had been installing a new water system. Barricades blocked off the street where I was walking, but not the sidewalks, which were very dark. Suddenly, I stepped off the edge of an unseen fifteen-foot ditch, my leg snapping like a toothpick as I hit a concrete culvert at the bottom. Screaming with pain, I could not move. I cried out to God for help, and he heard me.

At that moment, my best friend, Scott Oury, drove up to that very intersection and stopped for the stop sign. He heard my cries, got out of his car, cautiously worked his way through the darkness, lay down on the street, and peered over the edge of the ditch. Looking up out of

[1] I have always believed that any call to Christian service is a mixed bag. There are the more pious elements of Christian commitment, a concern for people in need, and those who have never heard the gospel, along with a deep desire to do "my utmost for his highest," as Oswald Chambers was wont to say. However, a sense of curiosity, a desire to explore, a yen for adventure, an ambition to do something beyond the ordinary, a willingness to rise to a challenge, and a keen sense of humor—all these are also used by God in the mix that is referred to as a "missionary call." From Paul to Livingston to Judson to the missionaries of the twenty-first century, in my view, those who have been most successful in crossing cultures and most effective in communicating the Christian faith fall somewhere between those missionaries who used to sit around our kitchen table and "Terry and the Pirates."

that black hole, I recognized his face and called out his name. Shocked, he lowered himself over the side and dropped down beside me. Others came as well and ran to call the fire department.

After an agonizing delay, the fire department finally arrived. It took them some time to figure out how to extract me from that deep hole, but they finally got me out and into an ambulance. Later, the doctor told me that had I stayed down in that hole for a few more hours, I would have died of shock. However, God had other plans for me.

I was in for a long ordeal. I underwent two surgeries and lost thirty pounds during my month-long stay in the hospital. A lot of prayers were said on my behalf, prayers that helped carry me through the long months of recovery until I could finally get back to college at the beginning of the second semester.

Meanwhile, I had taken a keen interest in all the medical procedures that were being performed, and in the life and routine of the hospital and its nurses and doctors. In fact, my sister, Nancy, was also training to be a nurse. Without paying too much attention to my native gifts or to what was needed to get high grades in such esoteric subjects as quantitative analysis, I decided then and there that I wanted to be a medical doctor—a missionary doctor, somewhat akin to Albert Schweitzer.

Discovery

My experience as a student at Wheaton College intensified my interest in missionary service. At Wheaton, we interacted with many cross-cultural missionaries who visited the campus, held up the high calling of missionary service, and made us more aware of the pressing needs of the world. It was also during those days that Wheaton grads Jim Elliot, Nate Saint, and Ed McCully, along with two other missionaries, were martyred by the Auca Indians in Ecuador. This event in 1956 had a tremendous impact on our campus and further stirred interest in overseas service, including my interest. A huge board on a prominent wall of the main college building listed hundreds of Wheaton graduates who had "followed the call" and served as Christian missionaries all over the world.[2]

It took four years of persistence for God (and the Science Department) to convince me that while I might be gifted for missionary service, I was not going to be another Albert Schweitzer. I did well

---

[2]   My name, my first wife Joyce's name, and my wife Renske's name are now, of course, also listed on that board.

The Gospel-aires l-r: Emery Cummins, Wendell Karsen, John Herzog, Paul Groen, Russ Bishop, Jim Ferris

enough academically and ended up with a Bachelor of Science degree, but I did not excel in science and so could not think about competing for admission to medical school. Undaunted, I applied to Purdue University and was accepted into a master's program in zoology, which could then be used as a back door into medical school.

However, just at that point, my life took another radical turn. While at Wheaton, I had participated in a number of Christian service activities, including singing with the college quartet. Having traveled to Europe on a seven-week intensive tour with a Wheaton Academy Concert Choir some years earlier, my quartet buddies and I came up with the idea of going on a European evangelistic mission during the summer following our graduation. Although we represented the college, we were responsible for our own itinerary and funds to cover the costs. A graduate student who was going into the ministry, and who played a mean trombone, joined us, as did our pianist, so we were six in all, and we named ourselves the Gospel-Aires.[3] The idea was to offer our services to local pastors in smaller towns in an evangelistic outreach to young people.

As secretary of the group, I was responsible for arranging engagements, managing the publicity, and dealing with the finances— the nitty gritty of mission. We ended up holding ninety meetings in seventy days in Northern Ireland, England, Scotland, France, Belgium, and Germany. We had a number of first-class wrestlers in the group who would put on exhibitions in a pastor's front yard as a means of attracting young people and then invite them to the evening meetings. We also did house-to-house calling, beach evangelism, and other activities to encourage people to attend. I began to discover that I had gifts for this kind of thing—working with young people, sharing the

---

[3] Paul Groen (bass), Russ Bishop (baritone), Jim Ferris (first tenor), myself (second tenor), Emery Cummins (pianist) and John Hertzog (evangelist).

gospel, leading singing, managing our engagements and logistics, etc. What a training ground for cross-cultural mission the summer was proving to be!

By the end of the summer, I was asking myself whether I should be considering seminary rather than medical school. The experiences of the summer had opened my eyes to new possibilities, but were these inner inklings my own, or was this the nudging of God? I decided to follow Gideon's example. I told God that I would postpone my dream of becoming a medical missionary, try theological studies for a year, and then see where things stood.

Destiny

When we returned to the States, the first thing I did was apply to the Wheaton Graduate School of Theology for a one-year preseminary program. As soon as I was accepted, I notified Purdue that I had changed my mind and wasn't coming to study zoology after all. It was while registering for the graduate school that I met the young lady I would eventually marry—Joyce Hughes.[4] As the year progressed, I became more and more convinced that my gifts and interests were pointing me in the direction of seminary. I became even more convinced that Joyce and I were meant for each other and that we would do well in ministry together. Fortunately for me, she eventually came to the same conclusion.

Part of what led us to that conclusion was our involvement together in weekend missions to African American families in the tenements and projects of Chicago's south side. As we taught Sunday school and called on families in their homes, we were getting a taste of what it meant to be cross-cultural missionaries, and it felt right. We were engaged in May of 1959 and married in June of 1960. During that time, we endured three long stints apart. While I began my seminary training at Fuller Theological Seminary in Pasadena, California, in September 1959, Joyce stayed on in Wheaton to finish up her master's degree in New Testament Studies. I managed three holiday dashes back to Wheaton to be with her, but most of our courtship was done by mail. The phone was too expensive!

---

[4]   For me, falling in love with Joyce was like falling off a cliff. For her, it was a process. She was from Greenville, South Carolina, had graduated from Bryan College in Dayton, Tennessee, and had just spent the summer at an Inter-Varsity Mission Camp in Michigan. She was registering for a master of theology course at the graduate school and was thinking of devoting her life to overseas mission service as well.

Perspective

I received a solid seminary education from a Reformed perspective at Fuller. My interest in cross-cultural mission was deepened through courses in world mission and evangelism and through exposure to a number of visiting missionaries who addressed us in chapel and talked with us in class. The strong theological foundation I received there, together with an exposure to the seminary's fervent evangelical outlook and its ecumenical make up, was to stand me in good stead throughout my years of ministry and mission. Joyce and I were married after my first year and shared life in Pasadena during my final two years at Fuller.

Fuller did nothing to dampen our enthusiasm for cross-cultural mission, but it did change our perspective about it. Dr. Clarence Roddy was my professor of practical theology. One day he startled our class by saying, "If any of you is thinking about being a foreign missionary, you had better make sure you have the goods to reach your own people in your own culture first." Joyce and I talked and prayed about this at length and decided that he was right. I still think he is right. We decided to put overseas mission on hold while I pursued graduate studies and practiced youth work, preaching, pastoral care, teaching, evangelism, counseling, administration, and the 101 other things that pastors did in those days before the advent of the church staff concept.

Transition

At that time, we were still members of the Christian Reformed Church. While attending Fuller, I had served the First Christian Reformed Church of Los Angeles as its Sunday school superintendent and preached in Christian Reformed churches in the Los Angeles area. During my final semester at Fuller, I applied to the Master of Theology program at Calvin Theological Seminary in Grand Rapids, Michigan, in preparation for ordination into ministry in the Christian Reformed Church. However, since I had attended a nondenominational seminary, Calvin asked me to repeat two and a half years of seminary work before I could even be considered for graduate studies. Following that, I would need to be approved by six committees and judicatories and then be granted a special dispensation from the synod before I could be ordained. As a result, I was confronted with another major fork in the road of my life.

I had been raised in the Christian Reformed Church, but my mother's family had all been members of the Reformed Church in America (RCA). During my boyhood, I had spent many a Sunday worshiping in my relatives' church, Westside Reformed in Cicero, attending vacation Bible school, and participating in other activities there. Although my mother had joined my father's church when they were married, she had never lost her enthusiasm for the Reformed Church and used to regale us with stories of her happy experiences in Christian Endeavor and in the Hasting Street congregation to which she belonged. Since attending seminary, I had also become more aware of the differences between the two denominations in mind-set, social outlook, ecumenical perspective, mission philosophy, and theological nuance.

After much thought, consultation, and prayer, Joyce and I decided that I should explore the possibility of being ordained into the ministry in the Reformed Church in America. The response to my initial inquiry to Western Theological Seminary in Holland, Michigan, was most encouraging. I would be welcome to begin a Master of Theology program immediately and to take a few additional courses that would introduce me to the denomination. The only other requirement would be to pass a series of examinations designed for those who had pursued their theological education in a non-RCA seminary. Upon passing those exams, I would be granted a "Professorial Certificate," which would qualify me for licensure by the Classis of Holland, and for ordination upon receiving a call from an RCA congregation. Meanwhile, we rejoiced in the arrival of our first child, Stephen John, born June 23, 1962, while we were at Fuller.

Ordination

The decision was not hard to make, and the fall of 1962 found us in Holland. There, I met Western's missiologist, the Reverend Dr. John Piet, who had been a missionary in India for many years. He sparked my interest in the Reformed Church's mission history and in its current outreach. I was amazed to learn that such a small denomination had had such a large impact on the world mission stage for almost two hundred years. I also learned that, at that point, the RCA still had some 150 cross-cultural missionaries in eleven countries who worked with ecumenical partners to create or support indigenous churches. I began to get the feeling that I had not come into the Reformed Church by accident. Here was a denomination that had mission close to its heart and whose mission philosophy and policies I strongly agreed with.

As I was working my way through courses and exams that year, the Reverend Dr. Henry Bast, professor of preaching, paid us a visit one snowy night in December. He had been called to return to a church that he had served before, the Bethany Reformed Church in Grand Rapids, Michigan, and he invited me to become his assistant there. This was a wonderful opportunity for me, since I was a comparative unknown in the denomination and was somewhat apprehensive that most of the churches looking for seminary graduates that year would have already found them. Bethany was a large city church that would provide me with ample experience in all aspects of the ministry, particularly since Dr. Bast, who was the Reformed Church's radio minister, would go on frequent speaking trips and leave me in charge. In addition, Bethany was known to be a mission-minded church. Our predecessor, the Reverend Dr. Gordon Van Oostenberg, had inspired the church to take its share of responsibility for the world's needs through mission projects, mission conferences, and the support of a number of RCA cross-cultural missionaries.

I gladly accepted the call to Bethany and began my ministry there in January 1963 on a part-time basis until I could finish my course work and exams at the seminary in May. I was then examined and licensed by the Holland Classis and ordained and installed as Bethany's full-time assistant pastor on July 13 of that year. That was a rewarding and inspiring day in my life. It was rewarding in that my call to the ministry had been confirmed and my gifts for the ministry had been affirmed. It was inspiring in that I was being afforded an opportunity to minister to people's needs and to hone the skills that I hoped to use someday among another people in another culture.

Although most of my time was spent ministering to young people, part of my responsibility was to nurture the mission vision of the church. This meant helping plan and promote mission conferences, organize mission projects for the vacation Bible school and the Sunday school, and welcome a steady stream of missionary speakers to the church. It was at Bethany that we began to forge close relationships with veteran missionaries like Sam and Lucy Noordhoff (Taiwan), Harvey and Margaret Doorenbos (Ethiopia), and Bob and Morrie Swart (Sudan). I was also in charge of neighborhood evangelism. During our time at Bethany, our second son, Philip Siebert, was born on June 9, 1965.

Ministry

In the fall of 1965, I received a call from the Lakeland Reformed Church in Vicksburg, Michigan. I accepted the call because the congregation had a strong outreach in the community, because it contained a mix of folks from different denominations, and because it

Lakeland Reformed
Church mission
festival display

provided me with an opportunity to try my wings as a solo pastor. While there, I had to find time in a busy schedule of teaching, preaching, youth work, visitation, counseling, and administration to finish my master's thesis on Paul's doctrine of union with Christ. I finally completed it in May 1967 and became a bona fide graduate of an RCA seminary. This process taught me the discipline of academic research. It also helped hone my writing skills. Both of these disciplines would be employed in the years ahead in ways beyond my wildest imagination (particularly since I had never gotten very good grades in English).

While at Lakeland, I stressed a mission-focused vision for the church. We held a week-long mission festival in the fall of each year that featured missionary speakers and that challenged the congregation to increase its contribution to the Reformed Church's mission program. Veteran missionaries like Ted and Harriet Bechtel (Taiwan), Paul and Dorothy Hostetter (Pakistan), Harvey and Lavina Hoekstra (Kenya), and Rowland and Judy Van Es (Taiwan) became our friends. We also had a very intentional "mission at home" outreach to our community, and neighborhood folks continued to commit their lives to Christ and to join our congregation. At the same time, I became increasingly interested in ministering to college-aged young people, an interest that would eventually blossom into full-time ministry abroad. Meanwhile, our third child, Rachel Lynn, was born April 21, 1968, the very Sunday we were celebrating Lakeland's tenth anniversary.

Decision

Throughout my ministry at Lakeland, the urge Joyce and I felt to get involved in the wider mission of the church in another part of the world had grown stronger. Bob and Morrie Swart, Reformed Church missionaries to Ethiopia, were the featured speakers for our mission conference in the fall of 1968. After their inspiring presentations, they spent the night at our place, where we talked further about mission in their part of the world, and about what it was like to serve as cross-cultural missionaries. We also shared our long interest in missionary service. They challenged us to apply to the RCA's Board of World Mission without further delay. We prayed together, and Joyce and I made the decision to do so that very night. There was no guarantee that we would be accepted, but we decided that our tutorial in ministry had been completed and that we should offer our services.

The next question, of course, was when and where? Having spent two summers in Europe with the Wheaton Academy Choir and the college evangelistic team, it seemed to us that Europe would be the best place for us to serve. Nevertheless, we felt that we should offer to go wherever the Reformed Church believed the need to be greatest, but we hoped that "wherever" would be somewhere in Europe. The only stipulation we put on our offer was that we did not want to go anywhere we would have to send our three young children to boarding school. After months of confidential negotiations with the secretary for the Board of World Mission, we were excited to learn that we had been accepted for missionary service and that we should aim at a departure date for missionary orientation training in June of 1969.

Assignment

However, we were surprised when the Reformed Church informed us that the place where our gifts could best be used was in Asia—in Taiwan doing campus ministry work, to be exact. Asia! We hardly knew a thing about Asia. It seemed a mysterious, even foreboding place to us—a place that conjured up my boyhood images of "Terry and the Pirates." As far as we knew, Asian culture was light years away from anything we had ever experienced or even read much about. The food seemed strange; the language seemed impossible; the customs seemed bizarre; the art seemed weird; the religion seemed incredible. And the list went on. However, a call was a call. How many times hadn't I preached that God calls us to do that which is difficult, not that which is comfortable, and that he equips us to do whatever he calls us to do. Now it was time to practice what I had preached. We told the denomination we would go.

On the plus side, our friends Sam and Lucy Noordhoff, Ted and Harriet Bechtel, and Rowland and Judy Van Es were serving in Taiwan, and campus ministry still had a strong appeal for me. We immediately wrote to them, asking a hundred questions about life and service there. We also began to read everything we could lay our hands

The Karsen family in 1969
l-r: Rachel, Joyce, Wendell,
Philip, and Stephen

on about Asia in general, and about China and Taiwan in particular. The world missions secretary supplied answers to our questions about the Presbyterian Church in Taiwan, under whom all RCA missionaries served, and about the practical side of how we would get our family of five over there, where we would live, and what we should take.

Sacrifice

We had, of course, consulted our families along the way. Knowing our keen interest in cross-cultural mission, and considering such service among the highest of callings, they were very supportive. Having been apprised of the unfolding developments, they were not taken by surprise. However, when the decision was firm, they were not without twinges of sadness at the thought of seeing their grandchildren go half way around the world with the prospect of seeing them only once every four years. This was the one thing that weighed heavily on us as well.

Much has been made of missionary sacrifice. Actually, in the end, the only real sacrifice that we made was to be so far away from our families for such long periods of time. But then, to keep even that in perspective, the pioneer missionaries only returned "home" every seven years, and some of them not at all. When we accepted the call, the advent of the jet plane not only made it possible for people to get back more often, especially in cases of emergency, but also enabled parents to come visit, something that would have been unheard of just a few decades before. There would be times, however, when the distance from family would be especially difficult. A beloved aunt dies, and by the time you come "home" on the next furlough, it seems that she has simply disappeared. Or sons or daughters go off to college in what has now for them become a strange culture, and the missionary parents send them off with much trepidation and many earnest prayers. But much of this was still in the distant future for us.

Questions

The remaining, and most difficult, thing left for us to do was to tell the Lakeland congregation. We had not wanted to share our mission service explorations prematurely. Had things not worked out, we would have continued to serve that church happily. We loved the people at Lakeland, and the feeling was mutual. Now it had come time to tell them that we were not only going to leave, but that we were going to Taiwan. I made the announcement at the end of our spring congregational meeting. The people had mixed feelings. They applauded our conviction that we had been called to missionary service, but they regretted the consequences of that decision for them. Following the meeting, some of the ladies who had come to love our kids followed me to my office with tears in their eyes. "How can you take those little children so far away to such a strange world! What will become of them so far apart from their culture, their families, their playmates?"

This was a legitimate lament. What *were* we doing to our little ones? We had thought and prayed about that for a long time. We were making a decision that would change their lives forever. Was it right for us to place their interests in possible jeopardy to follow "our" own calling? Apart from an assurance that God could and would love and keep and nurture them wherever we were in the world, their own response years later would answer these questions decisively. After our fourth child, Andrew, was born and then raised in Hong Kong until the age of seven, we were discussing the need to return to the USA to attend to the special needs of our two oldest children. "But Mom and Dad!" they protested. "How can you return to the States now? Andrew won't have the chance to grow up in Asia like we did!"

Other people wondered aloud why we should go to minister in another country when we were meeting people's needs effectively in our own. That was also a question we had pondered and prayed about for a long time. The more pious answer to that question was that there were far greater needs in third world countries, where only tiny minorities of the population were Christian and where there was a comparative dearth of Christian workers. The more human response to that question

Entrance to the
Missionary Orientation Center

was that "out there" in the cross-cultural trenches lay more challenges, more opportunities, more adventures, more discoveries than one could ever hope to have or make living and working in one's own back yard. The first answer played well. The second raised eyebrows.

Baptism

June arrived and we departed. Having packed a minimum of our earthly possessions for shipment abroad, and having dispensed with most of our household items through an all-day auction, we left with $1,100 with which to finance a new household upon our arrival in Taiwan. Meanwhile, we were headed for the Missionary Orientation Center in Stony Point, New York. This center, with its beautiful grounds not far from the banks of the Hudson River, was an interdenominational missionary training center cooperatively financed, staffed, and operated by the mainline denominations, including the Reformed Church in America. We never dreamed that our five months there would mean being yanked out of the cozy conservative cocoon within which we had been raised, educated, and employed.

In the first place, 1969 was the heyday of the student revolt. Among the one hundred trainees and forty-five children at the center that summer were a large number of student activists who wanted to have an adventure abroad, teaching English or doing some kind of social work, with the church footing the bill. More than a few were in open revolt against the church and its traditions and message. Those of us who were committed to that church, those traditions, and that message were accosted, particularly if we "wore the collar." The students confronted the staff and called for a complete reorganization of the program that had been planned. Participatory egalitarian democracy was to be the essential guiding principle that would dominate the action. Out with lectures! Out with books! Bring on the "T-groups." Challenge anybody in authority. Question everything, including our motives for evangelizing people of other cultures and faiths. For us, this was baptism for mission by fire.

However, what at first appeared to be a travesty turned out to be the best training course for mission among non-Christians in other cultures that we could have imagined. Here, right in front of our faces, was an opportunity to test whether we had what it took to serve people that were unlike us, to explain the faith to those who doubted it, and to demonstrate Christian love to those who derided it. In the end, once the barriers were patiently breached, these fresh-out-of-college self-styled "revolutionaries" turned out to be common human beings with common doubts, hopes, fears, and needs after all.

We older family types breathed a sigh of relief when this crowd shipped out and the remaining four months of our training could be conducted in an atmosphere that had at least some semblance of normalcy to it. However, we also missed the young people. They had taught us a lot about ourselves. They had caused us to re-examine the depth of our faith, to broaden our perspectives on society, and to practice love in a way we had never been challenged to practice it before. And many of them had changed too. They had come to respect us, to be interested in our understanding of the Christian faith, to listen to our perspective on the Christian life, and to admire our motivation for mission. We hoped the seeds that were planted that summer sprouted into shoots of faith once they found themselves abroad "doing mission."

Stretching

There were also more minor adjustments, but difficult ones nevertheless, for us who had grown up in the Christian Reformed Church and been nurtured within the evangelical community. Communion services with guitars and folk hymns seemed strange. Women serving Communion seemed even stranger. Various new perspectives challenged our conservative views on mission, evangelism, the kingdom of God, the church, and other subjects, and raised many questions. How do we respect other cultures while promoting change in them? How do we approach people of other faiths? How do we as foreign missionaries relate to regimes that practice systemic political and economic injustice? How do we, who were raised in a racist society, truly learn to love and accept people whose color and culture are so different from our own? How does the Republican Party, or any other party for that matter, differ from the kingdom of God?

Lectures on the relationship of the gospel to justice issues in the political, economic, social, and ecological realms exposed us to a plethora of thorny problems to which we had previously been underexposed. Cross-cultural exposure ventures at the Union Settlement House and its environs in the slums of East Harlem in New York City confronted us with the realities of how difficult "changing the world" would be on the ground. Linguistic courses forced us to face the difficulties of learning a foreign tongue, which, in our case, would be the formidable Chinese language.

Added to all that was my special training venture in campus ministry, since that was the area in which I was to minister in Taiwan. I was required to survey three campus ministry models on Long Island: one in a more or less traditional college setting, one as a "floater"—a campus minister serving several campuses, and one in a state university setting. My assignment was to absorb and evaluate how campus ministry was being done through these three models and to adapt my findings to the university scene in Taiwan.

The University of New York at Stony Brook was by far the most challenging assignment. UNYSB was known as the Berkeley of the East and was considered to be the eastern hub of student revolt. Among its eight thousand students, my survey revealed that 65 percent identified themselves as Jewish and 30 percent as Roman Catholic. The remaining students ranged from Zen Buddhists to Christian Science adherents. There was no interfaith center, no full-time campus minister, and no department of religion. One of the most popular professors was Thomas Altizer, a leading "death of God" theologian. Over a period of three months, I commuted between the Orientation Center and Long Island several times a week, usually spending at least one night in a particular campus setting. I once spent a whole eye-opening week living in a UNYSB dormitory. I interviewed every representative type on campus—from campus ministers to faculty to staff to students—and attended a broad sampling of campus groups and activities.

One night, I went to a meeting of UNYSB's Students for a Democratic Society (SDS). The purpose of the organization was explained to the 150 students who had gathered by hard-eyed youths with an evangelical fervor. The long-term goal, they said, was to form a coalition of students and workers who would bring down the imperialist ruling class of the country by violent revolution and establish a socialist society whose final form would be a communistic state as outlined by

Marx, Engels, and Lenin. Their program was to be spread on campus via dorm cell groups, book tables, demonstrations, strikes, debates, etc. There was no Sunday school apathy in this crowd. Never mind that most of these privileged young folks had never held a job of any kind, they had the solutions for all of society's ills and woe betide anybody who disagreed with them. I was a bit conspicuous by my age, my dress, and my note taking. Suddenly, one student stood up and demanded to know who I was. My explanation that I was a Christian pastor in training for campus ministry mission work in Taiwan sounded incredible to them. "You are an FBI informant!" they shouted. I demurred, but the meeting broke up in confusion, with people harassing me, and I left wondering if campus ministry in Taiwan was going to be anything like this.

Launch

By the beginning of December, I had submitted my research paper on campus ministry. We had finished our courses, been commissioned by the Reformed Church at its New York headquarters, and packed our bags. Our tutorial was over; now we would begin the real thing—what we had envisioned years before. We said good-bye to a place and to people that we had come to love—the staff, our teachers, and our newly made friends and colleagues. We boarded a plane at the JFK Airport to begin our long journey, first stopping in Greenville, South Carolina, and Chicago, Illinois, to bid tearful farewells to family and friends. Then it was on to Taiwan with a strong sense that we went with God.

Fast Forward

More than thirty years later, I returned to our beloved Mission Orientation Center at Stony Point. It had been renamed the Stony Point Center. Its program was still focused on cross-cultural international issues, but there were no more missionaries in training there. As I walked across the grounds and through the halls that used to ring with laughter, debates, and the sounds of the children of missionaries in the making, the faces of many people with whom we had bonded so quickly in 1969 flashed through my mind. I wondered where they were now, what they had ended up doing overseas, and how they felt about it all. So many things had changed since those days. The whole world had changed. What would it be like to be preparing for cross-cultural mission service today? Would I do it all over again? My answer was yes.

I walked into the Alpha dorm and into the open door of the three rooms that our family of five (along with a semi-legal cat) had

Wendell, Philip, Stephen, Joyce, and Rachel Karsen leaving the Missionary Orientation Center

occupied during our five months there. I opened a center desk drawer, pulled it out, and turned it over. The "Kilroy was here" message that I had penciled where nobody would see it was still there. "The Karsen's Five, Wendell, Joyce, Stephen, Philip, and Rachel, occupied these rooms during their preparation for mission service in Taiwan from June-December 1969." Tears rolled down my face as I recalled the faces of the three little tykes that had geared up with us then for the great unknown, and who were now grown up, some of them with children of their own. And there was the memory of a young Joyce who would be my partner through the many challenges and adventures of fifteen years of overseas service before she would succumb to cancer and leave us too early in life in 1989.

More than three decades later, with two and a half of those decades having been spent in Asia, I knew it had been a good go. God had remained faithful. Mistakes had been made, but much had been accomplished. I left with a good feeling.

PART ONE

The Cross of Fascism:
Mission in Taiwan, 1969-1973

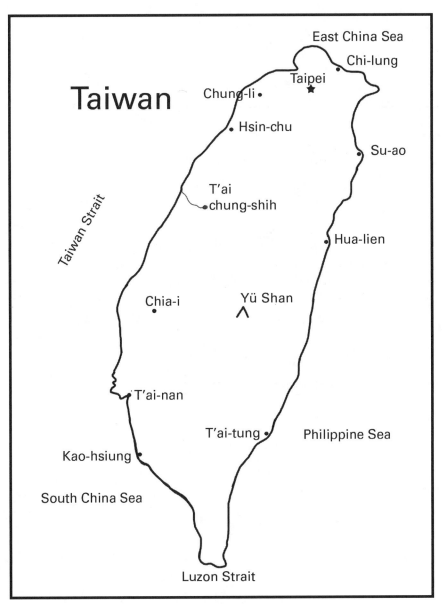

Map of Taiwan drawn by Renske Karsen

CHAPTER 1

Ilha Formosa

Guns and Groceries

It was December 6, 1969. Our plane was slowly descending towards the small Sung-shan Airport on the edge of Taipei, the capital city of Taiwan. As we broke through the clouds, with noses pressed against the windows, we could make out tall mountains to the east and long, lush green fields of rice along the western coast. Steve, at age seven, and Phil, then four, were especially excited—and tired of sitting. Back in America, they had watched a TV adventure program about an exotic place called "Danger Island." When they first learned that we had been assigned to work on an Asian island, they had let out a whoop and told their friends, "We're going to Danger Island!" Now, with visions of tigers and snakes and spear-hurling natives dancing in their heads, despite our dutiful disclaimers, they peered out the widows eagerly awaiting the adventure they were about to begin. And quite an adventure it would turn out to be!

We had been warned not to take any photos out of the plane windows. When we landed, we could see why. We taxied past a long line of vintage World War II Douglas DC3 twin-engine military transports. We also noticed pillboxes with antiaircraft guns poking out of them

Street scene in Taipei, 1969

and soldiers with rifles patrolling the premises. These were reminders that, although there had not been an attack in either direction for twenty years, the Republic of China (on Taiwan) was still technically at war with the People's Republic of China just ninety miles away.

As we emerged from the plane, Lucy Noordhof and other Reformed Church people who had come to greet us waved from behind a chain link fence next to the small terminal. There too were our old friends and fellow church members from Wheaton days, Paul ("PEP") and Ilene Peterson, who were serving in Taiwan as educational missionaries under The Evangelical Alliance Mission (TEAM). How good it felt to see familiar faces in a very strange place!

After customs formalities had been completed and hugs had been exchanged, PEP took me on an hour-long whirlwind orientation tour of downtown Taipei. Meanwhile, Lucy and Ilene took Joyce and the kids to the Carlton Hotel, where we would stay for a week until repairs to the house we were to occupy could be completed. The streets were filled with what seemed like thousands of bicycles, motor bikes, old buses, and taxis, along with some private cars. There were traffic lights and some police, but the rules of the road seemed quite different from those we were accustomed to.

And then there was the stench, particularly powerful in the lobby of the Carlton. A few weeks earlier, Taipei had been walloped by a deadly typhoon that had dumped a ton of water on the place. The rivers and what were then still open sewers had overflowed and flooded parts of the city. The still visible waterline on the walls of the hotel lobby was some three feet above the floor, and the carpets and furniture were still drying out. We would come to learn that typhoons and "benjos" (open sewers) were part of the fabric of life in Taiwan. In fact, our greeters laughingly told us that there was a saying that nobody lived in Taiwan longer than three months without falling into a benjo. I would prove them right when, less than three months later, I would accidentally step into one in my own back yard.

Our next step was to get Stephen situated in Bethany Christian School and Philip in a Chinese kindergarten. After we had procured a Taiwanese home helper to babysit our daughter, Rachel, and registered at the Taipei Language Institute for Taiwanese language study, we "moved in" to our home. I say "moved in" in quotes because besides what we had brought in our suitcases, we had a few loaned mattresses to lay on bedroom floors, a card table and chairs, a hot plate, and a tabletop refrigerator. The next few weeks were taken up with ordering Chinese-style furniture, equipping the kitchen, and procuring supplies. Since we didn't know a word of the language, we were glad we had had some experience in playing Charades. In the shops, we talked with our hands and our bodies and were only occasionally stumped. We also began to explore Taipei and to become acquainted with a few Chinese neighbors who could speak some English. Our RCA colleagues took us to church and assisted with our orientation to our new place and way of life.

Life with our Taiwanese "amah" (home helper) without any language proved intriguing. Again sign language, plus frequent phone calls to Lucy Noordhof for translation, worked most of the time. However, since our amah was new at the job, had never used a telephone, and didn't know how to open a can, things could get interesting. For example, one day we asked her to prepare tomato soup for lunch, assuming that the two cans marked tomato soup would be opened, milk added, and the soup warmed up, ready to be placed on the card table when we returned home from language school. When we sat down, the amah proudly placed bowls of hot water in front of us, each with one whole cooked tomato in the center. Lucy eventually found us a more experienced amah named Lu A-gim, who spoke quite good English, was a great cook, and ended up becoming like a daughter to us and a big sister to our kids.

Ten days after landing in Taipei, we journeyed south to the city of Tainan for the annual RCA missionary Christmas gathering. That trip gave us an impression of the island that was to be our home for the next four years. We were also able to visit the Presbyterian Church in Taiwan's Tainan Theological Seminary and to meet the entire RCA mission family. And family they proved to be. To this day the children still call the adults they encountered in Taiwan "uncle" and "aunt."

RCA "Family" Christmas gathering in Tainan in 1969

We enjoyed a festive weekend with Sam and Lucy Noordhof, Ben and Ruth Dykstra, Jean Walvoord, Bill and Ilene Estell, Bill Burke, Ted and Harriet Bechtel, Rowland and Judy Van Es, Dave and Judy Karduxe, and seventeen children. They took us in like long-lost relatives, and we felt at home immediately with people with whom we would not only serve as colleagues, but who would also become our lifelong friends.

Upon our return from Tainan, we placed an order for furniture with a small furniture shop in Taipei. It took a month for Mr. Chan to build the furniture by hand at his shop and transport it to our home. At last we could get our loaner mattresses off the floor and onto some bedsprings and our clothes from suitcases into drawers. We could also sit in comfortable chairs and eat around a family-sized dining table. However, our appliances, books, toys, records, bedding, an artificial Christmas tree, and a hundred other things were still aboard ship on their way to Taiwan—we *thought*. We had been told that our ship would reach Taiwan some six weeks after we did. It did, but our container wasn't on it. In fact, when RCA officials inquired about it in New York, the moving company couldn't find it.

Our container was finally located a few weeks later in the dark recesses of a New York warehouse and sent on its way. It would not reach us for another two and a half months. So we continued to semi-camp. The amazing thing about our first four months in Taiwan was that they proved to be among the most creative times in the life of our family. We had to make do with the little that we had and the simpler things that we could buy—like string to make "Charlotte's web" throughout the house, or paper bags that mischievous boys turned into cockroach traps. Then there were excursions into the interesting narrow lanes of the neighborhood, allowance spending at the little shack stores a lane away, and "big game" hunting in the empty lots that dotted the vicinity.

One day, for example, Steve and Phil came home proudly bearing a "wild turkey" they had "captured," which actually was somebody's discarded stuffed pheasant. When our real treasure finally arrived in early April, as we unpacked adult toys (stove, refrigerator, and library) and children's toys (clothes, books, and playthings), it was like three Christmases rolled into one.

Presbyterians and Partners

Our early orientation included a trip to the headquarters of the Presbyterian Church in Taiwan (PCT). There we were introduced to the general secretary, the Reverend Dr. C.M. Kao, and to other church officials who welcomed us warmly. Dr. Kao gave me a Taiwanese name—Ka Ui-Tek (meaning "great, good, and virtuous"), a name I have been trying to live up to ever since. We were introduced to the PCT's partner churches—the Presbyterian Church US (Southern), the United Presbyterian Church USA, the Presbyterian Church in Canada, the Presbyterian Church of England, the Church of Scotland, and, of course, our own Reformed Church in America. Fraternal workers from the Christian Reformed, Methodist, and United Church of Christ denominations were related to the PCT as well. In all, there were seventy-six missionary colleagues serving the Presbyterian Church in Taiwan at that time.[1] We were also briefed on the history, mission, and context of the PCT, subjects that we would explore in depth over the next few months.

The Presbyterian Church in Taiwan dated back to 1865, when Dr. James Maxwell, an English Presbyterian medical doctor, began pioneer missionary work in southern Taiwan.[2] He opened a hospital in 1868 and was joined by an English Presbyterian pastor, the Reverend William Campbell, in 1871. By 1873, fourteen mission stations with approximately nine hundred members had been established. Maxwell and Campbell were joined by an English theologian named Thomas

---

[1] RCA colleagues in 1969 were Sam Noordhof, Ben Dykstra, and Jeane Walvoord, who served at MacKay Memorial Hospital in Taipei; Bill Estell, who taught at Yushan Theological College in Hualien; Bill Burke, who taught at a university in Taichung; Ted Bechtel, who ran the Luke Student Center in Kaohsiung; and Roland Van Es and Dave Karduxe, who taught at Tainan Theological Seminary. Although full-time homemakers, Lucy Noordhof, Ruth Dykstra, Ilene Estell, Harriet Bechtel, Judy Van Es, Judy Kardeuxe (and eventually Joyce) also engaged in teaching English, conducting small group ministries, and the like.

[2] Tong, Hollington K., *Christianity in Taiwan: A History* (Taipei: China Post, 1961), 23-39.

Barclay, who established the Tainan Theological College in 1876 and began to train young converts for the ministry. Both boys' and girls' middle schools were also founded in Tainan in 1885 and 1887 respectively. From that point on, the Presbyterians would become the foremost educational body on the island and would raise up a highly educated Christian constituency.[3]

In 1872, a Canadian Presbyterian pastor, the Reverend Dr. George Leslie MacKay, pioneered Christian mission work in northern Taiwan in the town of Tamsui. Reading the account of his work was like reading the book of Acts. MacKay was a holistic missionary who did everything from pulling teeth to preaching the gospel. He learned the language by sitting with herd boys and imitating the sounds they made. By 1880, he had opened twenty chapels, baptized three hundred converts, and established the MacKay Hospital. In 1882, he founded Oxford College and in 1883 he opened a school for girls, both in Tamsui. By 1893, there were sixty chapels with 2,641 members in North Taiwan.[4]

These pioneers and the missionaries that followed them met with a good deal of opposition from the Taiwanese. For example, when MacKay built the first church building in Taipei, there was a big row over its steeple, which towered over the neighborhood. The locals objected to a structure that was taller than their temples. They believed it would disturb their gods and upset the *feng shui* ("spiritual balance") of the community, and they wanted it torn down. MacKay persisted, the gospel gradually took root, and the church grew steadily, both in the north and in the south.

When the island was ceded to Japan in 1895, the Japanese colonial government was quite tolerant of the church and it continued to grow. By 1931, there were 73 chapels, 72 Taiwanese ministers, and 3,167 communicants in the north, while in the south there were even more chapels, with 100 ministers and 7,700 communicants. However, when an aggressive military party later took over the Japanese government, Japanese Christians came under increased pressure while Taiwanese Christians were faced with overt persecution. Nevertheless, the Presbyterian churches more than held their own. After the Nationalist Chinese took over the island in 1945 at the end of World War II, this overt persecution ceased, but it took on new covert forms in subsequent

---

[3]   Lai, David, "The Christian Church in Taiwan: Past, Present and Future" in Karsen, Wendell, private papers (hereafter, pr.p.).

[4]   MacKay's fascinating account of his remarkable ministry in Taiwan is recorded in his book, *From Far Formosa: The Island, its People and Missions* (Toronto: Revell, 1895).

Presbyterian Church
in Taiwan
General Assembly
meeting in Tainan

years. By 1965 (the centennial anniversary of the PCT), there were 1,960 Protestant churches with 350,000 members, and 1,300 Roman Catholic churches with 300,000 members on the island. By then, Christians had established twelve major schools, ten hospitals, many mobile clinics, orphanages, leprosariums, social service centers, and other institutions.[5]

By the time of our arrival in 1969, the Presbyterian Church in Taiwan had 920 congregations with 176,000 members and adherents, by far the largest Christian presence on the island. It was organized into twelve presbyteries that covered the whole island, including the aboriginal areas that had been evangelized during the Japanese era.[6] The southern and northern synods had merged in 1957 to form a general assembly, which met once a year. The church had pioneered in the areas of music, education, and social service. It also operated a church press, two theological seminaries, a Bible school, a theological institute for aborigines, three middle schools, a business college, two hospitals, a nurses' training school, a clinic, and a family counseling center.[7]

Although the Presbyterian Church in Taiwan continued to receive some aid from abroad in the form of funds and personnel, it was completely indiginized and basically self-governing, self-propagating, and self-supporting. It had even sent out ten missionaries of its own to places like Japan, Brazil, Malaysia, and Tahiti. However, it still desired

---

[5] Lai, "Christian Church," in Karsen, pr.p.
[6] Swanson, Allen J., *Taiwan: Mainline versus Independent Church Growth, A Study in Contrasts* (Pasadena: Carey, 1970), 96-97.
[7] *Taiwan Christian Year Book Statistics 1972* (Taipei: Dixon Press), 1973.

a missionary presence from abroad. The missionaries were to assist the church in its specialized ministries and in the development of new approaches to mission and evangelism. They were also to be a cross-fertilizing presence in its midst and to serve as a link with churches and ecumenical bodies abroad.

The evangelistic task remained formidable. Ninety-four percent of the population had not yet experienced the fullness of life in Christ. The vast majority of Taiwan's people still adhered to an eclectic folk religion that mixed together elements of the three traditional Chinese religious streams—Buddhism, Taoism, and local folk beliefs. Underlying these were the basic concepts of Confucian humanism and the veneration of ancestors. The predominant presupposition was that there was safety in numbers. Over three hundred different gods were worshiped on the island. Along with these major religious currents were some minor ones. There were, for example, more than forty thousand Muslims in Taiwan, along with Mormons, Jehovah's Witnesses, Christian Science adherents, and Baha'is.

As a result of modern secular education, the inroads of materialism, and the advent of urbanization, the majority of Taiwan's young people no longer adhered firmly to the old religious beliefs. However, traditional folk religion was still a long way from dying out. Temples were still flourishing, and indigenous religious leaders were adapting to the new realities of a rapidly changing society.

Overall, 6 percent of Taiwan's population was Christian; of that, 2.5 percent was Roman Catholic and 3.5 percent was Protestant. However, among the Protestants, there was a confusing morass of Christian missions, denominations, groups, sects, and organizations. After the Nationalist regime fled to Taiwan in 1949, a large number of missions and missionaries that had been scattered all over the face of China had descended on the relatively tiny island after their expulsion from the mainland. Baptists, Lutherans, Methodists, Mennonites, Episcopalians, Seventh Day Adventists, and a host of parachurch personnel had all come to Taiwan and established churches, mission outposts, medical and educational institutions, and programs alongside those of the Presbyterians and the Roman Catholics.[8] Although much good had been done, the good had been mitigated by the triple scourge

---

[8]   Leonard Kip was the first RCA missionary to set foot on Taiwan. On a visit in 1867, he examined a group of new believers for church membership. (Tong, *Christianity in Taiwan*, 24). Jeanne Walvoord and Ruth Broekema were the first resident RCA missionaries in Taiwan, serving there from 1951-1974 and 1951-1964 respectively.

of denominationalism, division, and dogmatism. Although some effort had been made to work ecumenically, the distinctions and competition between groups were too often more obvious to the local people than their commonalities and cooperation.[9]

Tones, Tenses and Tests

In order to serve the people and share the gospel, we had to learn their language. There were two main languages spoken on the island—Taiwanese (or Hokkien) and Mandarin Chinese. We were assigned to study Taiwanese, the language of the majority of the people and the language predominantly spoken by Taiwanese Presbyterians. Only later would we realize what a momentous choice that would prove to be.

The various Chinese languages and dialects are tonal. Mandarin has four tones, which means that one vocabulary word has four different meanings, depending on the tone used. When the only differentiation between your cat and your hat, for example, is a slight inflection of the voice, things can get interesting. Taiwanese has *eight* tones, and those tones change depending on where one uses the word in a sentence. Then, there are sounds in the Taiwanese language that English speakers do not ever make. Try saying "ng" as a separate word, for example. We also quickly discovered that learning by association didn't apply to the study of the Chinese language either, since there are practically *no* associations between Chinese and English words.

The thought that crossed our minds on the first day of language school was, "This will be impossible!" And so it seemed for the first six months. However, patient teachers with twinkles in their eyes would urge us on by practically guaranteeing that within six months we would actually be able to use this draconian language in simple conversations. And, miraculously (along with a dose of dogged hard work), it eventually did happen that way. We had tremendous motivation, of course. We wanted to be able to talk to people, listen to people, and get what we intended to buy. We wanted to hear people's stories and be able to tell our own stories, as well as "The Greatest Story Ever Told." We were also greatly encouraged when, after stammering out some nearly incomprehensible simple phrase, we would see someone's face light up and hear the warm and affirming compliment: "Oh, you speak Chinese so well!"

We were forbidden to do any substantial "missionary work" during the first year of language study, although I did teach English

---

[9]   Swanson, *Taiwan: Mainline versus Independent*, 80-90.

and explain the Gospel of Mark to a group of twenty-five Taiwan Political University students one night a week. We cycled to language school every weekday, where we underwent four hours of linguistic brainwashing. After a break for lunch, three more hours would be spent at home gearing up for the next day. Physical conditions in the language school swung between too hot and too cold. When the hot and humid season was upon us, a few window air conditioners would be switched on, but most of their effect was offset by the local habit of keeping the windows wide open. The Chinese believed passionately in the preventative medicinal power of fresh air. During the three-month winter period, we went to the unheated concrete school building dressed like Eskimos. We were quite comfortable during the first period, but then the freeze would begin to set in. During the second period, our hands and feet would begin to get cold. During the third period, our legs and arms would succumb. During the fourth period, we would begin to shiver from head to toe. The only thing that kept our minds off the cold was the sweat of facing demanding teachers who could tell if you had fudged on your homework the day before.

The conversational part of language study was the easiest part. Reading and writing was another matter. Fortunately for us, Reformed Church missionaries had more than a century earlier invented a Romanized system that reduced the Chinese language to readable words written in Western script.[10] Since the Taiwanese used regular Chinese Mandarin characters, this meant that one could "read" Taiwanese without first having to master thousands of complicated Chinese characters. In order to read an ordinary Chinese newspaper, for example, one needed to memorize some four thousand characters. To read a book required seven thousand, while the perusal of a Confucian classic demanded ten thousand. However, Romanization didn't mean one was off the hook, since most local written communication was naturally done using Chinese characters.

During the second year of language study, we began to tackle the reading and writing of characters. My Chinese name is composed of only three characters, but to write them, you have to make fifty-six separate strokes. Not all characters are that complicated, but one can trip up even on the simple ones. The character for "ten," for example, is a simple +. However, the first time I wrote it, the teacher said, "Wrong."

---

[10]   One of John Van Nest Talmage's greatest contributions during his long missionary career in Amoy (1847-1892) was the development and publication of a Romanized Amoy/English dictionary.

"Wrong?" "Yes, you wrote it from left to right and then crossed it from top to bottom. Chinese always write it from top to bottom and then cross it from left to right. We originally wrote everything with a brush and ink, and you need to simulate the motion of a brush." So much for simplicity. In addition, unless one put a tremendous amount of continuous effort into it, Chinese characters had the bad habit of leaving one's brain at about the same rate they entered it.

There were three other complicating factors. One was that even though the Taiwanese used Mandarin characters, their vocabulary did not match those characters exactly. This meant that when one read characters out loud, one had to more or less transpose when expressing the Taiwanese meaning. Even church elders would trip up from time to time when reading the scripture or making announcements. A second complicating factor was that when engaged in daily conversation, one could speak in an informal way. However, when one spoke to a group or offered a prayer, then a more formal style of Taiwanese would have to be used. A third complicating factor was that on the small island of Taiwan, there were four Taiwanese dialects in use. Imagine walking out of language school equipped to dazzle the locals with your classic Taiwanese, only to encounter a Taiwanese southerner who has a hard time understanding you. Nevertheless, in time, we did gain the facility to function in this complicated language, and we began to fit into the culture and launch our ministry.

Language school was not all work and no play. Part of our program was an exposure to various aspects of Chinese culture. We enjoyed demonstrations of Chinese art, calligraphy (actually considered to be the highest form of art), and musical instruments, and we were introduced to Chinese traditions and customs. It was at language school that my teachers taught me how to play Chinese elephant chess during the breaks. We also enjoyed Ping-Pong tournaments, tea parties, and field trips and learned a lot about Taiwanese religion and culture through our conversations with our teachers and by observing how they did things. For example, we learned that the Taiwanese did not flaunt their wealth by the way they dressed or by the kind of houses they lived in. An old man dressed in ordinary work clothes monitored the entrance to the six-story building that housed the language school, while his shabbily dressed, stooped over wife swept the stairs and kept the rooms clean. Some of us were concerned about these old folks and asked a teacher whether we could organize a collection for them. The teacher hooted with laughter and exclaimed, "They own the building!"

Teacher Gui Ek-bin
teaching the author
Chinese chess

Practice and Perspiration

Once we had learned enough language at least to begin to figure out what was being said, we began to attend a Taiwanese-speaking Presbyterian Church in Taipei—Tiong-San Kau-hoe. It was quite a strain at first, but the congregation was very patient and friendly. We slowly began to be able to read the Romanized Bible passages, sing the Romanized hymns, understand the gist of the sermon, and have simple conversations with our fellow parishioners. For our young children, of course, it was quite a different story. We engaged a Taiwanese tutor for them, but this only gave them a rudimentary introduction to the language. We compensated for that by bringing English Bible story books to church for them to read during the sermon, and by home schooling them when it came to Sunday school.

It was another year before I took the fearsome step of attempting to preach in Taiwanese. The director of the language school's Taiwanese program, George Wu, was an elder in the First Presbyterian Church of Taipei, as was the director of nursing at MacKay Hospital, Jeane Walvoord.[11] Mr. Wu invited me to preach there on a Sunday evening, and with fear and trepidation, after a lot of practice at the language school, I did so. When the congregation chuckled on a few occasions, I was not sure whether I had made a humorous point or had missed a tone and ended up saying that my horse, rather than my mother, had been a good woman! Eventually I would be able to preach and teach in the local language, but it would never be easy.

Eventually, I was invited to conduct the morning worship service from time to time at a small Presbyterian Church in a Taipei suburb. To

---

[11] Interestingly enough, Jeane had been ordained an elder in that church long before the RCA sanctioned the ordination of women in America.

The author with members
of the little church
by the market

get to the church, our family rode the public bus to that neighborhood and then walked through the local market, with all of its wonders, to the church building. So did everybody else, and they brought what they bought with them and placed their purchases on the floor at the rear of the sanctuary. There were live chickens in baskets, fish swimming around in plastic bags, squirmy frogs tied together at the legs, and an assortment of other exotic purchases. This was the first time I had the experience of preaching to a menagerie, but the crowing of the chickens came in handy during a sermon on Peter's denial, and the whole collection made a wonderful illustration when dealing with Noah's ark. It was also the first time I had led worship wearing an overcoat and gloves. With no heat source, and with the windows wide open, the winter months in that little concrete church made me wish I were leading a Pentecostal service with a little more movement programmed into the liturgy. The cold didn't seem to faze the locals with all their layers of clothing—a custom that we soon learned to adopt.

The Taiwanese language also taught us much about the Taiwanese people's basic philosophy of life. We came to understand why heart disease and ulcers were comparatively rare in Taiwanese society as compared with the West. For example, *Ban-ban-a* meant, "Take it easy. Rome wasn't built in a day." *Cha-put-to* meant, "It's good enough. Don't try to be a perfectionist." *Bo-hoat-to* meant, "There's no way around it, so just accept it." *Bo-iau-kin* meant, "It doesn't matter. Don't take it so seriously." *M-si goa e tai-chi* meant, "It's not my affair, so don't bug me about it." *Goa u tai-chi* meant, "I can't be there because I have 'a matter' to attend to." (It was impolite to ever ask what "the matter" might be). *Chit po, chit po* meant, "Take it one step at a time. You'll get there eventually." This laissez faire attitude towards life demanded a huge adjustment for a punctual, activist, perfectionist, confrontationalist like me.

For example, I was driving to a meeting one day when a traffic jam developed at a busy intersection. I was becoming more and more irritated at the unexpected delay. However, I noticed eventually that the Taiwanese had nonchalantly turned their motors off and were closing their eyes for a little snooze. Rather than blowing their horns and getting all worked up or backing up and trying to unsnarl the traffic, they were simply waiting until a traffic cop could show up and get the mess straightened out.

Then there was the first meeting I attended at the Presbyterian Church office, which was to begin at 8:00 p.m. I showed up five minutes beforehand only to find locked doors and a darkened building. After I had waited about fifteen minutes and was beginning to think that I had gotten the date or the time wrong, somebody showed up, unlocked the doors, and turned on the lights. I asked whether I had gotten the time wrong. "Oh, no," said the man with a bemused look on his face, "people here usually turn up about twenty minutes after the announced time." I never went to another meeting "on time."

Chopsticks and Chicken Feet

We had only been in Taiwan a short time when I received an invitation to attend a young village pastor's wedding feast. Having had only a cursory introduction to the then strange world of Chinese food, and only being able to speak a few Taiwanese phrases, this occasion proved to be quite an educational experience. We were seated around a huge round table, with a Taiwanese elder who could speak some English seated at my right. I was the only honored foreign guest at the table.

The first few courses were served. I found them to be quite delicious and ate as heartily as I could while still learning to wield chopsticks. After the third course, I was getting quite full and assumed that the meal was coming to an end. I leaned over and quietly asked the elder if we were about finished. He looked bemused and said that since it was a wedding feast, we still had nine courses to go! I somehow made it through the rest of the meal without exploding, with the elder, as my host, continuing to put the choicest morsels on my plate. The grand finale was a large tureen of soup that was placed in the center of the table with the biggest chicken foot I had ever seen floating in the middle. All eyes at the table turned to me as my host fished the foot out of the soup and laid it on my plate. I shot a quick prayer upward and proceeded to do the best I could with it, all the while thinking about where that chicken foot had been. I would in time become an enthusiastic connoisseur of Chinese food and a formidable wielder of chopsticks, but I never would develop much of a taste for chicken feet.

With so much mass poverty and even starvation woven into their history, we soon became aware that food is a core value in Chinese society. Their equivalent of "how are you?" is "li chiah-pa-boe?" meaning "have you eaten yet?" They have another saying that shows how important food is to them: "Chiah-png, Hong-te toa" means, "If the emperor shows up at the door while you are eating, the emperor must wait because eating is more important than he is." They have learned how to cook *anything* and make it taste good, including much that goes into Western garbage cans. They are constantly inventing new dishes and turning out mouth-watering marvels.

Traffic and Topography

While learning the language, we were also learning about our adopted place and people, both in books and through personal encounters. Our first summer vacation was spent taking the family on a west coast driving tour from Taipei in the north more than two hundred miles down to Ko-lan-bi at the southern tip of the island. (The Noordhofs had kindly lent us their car while they were on furlough.) During that trip, we learned a lot about Taiwan and its people. We took Highway 1 south and Highway 3 on the return trip back north. Driving in Taiwan was quite an experience. The rules of the road were a bit different from the ones we had been used to, to say the least. First, the larger vehicle always had the right of way, no matter where or what. Second, bicycles could come sailing out of nowhere and whiz right in front of you, so you always had to keep your foot near the brake. Third, motorbike and taxi drivers resembled Kamakazi pilots who took death-defying risks. Fourth, a "circus" type of intersection operated on the principle that you either psyched out some driver coming around the circle and jumped in, or stayed at the edge of the circle forever. Fourth, left turns in front of two lanes of oncoming traffic were accomplished by hugging the tail pipe of the vehicle in front of you until somebody in the "turn column" chickened out and some dare-devil in the oncoming traffic broke through.

The two main highways were narrow two-lane affairs that were fraught with dangers. Highway 1, the main north/south route, had more traffic, especially trucks. In all the times we eventually made that north/south trip, we never saw fewer than five or six smashed up

Toroko Gorge
on the east coast

vehicles. The chief culprits were the pig trucks. The drivers were paid according to the speed with which they could get live pigs from the south to the market in Taipei. The results were predictable—a string of horrible head-on collisions between cars and pig trucks that were trying to pass on the curves or that misjudged while passing on the straight. Highway 3 wound through foothills and farms most of the way. Farmers thought the main function of that road was to be a drying ground for their peanut and rice crops. They would pile the crops on the road and protect them with big rocks. Drivers were forced to drive through an obstacle course as they zigzagged around them. Driving on that road at night was even more of an adventure. You would be driving along and suddenly come upon lightless bicycles tooling along the road, or, even worse, large oxen-drawn carts loaded with rice straw, with nary a light in sight.

Tai-wan means "terraced bay." Many Taiwanese preferred to call the island *Formosa*, a Portuguese word meaning "beautiful." When Portuguese sailors sailed by the island in the sixteenth century, they used to exclaim, "Ilha formosa!" meaning "beautiful island." It was an apt name for a gorgeous piece of God's real estate, but, as we shall see, the main reason *why* many Taiwanese preferred to call it that had more to do with politics than with scenery. The island lies 90 miles off the southeastern coast of China, directly across the Taiwan Straits from the city of Xiamen.[12] It is 225 miles north of the Philippine Islands,

[12]   Formerly called Amoy, the RCA was in mission there for more than a century, 1842-1951.

665 miles southwest of Japan, and 7,500 miles southeast of the U.S. mainland. It is shaped like a tobacco leaf and is 250 miles long (N/S) and 85 miles wide (E/W). Its total land area is approximately 14,000 square miles, slightly larger than the states of Massachusetts and Connecticut combined. It has a wide plain running along its western coast and a narrower one running along its eastern coast.[13] A huge chain of stunningly beautiful mountains forms the backbone of the island, including the tallest peak in Southeast Asia (called Mount Morrison in English), at 13,000 feet.[14]

Typhoons and Tremors

Taiwan's climate is subtropical. The average temperatures are seventy-one degrees in the north and seventy-six degrees in the south, and the humidity is consistently high. Summer lasts from May through October, while a mild winter (in Western terms) occurs from January through March. Rainfall is heavy, averaging 101 inches annually in the north. Taiwan is typically subject to at least three typhoons every summer, some of which cause extensive damage, especially to agriculture, and even loss of life. The most severe hit during our four years there was typhoon "Bess" in 1971. Windows were shattered, trees were uprooted, walls were blown over, scaffolding was demolished, power was lost—and we played Scrabble by candlelight while riding out the storm huddled in our home.

Since Taiwan straddles a major geologic fault, it is prone to frequent earthquakes. Buildings are constructed to deal with most of them, but once in awhile, a major one hits and inflicts severe damage, sometimes death. The worst earthquake we encountered while in Taiwan occurred when we were traveling over the "cliff highway" along the East Coast in 1972.

During the Japanese era (1895-1945), a narrow winding road had been constructed along the face of the extensive cliffs overlooking the Pacific Ocean. This spectacularly scenic road ran some 125 feet above the sea and through many small tunnels. Vehicles traveled by caravan at stated times, since most of the road was only one lane. A major

---

[13]   For a detailed description of Taiwan's physical features, see Hsieh, Chiao-min, *Taiwan—Ilha Formosa, a Geography in Perspective* (Washington, D.C.: Catholic Univ. Press, 1964), 3-120.

[14]   The mountain was named after the first Protestant missionary to China, an Englishman named Robert Morrison. Morrison arrived in Canton (today's Guangzhou) in 1807, served in China for twenty-seven years, and was the first person to translate the Bible into Chinese.

earthquake had occurred the night before, and our caravan suddenly came to an unscheduled halt. The earthquake had precipitated a huge landslide that had blocked the road. Heavy equipment was at work, and the estimate was that the road would be reopened to traffic by midafternoon. I had an important meeting in Taipei the next day, so we decided to wait it out.

The estimate proved optimistic. The workmen finally began waving the few vehicles that were left in our caravan through in the late afternoon. We were behind a big truck, and we noticed that, as we passed, all the road workers had their eyes glued on a big overhanging rock that towered above us. By then it was getting dark and there were no lights along the road. As long as we could follow the truck, we had a sense of where the edge of the road was. However, the truck eventually stopped in a small village for the night, and we drove on very slowly the rest of the way, breathing a deep sigh of relief once we reached the city of Ilan and the end of the cliff highway.

A small tourist bus that had followed us through the slide area had not been so fortunate, as we learned from the next morning's paper. The huge rock had come crashing down, and it knocked the bus off the highway, over the side of the cliff, and 125 feet down into the sea. All twenty-five passengers had been killed. We had come very close to having our missionary career in Taiwan ended when it had hardly begun.

People and Pirates

In 1969, 16 million people, 45 percent of them young people, were squeezed into Taiwan's 14,000 square miles—an average of 1,143 people per square mile, the highest population density in the world. The population was quite diverse. The first settlers of Taiwan were Polynesian aborigines who had landed on the island more than fifteen hundred years before. Their story reads like that of the American Indian. They had been pushed gradually off the plains and up into the mountains by waves of migrants from southern China.[15] By 1969, they numbered 200,000 (or 2 percent of the population), grouped in nine tribes speaking seven languages and still living a rather primitive life in the mountains.[16]

The first great migration from China had taken place during the early fifteenth century and was mainly composed of pirates,

[15] See Hsieh, *Taiwan*, 3-120. See also Chai, Chen Kang, *Taiwan Aborigines: A Genetic Study of Tribal Variations* (Cambridge: Harvard Univ. Press, 1967).
[16] Hsieh, *Taiwan*, 125-27.

Taiwan aboriginal women

fishermen, and farmers from Fu-jian province opposite Taiwan. Large waves of Hoklo, or Hokkien-speaking Chinese from the Amoy area (today's Xiamen), had followed during the sixteenth, seventeenth, and eighteenth centuries. These people and their language had eventually become known as "Taiwanese." In 1969, they comprised 78 percent of the population. The remaining 12 percent of Taiwan's inhabitants were made up of "mainlander" Chinese who had fled to the island from China after the collapse of the Nationalist Government there in 1949. They spoke Mandarin Chinese and a variety of local Chinese dialects as well, but they could not speak or understand Taiwanese.[17]

Taiwan's history is as complicated as its population. In 1624, the Dutch invaded and colonized the southern end of Taiwan. Two years later, the Spanish did the same in the north. In 1642, the Dutch ousted the Spanish and took over the whole island. They brought chaplains with them who were quite successful in evangelizing the local Taiwanese and forming them into Christian congregations. However, in 1661, a Chinese pirate by the name of Cheng Cheng-kung (known as "Koxenga" in the West) invaded Taiwan, defeated the Dutch, and set up an independent kingdom. He also pressured the now isolated Christians into giving up their "Dutch faith" and returning to their indigenous religion.[18]

In 1684, Ching Dynasty officials from the Chinese mainland arrived and exerted a rather lose control over the island. It was not until two centuries later, in 1887, that the Ching government declared

---

[17] Ibid., 149-50, 184-85.
[18] Campbell, W.M., *Formosa under the Dutch* (London: Kegan Paul, Trench, Trubner & Co., 1903; repr. Taipei: SMC, 1992).

Taiwan to be a province of China, even though it only effectively controlled one-third of the island. Just eight years later, in 1895, after suffering a defeat in the Sino-Japanese war, China, without asking the Taiwanese, ceded Taiwan to Japan in perpetuity. Japan ruled Taiwan as a colony for the next fifty years (1895–1945). Abandoned by China, the Taiwanese initially rejected Japanese rule and set up a short-lived Republic of Taiwan.[19] They eventually were subdued and forced to pay homage to the Japanese emperor and to adopt Japanese culture.[20] All education was conducted in the Japanese language, while higher education was denied to all Taiwanese except those who entered the medical and law professions.[21]

Older Taiwanese often told us of the subtle ways in which they had shown their contempt for their Japanese colonial masters. For example, every year some ten thousand workers and students would be assembled in the great square in front of the colonial administration's headquarters on the emperor's birthday to pay him homage. When the time came to shout, *"Banzai! Banzai! Banzai!"* ("May the emperor live ten thousand years!"), the Taiwanese would shout themselves hoarse yelling, *"Pang-sai! Pang-sai! Pang-sai!"* The Japanese guards would beam with approval, not realizing that with a slightly different inflection, the Taiwanese were actually shouting, "Shit on the emperor!"

Upon the surrender of Japan at the end of World War II in 1945, General Douglas MacArthur authorized Nationalist Chinese troops to occupy Taiwan on behalf of the Allied Powers until its future status could be determined. However, the Nationalist Government, without consulting the Taiwanese, immediately and unilaterally declared Taiwan to be an integral part of what since 1912 had been the Republic of China. When the Nationalists, under Chiang Kai-shek, lost the civil war to the Chinese Communists in 1949, a remnant of the Nationalist army and government fled to Taiwan, where they came under the protection of the United States. Chiang envisioned turning Taiwan into a bastion from which the Nationalists could eventually retake the Chinese mainland, but he never launched a counter attack. By 1969, a twenty-year stalemate had ensued between the Nationalist Republic of

---

[19] The short-lived republic even issued its own postage stamps, some of which are part of the author's Taiwan stamp collection.

[20] Mendel, Douglas, *The Politics of Formosan Nationalism* (Los Angeles: Univ. of California Press, 1970), 13-25.

[21] Since the Presbyterian Church valued education highly, many Presbyterian young people took up those professions. To this day, a large percentage of Taiwan's doctors and lawyers are Presbyterian Christians.

Generalissimo Chiang Kai-shek propaganda poster

China (on Taiwan) and the Communist People's Republic of China (on the mainland).[22]

Prosperity and Poverty

Although Taiwan had the most prosperous economy in Asia in 1969, except for Japan, there was quite a gap between the minority "haves" and the majority "have-nots." During the sixties, the economy had grown at the phenomenal rate of 10 percent per year, but it was obvious that the increased prosperity had not trickled down to the people who lived in the many villages and poorer areas of the cities. Traditionally, Taiwan had a basically agricultural economy and had served as Japan's rice bowl. Beginning in the early 1960s, however, rapid industrialization had taken place, so that by the end of that decade, the industrial sector outweighed the agricultural sector in terms of earnings, manpower, and exports.

As a result of its economic take off, by the time of our arrival, Taiwan had been propelled into the top twenty of the world's foremost trading nations. It was projected to increase its gross national product to $15 billion by 1980 and its per capita income to $1,000 per annum by 1983. Although the figures were impressive, there was evidence of the lingering presence of poverty for too many of Taiwan's people. The poor majority was paying an unequal share of taxes. Inflation was keeping their income level static while prices were continuing to

[22] Fenby, Johathan, *Chiang Kai-Shek: China's Generalissimo and the Nation He Lost* (New York: Carroll & Graf, 2003), 499-500.

rise. Too many Taiwanese were unemployed or underemployed. There were no independent unions, and strikes were forbidden upon pain of death. This, of course, resulted in the kind of longer hours, lower wages, and difficult working conditions that guaranteed fatter profits for the owners and greater revenues for the government. Foreign subsidiaries, like General Instrument and Philco Ford, were even allowed to hire children to work night shifts and to run factories in which the air quality was so bad that it had led to the deaths of some workers.

Except for timber, coal, marble, natural gas, and some minerals, Taiwan was rather poor in natural resources. Therefore, like Japan, it had to depend on trade to develop as an industrial nation. In 1969, the leading exports were textiles, electrical machinery, plywood and wood products, metal products, chemical products, and food. Its leading imports were machinery, electrical machinery, metal products, chemicals, transportation equipment, raw cotton, soybeans, timber, crude oil, and wheat. The major industries were construction, power production, textiles, electronics, petroleum, shipbuilding, food processing, metals, chemicals, and machinery.[23]

Taiwan produced enough food to sustain its own swelling population. This not inconsiderable achievement was attained through intensive farming methods and a climate that allowed two, and in some cases three, crops per year. Farms and orchards produced rice, sugar, sweet potatoes, bananas, pineapples, citrus fruit, peanuts, asparagus, soybeans, mushrooms, and tea. The hog, fishing, and poultry industries were well developed, while the development of both beef and milk herds was progressing rapidly. (I was glad to hear this last bit of news. I was a big milk drinker and ice cream fan, and all that was available in Taipei when we arrived was powdered milk, with ice cream nowhere to be seen.) However, with the migration of young people to big cities like Taipei in the north (2 million) and Kaohsiung in the south (1 million), the inequitable price paid by the government for rice, and the urbanization and fragmentation of farmland, Taiwan's farmers were in trouble. Some reforms had recently been enacted, but it was feared that unless farmers, who then made up 50 percent of the population, received a more equitable share of the economic boom, Taiwan would cease to be a self-sustaining nation as far as basic food was concerned.[24]

[23]   For a detailed analysis of Taiwan's post-WWII agricultural and industrial development up to the mid-50s, see Riggs, Fred W., *Formosa under Chinese Nationalist Rule* (New York: Macmillan, 1952), 61-127.

[24]   For a detailed analysis of Taiwan's agricultural and industrial development up to the mid-1960s, see Hsieh, Taiwan, 252-315.

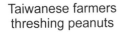

Taiwanese farmers
threshing peanuts

There was a very minimal social safety net for the poor in those days. Every family was expected to take care of its own, no matter what. Nevertheless, there were some unwritten social customs that tilted in favor of those who were poverty stricken. For example, people had to be very careful when driving, especially in the cities, because some people would become desperate to the point of throwing themselves in front of a car. The intent was to sustain a broken arm, or some other nonlethal injury, and collect what could be a fairly substantial sum of money. Most drivers would pay rather than risk going to court. Chinese judges would not settle such a dispute by concentrating on who was at fault but on who could afford to pay. Obviously, if somebody was rich enough to own a car, and was a foreigner to boot, she or he could afford to pay a settlement.[25]

Then there was the understanding that poor people had "squatter's rights." In other words, once people were not prevented from camping on a vacant piece of property, building a shack in a lane, or occupying some space in a building, they then had a "right" to be there. The only way they could be dislodged was to pay them a reasonable sum of money to move elsewhere.[26]

[25] A missionary colleague once got into serious trouble in a similar case. An old woman on a bicycle rode out of a narrow, obscured lane, ran into the *side* of his car, and was killed. The family demanded a huge sum. He refused to pay and was taken to court. The judge decided that he was the one who should pay and threatened him with prison if he didn't. The case dragged on over three years until, in order to avoid prison, he finally had to pay.

[26] For example, a missionary colleague who preceded me in student work at the Taipei Student Center hired a gate man and let him erect a shack near the gate where he and his family could live. Later, in order to get rid of the unsightly shack, she agreed to let him move into part of the center's basement. Still later, wanting to use that space for student programming, her mission agreed to pay the man a huge sum (the equivalent of US$10,000) to move out. Unfortunately, she gave him the money *before* he

These factors were important for us to know in order to be effective in mission in Taiwan. Unless we had a clear understanding of the context, we would not be able to relate the gospel effectively to people in their real situations.

---

moved. Several months later, he and his family were still there. When she pressed him to move, he protested that he had had to use the money to pay for his wife's surgery and recovery and that he could no longer move. When I came on the scene, we planned to use the basement as a coffee house for students. However, having lived there so long, the price of the gate man's "rights" had gone up—so far up that we had to give up on the plan. (He did not move until the Presbyterian General Assembly paid him off years later so it could tear the building down and build new headquarters on the site.)

CHAPTER 2

The White Terror

Nationalists and Communists

The roots of the "White Terror" period on Taiwan date back to 1911, when the Ching dynasty was overthrown by a revolution led by Dr. Sun Yat-Sen. Although a new Republic of China (ROC) came into being, a chaotic period ensued during which local warlords became powerful in their respective parts of the country. In response to this chaos, two parties were formed that would dominate the political scene in China into the twenty-first century—the Nationalist Party and the Chinese Communist Party.

Both parties originally proclaimed the same essential goals—the unification, modernization, and democratization of China and the end of foreign imperialist political, economic, and territorial encroachment. However, their philosophies and methodologies for attaining those goals were quite different. Simplistically speaking, the Communists wanted to champion the cause of peasants and workers by expelling the Western imperialists and their capitalist system that had exacerbated the great divide between the small wealthy class and the masses of the

Dr. Sun Yat Sen

poor in China. They also opposed the imperialists' Chinese cronies—big landlords, major industrialists, wealthy businessmen, and the powerful and corrupt warlords. The Communists were austere, intolerant of corruption, and ruthless with those whom they considered to be enemies of the people, namely, those whom they believed had been sucking the blood out of the Chinese nation.

The Nationalists also claimed they were attempting to unite the country and to introduce a better way of life, especially for the lower classes, through Sun Yat-Sen's Three Principles of the People—nationalism, democracy, and the people's livelihood (a form of socialism). However, the Nationalists' performance under the leadership of Generalissimo Chiang Kai-Shek grew worse as time progressed. Chiang allied himself with certain warlords, secret gangster networks, big business, and the big landlords. Increasingly, he allowed the privileged to get richer and the positioned to get more powerful (most notably the wealthy and powerful relatives of his second wife, Soong Mei-ling). This was done at the expense of the peasants, and all in the name of the three "people's principles." Chiang set up the façade of a democratic system to placate the intellectuals (and for Western consumption), but in reality he created a fascist regime and operated as the dictator of a totalitarian police state. For example, Chiang was dependent on Russian advisors in the 1920s and invited them to design his military and security systems. The Nationalists became notoriously corrupt and were as ruthless as the Communists with those whose ideology differed from theirs, or who got in the way of the Kuo-Min-Tang[1] (KMT) regime. Gradually, both the Chinese intellectuals and the masses of China's peasants and workers lost faith in Chiang and his Nationalists and were won over by the comparatively uncorrupted and dedicated Communists.

In 1931, the Chinese civil struggle was interrupted by Japan's invasion of Manchuria, China's northeasternmost province. The Japanese

---

[1]   A Chinese phrase literally meaning "country, people, party" and translated as "Nationalist" in English.

renamed it Manchukuo and ruled through a puppet, Pu-yi, the last claimant to the Chinese imperial throne. Six years later, after a contrived incident at the famous Marco Polo Bridge, Japan launched a full-scale invasion of China and eventually captured the entire eastern half of the country. Under these circumstances, the Nationalists were forced to declare a truce and to form a temporary alliance with the Communists in 1937. In 1938, they had to move their capital to a mountain fortress city named Chungking in the central Province of Szechuan.

Although the United States did not formally intervene, President Roosevelt did answer Chiang's pleas for material assistance. However, while Chiang conducted a war of passive resistance and strategic retreat, much of what was sent was stored up for use against the Communists after the conclusion of the war. Some of Chiang's officials even collaborated with the Japanese and became wealthy trading with the enemy. Meanwhile, in the north, the Communists were reported to be winning tactical victories using guerrilla methods. This impressed the Chinese people. Whenever the Communists "liberated" an area, the people were exposed to Communist propaganda and "converted" to their cause, often by ruthless means.

When World War II ended with the defeat and withdrawal of Japan in 1945, the uneasy alliance between the Communists and the Nationalists quickly fell apart. The struggle between them resumed and soon escalated into a full-scale civil war. Chiang had vastly superior firepower and military forces, but the people, even many of his own commanders, had had enough. When they compared the claimed accomplishments and utopian vision of the Communists to the collaboration, corruption, and broken promises of Chiang's regime, they began to go over to the Communists in droves. In the end, it was not so much that the lean and committed Communists had won the civil war, but that the Chinese people had become so thoroughly disillusioned by Chiang's regime that they had thrown the Nationalists out. By 1949, the Communists had decisively defeated the Nationalists and established the People's Republic of China (PRC). Chiang resigned the presidency before the end of hostilities so that he would not have to take official blame for the defeat. Then, with the rag tag remnants of his forces, he fled to Taiwan, where he was protected from a Communist assault by the U.S. Seventh Fleet. There he resumed the presidency and proceeded to rebuild his forces with massive American aid for what he hoped would be a decisive counterattack to retake the mainland.[2]

[2] For a comprehensive and detailed account and analysis of this complicated period and Chiang's part in it, see Payne, Robert, *Chiang Kai-Shek* (New York: Weybright and Talley, 1969).

Madame Chiang Kai-shek
on Republic of China postage stamp

Myth and Reality

During the turbulent decade of the 1940s, a strong China lobby had come into being in the United States to support the Nationalists and defeat the Communists. The most powerful member of this lobby was the American-educated Madame Chiang Kai-Shek herself, one of three daughters of the most wealthy and powerful family in China— the Soongs.[3] The Japanese attack on Pearl Harbor in 1941, and the subsequent entry of the United States into what had by then become World War II, was an answer to prayer for the embattled Chiangs. The glamorous "Madame" made a number of highly politicized trips to the United States, sometimes camping in the White House for long periods of time, much to Roosevelt's chagrin. She became the heroic darling of the conservative members of Congress. They were so enamored with her and so obsessed with defeating the Communists that they never bothered to look beneath the surface to see what was really going on within the Nationalist regime and how U.S. aid was being misused.

---

[3]   The twice-married Chiang had married Soong Mei-ling; a wealthy financier, H.H. Kung, had married her sister, Soong Ai-ling; while her brother, T.V. Soong, had become the Nationalist's finance minister. Sun-Yat-Sen had married her other sister, Soong Ching-ling (also a second marriage). It was said of the three sisters that Ai-ling loved money, Mei-ling loved power, and Ching-ling loved China. (Ching-ling was appointed a vice-chair of the government of the People's Republic of China and would hold other important posts in the PRC).

Under these circumstances, Roosevelt could deny her only to his political peril.[4]

Anna Chennult was another powerful member of the China lobby. When the Japanese had first attacked China proper in 1937, Roosevelt had allowed volunteer American fighter pilots to serve in the beleaguered Chinese Nationalist Air Force. One of them, General Claire Chennult, formed these volunteers into the famous "Flying Tigers"—a group that became the core of the Nationalist resistance to the Japanese in the air and captured the imagination of the American public. General Chennult's wealthy and well-placed Chinese wife, Anna, had influential political connections in both Chungking and Washington.

A third well-known member of the lobby was an American medical missionary who had served in China and then been elected to Congress from Minnesota—Walter Judd. Judd reflected the views of a number of American missionaries in China who had been displaced by the war and then expelled by the Communists. They were politically conservative and staunch supporters of Chiang's Nationalists and strong opponents of Mao's Communists. They viewed the Chiangs as devout Methodists who had promoted Christianity in China and who were continuing to do so in Taiwan. They had appreciated the carte blanche mandate they had been given to "preach the gospel" in China and Taiwan and therefore had became supporters of the regime, and of the China lobby, without closely scrutinizing who they were really identifying with and what they were really supporting.[5]

A fourth powerful member of the lobby was Henry Luce, along with his influential wife, Claire Booth Luce. Luce was the politically influential and wealthy owner and editor of *Time* magazine, which in effect became something of a propaganda sheet for the Nationalist cause in general, and for the Chiangs' welfare in particular.

The advent of the Korean War in 1952 and the subsequent entry of the People's Republic of China as an antagonist in that war froze U.S./China relations. This, along with Senator Joseph McCarthy's

[4]   For a comprehensive and detailed account of the Soong family and Soong Mei-ling and Chiang Kai-shek in particular see Seagrave, Sterling, *The Soong Dynasty* (New York: Harper & Row, 1986).

[5]   For example, in 1961 the beloved RCA missionary Tina Holkeboer, who served in China for twenty-eight years (1920-1948), wrote an impassioned defense of the Chiang regime in response to a proposal by the Reformed Church's Christian Action Commission to support the entry of the People's Republic of China into the United Nations at Chiang's expense. See Holkeboer, Tina, *Comments on a Study Document on the China Issue*, (New York: Christian Action Commission, RCA, 1961).

"red scare" witch hunt in the United States, gave the China lobby a terrific boost. If, the logic ran, the Chinese Communists were the devil, Chiang's Nationalists on Taiwan must be "Christian" knights in white armor. If "Red China" was a closed and oppressive society with a totalitarian regime, then "Free China" on Taiwan must be an open and progressive society with a democratic government. If the "atheistic Communists" were trying to stamp out Christianity on the mainland, then the Nationalists, led by the "godly" Chiangs must be trying to promote it on Taiwan.

The China lobby, through its powerful political connections and its effective propaganda campaign, successfully sold a number of myths to the American Government and the American people.

1. Generalissimo and Madame Chiang Kai Shek, as Sun Yat-Sen's legitimate heirs, had made a great effort to modernize, liberalize, and democratize the Republic of China.
2. The Nationalists, under the heroic leadership of the Chiangs, had fought a great war of resistance against the Japanese.
3. After the Japanese surrender, the Christian Chiangs had fought another heroic struggle against the atheistic Communists, which they would have won had they been better supported and equipped by the United States.

The China lobby continued to oppose Mao Tse-tung and the Chinese Communists by promoting Chiang Kai-shek and the Chinese Nationalists for decades. In so doing, they continued to ignore the facts on the ground and to spin even more distorted myths about Chiang's fascist regime in "Free China," i.e. Taiwan, for consumption by the American public and by American politicians.

1. Taiwan had always been an integral part of China, and its people were happy to once again belong to China after their liberation from Japanese rule.
2. Although the Chinese mainland had fallen temporarily to the Communists, Chiang's Nationalists, aided by the United States, would eventually prevail from their island redoubt of Taiwan by retaking the mainland and re-establishing Nationalist control over the whole of China.
3. Compared to the Communist mainland, the Nationalists had turned "Free China" (Taiwan) into a thriving bastion of freedom and prosperity.
4. Because the Chiangs were staunch Christians, Christian missionaries were welcome in Taiwan and had complete

freedom to "preach the gospel." Christian churches were prospering there, had great freedom to carry out their ministry and mission, and could freely address their concerns about life and society.[6]

Joyce and I, too, had once believed these myths to be the unvarnished truth about the Chiangs and their Nationalists on Taiwan. Shortly after our arrival there, we were shocked to discover that our opinions had been based on illusions, and that the truth of what had gone on, and what was going on, was too terrible to contemplate.

Slaughter and Subjugation

We were shocked, for example, to hear about the "Ji Ji Pat" (February 28, 1947) "incident," which led to the slaughter of more than twenty thousand innocent Taiwanese civilians by Nationalist troops. Almost every Taiwanese we met who dared to talk to us about this event had lost a family member at that time, or had friends who had lost somebody.

When Chiang dispatched troops and civil servants to Taiwan to take charge of the island on behalf of the Allies after Japan's defeat in 1945, the Taiwanese had welcomed them enthusiastically as liberators. However, the Chinese arrived with a different point of view. The Nationalist officials and their thirty thousand troops landed as conquerors and new masters of the Taiwanese. Contrary to their agreement with the Allies, they immediately claimed Taiwan as a province of China but gave it a legally inferior status to China's other provinces. Considering the island to be "degraded territory," and the Taiwanese "degraded people," the Chinese treated the Taiwanese populace like serfs. Military scavengers instituted an organized rape of the island, stole everything moveable (from the rails on the railroad lines to the hardware on the toilets), and shipped it back to the mainland to be sold for personal profit. Even the Taipei water supply system was dug up so that its lead pipes could be sold elsewhere. Desirable houses and other properties were commandeered and their Taiwanese occupants ordered to move out, or else. After a year and a half of this kind of maltreatment, the Taiwanese had had enough. On February 28, 1947, the powder keg exploded as the result of a dispute between police and

6   Chen, Lung-Chu, and Harold D. Lasswell, *Formosa, China, and the United Nations* (New York: St. Martin's Press, 1967), 201-05. For a comprehensive and detailed account and analysis of the China lobby, see Koen, Ross Y., *The China Lobby in American Politics* (New York: Harper & Row, 1974).

Nationalist soldiers

a Taiwanese woman hawker who was selling cigarettes on which taxes had not been paid. The Taiwanese staged a bloodless uprising against the corrupt governor and his Nationalist cronies and temporarily took over the island. Convinced that local officials were to blame for these offenses, they believed that once the central government learned of their distress, President Chiang Kai-shek would recall the corrupt governor, Chen-yi, and move to redress these wrongs. Meanwhile, the governor appeared to bow to their demands and arranged for a consultation with Taiwanese leaders. However, he was simply buying time while he secretly sent word to Nanking to send reinforcements.

Rather than investigating the real cause of the troubles in Taiwan, Chiang simply sent fifty thousand more troops to the island to put the peaceful Taiwanese uprising down forcibly without doing anything about their grievances. The reinforcements landed in March 1947 and began indiscriminately shooting every Taiwanese in sight. By the time they had made their way from Keelung in the north to Kaohsiung in the south, more than ten thousand unarmed Taiwanese had been slaughtered. The next phase was to root out and kill everyone who had played any leadership role in the uprising (down to the boy scouts who had acted as traffic police), or that had the potential of doing so in the future. Ten thousand more Taiwanese were executed in this second round of killings. The Taiwanese were cowed into sullen silence.[7]

---

[7]   Mendel, Douglas, *The Politics of Formosan Nationalism* (Los Angeles: Univ. of California Press, 1970), 31-41.

We were also surprised to learn that the Chinese claim to the island was historically bogus, and that the Taiwanese considered the Chinese Nationalists to be merely the latest in a fairly long list of occupying powers. Throughout the long history of Taiwan, the primary reason why various types of Chinese had come there was to *escape* the intolerable economic, social, and political conditions on the Chinese mainland. Over a period of two hundred years, Peking had sent a garrison force, magistrates, and a swarm of civil officers to the island to try to subdue it. However, the Taiwanese had fiercely resisted this attempt at colonization, encouraged by the thousands of Chinese intellectuals who continued to flee there to escape the totalitarian atmosphere on the mainland. The exasperated Chinese officials described the situation by exclaiming, "Every three years an uprising; every five years a rebellion." There were more than thirty violent outbursts in the nineteenth century alone. As we have noted, the Chinese government declared Taiwan a province in 1887, while controlling only one-third of the island. Just eight years later, China cavalierly ceded Taiwan and the Pescadores to Japan in perpetuity.

During the fifty years that Japan ruled Taiwan as its colony (1895-1945), the Japanese tried to wipe out any vestiges of Chinese culture on the island and "Japanize" the population. Although the Japanese officials were strict and oppressive, they did develop the island economically and industrially, so that by the end of World War II, Taiwan had become one of the most technically advanced territories in Asia. This period accelerated the evolution of a Taiwanese identity and culture distinct from that of the Chinese mainland.[8]

Toward the end of World War II, American planes had dropped leaflets over Taiwan promising the Taiwanese self-determination upon liberation, a promise that was never kept. The Nationalists were allowed to occupy the island on behalf of the victorious Allies and to disarm the Japanese. However, since China had ceded the island to Japan in perpetuity, its status had yet to be determined. The Nationalists' unilateral declaration that the island was Chinese territory was therefore illegal (and remains illegal to this day). The population of Taiwan, although for the most part Chinese in ethnic origin and culture, had by 1945 evolved a distinct, and in many ways unique, culture as compared to their mainland cousins. Given the choice, they would most likely have opted to become once again the Republic of Taiwan. However, the Taiwanese people were never consulted about

[8]   Ibid., 9-25.

their future. The Nationalists simply decided it for them and imposed it on them, without a dissenting voice among the world community.[9]

The situation did not improve for Taiwan after the Nationalists were defeated on the mainland in 1949. Chiang and a horde of about two million mainlanders descended on the island, many of them ragged soldiers without so much as shoes on their feet or a bicycle at their disposal. Many of the wealthy class, who had profited during the Nationalist era, also came, bringing their portable possessions and their Swiss and U.S. bank accounts with them. Planes loaded with gold and the portable national treasures of China were also flown over the Taiwan Straits. The mainlanders took over every civil service job of any consequence on the island (including schoolteacher posts, for example), every position above lieutenant in the armed services, and every central government political office (except for a few unimportant posts doled out as Taiwanese window dressing).[10]

In 1951, Chiang Kai-shek resumed the presidency of the Republic of China. He declared that the Nationalists would continue the civil war against the Communist "bandits" from Taiwan and, as the only legitimate government of China, would retake the mainland. He assumed that his wartime ally, the United States, in its extreme antipathy to the Communists (particularly after the advent of the Korean War), would risk another world war by assisting him. The U.S. did send massive military aid, both materiel and advisors, to help the Nationalists defend the island. However, President Truman also made it very clear that America would not support Chiang's fantasy of recapturing the mainland.[11] The Seventh Fleet continued to patrol the Taiwan Straits to prevent a Communist attack on Taiwan, but also to prevent Chiang from attempting to launch an attack on the mainland. Nevertheless, in order to maintain their legitimacy and their tight control over Taiwan, the Nationalists enshrined their "return to the mainland" ideology and enforced its acceptance by the Taiwanese people, who had not had a direct affinity with China for centuries.[12]

---

[9]   For a comprehensive and detailed account of this period, see Kerr, George H., *Formosa Betrayed* (Boston: Houghton Mifflin, 1965), 61-431.

[10] Lederer, William, *A Nation of Sheep* (New York: Norton, 1961), 46.

[11] For example, Chiang's offer to send troops to Korea to fight against the Chinese Communists there was declined.

[12] Mendel, *Politics*, 172-77. See also Riggs, *Formosa*, 31-58.

Propaganda on presidential palace depicting the ROC as ruling the whole of China

Propaganda and Pageantry

A huge propaganda campaign was launched to brainwash the populace. As with the Japanese before them, the Nationalists tried to strip the Taiwanese people of their culture. They decreed that Mandarin Chinese was to be the official language used in public affairs and in the schools, and they meted out punishment to those who did not comply. They systematically tried to wipe out the Taiwanese people's language, history, and culture. They constructed replicas of major mainland historical buildings like Peking's Temple of Heaven. The Kuo Min-tang Party song was promoted as the National Anthem and was sung at every event at every level. Even at the movies, the audience had to stand during the playing of this song while images of the Chiangs and their "return to the mainland" dreams were displayed on the screen. Sun Yat-sen and Chinag Kai-shek were raised to the status of the emperors of old, with their portraits and statues blanketing the island.[13]

For example, every October 10, the Republic of China's National Day, ten thousand school children, factory workers, and members of important organizations were marshaled into a huge square in front of the presidential office building in the center of Taipei. All were dressed in various uniforms and carried huge placards promoting the official line. The flag-draped tower of the building featured a huge display of Taiwan, with rays of light extending from the island across the whole

---

13 Payne, Robert, *Chiang Kai-Shek* (New York: Weybright and Talley, 1969), 299-301.

of China. The crowd witnessed a show of Nationalist military muscle, listened to propaganda speeches, and kow-towed ("paid their respects") to the Chiangs, with martial music blaring in the background.

In 1972, as foreign students at the language school, we were also invited to participate in this event, which was, as it turned out, the last time that the eighty-one-year-old generalissimo would appear in public. As foreign guests, we were lined up right at the front of the huge throng and given large colorful I.D. badges to wear. Since the program had not yet begun, I asked our director if it would be all right for me to mount the lower steps of the platform and take a few photos of the colorful throng, and he agreed. Before I could get back to our group, I was trapped near the platform by a large phalanx of soldiers who had rapidly moved into position between the crowd and the principal participants. Since my I.D. badge looked very much like those of the press corps, no one paid any attention to me, and I decided that I might as well act like one of them.

Having lost its United Nations seat to the People's Republic of China in 1971, the ROC's diplomatic position had continued to deteriorate rapidly. Many nations had already switched their diplomatic relations to the PRC, and the Nationalists had tried to stem the hemorrhage by wooing countries with right-wing governments or by bribing poor countries with aid. The guest of honor at the 1972 "Double Ten" (October 10) propaganda pageant was no less than "Emperor" Jean-Bédel-Bokossa of the Central African Republic. The "emperor," resplendent with so many medals pinned to his chest that he practically had to lean backward to support them all, emerged from his limousine some ten feet in front of my camera lens.

After he was seated, the speeches by military generals, the vice president, and the "G-mo's" son (and heir apparent), Chiang Ching-kwo, commenced, and my camera kept whirring. Finally, the officials on the platform turned around, as if on cue, and looked up at a small balcony near the top of the central tower of the presidential building as if they were expecting God. A signal was given, the music stopped, and a hush descended over the huge throng. Then, like the emperors of old, the generalissimo, resplendent in his military uniform and with the madame at his side, appeared on the balcony. The participants bowed, and the crowd was led in the equivalent of a "may the emperor live ten thousand years!" chant, the Chiangs all the while waving and acknowledging the adoration of the masses.

The propagation of the myth that the ROC on Taiwan was the only legitimate government of all of China was essential to keeping

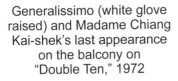

Generalissimo (white glove raised) and Madame Chiang Kai-shek's last appearance on the balcony on "Double Ten," 1972

the Chiangs and their Nationalist Kuo-Min-Tang Party in power. The whole of the party's central government structure had been transferred to Taiwan. Since elections could no longer be held on the mainland, those who had last been elected to represent their provinces in 1948 continued to represent those provinces in Taiwan at the National Assembly that was responsible for "electing" the president. Under that rigged setup, the sixteen million people of the "province" of Taiwan could only send a few representatives to the assembly. As the years passed, the representatives elected in 1948 had aged. Some had died, which meant that power had passed into fewer and fewer Nationalist hands. Some had grown gravely ill. Others had emigrated out of Taiwan. No matter! Every time the assembly met, people were flown in—some were even carried in on stretchers (along with their oxygen tanks)—to cast their dutiful votes for the G-mo. One can hardly imagine the frustration of the Taiwanese.[14]

While still in the States, Joyce and I had heard the China lobby extolling the Nationalist Government on Taiwan for having conducted the most successful land reform in the world and for building Taiwan's economy up to the point where it had become the second most prosperous "nation" in Asia. After we arrived, we quickly found out why this was the case—the land that the Nationalist mainlanders had parceled out had all belonged to the Japanese and the Taiwanese! However, by 1969, Taiwan's agriculture was in trouble because the government had divided the land into such small plots that farming had become impractical—so impractical that farmers were being encouraged to form cooperatives.

---

[14] Mendel, *Politics*, 89-121.

Women workers
at a marble factory

The Nationalists inherited a relatively developed island from the Japanese, so, in a sense, they started with silver spoons in their mouths. They got a windfall when they confiscated all Japanese assets after the war and sold some of them to finance the land reform. By 1969, the government still owned such major monopolies as sugar, salt, wine, tobacco, oil, and gasoline, and the Kuo-Min-Tang Party owned a fortune in property, real estate, and communications in its own right.

The regime used totalitarian methods to control every aspect of the economic machine. There were rigid wage and price controls. Collective bargaining was prohibited upon pain of death. Unions (other than KMT rubber stamp farces) were also prohibited upon the pain of death. There was a heavy and discriminatory tax structure. For example, if a businessman, especially a Taiwanese businessman, cooperated with the regime, the tax man would examine his company's books with "one eye open and one eye shut." However, should somebody dare to cross the regime in even a small way, they could easily be sent to prison for "tax fraud" by that same tax man.

Industries favored the wealthy and influential by paying workers low wages for long hours under difficult conditions to produce cheap goods. The minimum wage for factory jobs was the equivalent of US$15.00 per month. Madame Chiang Kai-Shek personally owned the controlling interest in the Yue Loong car manufacturing company—the only one on the island. Low-income taxi drivers had no choice but to pay the equivalent of US$4,000.00 (a princely sum in those days) for a compact car that literally began falling apart after one year of use. The company was protected by a 135 percent import tax on foreign-made cars. Under these conditions, foreign investment companies earned huge profits, while the government skimmed off huge tax revenues. Add to this the US$4.75 billion that the United States poured into the ROC's economic development and military buildup from 1950–1970, with more billions given in hidden ways, and Taiwan's "miracle economy" seemed to us to be a little less miraculous.[15]

Spies and Censors

When Chiang resumed the presidency in 1951, he announced that the island was under a state of emergency. The constitution was suspended, martial law was declared, and Taiwan was turned into an armed camp under the watchful eye of the Chinese Nationalist "Garrison Command," (read "occupation forces"). All constitutional human rights were suspended. The one-party regime turned Taiwan into a fascist police state by creating a massive security apparatus, and that's how things remained for another thirty-eight years.[16]

The Nationalists employed exactly the same practices and policies they had used on the mainland, most of them carried out by the very same people. Corruption was rife at every level. The secret police were in everything and everywhere. All media was strictly censored, and great efforts were made to keep Taiwan's people in the dark. The government ran the only television station, with predictable results. Newspapers and magazines could only print the party line. For example, even we foreigners sometimes received our foreign newsmagazines with news or photos about the mainland blackened out. If there was a feature story on "Red China," or if the magazine was even mildly critical of the Nationalist regime, we would not get any magazine at all. When President Richard Nixon visited China in 1972, we who were only ninety miles offshore from the place where this astounding news was breaking could find out nothing about it.[17]

The Nationalists sealed off the island from the rest of the world. In addition to the normal security operations to prevent Communist infiltration, they were very picky as to whom they let into the island and whom they let out. Journalists, politicians, church leaders, and anybody else that the regime considered unfriendly could not get a visa. Those who did had to be very careful not to offend the regime or their visas would be canceled, and they would be asked to leave. In cases where the offense was considered to be serious enough, even at the risk of incurring diplomatic consequences, they would be deported. In the opposite direction, right-wing politicians, economists, and even

---

[15] Mendel, *Politics*, 64-95.
[16] *The History of Taiwan's Democratic Movement* (Taipei: Tsunah Foundation, 2003), 30-31.
[17] Ibid., 52-54.

churchmen (like the Orthodox Presbyterian Church's Carl McIntire, for example) were invited to Taiwan and treated like royalty.

As for letting their own people out, it was extremely difficult for a person without KMT connections to get an exit permit to go abroad for any reason. Those who did manage to get one were held on a tight leash while abroad. The regime had spies all over the world—and especially in the United States. People never knew who might turn up at a meeting they were addressing or who might read what they were writing. The safety and security of their families back home was always a concern should they be caught doing, saying, or writing anything that the regime considered unfriendly. In effect, the great majority of the people on Taiwan were imprisoned on their own island.

The regime paid thousands of people to spy on their neighbors and to report any expression of dissent or disagreement to the secret police. Taxi drivers were paid to listen in on their passengers' conversations and report any suspicious comments. Garbage collectors were paid if they discovered any documents in the garbage that were useful to government agents. Home helpers were paid to listen in on their employer's conversations and to track their visitors. Telephones were regularly tapped and mail opened by government censors. Restaurants and other public places were bugged in order to pick up conversations between unsuspecting people. Paid informants infiltrated every organization, attended every meeting, and sat in every classroom.

People were also under pressure to disclose information. A government agent, for example, might level some criticism of the regime in front of someone just to see if that person would report what he had heard. If he didn't, he was suspect. There were enough vague and ridiculous laws on the books to enable the police (of which there were fifteen varieties) to deport anybody or throw anybody in jail that the regime wanted deported or thrown in jail. In other words, many laws could normally be broken with impunity *until* an infraction became a way of disposing of someone who had made a political mistake. It was also not uncommon for people whom the regime did not like, or who could not be "caught in the act" to be framed by the secret police, with the same result. Even we missionaries were warned to be very careful about what we said in public or over the telephone, what we wrote and mailed, what we threw away, and with whom we discussed any politically sensitive matters. Living under these conditions was like living under a suffocating blanket, even for us.[18]

18 Ibid., 111-21.

New Life "Correction" Center on Green Island

All this was excused as necessary to keep the island on a war footing and to foil any attempt at infiltration by the Communists. In truth, the large number of military encampments spread throughout the cities and rural areas of Taiwan under the garrison command were not only there to defend the island against a Communist attack, but also to intimidate the Taiwanese people. Over eighty percent of the national budget was spent on building up the ROC's military might for an invasion of the mainland, an invasion that would never come. Meanwhile, the constitutionally mandated allocations for education and other social needs were woefully underfunded, and the people of Taiwan suffered accordingly.[19]

If anyone, particularly any Taiwanese, had the temerity to criticize or even question what was going on, he or she was immediately and ruthlessly silenced. Thousands of political prisoners were incarcerated in special prisons, like the infamous New Life Correction Center on Green Island, under abysmal conditions. In a confidential report describing the conditions we discovered in Taiwan, smuggled out to the States in 1971, I described this dire situation in some detail.

> When an informer reports another person for alleged antigovernment sentiments or activities, he will be arrested immediately and held by the Taiwan Garrison Command incommunicado for several months or even years. His home will be thoroughly searched. He will be asked to write a detailed biography, and if a confession is not forthcoming, he may be promised a release after a confession. Intimidation, by threats of the arrest of his family or friends and by torture, is often used to

---

[19] Ibid., 122-35.

obtain the desired results. After charges are made, the prisoner may have a lawyer, but all conversation is taped, typed, and sent to prosecutors and judges for study. Martial law is such that a just trial is impossible because the government can interpret the criminal code as it sees fit.

The total number of political prisoners is a closely guarded secret. We do know that between 1949 and 1955, over 90,000 anti-Kuo-Min-Tang elements, by no means all Communists, were arrested. Over half of them were executed. Now we hear first-hand reports that there may be over 1,500 arrests and 200 executions for "political offenses" per year. Some 30,000 families of political prisoners are severely curtailed in their activities. Wives are only permitted to hold menial jobs, and families are ineligible for even meager welfare assistance. This means that families of political prisoners are among the most destitute persons in Taiwan.[20]

[20] Karsen, Wendell, May 1970 letter to Paul Yont, NCCUSA, pr.p., 2.

CHAPTER 3

A Courageous Church

Missionaries and Mythology

As we have seen, the China lobby, particularly its missionary supporters, made much of the Chiangs' Christian commitment in their effort to mobilize American politicians and the American people to back the Nationalist cause. However, Chiang Kai-shek's history paints a different picture. In 1901, he married a peasant woman named Mao Fu-mei in the village of Xikou in Zhejiang Province who bore him a son—his heir-apparent, Chiang Ching-kuo. However, when he gained political and military stature in the aftermath of the 1911–12 revolution, he abandoned her. By 1905, during a brief stay in Japan, he had "acquired" another son, Chiang Wei-kuo, whom, he said, had been fathered by a close Chinese friend and whom he had adopted. It was rumored that he was, in fact, the boy's father. After taking a concubine named Yao and living a life of debauchery in Shanghai, Chiang married a fifteen-year-old girl named Chen Ah-Feng in 1921.[1]

---

[1]   Fenby, Jonathan, *Chiang Kai-Shek* (New York: Carroll & Graf, 2004), 22-23, 44-53.

Chiang Kai-shek
and Sun Yat Sen

It was while contending for the leadership of the Nationalist Party after the death of Sun Yat-Sen in 1925 that Chiang sought to consolidate his position by wooing Sun's sister-in-law, Soong Mei-Ling, daughter of the most wealthy and politically influential family in China. Sent on a "study trip" to America in 1927, Chen Ah-Feng was stunned to learn upon her arrival in New York that Chiang had publicly dismissed her as his "concubine" and claimed they had never been legally married. Chiang's immoral behavior, his association with gangsters, and his penchant for violence did not endear him to Mei-ling's mother, a staunch Methodist. She made it clear that she would only allow him to marry her daughter if he would consider becoming a Christian. Upon his promise to begin reading the Bible, she reluctantly gave permission for the marriage to take place in December 1927. This marriage brought Chiang the economic, political, and personal connections that would eventually enable him to emerge as the supreme leader of the party and the country. He was baptized in the Soong's living room two years later, explaining that he had decided to become a Christian after making a bargain with God that he would do so if God would deliver him from a desperate military position in a recent battle at Kai-feng. Obviously, he thought God had delivered him.[2]

Chiang's newfound faith did not have much effect on his associations, his lifestyle, or his policies. Neither did it seem to temper the couple's lust for power or the corrupt and ruthless nature of the Nationalist regime. "The Madame," as she demanded to be called, lived a double standard. While championing the cause of China's suffering masses at home and abroad, she lived extravagantly, demanded royal

[2]   Fenby, *Chiang Kai-Shek*, 163-71.

treatment, and privately practiced habits that she publicly exhorted the Chinese people to eschew.[3]

The Chiangs were astute enough to realize that Christian missionaries could not only bring some social benefits to China, but that they could also become a powerful influence on public opinion on behalf of the Nationalists in the countries from which they came, the United States in particular. So the couple supported the missionaries who were already in China and encouraged more to come. However, missionaries were only welcome if they stuck to their Bible studies, prayer meetings, worship services, and social service work; supported the regime; and ignored the dark side of its practices. A number of missionaries, happy to have an "open door to spread the gospel in China" at the invitation of a "Christian" president, by and large closed their eyes to much of what eventually led to the Nationalist defeat and the Communist takeover in China.

Nothing changed after the retreat to Taiwan in 1949. The Chiangs again appealed for missionaries to come to "Free China" to join them in strengthening their position on the island and in their crusade against the godless Communists. A flood of Protestant missionaries, particularly those who had served on the mainland and had been expelled by the Communists, responded enthusiastically. Since most of them had ministered to Mandarin-speaking Chinese, were strongly anti-Communist, and had benefited from the support of the Nationalists, they simply carried on as though nothing had really changed. They spoke the language of the rulers, supported the regime, and mainly ministered to the Mandarin-speaking minority.[4] Despite evidence that the Taiwanese people were suffering, they chose, for the most part, to ignore their plight.[5] Since most of their denominations represented comparatively small groups of Christians, they were not perceived as a threat to the regime.

The Roman Catholic Church, although larger, was by and large an ardent supporter of the Nationalists. The Vatican continued to recognize them diplomatically as the sole legitimate government of the whole of China (which it does to this day). While a handful of

---

[3] Ibid., 387-407.

[4] For example, the interdenominational publication, *Taiwan Christian Yearbook 1968*, includes Chiang Kai-shek's October 10, 1967, speech outlining his goals and objectives in retaking the mainland and defeating Mao Tse-tung, pp. 149, 151, 190, 195.

[5] By contrast, all RCA missionaries on Taiwan served under the Presbyterian Church of Taiwan, and most spoke Taiwanese.

Presbyterian Church in Taiwan
headquarters in 1969

foreign priests worked with the Taiwanese and were passionate about
their distress, the Mandarin-speaking church hierarchy largely ignored
them.

Presbyterians and Persecution

All of this affected the church we had come to serve—the
Presbyterian Church in Taiwan. This church *was* perceived to be a threat
to the regime—in fact, the biggest threat on the island. The Presbyterian
Church was made up almost entirely of Taiwanese and tribal peoples,
was 167,000 strong, and was well organized. It had a highly educated
leadership and constituency, was involved in every aspect of society, was
the repository of Taiwanese culture, and had dared to passively resist
the occupying power. In turn, the regime had tried its utmost to bribe,
coerce, tame, intimidate, infiltrate, and threaten the church. It was truly
a church under the cross—the cross of fascism.

Since the Presbyterian Church was Taiwanese, it used the
Taiwanese language in its churches, schools, and other institutions.
It also published Bibles, hymnbooks, and educational materials in
Romanized Taiwanese. As we have seen, in its campaign to convert
the Taiwanese people into good Nationalist Chinese, the regime did
everything it could to erase the core of Taiwanese culture from the
island—the Taiwanese language. All educational institutions, including
those run by the Presbyterian Church, were forced to use Mandarin
Chinese as the language of instruction. Any student caught speaking
Taiwanese on school premises was punished. All educational materials
had to be printed in Chinese characters. From time to time, the secret
police confiscated large stocks of Romanized Taiwanese Bibles and

destroyed them. The church was pressured to use Mandarin Chinese at any official public function and even in worship (which, for a Taiwanese pastor, amounted to trying to preach and pray in a foreign language).

The church had to comply with the government's educational policies or risk losing its schools, including its two seminaries and two Bible institutes. However, it steadfastly refused to use the language of the rulers in worship and in internal church affairs. The Taiwan Church Press, which published a weekly newspaper, was a particular irritant to the regime. Its editors bravely probed the parameters of what the regime would tolerate as the paper commented on church and social news and concerns. Sometimes entire issues were confiscated when they were deemed to have crossed the invisible political boundary.

The church was under constant surveillance. The secret police came to the General Synod office in Taipei weekly to interrogate church leaders and to search files. All phones at the church headquarters were bugged, and constant efforts were made to obtain information by attempting to bribe or intimidate support staff. Agents roamed the church's college and seminary campuses. "Professional students" were infiltrated into classrooms and church programs by the Kuo-Min-Tang. Agents sat in the rear of rooms listening, observing, and asking teachers or speakers tricky questions. They demanded copies of all programs and lists of all participants. They interrogated college and seminary heads and faculty members periodically. They sat in the backs of churches taking notes on every sermon preached.

The KMT presence was everywhere. The Ministry of Education dominated all activities in all schools, from propaganda posters to elections for student governments. At one church-related college, for example, only students whose parents were KMT members in good standing were permitted to run for the student council. Even though a graduate might have a perfect academic record, if his or her parents were not good KMT people, permission to study abroad was seldom given. Such students usually had a difficult time even getting a good job. Professors were forbidden to fail any student who had come from a mainlander family.

Slander and Stool Pigeons

The most devastating problem for the Presbyterian Church to cope with was the mistrust that was successfully sown by KMT agents among its leaders, teachers, colleagues, pastors, and church members. Four methods were used. One was to recruit visible stool pigeons that could intimidate and influence people at church meetings and gatherings. (One infamous traitor was nicknamed "five eyes" because, beside his natural pair of eyes, he wore glasses and used a magnifying glass with which to read. We all knew that he was an informer, so whenever he was present, no sensitive subject could be discussed.)

A second method was to use the carrot and the stick approach. For example, if you were a pastor, an agent might make an appointment for an afternoon tea visit. He would remind you pleasantly that you had a son who was about to graduate from high school. He would then suggest that if your son had any plans for studying abroad (a very high priority for Taiwanese parents), it would be much easier for him to get the necessary exit permit if you were to simply cooperate with the party. If the carrot approach didn't work, he would take out the stick and tell you that if you didn't cooperate, you and your family would be under constant surveillance. The pastor knew that once he was under the KMT's microscope, any misstep, or even a slip of the tongue, could land him in prison or maybe even cause him to disappear in the night.

A third method used was to spread false rumors. Even during the best of times, gossip spreads like wildfire. Under these circumstances, a stool pigeon could blackball somebody in the church that the regime wanted to discredit simply by starting a whispering campaign. Or, when someone was discreetly trying to find out whom he or she could really trust about some sensitive matter, stool pigeons could have a field day by simply sowing subtle doubts about people.

A fourth method used was to test people by sending them something that was critical of the regime in the mail, or to use someone to confide some politically sensitive piece of information to them. If people did not report they had received a mailed item or had heard a bit of confidential information, they would be trapped. If they did report, they would not know for sure whether they might inadvertently be implicating an innocent colleague.

Pastors were in a terrible dilemma. They knew that they needed to speak to the real needs of their oppressed people, but how could they even mention that they *were* oppressed? They read and preached from the prophets of old and knew that they had a similar prophetic duty to decry the evils of their own day, but how could they spell those out without risking arrest and without the people then losing their pastor?

One day, our pastor at Tiong-San Church (and one of the leading Presbyterian pastors), the Reverend Chhoa Chin-Li, came to our house in obvious distress. He had come to me, he said, because he knew that as a foreign missionary, he could trust me. A few days earlier, a copy of a

l-r: Chhoa Jin-li, Mrs. Chhoa, Joyce Karsen, the author (in Hong Kong, 1979)

speech made by Representative Donald Frazier of Minnesota outlining the terrible events of the 1947 massacre, decrying further support of the Nationalist regime, and pleading the cause of the Taiwanese people had been placed in his mailbox. (Frazier was one of the few enlightened American politicians who had done his homework on Taiwan and who had not been intimidated by Joe McCarthy or the China lobby.) Chhoa did not know and dared not ask if any of his colleagues had received this pamphlet, or if they had had anything to do with its distribution. If the secret police had placed it in his mailbox, he would need to report it. However, if they hadn't, and he did report it, perhaps he would be helping them trace it to the brave person or group who had risked distributing it. Would I please see if I could find out whether or not this had been privately distributed? I agreed to do so.

Then we talked heart to heart about what it was like for him to serve as a pastor under such awful circumstances. With tears in his eyes, he told me how torn up he was inside by the dilemma of knowing what he *should* preach and knowing what he *could* preach. Was it a pragmatic love to spare his flock the consequences of boldly "telling it like it was" that restrained him, or was it his fear of what would happen to him and to his family? He shared the agony of trying to "preach between the lines," not really knowing from one Sunday to the next whether or not he might end up crossing a line. We prayed together, hugged, and he left to resume his ministry under the cross. In the end, I found out that the pamphlet had been mailed by trusted dissidents and notified him that he therefore did not have to report receiving it.

Others were not as brave as he was. Although knowing they would be despised, some went over to the other side because they were either offered bribes that they couldn't resist or threatened with consequences that they were too weak to face. Knowing the pressures they were under, it was hard to judge them. But becoming a "Judas" meant terrible consequences for others, and eventually for them.

Isolation and Intimidation

Besides harassing the church at home, the regime tried to isolate it from its partners abroad. In 1972, for example, when the World Council of Churches called for the recognition of the government of the People's Republic as the legitimate government of all of China, the ROC government on Taiwan forced the Presbyterian Church to pull out of the council. Presbyterian delegates to international church meetings of various kinds were often denied exit permits, or the permits were delayed just long enough for them to arrive too late to be elected to important committees or to be scheduled to report on the church's state of affairs. Whenever delegates *were* allowed to attend such meetings, they had to submit agendas, delegate lists, reports, and a detailed description of anything they or anyone else had said about Taiwan or China. Even far away from home, Presbyterian leaders could not escape the long arm of the secret police, which had informants in various parts of the world to check on these things.

The regime also tried to deprive the Presbyterian Church of any of its foreign missionaries who might get too close to learning the truth and dare to stand with their brothers and sisters in their time of trial—especially those who spoke Taiwanese. Beginning in 1970, one such missionary colleague after another was either deported or not allowed to return to the island once he or she had gone on furlough. The intent was to raise a sword of Damocles over the heads of all Presbyterian missionaries to keep them from reporting to the outside world whatever truth they might know about the regime and its oppressive policies.

A Rock and a Hard Place

As Joyce and I learned the Taiwanese language, became acquainted with Taiwanese people and foreigners who knew the truth, read smuggled-in materials, and observed life around us, we knew in our hearts that true Christian service to the Taiwanese people would compel us to join them in their struggle to free themselves from the oppression and exploitation of the Nationalist regime. We also knew this would mean taking risks, but that these would be small in comparison to the life-threatening risks being taken by many of our Taiwanese colleagues every day.

Some missionary colleagues disagreed with us. Some believed that the Nationalists, no matter what their deficiencies, should be supported at all costs in order to defeat the Communists. We believed that combating one evil should not excuse supporting another. Others

Former PCT general secretary,
C. M. Kao

felt that it was a mistake to engage in activities that put one's visa at risk, and therefore one's opportunity to continue to preach the gospel in Taiwan. We were compelled to ask what kind of a gospel we were preaching if it did not include emancipation for those who were being exploited and oppressed. Still others thought that since we were guests in a foreign country, we should keep out of our hosts' internal political squabbles. We argued that if we were guests in someone's home and heard screaming in the bedroom in the middle of the night, we would have a moral responsibility to investigate and try to stop the violence, or at least to call the police. Could we, knowing what we knew, simply go about our "Master's business" without paying any attention to that part of his business that had to do with suffering people?

Some did not think it wise for foreign missionaries to get involved and thereby put their Taiwanese colleagues at risk. We could always leave, but they would have to bear much more serious consequences. We thought they were absolutely right. But what if the Taiwanese themselves *asked* us to become involved, *asked* us to help them do what they themselves could not do alone, and *asked* us to stand with them in their trials? Should we reply that it would be too risky for them, and incidentally for us, if we did so? We agreed that they, not we, should take the initiative and should weigh the risks and the consequences, but that we had a duty to join them in their struggle when invited. Or, if we did become involved in some activity that might put them at risk if they knew about it, we had an obligation not to tell them about it. Others believed that security was so tight that it was foolish to think one could engage in such activity without the secret police finding out about it. We believed that Jesus' own principle applied here: "Be wise as serpents and (appear) innocent as doves."[6]

---

[6] Matthew 10:16.

We understood why some of our colleagues thought the way they did. Some had been expelled from China by the Communists and were still licking their wounds. Others spoke Mandarin and worked mainly with Mandarin-speaking people whose perspective on things was, of course, entirely different. Still others were heavily invested in institutional work and were not as involved in the inner workings and struggles of the Presbyterian Church and therefore not privy to the back-hall conversations of its leaders. Some showed little interest in the *context* of their mission and were consequently rather unaware of the real plight of the Taiwanese people, while others had a rather narrow theology of mission.

When persecuted and oppressed compatriots and colleagues began to come to us and ask us to assist them in the cause of justice and human rights, we believed that we had a responsibility discreetly to do all that we could to help them. How could we, in the name of protecting our visas and our "missionary work" refuse to join them in difficult, at times even dangerous, activities in the cause of justice, when they were willing to risk imprisonment and even their lives for the same? And then, was not this kind of judicious participation *part* of our mission work? Were we not called to join them in *exposing* the evils that were going on around us, *opposing* those evils in any way we could, and *deposing* the perpetrators of those evils when and where possible? Under these circumstances, we came to see that the gospel is not only about *a*nnunciation, but also about **de**nunciation.

CHAPTER 4

Mission in Tense Times

Students and Strategies

Upon completion of language study in 1971, I was appointed as the island-wide associate coordinator for University Student Ministries by the Presbyterian Church in Taiwan (PCT) and served in that capacity along with my able Taiwanese colleague, the Reverend Andrew Hsieh. I could not have been assigned to a more sensitive area. All education, particularly university education, was strictly controlled by the government and was used to disseminate propaganda and exercise social control. I knew that because I was a Presbyterian Church missionary and a Taiwanese speaker, the government security agencies would watch me like a hawk.

Our mission in Taiwan was to assist the Presbyterian Church in its ministry to university students. I say "our" because my wife, Joyce, was also very much involved in this ministry. She warmly welcomed the many students who came to our home, entertained and counseled Reformed Church in America volunteers who came from the United States to help us with our student programs, and participated in many student outreach activities.

Andrew Hsieh and
the author
at a 1993 reunion

The Chinese people have traditionally placed a high value on education. Over 27 percent of Taiwan's population was in a school of some kind, while over 93 percent of its people were literate. Each child was entitled to nine years of free education through junior high school in a system patterned on the American system. Those wishing to continue their formal education past junior high had to compete for the right to do so through a national examination system. Some one million students were enrolled in high schools, but only 222,000 had been fortunate enough to make it into one of Taiwan's nine universities and eighty-four colleges, some of which were operated by various churches, the PCT among them. Three universities offered masters and doctoral programs, with an enrollment of approximately 2,500. However, about 3,500 students went abroad annually for their graduate and postgraduate studies, most of them to the United States. Because the academic and political environment in Taiwan was so stifling, 95 percent of them never returned—a crippling brain drain.[1]

The Presbyterian Church's university student work was a key ministry intended to reach out to those who would become Taiwan's future leaders. The overarching goal of the ministry, of course, was to introduce students to the Christian faith and to invite them to become followers of Christ. Many lives were touched through our programs, and not a few students answered Christ's call. A key component of our ministry was to help students become aware of the true situation of the society in which they lived and to motivate them to do something to

[1]   Mendal, *Politics*, 47-52.

address its problems and serve its people. In order to achieve this goal, we introduced students to the ideas, ideals, and lifestyle of Jesus Christ and developed programs that would get them out of their academic ivory towers and into the realities of Taiwanese society. There they could apply those ideas and ideals and live out that lifestyle.

The gospel message and their social exposure experiences led students to draw their own conclusions as to what their society was facing and what their role in its struggles should be, conclusions that we could not, of course, articulate publicly. Campus ministers and RCA volunteer "Interns in Mission" offered programs and activities at a string of seven student centers run by the Presbyterian Church and strategically located near key university campuses. Each center also had a student hostel where students could live together, build community, and explore ideas that were not being addressed in their university courses. Along with my colleague Andrew Hsieh, it was my responsibility to design these courses, train these campus ministers and volunteers, form and administer an island-wide Presbyterian campus ministry network, and oversee these programs. To carry out this ministry effectively, we needed an overall rationale and approach. I worked out a philosophy and strategy for campus ministry in a paper entitled, "A Suggested Approach to a Ministry to Higher Education in Taiwan." This paper was translated into Chinese, published in the *Ambassador* magazine,[2] and became the underlying basis for the PCT's university campus work and the training of its student workers.

The Way and the Life

Beginning in 1971, I also had the privilege of interacting personally with students attending Taiwan's prestigious Taiwan National University in our student work complex in Taipei, where I had my office. The complex was located one block from the entrance to the university and contained a student hostel and student center, which we named "The Way." As I taught and counseled students there, I became acutely aware of their academic, social, personal, and spiritual needs. I also became aware of the conditions on their campus, although it was off limits to foreigners unless one held an official teaching position. I learned that there was no academic freedom. All professors taught the same line. There were no courses in philosophy, ethics, values, or spirituality. Students were left to figure these things out on their own. There was no counseling to help them cope with personal,

---

[2]   March 1972.

Student work coordinators
Ng Choan-cheng
and the author
in front of
The Way Student Center

family, academic, and career problems and decisions. There was little discussion, because discussion could be dangerous—especially for the professor. There was too much emphasis on authoritarianism and the rote memory of formal facts. There was very little connection between what students were learning and what they were experiencing in their own lives. There was a strong emphasis on competition, which was out of sync with the traditional Chinese emphasis on community and cooperation.

Students were often not very interested in what they were studying because they had been "streamed" into a subject area as a result of their performance on the national exam. There was a great deal of distrust because government agents were everywhere, many of them in the guise of professional "students." No student and no professor dared to express a real opinion on what most mattered, even on the university grounds, which could be bugged. The universities were supposed to be secular, and therefore no religion was to be taught or practiced on campus. This put the Christian faith at a distinct disadvantage, since all subjects were taught within a broadly traditional Buddhist context. In other words, if a professor made a remark about something from a Buddhist perspective, nobody would raise an eyebrow since it was, more or less, "part of the woodwork." However, if somebody were to say something from a Christian perspective, everybody would immediately sit up and take notice.[3]

These conditions left us with a wide-open opportunity to minister to a host of needs. Our student center had a staff of four student workers, including a particularly gifted and effective worker named Susan Chang. We offered students what the university did

[3]   Mendal, *Politics*, 47-52.

Student residents
at The Way's
student hostel

not—counseling, goal setting, community, spirituality, courses in faith and life, and plenty of free-ranging discussion. I offered a number of courses in English, since many students were interested in listening to and practicing English with a native speaker. Some of my courses, like "Music with Meaning," "Movies with Meaning," and "The Art of Living," were "teaser" courses designed to attract non-Christian students to the center by analyzing contemporary songs and films from a Christian perspective and then challenging students to think through the implications for their own lives. For those who then became interested in a deeper understanding of the gospel, I offered a course exploring the basic tenets of the Christian faith entitled, "The Word and the Way."

Students were also curious about Christian festivals like Christmas and Easter. We capitalized on their curiosity by offering special parties and programs to help them understand that there was a lot more to these festivals than Santa Claus and the Easter Bunny. The discussion provoked by our courses and special events proved to be risky at times, since we had to assume that anything that was done or said at the center would be reported to some authority. I prayed for wisdom and practiced being "wise as a serpent, and innocent as a dove." For example, if an earnest student (or perhaps a KMT plant?) asked a sensitive question, I would reply, "Well, some people think this, others think that, and still others think something else." I would include the "forbidden view," but never say that it was mine. Only when I had known a student for a long time would I risk telling him or her what I personally thought in private. These were tough conditions under which to minister, but I kept reminding myself that God had sent us to Taiwan "for such a time as this."

Our ministry to students was challenging and fruitful. During the course of my two-year involvement in student ministry in Taiwan, it was gratifying to see Christian students grow in their faith and a number of non-Christians become followers of Christ. Several stand out in my mind.

The first is David Chen. I first met David in 1971 when he was a second-year university student. He began to attend a class at the student center and was soon a regular fixture at our home whenever we had gatherings there. David was a fifth-generation believer, but he was struggling. His grandfather was a Presbyterian minister who received a pittance for a salary. His father had been severely injured in a shipwreck and had barely survived. He was unable to hold a steady job and could not provide adequately for a family with seven children. When David attended primary and then high school, he had a few beans and a little rice in his lunchbox to barely keep him alive. He attended his local church regularly, but nobody really seemed to show much interest in him or in the plight of his family. David began to question how a God of love could allow such suffering in his family.

For the first time in his life, David felt noticed, accepted, and loved as part of our student center "family." He thrived at our home gatherings—and ate a lot! He became particularly close to our family and was a regular attendee at the student English worship experiences that we conducted at the Tiong-san Church on Sunday afternoons. Slowly he began to understand that God really did love him and his family. God was working to recycle all the difficulties that he had been through in a way that would open a door of hope for him in the future. His faith grew stronger, and he became a firm and enthusiastic believer.

One Sunday after worship, David asked if I would baptize him and serve him his first Communion. I was thrilled to do so and made arrangements with our pastor, the Reverend Chhoa Jin-li, to incorporate his baptism, along with that of another student, into the regular Taiwanese morning worship service. His baptism was a moving event for us all, and David became a regular member of the congregation. He went on to graduate from university, attend our Summer English Program, and then serve his compulsory time in the ROC military. Our family gave him a Bible as a parting gift and we kept in touch by mail.[4]

---

[4] We are still in touch. David went on to marry a Taiwanese girl who honored us by taking the English name "Joyce" after my first wife. Although we would not be able to communicate by mail after our expulsion from

David Chen and
the author after Chen's baptism

A second student that comes to mind is Beaver Lee. When I first met him and asked him why he had chosen the English name "Beaver," he replied, "From the TV program, "Leave It to Beaver." He was an earnest and likeable young man with a devout Buddhist background who was searching for the truth. He also warmed to the Christian fellowship that was offered at the student center and in our home. I tried to show him that Jesus and Buddha agreed on many things, but that Jesus went much farther and deeper when it came to living life fully now and having a hope for the life to come. I stressed that Jesus sacrificed himself for us and then rose from the dead to make it all possible. Beaver became very interested in the Christian faith, but he continued to struggle with the implications becoming a follower of "The Way" held for his relationship with his friends, his family, and his culture. He was like the rich young ruler—so close and yet so far. When we left Taiwan for a furlough in 1973, he was still struggling to come to a decision.

Little did I know it then, but Beaver Lee would become a living example of the way in which God works. We are called to plant seeds and water plants, but God gives the increase—and in his own time. Twelve years after I had lost contact with Beaver Lee, I received a letter

---

Taiwan, David, Joyce, and their daughter would come to visit us in Hong Kong. They eventually immigrated to the USA where David changed his name to Patrick and become eminently successful in the import/export business in Chicago. He also conducted an active campus ministry for Chinese university students on the Chicago campus of the University of Illinois and helped begin a Chicago branch of the Glendora, California, based Logos Evangelical Seminary. We reconnected in Chicago in 2006, some thirty years after we had last seen each other in Hong Kong.

Student group at Karsen home:
Beaver Lee in front row
(third from left) next to David Chen

in my mailbox in Hong Kong written in broken English. Beaver had met somebody who knew my address and wanted to write to tell me that after all these years, he had become a Christian.

> Feb 20, 1983
>
> Thanks God let me write this letter to show my thanksgiving that you giving me so much while we were together at Taipei Student Center. Sir, please forgive me for I am so stupid that I finally understand your teaching the meaning of "Art of Living" class after twelve years later! I seldom go to Church after graduation until last December. Within this ten years, I only learned busy for job and for choosing one girl to be my wife. But as the matter of fact, I lost my job and I am still single.
>
> Now I realize that all of the test are from the message of God. God let me have confidence to follow the way of Bible and to search the truth for the better life. No matter what happen in the future, God would be with me. Recently God guide me to find the job in one computer components producer to be a buyer. I know if not the blessing from God, I should not have chance to get this one vacancy....
>
> I love the song, "Amazing Grace." I was the sheep and missed the way, but God guide me the right way at the right time. Thanks God, you are my first teacher in Christianity....May God be with you and bless your sweet home forever.
>
> Very truly yours, Beaver Lee[5]

Obviously, I had not been too effective as an English teacher, but God had used my feeble efforts to touch Beaver's heart. I sometimes wonder how many other seeds that were planted and plants that were watered in Taiwan also bloomed into faith unbeknownst to me. Only God knows, and that is enough.

---

[5]   Feb. 20, 1983 letter from Beaver Lee, Karsen, pr.p.

A third "student" that comes to mind was Lu A-gim. I put "student" in quotation marks because A-gim, as we have seen, was actually our Taiwanese "amah," or home helper. A-gim was young, good looking, and very intelligent. Unfortunately, she had only received a rudimentary education, but she had succeeded in picking up English on her own. When she first came to us, although repeatedly invited to sit around the table with us, she demurred, believing that it was not an amah's place to eat with the family she was serving. However, in time she overcame her shyness, ate with us, and began to be exposed to our practice of prayer and table devotions.

Since her perspective on the world was limited, when I offered to teach her rudimentary information about geography, history, mathematics, science, and other subjects, she accepted and learned with alacrity. I also taught her how to play chess, and she improved so rapidly that she began to win (to her great delight, and to her teacher's chagrin). Since I had learned how to play Chinese chess at language school, we also played that game. However, when I invited her to join an English Bible study on the Gospel of Mark that I was conducting for university students in a local Presbyterian church, she demurred. As a poor farm girl, she did not believe she could mix with people out of her class. I persevered, arguing that from the Christian perspective, all people are equally valuable and accepted in God's sight. I also assured her that her English was actually better than that of most of the students. So she came, and she learned about the gospel and what it meant to become a follower of Christ.

When we first began to host student parties and events at our home, A-gim would help with all the preparations and serving but then retire to the kitchen or to her room. At first, we could not coax her to become part of the event. That was "above her status." Eventually, however, she began to join in some of the activities and then to participate fully. I noticed more than a few boys look her way or try to sit next to her. She was a gem, and they sensed it. Secretly, Joyce and I hoped and prayed that A-gim would not only become a Christian, but that she would develop a relationship with one of the Christian boys in the group.

A-gim had truly become one of the family. She loved our kids, and they loved her. She and Joyce enjoyed working together in the kitchen. She could see that our family was no different from other families in that we had our arguments and our failings. But she could also see that we deeply loved each other, that we could confess to and forgive each other, and that, above all, we felt loved and forgiven by God. She enjoyed

l-r: Stephen, Philip,
Rachel, A-gim

participating in our family events like birthday parties, a Mexican fiesta complete with piñata, game nights, Chinese New Year fireworks, story times, Christmastime, outings, and all the rest. We came to feel as though she was the kids' big sister and our daughter, and the feeling was mutual.

We had, of course, asked her many questions about her family—their heritage, their village, and their farm. We expressed an interest in visiting the farm and meeting her family. At first, this was unthinkable to her. I was, after all, a "professor" and her father was a mere farmer. Professors and farmers just did not mix in Taiwan, nor did the Taiwanese usually invite people to their homes except for relatives and close friends at Chinese New Year. However, we finally convinced her that in God's eyes, there is no caste system when it comes to his children, and that we personally would be delighted to mix with her family. Convinced, she arranged a memorable visit to her village of Pat-li and to her family on their farm.

We all had a delightful time. Her brothers took our boys out shooting birds; her father included me when dickering with another farmer over the sale of a water buffalo; her mother introduced Joyce to a Taiwanese farm kitchen. We were invited to be present when a Taoist priest showed up to conduct a ceremony to scare away the fire ghost since a hay stack had mysteriously gone up in smoke the day before. After an enjoyable conversation around a sumptuous Chinese meal, we bid a grateful farewell, feeling that there was now even a stronger tie between A-gim and us. The one amusing event of the day was when A-gim's father observed Rachel, our freckle faced four-year-old redhead, leaned over, and loudly "whispered" in Agim's ear, "What kind of a disease does that girl have?" (Unlike Westerners, Chinese do not have freckles, nor do they grow body hair or have long noses). A-gim and our family tried hard not to laugh. We were grateful for the opportunity to

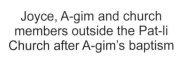

Joyce, A-gim and church members outside the Pat-li Church after A-gim's baptism

make this visit. It was important that her family meet us so that some kind of trust could be developed if and when A-gim decided to follow a different spiritual path from their own.

Of course, this visit provoked much discussion about how such a change could ever be accomplished. A-gim loved her family and did not want to hurt them or to cut herself off from them—a common struggle for any Taiwanese who considered becoming a Christian. What would she do when the family engaged in Taoist ceremonies, visited the Buddhist temple, or worshiped their ancestors? We encouraged her not to think of this as an either/or choice, but in some ways to see it as a both/and decision. With Naman the leper's dilemma in mind,[6] we explained that if she were to become a Christian and be baptized, she could tell her family that this would not mean that she was rejecting them or the ancestors, but that she now looked at the meaning of what they were doing differently. She could participate in these ceremonies out of love and loyalty to the family, but she would not be worshiping the Buddha or the ancestors. She would be respecting the Buddha and his teaching and venerating the memory of her ancestors, but her spiritual commitment would be to Jesus Christ and his way of life and salvation alone.

We were thrilled when A-gim made a decision to follow Christ openly. We were privileged to attend her baptism in the little village church in Pat-li, where I was asked to preach the sermon. She was able to work things out with her family and maintain strong ties with them. However, when it came to marriage, tradition proved to be stronger

---

[6]   See 2 Kings 5:17-18.

than personal choice. Several Christian male students were interested in developing a romantic relationship with A-gim, but her family and another prominent family in Pat-li had long before decided that the daughter of one and the son of the other should be married. And so it proved to be. A-gim felt free to bring her fiancé to our home to meet us, and we were very impressed with him both in terms of his looks and his character. However, he was "not yet" (as the Taiwanese are wont to say) a Christian.

We were invited to the wedding ceremony and were very proud of "our daughter" that day. Still, our emotions were mixed. We were glad for her, but sad that she would no longer be our amah. She would instead help her husband begin a small appliance business in Pat-li. Although he would not accompany her to church, he would not oppose her going either, and we continued to pray that he might one day come to faith through his wife.[7]

Programs and Propaganda

We were acutely aware of the KMT's brainwashing program to which all university students were constantly exposed. This was particularly true during the summer months when students were encouraged (read "pressured") to join the *Kiu Kok Thoan* ("National Salvation Youth Corps") camps, which were modeled after similar Soviet camps and Nazi youth programs. Students were enticed to these camps through sports and other types of enjoyable activities and fed a steady diet of KMT propaganda.[8]

We were determined to give students another choice by developing a number of summer programs that aimed at furthering our student work goals. In 1972, we ran a summer music camp at the Tung-Hai Christian University in Taichung. We also designed an "around the island" study tour for Presbyterian students. These students rode a bus around Taiwan, talking to people and analyzing social, economic, and political realities at each stop. They lodged overnight at Presbyterian churches, discussed their findings, and explored what those findings suggested for ministry and for the future of Taiwan.

---

[7] We enjoyed one more visit to Pat-li before our departure from Taiwan in 1973, but then, sadly, we would lose touch with our dear A-gim except for one last contact when Steve and Phil went to camp in Taiwan in the summer of 1976 and had a brief reunion with her. Renske and I searched for her in Taiwan in 1992, but, unfortunately, we were not able to find her.

[8] Mendal, *Politics*, 54.

We offered English camps in seven university towns. The camps featured English lessons, spiritual exercises, physical activities, and social service projects, and they were conducted by native-speaking American volunteers from the Reformed Church in America. Students lived in community for five weeks at PCT campus ministry centers and discussed current personal, spiritual, and social concerns. An island-wide "Round Up" was held at Tung-hai over the final weekend, which brought together the entire teaching staff and student participants from across the island, some 170 people in all. A number of the volunteer teachers stayed on for a year as "Interns in Mission" and lived in student hostels. They acted as bridges between the university campuses and our student ministers, student centers, and student hostels. The interns earned their keep by teaching English at the universities, which also served to give them a legitimate entrée to the university campuses.[9]

We designed two social immersion experiences for seminary students. One group went to rural areas to live and work with farm families. They learned about rural life in Taiwan, discussed their observations, and explored ideas for addressing the concerns and meeting the needs of rural people from a Christian perspective. Another group went to Taipei and took up factory jobs. They lived together in a student center hostel and spent their evenings talking with fellow workers and observing the conditions under which people worked. They too explored the spiritual, social, economic, and political implications of their findings and formulated strategies for future ministry and mission.

In all, around three hundred students participated in our demanding and challenging programs while resisting KMT pressure to join the KKT. As our student centers and summer programs developed and grew in popularity, they did not, of course, escape the notice of the regime. A number of efforts were made to sabotage them. Perpetual "students," recruited by the secret police to be their eyes and ears on university campuses around the island, were sent to infiltrate our student centers and to apply for our summer programs. They were easy to spot. In fact, we would always accept a few obvious ones so we would

---

[9]   For a full description of the Summer English Program during our time in Taiwan, see Karsen, Wendell, "Summer With a Purpose," *Church Herald*, October 15, 1971, and "Lighting a Candle at Both Ends," *Church Herald*, December 1, 1972. See also Karsen, Wendell, "An Experience Overseas," September 1972 (unpub. ms.), and "Bringing People Together," September 1973 (unpub. ms.), pr.p.

The author conducting staff training session for the Summer English program

know whom we were dealing with. Only when they were not around would the "real" conversations take place.

However, when a program went beyond the limits tolerated by the regime, more direct action was taken. A case in point was the summer industrial exposure program. Seminary students working and talking with factory workers about their working conditions, their problems, their opinions, and their concerns made the secret police very nervous. In the end, they moved to shut the program down. One night in the summer of 1972, the police swooped down on the Taipei student hostel where the students were living, arrested the lot, and clapped them in jail. The charge was disturbance of the peace. People in the neighborhood surrounding the student hostel had supposedly complained that the students were gambling, drinking, and raising a ruckus. The charges were, of course, completely false.

Andrew Hsieh and I learned what had happened in the wee hours of the morning. Taiwan was still under martial law, and Andrew bravely volunteered to go to the jail well after curfew and demand their release. (I could not go because my presence would have increased the problem rather than contributing to a solution.) The police said they would release the students under one condition—the program had to be shut down and the students sent back to their homes. Andrew and I decided by phone that we had no choice but to comply, since not to do so would have unduly endangered the students, their families and friends, and Tainan Seminary.

Events like this, although appearing to be defeats at the time, had a great impact for good on the young people who went through them, along with their families, friends, and classmates. Such experiences underlined the oppressive nature of the regime and exposed its hollow rhetoric for what it really was. In the end, when the students eventually became pastors, they would be among those who would courageously back the struggle for justice, human rights, and democracy in Taiwan in the name of the Christ they preached.

Research and Reports

Throughout 1970, as we learned the truth about what was going on in Taiwan from trusted sources, I took careful notes. I also began reading whatever I could get my hands on to document what I was hearing. This was not always easy to do because much of this type of material was banned in Taiwan. Some of my colleagues lent me sensitive material that they had managed to smuggle into the island in one form or another. Sometimes I had to resort to creative methods of educating myself. For example, during a vacation trip to Hong Kong in 1971, I bought a copy of George Kerr's *Formosa Betrayed*, a top book on the KMT's banned list. I disguised it as a birthday present, complete with birthday wrappings, ribbon and card, and mailed it to a friend's address, using a fictitious name. It got through.

The question kept nagging at me: "What are you going to do with the information you have gathered, just sit on it?" After consulting with colleagues, I decided to take a first step. Based on the information I was gathering, I began to send periodic reports out with trusted friends. These friends then mailed them to Reformed Church leaders, friends at the National Council of Churches USA, and other key people and organizations.[10] My reports always included a plea for action on behalf of the Taiwanese people in general and for the Presbyterian Church in Taiwan in particular. I also wrote letters to major newspapers and magazines under fictitious Chinese names exposing the human rights abuses of the Chiang regime and advocating self-determination for the people of Taiwan.[11]

Questions and Answers

Dr. Wolfgang Grichting, a German sociologist, had obtained permission to come to Taiwan at the beginning of 1970 to do a

---

[10]   See Karsen, pr.p.: December 1969, "Notes"; May 1970, "Report to Paul Yont, NCCUSA"; May 1971, "Report to Marvin Hoff, RCA"; July 1971, "Things You Should Know About Taiwan: A Report to Supporting Congregations"; November 1971, "Taiwan After the U.S. Expulsion Vote: Report to Marvin Hoff, RCA."

[11]   Karsen, pr.p.: March 2, 1972, letter to ten leading American newspapers and magazines with the alias "Chen Ping-chung."

study on religion and society (politics excepted) and to publish a book detailing his findings. He circulated an extensive questionnaire throughout various levels of society via churches, universities, and other institutions and organizations. After he had collated the results, he looked for people (particularly PCT missionaries) living in Taiwan who had an informed understanding of Taiwan's society to help him interpret his data. Grichting was introduced to Milo and Judith Thornberry, American United Methodist missionaries, seconded to the Presbyterian Church in Taiwan, who had arrived in 1965. They lived on the campus of the Taiwan Presbyterian Seminary in the Yang Min-Shan mountain area near Taipei where Milo taught church history. Like us, it had not taken the Thornberrys long to come to an understanding of the plight of the Taiwanese people and to become engaged in various activities to further the cause of human rights in Taiwan. They, in turn, introduced Grichting to other Presbyterian missionaries and friends (including Joyce and me). Our goal was to help him understand the real situation in Taiwan, including human rights questions that were not included in the survey.

A series of confidential evening meetings was quietly arranged by the Thornberrys in their home to help Grichting process his findings. He assigned different aspects of his data to various participants according to their expertise and asked them to write up their assessments. These were then discussed by the group as a whole, edited by Grichting accordingly, and incorporated into his book anonymously. The book was subsequently published under the title, *The Value System in Taiwan 1970*.[12]

I was responsible for the section on the Presbyterian Church in Taiwan's ministry to the aged and the young, and my analysis and suggestions for action were published almost as I wrote them. One of my recommendations read: "The PCT needs to prophetically and courageously attack the roots of the present social problems in Taiwan from the perspective of the Gospel with the spirit of speaking the truth in love, letting the chips fall where they may, and being willing to bear passively and patiently whatever consequences this may elicit."[13] Little did I know that this was exactly the course the church would take, beginning that very year. For a number of years, I did not think the Bureau of Investigation (BOI) or the Garrison Command ever knew about these meetings or who had participated in them, but I was mistaken.

[12] Taipei: 1970.
[13] Ibid., 195-99.

Wolfgang Grichting's book,
The Value System in Taiwan 1970

Expulsion and Exile

The Thornberrys continued to be a thorn in the side of the KMT through their discrete but active involvement in various Taiwanese human rights issues. They also masterminded the successful escape of their good friend, Dr. Peng Ming-min, from the island in January 1970.[14] Peng, a leading space law expert, had been under house arrest for a number of years for daring to publish a manifesto calling for self-determination for the people of Taiwan and had been threatened with assassination shortly before his escape.[15] The regime decided it could no longer tolerate the Thornberry's presence on the island.

In April of that same year, the Thornberrys were accused of having imported a bomb by courier from Japan, concealed it in a cake box, and planted it at the railway station in central Taipei, where they intended to commit an act of sabotage against the Nationalist Government. The charge was so ridiculous and so obviously an invention of the security apparatus that it was laughable. However, for the Thornberrys, it was no laughing matter. Government agents suddenly descended on their home, cut their phone line, forbid them to contact anybody, and said they had two days to pack up to leave. The Thornberrys finally smuggled word out to colleagues through their five-year-old daughter by folding a message into a package of gum and sending her to "play" at the neighbors, but to no avail.

[14] Phipps, Gavin, "Turbulent Times Recalled," *Taipei Times*, December 13, 2003, 16.
[15] Mendel, *Politics*, 117-18.

l-r: Peng Ming-min, the author, and Milo Thornberry
at 2003 reunion

The next day, they were unceremoniously expelled from Taiwan and treated like terrorists. Nationalist troops were stationed along the entire route of the considerable distance from their home on the seminary campus to the Sung Shang airport. The word had spread, and I wanted to go to the airport to demonstrate our solidarity with these colleagues, but I had been warned that this would be a suicidal thing to do. Little did I realize that theirs would be the first in what would eventually become a string of such expulsions or re-entry refusals for PCT missionaries who were involved in the Taiwanese struggle, in an effort to further isolate and intimidate the church.[16]

Secrets and Soul Mates

Following President Franklin Roosevelt's mistaken prognosis of the post-World War II Asian world, the United States continued to pursue his policy of propping up the Chiang regime's Republic of China as the future hope of the region, even after Chiang's civil war defeat and his Taiwan retreat. As we have seen, the regime's American supporters, the powerful China lobby, continued to spin and promote the myth of Chiang's benevolent rule in "Free China" and the KMT's democratic credentials. Fortunately, there were some who suspected otherwise, even among the U.S. Embassy staff in Taipei, and who were trying to uncover the truth and report it to the U.S. State Department.[17]

Sydney Goldsmith and Burton Levin were two such staff members. Since the "Taiwanese question" was such a sensitive one,

[16] Thornberry, Milo and Judith, "Our Human Rights Activities in Taiwan," in *International Friends and Taiwan's Democracy and Human Rights* (Taipei: Taiwan Foundation for Democracy, 2003, 27-34).

[17] Lederer, *Nation of Sheep*, 39-65.

Syd Goldsmith and the author at a 2003 reunion

they had to be careful and quiet in the way they went about gathering information. They gleaned what they could from intelligence sources and local opposition publications and dined discreetly with opposition politicians like Kang Ning-hsiang.[18] I was introduced to Syd and Burt at a public function in 1971. When they realized how much I knew about the Taiwanese scene and what kind of connections I had, they asked if I would be willing to meet with one or both of them quietly from time to time at the embassy. They guaranteed that my name, the RCA, or the PCT would never appear in any report they would give. I was hesitant, because I believed that I could be linked with U.S. intelligence, even though they assured me that they were not working for the CIA. On the other hand, here was a rare opportunity to argue the Taiwanese case at the highest echelons of the American embassy and to feed them accurate information. After consulting with a trusted Taiwanese church leader, I accepted.

Syd, Burt, and I worked out a way that I could enter a back door of the embassy unobtrusively and go directly to the meeting room without being seen by anyone other than an alerted security guard. I used to take a very circuitous route to the embassy to make sure I was not being followed. Throughout the next few years, until my departure from Taiwan in July 1973, I made periodic visits to the embassy for this purpose. I passed on any relevant information that I had on the regime's harassment of the PCT, its treatment of political prisoners, news about

18 Kang, who I met several times, was a well-connected and outspoken member of the fledgling Taiwanese opposition who was first elected to the Taipei City Council in December 1969, the month we arrived in Taiwan.

Taiwanese dissidents inside Taiwan and in the United States, material on Taiwanese concerns and aspirations, and the like.

How much of this information was passed on to the State Department and what effect it may have had on U.S. Taiwan policy I will probably never know. However I believed that I was at least doing *something* to counter the myths being fed to the U.S. Government and to the American people by the Chiang regime and the China lobby.[19]

Conviction and Courage

The expulsion of the ROC regime from the United Nations in October 1971 and the impending visit of President Richard Nixon to the People's Republic of China in February 1972 produced considerable anxiety among the Taiwanese. They were afraid that a deal was going to be made between the United States and the People's Republic (with the connivance of the ROC regime) at the expense of, and without any consultation with, the people of Taiwan. Presbyterian Church leaders believed that somebody must speak on behalf of the Taiwanese people and that it was now or never.

Dr. Dan Beeby, an English Presbyterian missionary and president of the PCT's Tainan Theological Seminary, drafted a public statement entitled, "The Fate of Our Nation." The statement was translated and edited by Dr. John Tin and other faculty and sent to the PCT General Assembly Office in Taipei. Church representatives then presented it to the Taiwan Ecumenical Cooperative Committee (ECC) (loosely akin to a national council of churches) as a draft, with the request that it be adopted and issued as a joint statement by the committee. However, agreement could not be reached. The PCT then courageously decided to issue the statement on its own. The executive committee secretly met at the General Assembly headquarters on the evening of December 17, 1971, to discuss and refine the statement and to organize its distribution throughout the island and abroad.

That evening, a courier from the General Assembly office knocked on our door at 11:00 p.m. and got me out of bed. He said the executive committee was assembled at the office, was working on an important public statement, and would like me to come and help. I had heard nothing about the issuing of such a statement at that point, but I threw on my clothes and immediately went to the headquarters, knowing that something big must be up.

---

[19] Ironically, as I wrote this sentence on October 24, 2003, news came that the greatest proponent of the ROC/KMT myth, and the darling of the China lobby, Madame Chiang Kai-shek, had died in New York at the age of 105.

The 1971 PCT Statement as displayed in a Taiwan museum

When I arrived, the general secretary, the Reverend Dr. C.M. Kao, explained the circumstances surrounding the issuing of the public statement. We all then discussed the text line by line. I suggested a number of changes in the English version, almost all of which were adopted in the final text that was released.[20] There was also a concern that the English translation, which was to be sent to news and church agencies around the world, should *exactly* reflect the double meaning of the Chinese text. In other words, when government officials would read the statement and accuse the church of promulgating "seditionist ideas," the church could point to the literal words of the text and rightly say that the statement did not, in fact, say anything of the kind. However, for those who knew the true situation, whether inside or outside of Taiwan, the text was worded in such a way that they could read between the lines and discern the real message. That message was a call for a new constitution, for elections that reflected the true political situation on the island, and for self-determination for the people of Taiwan. It said in part:

> We long to live here in peace, freedom, and justice. And we do not wish to be governed by Peking....We oppose any powerful nation's disregarding the rights and wishes of fifteen million people and making unilateral decisions to their own advantage, because God has ordained, and the United Nations Charter has affirmed, that every people has the right to determine its own destiny....We earnestly request that within the Taiwan area it [the government] hold elections of all representatives to the highest government

[20] Karsen, pr.p.: hand-corrected English draft of the PCT's "Public Statement On Our National Fate."

bodies to succeed the present representatives who were elected 25 years ago on the mainland...under a temporary constitution....[21]

The next task was to decide how to disseminate the statement throughout Taiwan and the world, both in Chinese and in English. We drew up a list of churches, Christian organizations, and news services abroad to which we wished the English version to go. I agreed to contact trusted colleagues who were going off island during the next few days through whom we could get the statement smuggled out and sent to the list.[22] Meanwhile, the statement would be issued on December 29 and published in Taiwan's newspapers as a paid advertisement. All PCT pastors would be asked to read the statement from their pulpits the next Sunday, January 2, 1972. The meeting was finally adjourned, and we returned to our homes in the wee hours of the morning, tired but elated that such a momentous step had unanimously been taken, yet a bit apprehensive at the possible fallout.

The plan was implemented but, not surprisingly, ran into immediate difficulties. The newspapers at first agreed to run the paid ads. However, once the government censors saw the text and reported to their superiors, the security people ordered the newspapers to cancel them. The cat was now out of the bag. The head of the garrison command called C.M. Kao and demanded that the statement not be issued. Kao replied that since the statement was an official act of the PCT executive committee, he was duty bound to carry it out. Meanwhile, ecclesiastical stool pigeons within the PCT alerted their security handlers, who reported the plan to have the pastors read the statement from their pulpits. The secret police immediately scheduled "tea times" with all PCT pastors and, using both carrot and stick, tried to prevent them from reading the statement on the following Sunday by bribery or intimidation. Some caved in, particularly in the capital, the security hub of the island where the pressure was the greatest, but most of them courageously read the statement.

Meanwhile, I had found people and means to get the English version of the statement out to the world with immediate effect. The major news agencies carried the story, while many church publications, particularly in the United States, featured it. Some called upon their governments to take action to protect the rights of the people of Taiwan. The *Church Herald*, in response to my urgings and those of other colleagues

---

[21] "Public Statement on Our National Fate," General Synod Executive Committee, Presbyterian Church in Taiwan, December 29, 1971.

[22] See official English version plus December 29, 1971, covering letter signed by C.M. Kao, Karsen, pr.p.

who were knowledgeable about and committed to the Taiwanese cause, published a particularly strong editorial calling for action.

> We think of Taiwan. What is going to happen to this little island, hovering under the shadow of the Communist Chinese dragon?... Will [President Nixon] surrender Taiwan for the sake of some paper-reconciliation with Communist China?...The position of Nationalist China would be far stronger today were it not for two disappointing factors. The first is the foolish insistence of Chiang Kai Shek's government that it was the real government of China, including the corollary that Taiwan is an integral part of China.[23] This has now backfired, with disastrous consequences. Though it supported Chiang Kai Shek, the United States should have repudiated this unrealistic and false thesis long ago. The second is that we have not insisted more strongly and publicly that Chiang Kai Shek's government become more representative of the people of Taiwan....Where have our often proclaimed principles and morality been in regard to these, the real Taiwanese people?...The cry of the Christians in Taiwan, in the words of the leaders of the Presbyterian Church on that island should ring in our ears and hearts. Out of their agony and peril they plead for our understanding, our help, and our prayers....Now is the time to pray and to write [government leaders], expressing our concern for freedom and independence for the people of Taiwan.[23]

Issuing the 1971 statement turned out to be a catalytic act. For the first time, the largest, best-educated, and best-organized group of Taiwanese on the island, the 167,000 strong Presbyterian Church in Taiwan, had publicly challenged the regime. Even though every effort had been made to suppress the statement, enough people eventually learned about it to boost the sagging morale of the Taiwanese people. The statement also brought the plight of Taiwan's people to the attention of the global church and the world in a dramatic way. Many were moved by the courage of the Presbyterian Church and its leaders and rallied to their side.

Cruelty and Compassion

Joyce and I had been in Taiwan only a few months when we began to hear gruesome tales of how political prisoners, who were arrested simply because they advocated justice and self-determination for the

---

23 Benes, Louis, "Are We for Righteousness, Freedom, and Peace?" *Church Herald*, January 28, 1972.

Taiwanese people, were treated. "Confession" under torture was the norm. The majority of these political prisoners were not executed, but without adequate blankets in winter, nutritious food, medical care, and sanitary conditions, they slowly deteriorated physically, mentally, and emotionally, and many died.[24]

Once a person had been imprisoned for political reasons, the secret police would visit the employers of every member of the person's extended family and order that they be fired. This left the family destitute, since nobody else would dare to hire them. The prisoner's family was made an object lesson to others who might be thinking of speaking up on behalf of the Taiwanese people or of questioning the Nationalist mythology.[25]

These reports aroused both anger and compassion within me. When an opportunity presented itself, I was more than ready to help these political prisoners as best I could. While in Hong Kong on vacation in 1971, I met an Amnesty International representative. When he heard what I had to say about Taiwan, he asked if I would be willing to be a contact person for Amnesty there. Since the deportation of the Thornberrys, the organization had found it very difficult to obtain accurate information on political prisoners in Taiwan. I agreed.[26]

Later, trusted people at Tainan Seminary asked me if I would serve as a conduit to funnel funds provided by the Presbyterian Church USA to families of political prisoners. Although I knew that I was getting into very risky territory, I also agreed to try to find a way to do that.

I had learned most of what I knew about political prisoners and their families from one of my Taiwanese tutors at the Taipei Language Institute who seemed trustworthy at the time—Gui Ek-bin. We had had many conversations about the real situation of the Taiwanese people, and he had been very vocal about the need for political change leading to their freedom from oppression. I assumed that from what he had divulged to me, he could be the source both for information on political prisoners for Amnesty and for trusted contacts to get the Presbyterian funds to those who most needed them. When I asked him if he would be willing to help his people by getting me specific information and by delivering funds, he agreed.

[24] Evidence compiled by DPP legislator, Hsieh Tsong-min, in 2005 shows that during the 1949-1987 martial law period, there were 29,000 cases of political persecution involving 140,000 people, of whom 3,000-4,000 were executed.

[25] Mendel, *Politics*, 119-31.

[26] See July 1, 1972, letter from Marlies Piontek, head of the Taiwan Coordination Group in Germany, Karsen, pr.p.

Gui began to feed me detailed information on the names and conditions of political prisoners during my private Taiwanese lessons at the institute, and I passed that on to Amnesty International through safe channels. He did not divulge the sources of his information to me, and I did not ask. Later, he also gave me specific information as to which families of political prisoners needed help, what kind of help they needed, and how much it would cost. I then secretly delivered funds to him in the privacy of our classroom at the institute, and he in turn delivered signed receipts to me from the families who received help that I then passed on to Presbyterian Church USA people through safe channels.

This went on for some time until shortly before our family was to leave Taiwan for a furlough in the United States in the summer of 1973. One day, the Reverend Ng Choan-cheng, the PCT's new associate coordinator for student work, with whom I worked, asked me to come with him to see the brother of a leading Taiwanese theologian, C.S. Song. This man, Song Choan-chong, was a top executive at the state-run oil company. When we arrived, Song startled me by asking how involved I was with Gui Ek-Bin. I replied that he had been one of my teachers at the language school and that I continued to visit him on occasion. Song then made it clear that he suspected there was more to it than that but did not spell it out. He said he was trying to help me by warning me that Gui could not be trusted and advised me not to see him again.

I left unsure as to what to do. On the one hand, Song's information could be true and Gui could be suspect. On the other hand, as a top oil executive, Song could well have had some kind of connection with the regime. Perhaps he was simply being used to sow seeds of suspicion to disrupt a relationship that had become suspect in the eyes of the security apparatus. Since I was about to leave Taiwan on furlough anyway, I decided not to see Gui again until after my return.[27]

Expulsion and Exposure

The Reverend Dr. Rowland Van Es, a fellow Reformed Church in America missionary and professor of Old Testament at Tainan Theological Seminary, shared my concern for human rights in Taiwan, as did most of the faculty and student body at that institution. Rowland

[27] Later, I heard that Gui had been arrested and that he had divulged our activities after being threatened and bribed. To this day, I do not know if that report was true.

l-r: Rowland, Judy, Rody, Scott, and Amy Van Es in their yard at Tainan Seminary

and I had worked out a code, based on Old Testament characters and events, which we could use to communicate with each other concerning sensitive subjects. Since our mail was censored and our telephones were tapped, we used this means to communicate via the one-day delivery Han-si-e (postcards). In this way, we could safely exchange messages and pass on information with a one-day turn around between Tainan in the south and Taipei in the north.

In late February 1972, I received an urgent coded postcard from Rowland. The Reverend Dr. Dan Beeby and his wife, Joyce, had received the shocking word from the police that they were to be expelled from Taiwan in ten days' time. Beeby, an English Presbyterian missionary, had become an ardent but discreet supporter of human rights for the Taiwanese during his many years as president of the seminary. He had managed to walk a tightrope. On the one hand, he had quietly encouraged the faculty and students to become discreetly involved in these issues. On the other hand, he had avoided precipitating the kind of overt action that would have brought down the wrath of the secret police on the institution and its parent body, the Presbyterian Church in Taiwan. The agents on campus and the security apparatus behind them had been unable to accuse him of fomenting any direct action against the regime. However, over the years, police reports and security innuendoes had added up until the government decided it could no longer tolerate him, and that it would quietly expel him from the island.

Apart from a concern for the Beebys and the personal trauma of their being suddenly uprooted from a place, people, and work that they loved, the church, particularly its missionary community, was alarmed. This would be the second PCT missionary couple to be expelled within a year's time. Should this continue, the regime's goal of isolating the Taiwanese church from its overseas partners and getting rid of or silencing any foreign missionaries who knew the truth about Taiwan would in time be accomplished.

The only way this could be prevented was to make sure the Nationalists paid a heavy price in world opinion—and thought twice about taking such action against anybody else. The Beeby case also presented another opportunity to let the world know the real story about Taiwan and to gain support for self-determination for the Taiwanese people. But how could that be done?

Because this crisis was too sensitive and the time was too short to convene confidential meetings with officials and colleagues in Taipei to decide on a commonly agreed course of action, I had to use my own judgment in replying to Rowland. By coded postcard, I learned from Rowland the exact timing and method to be used by the authorities in expelling the Beebys. He reported that they had been told the Kaohsiung chief of police, along with other officers, would quietly escort them from Tainan by a certain train on Monday, March 6. Once they arrived in Taipei, they would be moved to the airport by car under police escort and immediately flown to Hong Kong on a certain flight.

Several aspects of this plan were in our favor. Dan Beeby had been interviewed so often by this particular police chief that they had become personal friends. The chief would be in charge of the escort. However, he was chagrined that the Beebys were being expelled in such a manner and was only reluctantly carrying out his orders. Also, President Nixon was completing his earth-shaking visit to the People's Republic of China and had just signed the Shanghai Communiqué. Consequently, a number of reporters for the major newspapers and news services of the world were en route to Taipei to see how Taiwan would react to this shock.

I thought up a plan and relayed it to Rowland for his and Dan Beeby's approval.

1. I would write an anonymous letter to these reporters. It would explain the situation and invite them to a press conference with Dr. Beeby in the President Hotel's Philippine Room after his arrival in Taipei.
2. I would reserve the Philippine Room for March 6 at 2:40 p.m. and pay for it in advance under a fictitious name.
3. Rowland would unobtrusively board the same train and sit as far away from Beeby's car as he could.
4. Upon arrival in Taipei, Dr. Beeby would ask his police chief

"friend" if he would do him one last favor and let him say goodbye to a dear friend staying at the President Hotel on the way to the airport.

5. If granted, he would lead the police to the Philippine Room and proceed to hold a press conference about his expulsion from Taiwan with the gathered journalists. (If the police tried to remove him from the room forcibly, the reporters would, of course have an even bigger story.)

6. Rowland would proceed to the airport where he, I, and other missionary colleagues and friends we had notified would wait for Dan and Joyce's arrival. Upon bidding us a normal farewell, Dan would give a stealthy thumbs-up to indicate if he indeed had held the press conference.

The word came back by postcard that, although the chances of the plan succeeding were slim, the people at Tainan thought it was worth trying and I should proceed. I immediately went to the President Hotel (with my three-year-old daughter Rachel in tow to allay suspicion) and booked the Philippine Room (complete with tea and cookies) using a false name. I told them that I had invited a group of businessmen for a tea party for a friend, but that since I myself would be out of town and unable to attend, I would pay for the room in advance. They bought my story, collected the cash, and wrote me out a receipt. So far, so good.

I returned home, wrote the anonymous invitation letter, and made a series of discreet inquiries to determine where the news people were staying. I then hand-delivered the invitations by slipping the addressed envelopes under the various reporters' hotel room doors.[28] Again, no problems were encountered.

Now, the big questions were, of course, would the exit schedule and arrangements given the Beebys be changed? Would Dan Beeby's request to visit his "friend" at the President Hotel on the way to the airport be granted? Would the news reporters think these invitations were some kind of a hoax and not show up?

Rowland sent a last-minute coded postcard saying that all was in order, that the Beebys would leave as scheduled, and that he would be on the train and proceed to the airport once the Beebys had left the train station. Amazingly, all went according to plan. The train journey proceeded without incident, the police chief granted Beeby's request, and thirteen reporters showed up for the press conference, which lasted

---

[28]   See March 4, 1962, letter to Donald Shapiro of the *New York Times* and list of twelve other correspondents to whom the letter was delivered, Karsen, pr.p.

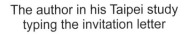
The author in his Taipei study
typing the invitation letter

half an hour. The police were flabbergasted but realized that they could not intervene. Beeby proceeded to tell them about his service to the people of Taiwan and the circumstances surrounding his expulsion. He then answered questions.

The police chief finally intervened by reminding the Beebys that their plane was due to leave shortly. The police then escorted the Beebys to the airport. Dr. C.M. Kao and a few other church leaders bravely came to the airport to bid them farewell. By that time Rowland and I, along with other Taipei friends and colleagues that we had notified, had also arrived. We all gathered around Dan and Joyce, bid them farewell, prayed together, and escorted them to the immigration gate. Meanwhile, Dan had given us the thumbs-up and whispered to me, "Someday we will meet again in Taipei and drink a toast in celebration of a free Taiwan."[29] Meanwhile, every security branch of the government had agents and photographers there who snapped pictures left and right of everyone who greeted the Beebys.

The word had already flashed around the world. When the Beebys arrived in Hong Kong, a group of reporters were there, and they held another press conference. When they arrived in England, there was a further press conference. We were thankful. The Beebys had been expelled, but in the process the Nationalist regime had received a black

29 Sadly, we never got to do so. Rowland and I kept in touch with Dan by correspondence and phone during our years of mutual exile. Years later, we would all be allowed back into Taiwan, but on different occasions. After teaching at Selly Oaks Colleges in Birmingham, England, for many years, Dan Beeby died at a ripe old age, mourned by us and by the hundreds of Tainan Seminary students whose lives he had touched during his time in Taiwan.

eye in terms of world opinion. More importantly, a small but significant step had been taken to expose the fraudulent nature of the regime and to plead the people of Taiwan's case. We hoped the regime would learn a lesson and not blacklist any more PCT missionaries. But, as we were to discover, that was a forlorn hope.

The Scholar and the Smuggler

As we have seen, since its occupation of Taiwan after World War II, the Nationalist regime had embarked on a systematic program of destroying Taiwanese culture and replacing it with a mainland Chinese culture permeated with Nationalist ideology. A key element in that program was an effort to wipe out the Taiwanese language, which is the core of Taiwanese culture.

Dr. Bernard Embree, a professor at the Presbyterian Church's Taiwan Theological College in Taipei and a skilled linguist, was dedicated to the cause of keeping the Taiwanese language and culture alive. Over a number of years, he had quietly developed an updated Romanized dictionary of the Southern Min dialect. Had he tried to have it published in Taiwan, the regime would have confiscated it. In 1972, he secretly communicated with the Hong Kong Language Institute Press in Hong Kong and asked if it would publish the work. The institute agreed, even though it knew that sales for this highly specialized work would be sparse. The problem then was how to get the manuscript to Hong Kong without its being discovered and confiscated by the regime.

Knowing that our family was about to take a vacation trip to Hong Kong, Dr. Embree asked me if I would be willing to smuggle the dictionary manuscript out in our luggage and deliver it to the publisher there. Joyce and I agreed. Embree delivered the manuscript to our home in person. To reduce the risk of discovery, I took a large number of files of papers of all sorts and scattered the pages of the substantial manuscript between them in a briefcase that I carried on board our aircraft. At the airport, a security agent took a quick peek into my briefcase, shut it, and waved us on board.

We landed in Hong Kong, I delivered the manuscript to the publisher, and the dictionary was published in 1973.[30]

---

[30]   Embree, Bernard L.M., *A Dictionary of Southern Min* (Hong Kong: Hong Kong Language Institute, 1973).

The Karsens in Hong Kong
with RCA missionaries
Walter and Harriet DeVelder in 1972

A Movement and a Mailing

In 1971, a group of Taiwanese Christians in the United States formed a movement called Formosan Christians for Self-determination. Most of them were well known Presbyterian pastors and scholars like Hwang Wu-tong, Lin Tsung-yi, Hwang Chiong-hui, and Song Choan-seng. Their goals were to make the plight of the Taiwanese people better known in the United States, to encourage their compatriots in Taiwan to demand the right to determine their own future, and to mount an organized campaign for Taiwanese self-determination among Taiwanese exiles in the United States.

In 1972, on Christmas Day, they issued a courageous statement calling for self-determination for the people of Taiwan. The statement was published in American newspapers; sent to U.S. senators and representatives; widely disseminated among Taiwanese groups in universities and churches; and promoted by PCT partner denominations, the Reformed Church in America included. The effect in Taiwan was immediate. Secret police agents came to the PCT headquarters and accused C.M. Kao and other Presbyterian leaders of having been involved in the development of this organization and in the formulation of the statement. He could honestly say that he had known nothing about it, and that even though the signatories were indeed Presbyterian pastors, they had taken this action on their own initiative while abroad.

Since the statement reflected the PCT's own stance in its 1971 statement, it would be a great encouragement to the church's pastors and other key Taiwanese to learn about this action and to receive a Chinese copy of the statement. However, it was equally important not to involve the Presbyterian leadership in such a project, even though they would welcome it, so that they could continue to honestly report

C.S. Song (second from left) and author (right) at 1981 CCA Assembly in Bangalore, India with David Lai (left) and other Taiwan representatives

that they had had no part in it. Unfortunately, it was too dangerous to print and disseminate such a sensitive document in Taiwan.

I immediately sent a letter by courier to C.S. Song and to a confidential colleague in the United States, suggesting a plan code-named The Bible Project and including relevant address lists.

1. The statement should be printed on official FCSD stationery and mailed from the United States. This would immediately remove any grounds for accusing the PCT of being involved and would give the statement a ring of authenticity, as over against locally produced and surreptitiously mailed mimeographed copies.
2. A Chinese copy of relevant data and statements concerning the FCSD, along with an up-to-date progress report, should be printed on official stationery and be included in the mailing.
3. The mailing should be sent to all Presbyterian pastors; university professors; religious leaders; foreign correspondents; central, provincial, county, and city government officials; and Taiwan newspaper and news magazine editors, as listed.
4. The mailing should not be uniform. As many different types of plain envelopes and fictitious return addresses should be used as possible. Addresses should be mixed, with some done by hand, some typed, some written in English, and some in Chinese.
5. The mailing should not be done in bulk. A batch of fifty envelopes with addresses in ten different cities should be mailed every other day.

I cautioned them, "If we don't use these procedures, the secret police can alert the post office to confiscate the entire mailing once they discover its contents. It is inevitable that they will discover some, but they will have no way to discover the majority if we are careful to follow these procedures."

The coded response came back in the affirmative. The "Bible project" was a go. The FCSD produced the materials, the confidential colleague financed and helped with the complicated mailing project, and the letters were sent out. It was too dangerous to inquire as to how many people received them, but I knew that the project had succeeded by the number of "rumors" I heard among my colleagues about the FCSD and its call for self-determination.[31]

The Preacher and the Politician

I had heard about Kuo Yu-hsin from PCT leaders I trusted. He was a Presbyterian layman who was referred to as a "father figure" among the Taiwanese opposition. He was a long-term representative of the Ilan constituency in the relatively powerless Taiwan Provincial Legislature and eventually became its speaker. Kuo was one of a handful of Taiwanese politicians who continually tested the parameters of criticism that would be tolerated by the Nationalist regime. He was also an articulate voice for the aspirations of the Taiwanese people. The Kuo Min-Tang had done its utmost to defeat him with bribes, intimidation, slander, accusations, etc., but he was so popular with his constituents that it had never succeeded.[32]

My colleagues must have also told him about me. In 1971, we met casually at church and at other general functions a few times. He then asked me to correct a letter that he had written in English to Minnesota Congressman Donald Frazier and send it out by courier, which I did.[33] However, I was cautious. I did not think that I should become directly involved with a Taiwanese politician who was also a well known opposition figure. Nevertheless, when he thought his life was in danger and personally appealed to me for help, I believed that I had a duty, as a fellow Christian, to assist him even though I knew it would be highly risky.

One day in 1972 he sent a message to me by courier saying that he feared he was going to be assassinated and asking for a meeting. The message explained that political tensions had been building for some time between the regime and the few local Taiwanese opposition politicians that had been tolerated. Several had recently been arrested.

---

[31] See May 1, 1972, letter to Song Choan-seng, Karsen, pr.p.

[32] Armbruster, William, "Jailings: A Warning to Dissidents," *Journal of Commerce*, June 11, 1976, 37. See also *History of Taiwan's Democratic Movement*, 38-39.

[33] See January 22, 1971, letter to Rep. Donald Fraser, Karsen, pr.p.

Tensions were rising ahead of the next provincial election. He had received word from reliable sources that an attempt was to be made on his life. He had been advised to escape from Taiwan and to ask for political asylum in the United States while he still had a chance. Before, the regime would have been only too happy to grant him an exit permit and let him "visit" his daughter in the States. He had never done so, knowing that he would be denied re-entry into Taiwan. Now, however, that route was no longer possible. He knew too much and would be too outspoken abroad, so the regime was out to get him within the next few months. Could I possibly figure out some way to get him out of Taiwan alive? And could we meet to discuss it?

Escaping from Taiwan was no small matter, especially for a well-known personality like Kuo. The island was a tightly controlled fortress, and people like Kuo were carefully tracked by the secret police. But how could I in good conscience refuse to try to help a fellow Presbyterian under these circumstances? I gave the courier a return message that included a code for all future "discussions" of this matter. I said I would do what I could and then let him know.

"Henry" (his code name) and I "discussed" several possibilities by coded correspondence delivered by courier. One was spiriting him off the island via a hired Japanese fishing boat off the rugged and less guarded East Coast. I had contacts in Japan through the East Asia Christian Conference who would have been willing to try to arrange this, but in the end we agreed that it would be too risky. Instead, I suggested getting him out by using a ruse similar to that which the Thornberrys had used to help Peng Meng-min escape in January 1970. We agreed that this would be the best route to try.

Meanwhile, a Presbyterian missionary friend from Japan, Jim Atwood, was in Taiwan as a tour leader for a group of Japanese students. I explained Kuo's situation to him and asked if he would be willing to help. He said he would be glad to. I asked him to explain the situation and the proposed plan to my friend, John Nakajima, the general secretary of the United Church of Christ in Japan, and ask if he would be willing to set it up on the Japanese end. We worked out a code so that we could correspond freely. The operation was referred to as "the student center construction project." A week later, I received a coded letter from Jim saying that Nakajima had agreed and that he would implement the plan as soon as they got the go-ahead from me.

The plan was as follows:

1. Kuo would send me clear passport photos for use in the project.

Interesting

2. I would send the photos to Japan by courier.
3. Nakijima would find a Japanese man who generally resembled Kuo in terms of height, weight, features, etc.
4. The Japanese man would wear a fake mustache, glasses, and a distinctive suit, shirt, and tie to have his passport photo taken. He would then apply for a passport.
5. The Japanese man would fly to Taiwan and enter the country as a tourist wearing a hat. He would then deliver his passport and his fake mustache, suit, shirt, tie, and hat to me. I would get them to Kuo by courier.
6. Kuo would don the disguise and fly to Japan using the Japanese passport. Nakijima would then work out arrangements from there to gain him entry to the States on the grounds of political asylum.
7. A few days later, the Japanese "tourist" would go to the Japanese Embassy in Taipei and report that his passport and air ticket had been stolen. He would be assisted to get a new passport and air ticket and fly back to Japan.[34]

Now Kuo and I had to talk things over face to face. I thought my office at the Presbyterian Student Center would be the safest place to meet. We could meet there at night after the center was closed, the lights were out, and no one was around. His driver would do his best to throw any agent who might be tailing him off the track.

We met at the student center, and he agreed to the plan. I notified Atwood in Japan by coded letter to proceed. However, no sooner had I sent the letter than Kuo sent me an urgent message saying that he now had reliable information that the secret police had been ordered not to carry out their plan to have him eliminated and that we should put our plan on hold. I immediately notified Atwood.

In the end, Kuo was "encouraged" to leave the island and immigrate to the United States. There he carried on his fight for self-determination for the people of Taiwan.[35] I, along with C.M. Kao and other PCT leaders, received an invitation to attend a farewell dinner in his honor. However, distressing as it was to decline, I did not dare participate. Apparently Kuo *had* been followed to my office. When I went to the travel agency that handled all the PCT's travel arrangements

---

34 See April 20, May 3, and June 16, 1973 coded correspondence with Jim Atwood (alias Stenztel), Karsen, pr.p. See also Kuo's undated passport photo and list of items needed for the hoax sent to him by courier.

35 Kuo Yu-hsin was very active among Taiwanese dissidents in the United States. In 1978 he even ran for president against Chiang Kai-shek's son and

Kuo Yu-shin, as portrayed
on a Taiwan stamp

to pick up some tickets a few days after our meeting, the Presbyterian owner of the agency looked me in the eye and said, "I am trying to help you. I understand that you had a meeting with Kuo Yu-Hsin in your office a few nights ago. That was a very dangerous thing for you to do. You must have nothing further to do with him if you want to continue to work in Taiwan." I had heard rumors that this man was a KMT sympathizer, so I looked him in the eye and, hard as it was, lied through my teeth. "There never was such a meeting. Somebody must be spreading false rumors about me."

---

designated heir, Chiang Ching-kuo, in absentia. (See campaign articles and correspondence in Karsen, pr.p). He corresponded with me from time to time through that year. He was always grateful to me for having taken such a risk to help him when he thought he needed it. When I was banned from Taiwan and put on the regime's black list in 1974, he suspected that one of the reasons why this had happened was that I had been linked to him and to his efforts on behalf of the Taiwanese people. His card to me upon hearing the news read: "For whom doth the bell toll? It tolls for thee."

CHAPTER 5

On the Black List

Censors and Consequences

As we became more involved in the human rights struggle in Taiwan, Joyce and I knew that, despite our efforts to keep our activities as clandestine as possible, the risk of expulsion or of visa denial was increasing. We had been given the postal censor code by a trusted friend, so we knew by the markings on our envelopes that our mail was being read on a regular basis. We had therefore been very careful not to discuss any sensitive matters in our letters and to warn people who wrote to us to refrain from doing the same. We had also been careful about what we said on the phone or in public and to whom we said it.

However, it had become clear that we were under more than routine surveillance, even for a Presbyterian missionary engaged in university student work and speaking Taiwanese. Private warnings by Song and others made it clear that we were becoming increasingly suspect in the eyes of the secret police, and that we might be in danger of having our application for a re-entry visa denied. This was confirmed when A-gim courageously reported that she had been followed home by

The author and C.M. Kao

the secret police on several occasions. They were pressuring her to report on the comings and goings at our house and on the conversations that were held there and offering her money to cooperate. Her dilemma was solved when we encouraged her to cooperate with the police and gave her safe "information" to report.

The time had come to make arrangements for our furlough in the United States. Figuring that we might run into difficulty trying to obtain a multiple re-entry visa from the central government, we decided to apply for a one-time re-entry permit that could be obtained at the provincial level. We thought that we might in this way be able to do an end run around the central government's security apparatus. We applied and were relieved to receive the permit a short time before our scheduled departure.

Upon our departure in July 1973, however, the warning bells grew louder. After saying farewell to C.M. Kao and other Presbyterian officials and friends at the airport, our family was pulled out of the immigration line and asked to go to a private room. There, uniformed personnel from the Bureau of Investigation and other security agencies proceeded to go through our luggage with a fine-tooth comb. On the previous afternoon, I had paid a farewell call on Dr. Kao at the General Assembly headquarters. During our talk, he had given me some confidential documents and asked me to deliver them to the Formosan Christians for Self-determination leaders in New York. Believing that the average agent could not speed read in English, I had scattered the documents in among scores of other papers in files in my large carry-on briefcase.

When I saw how extensively the agents were going through our things, even paging through children's books page by page, I quietly shoved my briefcase behind the seat on which I was sitting. After they had delayed the entire flight for more than half an hour and had found nothing suspicious, they allowed us to board. I walked ahead of my wife and children to conceal the briefcase that I had quickly slid out from behind my chair. It was only when we were almost to the end of the hallway leading to the door of the plane that I overheard someone exclaim, "We forgot to check his briefcase!"

We boarded the plane before they could catch up with us and were taking our seats when they came running into the plane loudly demanding that we return to the inspection room. By that time, the other passengers, who were disgruntled at being delayed and wondering what was going on, were all ears. I said in a voice that all could hear, "You have held up this plane long enough! My wife and children are now finally seated and I do not want to delay these people any longer. I have nothing to hide. You can search through anything else you want to search, but please do it here."

The security agents became flustered at the prospect of trying to force a family to get off the plane against their will. They looked quickly through our hand luggage, which was crammed with cassette tapes, boxes of slides, and files. Some of the passengers began to grumble about holding up the flight any longer and about hassling a family with three little children. The agents finally retreated in embarrassment without searching my briefcase (which I had shoved out of sight behind a seat), and the plane pulled away from the gate. However, these had been ominous signs.

After visits to several countries en route, we finally landed in Chicago, where we emerged from customs and immigration to our family's squeals of delight and tears of joy as hugs were exchanged all around. Then we were off to our temporary home in Wheaton, Illinois. There we unloaded the car with everybody excitedly talking at once, trying to catch up after almost four years of separation. The food was about to be placed on the table when my father handed me an express letter from Taiwan that had arrived the day before. I went into the bedroom to escape the hubbub and, puzzled, opened the letter.

The letter was from the Reverend David Lai, a Presbyterian Church colleague who had served as my official "sponsor" in Taiwan, as required by the government. He had been visited by the provincial police who had informed him that he could no longer be my sponsor, since my provincial visa had been revoked. Although he regretted having to do it, he had been instructed to write this letter and had sent a copy to the Presbyterian Church of Taiwan's headquarters. Reading between the lines, I knew that he had been forced to take this action, with a policeman looking over his shoulder.

Karsen family
"welcome home"
picnic

I was stunned. It seemed like only yesterday that we had said our farewells at the very airport where we had just landed and launched our missionary career on that beautiful island among those wonderful people. Now we were being told that our ministry there was over.

I returned to the family celebration and masked my inner turmoil, saying nothing to the family or to my wife until two days later, after I had spoken with Reformed Church officials about the letter. They were overwhelmingly supportive. They would send an inquiry to the ROC Ministry of Foreign Affairs, with a copy to the Presbyterian Church in Taiwan, asking if there had been some error. If not, on what basis were we being denied a re-entry permit by the provincial authorities?[1] They never received a reply, but Presbyterian leaders in Taiwan assured the RCA and us that they would do their best to work things out.

Hopes Raised...and Dashed

After discussing our case with people at the Ministry of Foreign Affairs, Presbyterian Church officials advised us by phone to apply to the ROC central government for a multiple re-entry visa. Since the re-entry permit had been revoked at the provincial level, a visa application at the central level would allow them to override the provincial authorities without having to rescind anything they had already decided. The PCT was quite hopeful that this strategy would succeed.

After several months of negotiations, the PCT informed us joyfully by phone in early January that their hopes had been realized. The foreign ministry had finally informed them that we had been

[1]   See Marvin Hoff's February 22, 1974, letter to me and his February 25 letter to Hugh O'Young, the ROC consul general in Chicago, Karsen, pr.p.

granted four-year multiple re-entry visas and that a telegram had been sent to the ROC consulate in Chicago with instructions to issue them. Overjoyed, but wondering if the news was too good to be true, I phoned the consulate to make an appointment to get the visas stamped in our passports. It turned out that the official I dealt with was a Taiwanese who was familiar with the Presbyterian Church and with missionary activity. However, when he checked his cable file, the only back cable that he had not yet received was the one with the number that the PCT had given us. Nevertheless, since it was a missionary case, and since I had given him the correct number, he agreed to give us the visas, figuring that it was simply a bureaucratic error. Feeling somewhat apprehensive, I went to the consulate on the next day, and our visas were promptly stamped into our passports. We were going back!

I immediately phoned the good news to RCA and PCT authorities, to our family and friends, and to our supporting churches. Having been scheduled to return to Taiwan in mid-January, we went into high gear—purchasing airline tickets, holding a garage sale, buying last minute supplies, packing our suitcases, and bidding our farewells. The Lombard, Illinois, Reformed Church, which had been our home church while in the States, hastily arranged a farewell dinner and gave us gifts.

Two days before we were to depart, in the middle of a garage sale, the phone rang. It was the Taiwanese official at the Chicago consulate. He said he was sorry but that he had received an urgent cable from Taipei ordering him to cancel our visas. Dumbfounded, I asked him why. He didn't know, but could I please come down so that they could put an official cancel chop on the visas. I was stunned and inclined to tell him no. However, because he had been kind to us and could be in trouble if the visas were not canceled, I agreed.[2] Upon hearing the news Joyce dissolved into tears, and I got a great lump in my throat. We were not, after all, going to be able to go back to the place and people that we had grown to love.

When I arrived at the consulate with the passports, the counsel, with many apologies, chopped them "Canceled." Then he and his colleague, realizing this could give their consulate and ROC-U.S. relations a black eye and to soothe our frustrations, invited us to a Chinese dinner and cultural performance. I politely declined and took my leave. It was a long drive home.

I phoned the bad news to RCA and PCT officials, who were as sad and frustrated as we were. When we returned to the Lombard church

---

[2]   See passports with ROC canceled visas dated February 1974, Karsen, pr.p.

that Sunday and I walked in to sing with the choir, there was an audible gasp from the congregation, who had assumed that we would have been safely back in Taiwan by then. The pastor invited me to tell the congregation our story, and I did—the first of many times that story would be repeated verbally and in print.

Communication and Call

The Reformed Church General Program Council voted to send a stiff protest to the ROC Government.[3] The Program Council was concerned about potential fallout for their other Taiwan missionaries and about the plight of the Taiwanese people in general and the Presbyterian Church in Taiwan in particular. I wrote a letter explaining our circumstances and the situation in Taiwan and sent it to our forty-two supporting churches.[4] I also wrote an article about the human rights situation in Taiwan for the *Church Herald* [5] and contributed to an information packet containing suggestions for action that was sent to all Reformed Church pastors and their congregations.[6] I spoke in scores of Reformed churches and to other groups about the situation in Taiwan and asked our people to press their legislators to advocate self-determination for the Taiwanese people. In short, the RCA and I used the publicity generated by our visa denial as a launching pad for an educational campaign concerning Taiwanese human rights throughout our denomination and beyond.

One of my speaking engagements was organized by Dr. Peng Ming-min, the leading Taiwanese dissident and an expert on international space law. Peng had escaped from the island in 1970 and had been teaching at the University of Michigan. Hearing that I would be speaking at the University Reformed Church in Ann Arbor, he invited me to meet afterwards with a group of Taiwanese university people in his home. I was able to give them a firsthand account of recent events in Taiwan, along with the details of my visa denial episode. They filled me in on the latest Taiwanese efforts in the United States. Finally, we discussed what could be done to further the cause, both in Taiwan and in the States. Little did he or I dream then that two decades later Peng would be able to return to Taiwan—and even run for president![7]

---

[3]   Reformed Church in America, *Hotline*, April 10, 1974.

[4]   See February 11, 1974, letter to partner in mission churches, Karsen, pr.p.

[5]   Karsen, Wendell, "A New Cry from Barmen!" *Church Herald*, June 14, 1974, 9, 25.

[6]   See Marvin Hoff's June 6, 1974, letter and accompanying materials, Karsen, pr.p.

[7]   An election that he unfortunately lost.

The author and Peng Ming-min at 2003 reunion

Still wanting to serve the Chinese people, Joyce and I responded to a call from the Church of Christ in China, Hong Kong Council, to go to Hong Kong to do youth and education work, beginning in May 1974. Meanwhile our entire household, including my extensive library, was still in our home in Taipei. Colleagues kindly packed our things and shipped them to Hong Kong. With sad spirits, we were forced to leave Taiwan behind, but "Ilha Formosa" and especially the Taiwanese people would always have a big place in our hearts.[8]

Probes and Rebuffs

From 1976 on, Joyce and I made several attempts to return to Taiwan. At first, we entertained the hope that getting back, even for a short visit, might make it easier to return there eventually and take up our work once again. In 1976 while planning a speaking trip in the USA, I booked my return flight through Taipei, intending to see whether I might be allowed back in, at least as a tourist. I walked into the ROC consulate in Chicago and casually asked for a tourist visa. To my surprise, without bothering to check a computer, they stamped one in my passport.

My hopes were dashed, however, upon arrival at the new Chiang Kai-Shek Airport near Taipei. As soon as the immigration official punched my name into her computer, all havoc broke loose. Several officials at the rear ran over and ordered me to stay where I was. They then went into the immigration chief's office and conferred for a long time. When they emerged, I asked if I might join them there and explain my situation. They declined curtly and announced that I was going to be placed on the next flight to Hong Kong. I asked them to call the office

---

8   Joyce, who died of cancer in 1989, would never be allowed to set foot in Taiwan again, and I would remain on the regime's official black list for nineteen long years.

The Karsens bidding
farewell to Steve (right)

of the American Institute in Taiwan (AIT, formerly the U.S. Embassy) and let me talk to the officials. They again declined and indicated that if I wanted to make a call, I would have to use a public phone in the transit area. I explained that I had no Taiwan coins to operate the phone and that there were no moneychangers there. Would they please lend me a coin? "No!"

A man, who turned out to be a newspaper reporter, was standing nearby and had overheard the whole conversation. He offered a coin and helped me put the call through. I explained my case. The AIT official promised to contact the ROC Foreign Ministry immediately and to call back at the public phone. He did, but with the expected news. All contacts at the ministry were "busy." When my flight was announced, the security agents escorted me aboard the plane and made sure I stayed there until it took off. Later I learned from the AIT that the Foreign Ministry returned its call immediately thereafter.

The AIT advised me to write them concerning my case. They promised to take it up with the Foreign Ministry and to press for a reason for denying me re-entry into Taiwan. After a series of letters between the AIT, the Foreign Ministry, and me, the AIT finally received a letter charging me with having helped Peng Meng-min escape from Taiwan. I wrote a letter of protest, pointing out that I could not possibly have been involved, since Peng had escaped only one month after my arrival. The AIT made one more effort on the basis of my letter, but the Foreign Ministry refused to budge. Apparently, it was a case of guilt by association with our colleagues Milo and Judith Thornberry who *had* arranged Peng's escape.

Although neither Joyce nor I were allowed even a brief visit to Taiwan during our Hong Kong years, our children were. When our two sons, Stephen and Philip, applied for visas to go to a summer camp there, the requests were granted. A few years later, Steve asked if he could transfer to Morrison Academy in Taichung to finish his high school course. He had been invited to live with our good friends, Paul and Ilene Peterson, Paul being the principal of the academy. Again a visa was granted. However, a year later, when he was about to graduate, Joyce applied for a visa for herself and our two-year-old son, Andrew, who had been born in Hong Kong. In an accompanying letter, she explained that her sole reason for traveling to Taiwan was to represent our family at Steve's graduation. (I did not even bother to apply, thinking that I was the main culprit and would spoil her chances of receiving a positive reply.) Ironically, they granted two-year-old Andrew a visa to come on his own but denied one to his mother.

In the spring of 1979, the Hong Kong Oratorio Society, a one-hundred-voice international choral group in which I sang, was invited to perform a concert tour in Taiwan. Here was an excellent chance for me to more or less sneak back into Taiwan on the shirttails of this huge choir. I was wrong. Out of the one hundred visas requested, only mine was turned down.

CHAPTER 6

Aiding the Cause in Exile

Conduit and Colleague

Although we had been reassigned to Hong Kong, we could not, of course, simply walk away from our Presbyterian colleagues and friends in Taiwan and from the Taiwanese human rights issues. I continued to keep in touch with Amnesty International people in Germany; Ronin Publications people in Japan; Formosan Christians for Self-determination people, church officials, and publication editors in the United States; and representatives of other human rights organizations.[1] Whenever I could contribute something relevant regarding the human rights struggle in Taiwan, I did so.[2] Since I was acquainted with some top people in the U.S. consulate in Hong Kong through our church, I met periodically with them and with official guests who were passing through, who were interested in my information about and opinions

[1] E.g., see Marlies Piontek, Amnesty International, July 1, 1974, letter and my July 16 reply, Karsen, pr.p.
[2] For example, beginning in 1978, during my twelve years as editor of the Hong Kong Christian Council's English Quarterly, *News & Views*, I was able to publish ten articles on current events in Taiwan.

Amnesty
International logo

on Taiwan issues. I also continued to urge Americans to write their representatives in Congress concerning Taiwan.[3]

Officials of the Presbyterian Church in Taiwan were happy to talk whenever they came through Hong Kong and when we attended common meetings together in other places. Through these encounters I learned the latest PCT and human rights news. People like C.M. Kao, Andrew Hsieh, and others could, in turn, learn from me how Taiwan's situation was perceived in the outside world. I could also help them send sensitive communications to churches and organizations around the world when that was needed. Furthermore, since I had begun to make regular visits to the People's Republic of China (PRC) in 1977, I could report on the situation on the mainland and on the emerging church there. These meetings were also very helpful to them emotionally. They had a safe place and a trusted friend with whom they could openly discuss in their native tongue all the difficulties they faced. They knew that I had an insider's view and that I was a committed supporter of the Taiwanese cause.[4]

Struggle and Solidarity

During our early years in Hong Kong, tensions between the ROC regime and their political opponents (particularly the PCT) rose steadily. The Presbyterian Church issued several more courageous public statements that had strong political overtones.

In a lengthy statement issued November 18, 1975, entitled "Our Appeal Concerning the Bible, the Church and the Nation," five demands were made.

1. The government should "preserve the freedom of religious faith which is guaranteed to the people in the constitution." Specific

---

[3] E.g., see Rep. Guy Vander Jagt's August 27, 1974, correspondence with my cousin, Ruth Custer, Karsen, pr.p.

[4] See January 14 through November 19, 1975, correspondence with Marvin Hoff, Karsen, pr.p.

objection was made to the recent confiscation of a large stock of Romanized Taiwanese Bibles, including a new translation.

2. The government should "help overcome our isolation in foreign relations." Specific objection was made to the government-imposed ban on membership in the World Council of Churches.[5]

3. The government should "establish a relationship of mutual trust and confidence between the government and the church." Direct dialogue between government and PCT officials on the reformation of society was called for.

4. The government should "help toward the reconciliation and working together of all people living in Taiwan. The end of "discrimination based on provincial origin or party membership" was advocated.

5. The government should "preserve human rights and the welfare of the people." Specifically, the government was asked to "focus its attention on the problems of corruption in society, of the unequal distribution of wealth, of avarice, of public peace and order and of pollution." The government should "also adopt effective measures to safeguard human rights and the welfare of the people."[6]

On August 16, 1977, the PCT issued a strong statement, entitled "A Declaration on Human Rights," calling for the recognition of Taiwan as an independent nation. Among other things it stated:

> We request President Carter to continue to uphold the principles of human rights while pursuing the "normalization of relationships with Communist China" and to insist on guaranteeing the security, independence, and freedom of the people of Taiwan.
>
> As we face the possibility of an invasion by Communist China, we hold firmly to our faith and to the principles underlying the United Nations Declaration of Human Rights. We insist that the future of Taiwan shall be determined by the 17 million people who live there....

---

[5] The regime had forced the PCT to pull out of the WCC when it acknowledged the legitimacy of the government of the People's Republic of China.

[6] See "Our Appeal Concerning the Bible, the Church and the Nation" issued in the name of the PCT's General Assembly and signed by N.C. Wang and C.M. Kao, November 18, 1975, Karsen, pr.p.

PCT poster celebrating
thirtieth anniversary of
issuing of 1977 statement

In order to achieve our goal of independence and freedom for the people of Taiwan in this critical international situation, we urge our government to face reality and to take effective measures whereby Taiwan may become a new and independent country.[7]

The statement reflects great concern over the possible recognition of the People's Republic of China by the United States as the sole legitimate government of China (a possibility that became a reality on December 16, 1978). The Taiwanese once again believed that they might be sold out by the KMT regime through some accommodation with the PRC at their expense. Also, an impending December election, with the possibility that opposition politicians could make significant gains over the increasingly embattled KMT, was about to be held. Under these conditions, the KMT's security apparatus had continued to tighten the screws, with the result that the people of Taiwan in general, and the Presbyterian Church in particular, felt more isolated than ever.

The reaction of the regime was predictable. It confiscated almost all five thousand copies of the August 21, 1977, issue of the *Taiwan Presbyterian Weekly* in which the statement appeared. The government demanded that a new statement be issued stating that some people had apparently misread the original statement's meaning. The church refused, saying that it stood by what had been written. The church

---

[7]   See "Declaration on Human Rights by the Presbyterian Church in Taiwan" issued in the name of the PCT's General Assembly and signed by H.E. Chao, H.K. Weng, and C.M. Kao, August 16, 1977, Karsen, pr.p.

was accused of offending the good name of the late president Chiang Kai-shek. The PCT responded that President Chiang's ideas could not dictate what the church should hold on these issues. The church's position was based on its theological contemplation and church tradition. It was not the intent of the PCT to try to overthrow the regime, but to push it to change its suicidal policy of claiming to be the government of all China and thereby risking the diplomatic isolation of Taiwan without even consulting its people. The regime accused the PCT of being pro-Communist and antipatriotic. The PCT replied that being anti-Communist and patriotic did not necessarily mean being pro-KMT. Reprisals were threatened, but the church bravely stood its ground.[8]

In light of these developments, in late October 1978, Presbyterian leaders decided to explore whether they could quickly organize a conference on the mission of the church in Asia and thereby garner support from partner churches and Christian organizations around the world. Such a conference would have two goals:

1. To explore with partner churches ways in which the PCT, as a "church under the cross," could creatively strengthen its life and witness under the difficult circumstances in which it found itself.
2. To show the regime and the world that the PCT was not an isolated and forgotten church, but a church with partners around the world that would stand with it during this critical time.

To have maximum impact, the conference would need to be convened as soon as possible; it was hoped within five weeks.

Some PCT people involved in these preliminary discussions believed that time was too short to plan and implement such a major conference. In their opinion, the most that could be done would be to gather a few people who had ready access to Taiwan and hold a small meeting. However, it was agreed that Dr. David Gelzer of Tainan Seminary, a UPCUSA missionary, would be sent to Hong Kong to meet with a few leaders there to explore possibilities.[9]

David arrived in Hong Kong and met with a few people who were not very encouraging. The time was too short; the logistics

---

8   See November 17, 1977, "Presbyterian Church of Formosa and the Kuomintang—Continuing Conflicts." Karsen, pr.p.
9   I was then serving as the executive secretary for education for the Hong Kong Christian Council.

l-r: David Gelzer, the author, and Tan Lam-chhiu at 2007 reunion

were too difficult; the ROC/PRC struggle was too sensitive an issue in Hong Kong. He then came to see me. Having been involved in the Presbyterian Church's ministry and in the human rights struggle in Taiwan personally, and knowing that I was being asked to help very close friends and colleagues, I had quite a different view. In the end, I convinced David that not only could such a conference be pulled off, but that the PCT should think in terms of a *worldwide* conference that would involve church leaders from partner churches in Asia, Europe, and North America. In my view, only this kind of a gathering would have the desired impact.[10]

I offered to act as the conference coordinator, since such a gathering could be organized from Hong Kong through my contacts with church leaders around the world. The organizing would have to be done outside of Taiwan anyway, since every effort would be made to sabotage the conference, should the regime get one whiff of what the PCT was up to. David was very encouraged. We set up a code that we could use to communicate publicly. I was to be "Wanda Wilke," and the conference was to be referred to as our "Secondary School Religious Education Project."[11]

David and I immediately made phone calls and sent a series of cables to friends abroad: to Yap Kim-Hau (general secretary of the Christian Conference of Asia) in Singapore; Newton Thurber and Marvin Hoff (officials of the UPCUSA and the RCA) in the USA; Dan

---

[10] See David Gelzer's October 23, 1978, letter to Bishop Yap Kim-Hao, Karsen, pr.p.

[11] See my November 10, 1978, coded letter to David Gelzer, and his November 16 reply to me, Karsen, pr.p.

Beeby (United Reformed Church professor at Selly Oaks Colleges) in the United Kingdom; John Nakajima (general secretary of the United Church of Christ) in Japan; Kim Kwan Sung (general secretary of the Korean National Council of Churches) in Korea; LaVerne Mercado (general secretary of the NCC Philippines) in the Philippines; Earle Roberts (general secretary of the Canadian Presbyterian Church) in Canada; Hartmut Albruschat (official of the German Evangelical Church [EKD]) in Germany; Richard Deutsch (chair of the Basil Mission) in Switzerland; Kwok Nai-Wang (general secretary of the Hong Kong Christian Council) in Hong Kong; and others. All we had to tell them were the proposed dates, December 4–6, and the general nature of the conference. The Presbyterian Church would provide meals and lodging, but participants would need to cover their own travel costs. People would need to clear their schedules, provide travel funds, and trust our word in lieu of an official invitation which, of course, could not be sent for security reasons. Everything had to be kept secret.

David returned to Taiwan and conferred with PCT officials. A coded cable came back. Our "project" was a "go!" Phone calls and telegrams flew back and forth between Hong Kong and key contacts. News was relayed to Taiwan, and detailed conference plans relayed back to Hong Kong, by coded letter and telegram. In the end, after four weeks of intense communication and planning, eighteen church leaders from nine countries arrived in Taiwan as individual "tourists" and made their way to the conference venue. There they met with twenty-eight participants from the Presbyterian Church in Taiwan. Only the South Koreans did not show up. They were denied exit permits by their own repressive regime.[12]

The results and timing of the conference were gratifying. Leaders of the Presbyterian Church in Taiwan were greatly encouraged and partner church leaders could experience firsthand the hopes and fears of the Presbyterian Church and the people of Taiwan. They returned to their home countries strongly recommitted to supporting the Taiwanese people in their struggle for human rights in general and the Presbyterian Church in its struggle with the KMT regime in particular. Full reports of the conference were published in church periodicals and elsewhere, and Christians in the countries represented were called upon to pray for the Presbyterian Church and for the people of Taiwan. They were also encouraged to petition their political leaders to press the ROC

---

[12]   See my November 24, 1978, communication to the conference participants, Karsen, pr.p.

regime to grant full human rights to the people of Taiwan and to give them an opportunity to determine their own future freely.[13]

The timing of the conference proved providential. Just ten days after its close, the United States recognized the People's Republic of China, and President Chiang Ching-kuo abruptly canceled the island-wide elections. Tensions between the regime and the Presbyterian Church continued to tighten, but the conference had reassured church leaders that they were not bearing their cross alone.[14]

Crisis and Courage

On December 10, 1979, a large rally was organized by Taiwanese opposition leaders to celebrate Human Rights Day. The rally took place in the large southern city of Kaohsiung. Although speakers were critical of the government and the KMT, not one of them made any attempt to incite the huge crowd to violence. Nevertheless, a serious riot did ensue. The cause of the riot was hotly debated, but, in the end, the evidence pointed clearly to the Taiwan police and their security bureau handlers. Instead of merely keeping order, the police used the rally to create an incident. Surrounding the ten-thousand-strong crowd in a threatening manner, they began drawing the circle tighter and tighter until they eventually provoked physical resistance. Using this as an excuse, they then launched an attack on the crowd with predictable results. A melee erupted in which, according to government reports, 183 policemen and hundreds of "rioters" were injured.[15]

Using this as a pretext, the regime then launched an all-out attack on opposition politicians and on well-known dissidents and their supporters. Hundreds were detained, some disappeared, and others went underground. Three opposition publications, *Formosa*, the *Eighties*, and *Spring Wind*, were closed down and their editors arrested. Sixty-five prominent people were arrested, and forty (including eight

---

13 See the TPC's "Report on a Consultation on THE MISSION OF THE CHURCH IN ASIA TODAY" and a comprehensive personal report by Richard R. Deutsch, chair of the Basil Mission, Karsen, pr.p.

14 The RCA delegates to the consultation were former Taiwan missionaries Carl and Lucile Schroeder. Their participation, and the subsequent American recognition of the People's Republic of China, stimulated the *Church Herald* to run a cogent and comprehensive cover story on Taiwan and the PCT written by J. Martin Bailey, editor of *A.D.* magazine, entitled, "Taiwan: the Church, the Government and American Reality" (January 26, 1979).

15 *The History of the Democratic Movement* (Taipei: Tsunah Foundation, 2003), 51-57.

2003 display showing 1979 Human Rights Day rally leaders

Presbyterians) were eventually charged with fomenting sedition against the state. It was obvious that the embattled regime was out to smash the growing opposition movement once and for all.[16] However, the key organizer of the Kaohsiung rally, Hsieh Ming-teh (who had spent many years in prison as a political prisoner), escaped the net.

As soon as word of the "riot" and its aftermath reached Hong Kong, I immediately notified my contacts around the world.[17] Marvin Hoff from the Reformed Church, Newton Thurber from the UPUSA, Amnesty International, the Asia Human Rights Group, and others responded quickly by telegraphing protests to the ROC government and asking for the release of the victims of these events, particularly the Presbyterians. Nevertheless, in the end, the regime put them all on trial and gave most of them long sentences. However, the authorities were not going to let things rest there.

Hsieh Ming-teh, the organizer of the rally, hid out in friends' homes for twenty-five days. He even underwent plastic surgery to try to escape detection. Some of those who helped him were Presbyterians. They informed the PCT's general secretary, C.M. Kao, of the situation and asked for his advice. He took a pastoral approach and said that the church had a duty to be merciful to Hsieh, since he had come to them for help and had not committed any crime.

Kao's involvement became known to the regime, and it seized this opportunity to arrest a person whom it considered to be a chief nemesis. PCT supporters abroad were shocked to receive this news.[18]

16 Kurata, Phil, "The Sound of Silence," *Far Eastern Economic Review*, June 13, 1980, 16.

17 See the series of telegrams, letters, and statements dated from Mid-December 1979 through February 1980, Karsen, pr.p.

18 See the Reformed Church in America's April 30, 1980, *Hotline*, Vol. 9, No. 8, for a typical reaction.

We were also galvanized into action. Again, even stronger protests were lodged with the ROC government, this time addressed directly to the president, Chiang Ching-kuo. In Hong Kong, I obtained fifty-four signatures of Hong Kong missionaries and church members on a letter that read,

> Mr. President. We Hong Kong residents are alarmed that your government has arrested the Rev. Dr. C.M. Kao, general secretary of the Presbyterian Church of Taiwan. We believe the charges against him are unwarranted, and we request you to order his release. We believe that any trial or imprisonment of the Rev. Kao will discredit your government in the eyes of all who uphold freedom and democracy around the world."[19]

Prayers were offered around the world on Kao's behalf, and on behalf of the other seven defendants. Our May 2, 1980, follow-up letter to President Chiang stated,

> This letter is to register our continuing and growing concern for the Rev. Dr. C. M. Kao....We note that he has now been formally charged, that he is to be tried in secret by a military court and that, if convicted, he could draw a sentence of between 10 years in prison to death. Mr. President, we again appeal to you to order the release of the Rev. Dr. Kao without delay."

However, Dr. Kao and the others were tried on May 16, 1980,[20] in an "open" trial. The decision to not hold the trial in secret was probably made because of the worldwide protest that it had engendered. Dr. Kao and his codefendants were eventually sentenced to seven years in prison.[21]

During his imprisonment, my colleagues and I made every effort to keep Dr. Kao's unjust incarceration at the forefront of people's minds and prayers. His moving writings from prison were printed and circulated. Letters continued to be written to newspapers and to the ROC government calling for his release.[22] In a series of radio broadcasts

---

[19] See May 2, 1980, letters addressed to President Chiang Ching-Kuo and list of signatories, Karsen, pr.p.

[20] King, Bob, "The Church under Fire," *Far Eastern Economic Review*, May 23, 1980, 22.

[21] In the end, Dr. Kao served four years and three months and was then released on parole.

[22] See the series of letters, statements, and articles concerning Kao's imprisonment from mid-1980 to mid-1984, Karsen, pr.p.

The author
broadcasting in
Hong Kong

over Radio Television Hong Kong that highlighted stories of Christians who had been imprisoned for their opposition to injustice, I dedicated an entire broadcast to Dr. Kao's story and included his poems and songs written from prison.

In a letter to his wife, Ruth, marking the third anniversary of his imprisonment, he wrote,

> Today is the third anniversary of my imprisonment. I bought two chicken legs and celebrated the day with my cellmates. These past three years have been very important and meaningful to me.
>
> 1. These three years of suffering have disciplined my faith, my body, and my spirit.
> 2. These three years of quiet thought have given me a deeper understanding of my own shortcomings and weaknesses.
> 3. The concern and love which you and other relatives and friends have shown me over the past three years have helped me understand more clearly how precious and reliable are the strong ties which Christians have for each other in the family of God.
> 4. In the last three years, those with whom I have been in contact— the sea captain, the truck driver, the company director, the army officers, the important underworld figures—have all helped me to a deeper knowledge of many facts about a different life and society than my own.
> 5. In these three years, I have read the Old Testament four times and the New Testament six times, as well as reading about 170 good books. This has been of considerable benefit to me.
> 6. In these three years I have been able to share in the sufferings of more than thirty friends and share the love of God with them.

The Bible says, "Strengthen the weak hands, and make firm the feeble knees. Say to those who are of a fearful heart, 'Be strong, fear not! Behold your God will come with vengeance, with the recompense of God. He will come and save you.'...For waters shall break forth in the wilderness, and streams in the desert" (Isaiah 35:3–6).

Yes, I am certain that God can really make waters of joy break forth in the wilderness and cause the desert of despair to be transformed by streams of hope. (He enclosed a poem that he had composed in prison).

God's Way Is the Best Way

I asked the Lord for a bunch of fresh flowers,
    but instead he gave me an ugly cactus with many thorns.
I asked the Lord for some beautiful butterflies,
    but instead he gave me many ugly and dreadful worms.
I was threatened, I was disappointed, I mourned.
But after many days, suddenly, I saw the cactus bloom with many flowers,
And those worms became beautiful butterflies flying in the spring wind.
God's way is the best way.[23]

More than another long year later, on August 15, 1984, Dr. Kao was finally released.[24] We were proud of his colleagues in the Presbyterian Church in Taiwan, who, despite tremendous pressure from the regime to do otherwise, had maintained Dr. Kao as their general secretary during the whole time of his imprisonment. It was obvious that his courageous example, his transparent humility, and his strong faith and hope in the face of suffering had galvanized the church and all who were struggling for human rights in Taiwan, turning them into an unstoppable force.[25]

---

[23] See April 24, 1983, letter from Chun-ming Kao to Ruth Kao, Karsen, pr.p.
[24] See official announcement by the ROC's Coordination Council for North American Affairs' spokesman, Fredrick F. Chien, addressed to the UPCUSA's Newton Thurber dated August 15, 1984, Karsen, pr.p.
[25] See "Report of the April 21-24, 1981, Meeting of the General Assembly of the Presbyterian Church in Taiwan," 3, Karsen, pr.p.

A Time of Trial

Due to the critical needs of some of our children, Joyce and I had returned to the States in July 1984.[26] During what would end up being a six-year hiatus in my cross-cultural missionary service, I first served as a visiting professor at Western Theological Seminary in Holland, Michigan, for a year and then as the Reformed Church in America's coordinator for mission communication for five years. This job entailed scheduling all RCA missionary speakers, leading denominational mission education workshops and other events, serving as the mission secretary for the church's work in Kentucky, and leading mission education tours.[27]

In November 1986, I underwent major gallbladder surgery. I was barely back on my feet and in the office when our family was hit with the shock of our lives. Shortly after Christmas of that same year, Joyce was diagnosed with ovarian cancer of the worst type, for which there was no known cure. Our lives were to be changed forever. After an initial surgery in January 1987, we were told that she had three to six months to live.

After recovering from the surgery, Joyce began an intensive chemotherapy program. This meant semimonthly overnight stays in the hospital followed by horrible after-effects for almost a week each time. We would then have a fairly normal few weeks before repeating the process. We had not given up hope but hung on every blood count report and prayed that she might receive one of those breakthrough kingdom miracles. In a way, she did. Through a series of surgeries and various types of chemotherapy, Joyce fought a brave two-and-a-half-year battle against a disease that had come straight out of hell. The way she dealt with her illness was an inner miracle of the spirit. As I often said to people, Joyce was built of faith and piano wire. She continued on as administrative assistant at the Grace Episcopal Church in Holland as long as she could. She taught an adult education course on suffering and the presence of God at the Third Reformed Church. During a period when the congregation experienced several tragic

---

[26] For a reflective article on our ten years of mission service in Hong Kong, see Karsen, Wendell, "The Beat Goes On," *Church Herald*, January 4, 1985, 18.

[27] The first such tour was a trip west with a group of sixteen people to learn about the RCA's mission to Native Americans. See Karsen, Wendell, "The Dawn of a New Day," *Church Herald*, September 5, 1986, 6-9.

Hudson and Amy Soo
and son meet
Karsens at the
Hong Kong airport

deaths, somebody in a small group once asked her how *she* was doing. She replied, "I'm struggling to live while preparing to die." Our family struggled and prepared with her to keep hope alive while not denying the realities of increasingly pessimistic medical reports.

The Reformed Church was very gracious to me as I struggled to cope with Joyce's illness, the needs of four children (including one nine-year-old who was still at home), and my responsibilities as a staff member. My position also demanded quite a bit of travel, and my schedule often had to be adjusted to enable me to give Joyce and the family the support they needed. Joyce was able to stave off the cancer long enough to enjoy one more trip to Hong Kong with our son Andrew and me in August 1988. Although short on energy, she enjoyed reunions with friends and colleagues and visited the Wai Ji Center for the Mentally Challenged that she had done so much to help bring into being.

On June 17, 1989, Joyce died. After her death, I felt like walking out into the woods, sitting down under a tree, and never getting up again. But I had a twelve-year-old boy to take care of, the loving Third Church congregation around me, and caring Reformed Church colleagues to help me through this dark valley. I also sensed the hand of the loving God that I had told others about for so many years reaching out to me in a special way and lifting me up.[28]

---

[28] For a synopsis of Joyce's life and work, see "Joyce Hughes Karsen," Ratmeyer, Una, ed., *Hands, Hearts and Voices: Women who Followed God's Call* (New York: Reformed Church Press, 1995), 57-58.

Fast Forward

The DPP and the KMT

In May 1992, the Christian Conference of Asia (CCA) sponsored a subregional consultation, "Co-working with Ecumenical Solidarity in the Mission of God." It was to be held in Hsinchu, Taiwan, and I was invited. I was concerned about having visa problems, but Presbyterian colleagues assured me that things had changed. Ninety percent of the names on the black list had been removed. They were sure my name must have been among them, but they were wrong. When I applied for a tourist visa to attend the meetings, it was denied, even though my new wife Renske's application had been approved.[29]

At that time, I was serving the Hong Kong Christian Council as its secretary for education and communication. Our general secretary, Dr. Tso Man-king, was confident that he could prevail upon the ROC Foreign Ministry to change its mind, since the foreign minister, Dr. Frederick Chien, had been a member of his church in Washington, D.C., when he was the ROC ambassador to the United States. He was also wrong. He made several calls to the Foreign Ministry, but the minister was always in a meeting or somewhere else, and Tso's calls were never returned. Apparently, I was one of the remaining ten percent whose names were still inscribed with indelible ink on the infamous black list.

The Presbyterian Church in Taiwan was bound and determined to change this and by then was in a position to do so. Times had indeed changed. The Taiwanese opposition had continued to grow stronger, and, after years of struggle, a new political party had forced its way into being—the Democratic Progressive Party (DPP). The KMT, under intense pressure, had created some "temporary constitutional measures" that had resulted in the entire legislature being elected from candidates residing in Taiwan. The DPP had continued to gain seats, and, in this very year, the still KMT-dominated National Assembly had elected the first Taiwanese president in the ROC's history—a Presbyterian layman by the name of Lee Teng-hui. Lee appeared to be a man who would toe the party line, but in fact over the next eight years he would transform Taiwan step by step into a two-party democracy with a president elected directly by the people.[30]

---

[29]   Renske Greve and I had been married in the United States June 19, 1991, and she had joined me in missionary service in Hong Kong that same month. For details, see chapter 12.

[30]   *History*, 58-75.

The author with
Hong Kong
Christian Council
staff

A Presbyterian layman who held a DPP seat in the ROC Legislative Yuan attached a rider to a bill allowing me permission to enter Taiwan for a two-week period. It passed in the nick of time—the day on which we had hoped to leave for the consultation. I had not contacted friends and colleagues in Taiwan about my coming, fearing to put them in an awkward position.

Meanwhile, it seemed that even nature was against us. That day Hong Kong was hit by one of the biggest floods it had seen in years. All transportation ground to a halt and many stores and offices closed. Determined to get my visa at last, I took off my socks, put on an old pair of shoes, rolled up my pant legs, and waded through a half mile of swirling waters to the ROC's downtown office. It was open! With visa at last in hand, I waded to my office, called Renske, and made preparations to leave for Taipei the next morning. There was no time to contact anybody. We would need to do that after our arrival.

Upon arriving at the Chiang Kai-shek (CKS) Airport, I was still a bit apprehensive as to whether this time the immigration people would actually let me cross that magic line or not. Renske went through first, figuring that if she were on the inside, I stood a better chance of making an argument in case of difficulty. She sailed through, but sure enough, when I stepped up to the counter and had my name punched into the computer, all the bells and whistles went off again. The chief officer in the back jumped up and told me to wait. He disappeared into the chief of immigration's office, and I thought, "Here we go again!" However, upon emerging some five minutes later, he barked "Okay!" to the officer, and I was in. Home at last after nineteen years![31]

---

[31] I suspect the delay was caused by the data regarding my newly approved visa not yet having been entered into the airport computer security system. The official's five minutes in the chief's office had probably been spent phoning "downtown" to check it out.

Friends and Festivities

When we arrived at our hotel in Taipei, I phoned a number of old colleagues and friends, who were astounded to learn that I was back in Taiwan. Esther Tien, a veteran Presbyterian human rights campaigner, invited us to a dinner that very evening. The event was being staged to raise funds for the Presbyterian Church's work among aboriginal girls whose families had sold them into prostitution in Taipei in order to make money to send home. A center had been set up to enable these girls to escape from their handlers and to give them a place to live until they could learn a legitimate trade and become self-sustaining.

Upon entering the banquet hall with Esther, I immediately spotted many familiar faces. We were seated next to C.M. Kao's wife, Ruth, whom I had not seen in almost twenty years. One of my former student workers, Chhoa Cheng-it, was also there. We didn't eat much as we had so much to catch up on. Some of these friends had not known about Joyce's death. Nobody had met Renske, of course, and I proudly introduced her all around. When it came time for the charity auction, I was surprised to be invited on stage to make some comments and to help run the auction. Not having used the local language much during all those years away, my Taiwanese was very rusty. However, the auctioneer helped me, and the festive crowd appreciated my effort. Nevertheless, I almost fainted to see Go Tai Tai, one of my former language teachers, sitting in the front row. Despite my stumbling efforts, though, she was beaming and proud to tell everybody afterwards that *she* had taught me Taiwanese.

The next day was a Sunday, and we made our way to the Tiong San Presbyterian Church that our family used to attend. Upon entering the sanctuary, I recognized one of the elders. He called the pastor over and introduced me before we took our seats. This was quite an emotional experience for me, especially when we sang the old Taiwanese hymns and the pastor gave the benediction. Tears of sadness rolled down my cheeks when recalling our family, and especially Joyce, worshiping there so many years before, mixed with tears of gladness for the blessing of worshiping with my old congregation again. At the conclusion of the service, many people crowded around us, some still recognizable and others new to me, but all eager to welcome me "home" and to meet Renske.

Following the church service, we were picked up by a former colleague, Susan Chang-Lee, and her husband, Michi, who was a medical doctor. It was a special delight to see Susan again and to

The author with Susan
Chang-Lee at 2003 reunion

introduce her to Renske. Susan, Joyce, and I had become close friends
during our Taiwan days. Susan and I had enjoyed working together
as student work colleagues at The Way Student Center in Taipei, and
she had often been in our home. When she was married, our entire
family had been her family's special house guests during the three-day
wedding festivities. She had also visited us in Hong Kong.

Susan and Michi whisked us to the Gi-kong (Righteous Light)
Presbyterian Church, where a celebration of the tenth anniversary of the
opening of the church was underway. Dr. and Mrs. Kao, Esther Tien and
her husband, and a number of other Presbyterian leaders and human
rights activists were there. I was asked to give some remarks to the
gathering and again strained to do so in my rusty Taiwanese. Knowing
the history of the church, it was quite an emotional experience.

When a Taiwanese lawyer named Lin I-hsiung had been on trial
for participating in what became known as the "Kaohsiung incident"
in 1979, his wife had attended the trial, leaving their three young
daughters at home in the care of Lin's mother. Suddenly, hooded
thugs had descended on their home and stabbed the grandmother
and two twin girls to death. The third daughter had been stabbed
six times, but, although badly wounded, she had escaped through a
window and hidden in some bushes. When Lin's secretary discovered
the murders, the wounded daughter had been rushed to a hospital. She
had miraculously survived and had eventually been able to describe
what had happened. All were convinced that the Nationalist secret
police were behind these murders and that they had been intended
to send a message to other would-be dissidents. Security agents had
surrounded the Lin's home for days, but they had suddenly been struck
with amnesia when questioned about what had taken place, and the
murderers had never been "found." These murders had shocked the
nation and the world, especially when the Nationalist regime had only

allowed the distraught father to leave his cell for two days to help his devastated wife deal with the aftermath.[32]

Lin had been sentenced to six years in prison, and his wife was left to cope with this disaster on her own. She had been destitute, but Presbyterian Christians had reached out to her and to all the wives and families of the other jailed dissidents, and Lin's wife, Fang Su-min, and her daughter, Huan-jun, had eventually become Christians. It had been their wish that the house where the murders took place should be transformed into a small Presbyterian church that could become "a place of love and healing and be used to share the love of Christ who brought us new life!"[33] The Presbyterian Church in Taiwan had approved the request, purchased the house (and thereby providing Mrs. Lin with some badly needed income), converted it into a small church, and began services there in May 1982.[34] It was that church whose anniversary we were gathered to celebrate. Little did I know then that, eleven years later, Renske and I would have an opportunity to meet the Lins and to hear their account firsthand.

After lunch, Susan, Michi, Renske, and I drove to Pat-li, the village of our former amah, to see if we might find some clue as to A-gim's whereabouts. I had heard that she and her husband had moved their appliance business to Taipei some years before but had no idea where they might be in that huge city. We arrived in Pat-li to discover that where there used to be farms and a small village now stood a large town with modern buildings. The Lu family farm no longer existed. The small church that A-gim had attended had also disappeared. We went to the local police station to ask if anybody knew about the Lu family and where they might now live, but without success. Nobody else we asked could give us any clue either, and it was with great disappointment that we finally gave up the search.

---

[32] *History*, 52, 96-97. Many of these brave but politically inexperienced wives, along with the young lawyers who dared to defend their husbands, ran for public office against the KMT, and a number of them won, including Fang Su-Min. Ruth Kao lost by a narrow margin in the city of Tainan in an election that most charged was rigged.

[33] For a description of the PCT's role in this event, see "Cross of Courage in Taiwan," *Disciple*, Sept. 19, 1982, 14-15.

[34] For an eyewitness account of the Lin murder story and its aftermath, see "2-28, 1980. The Lin Family Murders; the Surviving Daughter's Account," *Jerome F. Keating's Writings*, Tuesday, March 03, 2009, http://zen.sandiego.edu:8080/Jerome/1196920787/index_html, September 9, 2009.

Karsens and Kaos at tenth anniversary of Ki-Kong (Righteous Light) Presbyterian Church

Susan and Michi dropped us off at the gate of Reformed Church medical missionaries and longtime friends, Sam and Lucy Noordhoff. After hugs all around, since it was Mother's Day, they took us along to son Sam Jr.'s nearby home, where we enjoyed meeting his wife and children and eating a scrumptious meal together. The last time I had seen "Sammy," he had been a teenager and a student at the Taipei American School. Now he was in business in Taiwan for the Amway Corporation. We talked long and hard, reminiscing, catching up on family and mission news and on Sam Sr.'s pioneer work in cleft palate surgery at the private Chang Kung Hospital, which he had helped set up.[35] We owed an eternal debt to Sam and Lucy who had borne the brunt of emptying our home and shipping our things to Hong Kong after we had been denied re-entry into Taiwan in 1974. It is hard to imagine the joy of spending a day visiting old friends and colleagues again after so much time and such significant events had transpired.

The next morning, we had the privilege of eating breakfast with my old friend, mentor, and Taiwanese teacher, George Wu. During our time in Taiwan, George had become more than a teacher to us; he had also become a friend. Joyce and I had also come to know his wife, Ruth, and their children. We had kept in touch through occasional correspondence.

George had stepped down as director of the Taipei Language Institute's Taiwanese Department in 1972 and taken a position as the World Home Bible League's representative in Taiwan. In 1975, he had run afoul of the KMT regime when he had introduced an anti-KMT political candidate to a printer who was willing to risk printing his campaign literature. The printer, politician, and George were all arrested and subjected to abject treatment at the Taiwan Garrison Command interrogation headquarters. It was only through the strenuous efforts of Dennis Mulder, a former Christian Reformed missionary colleague

---

[35] For an overview of Sam Noordhoff's impressive medical ministry in Taiwan and elsewhere, see Karsen, Wendell, "The Miracle of Mackay," *Church Herald*, February 2003, 16-19.

Presbyterian Church in Taiwan's new headquarters building

who had become the director of the World Home Bible League, that George had finally been released.[36]

It was a wonderful reunion. We talked about Joyce and her untimely death. He had heard about my marriage to Renske and was delighted to meet her. We reminisced about our time at the language school and laughed about the sometimes hilarious things that had happened while learning Taiwanese. We talked about his arrest and interrogation by the secret police and about the unbelievable changes that had come about in Taiwan since then. We also talked about the Presbyterian Church and the long ordeal that it had been through. It seemed as though it had only been yesterday that he had come up to encourage me after I had preached one of my first sermons in Taiwanese at the Presbyterian church where he served as an elder. It was hard to say goodbye again.

After bidding George farewell, we headed for the impressive new headquarters building of the Presbyterian Church in Taiwan, erected on the site where my old student center and office had once stood. We were warmly greeted by the staff, some of whom I still knew, and by the general secretary, Yang Chi-sou, who had been the principal of Yushan Theological College during our time in Taiwan. He had also earned his Th.M. degree from Western Theological Seminary, my alma mater, so we were old friends. I thanked him for the PCT's efforts to help procure our visas, told him how thrilled we were to be back in Taiwan after so many years in exile, and brought him greetings from the Hong Kong Christian Council. We had an informative talk about the politically

---

[36] Interestingly enough, George eventually made many trips to the mainland when it became possible to do so. He became the World Home Bible League's main conduit through which it clandestinely sent Bibles to the unregistered churches there.

evolving situation in Taiwan and about the work and mission of the Presbyterian Church in the new era that was dawning under Taiwan's president, Lee Teng-hui (who was also a member of the PCT). Yang reported that the Presbyterian Church had continued to thrive and was more than holding its own in overall membership and number of congregations. I was also happy to see a former Mennonite missionary colleague, Ed Senner, who had been in community development work on the East Coast in the seventies. Ed was now serving as the associate general secretary of the PCT.

Our next stop was the Mackay Memorial Hospital where the Reformed Church's Sam Noordhoff, Jeane Walvoord, and Ben Dykstra had all served as medical missionaries when we were in Taiwan. The old Canadian-built staff residences had all been pulled down and a new high-rise hospital erected. The old section of the hospital, where our nine-year-old son Steve had had his chin sewn up after being bitten by a dog, was still there. However, it was scheduled to be demolished within the next few months and a new wing built in its place. A lump rose in my throat as I remembered holding Steve's hand with my left hand while using my right to wipe the sweat off the doctor's brow with my hankie. The setting had been rather primitive, but the outcome had been superb.

We walked into the hospital chaplain's office and Abraham Chen just about fell out of his chair. Abraham had been a student at Western Seminary during the 1984–85 year when I was teaching there. He, his wife Carol, and their son had often been to our home for dinner and, as fellow Taiwanese speakers, we had become good friends. He had not known, of course, that we were coming to Taiwan, and it was a great delight to surprise him. He showed us around the new hospital, explained his ministry there, and we enjoyed a brief chat before we had to move on.

We then walked a half mile to the neighborhood where our family used to live, in search of our old house. Many large new buildings had been built around it, and it looked rather run down, but it was still there. I stood on tiptoe to peer over the wall into the small yard where our kids used to play. I could still see them in my mind's eye, running and playing with our dog, Labby, while Joyce was busy in the kitchen and I sat working in my study. Those had been rich times.

Across the busy street stood the complex where Bill and Zoe Glysteen had once lived. Bill had been the deputy chief of mission at the embassy in Taipei while we were there, and our boys had become friends. The Glysteens were very knowledgeable about China, since both of them had been born and raised in Beijing. Zoe's father had been a career foreign service officer and had written a definitive history on China,[37] while Bill's parents had been long-time missionaries there. Bill spoke fluent Mandarin and was an expert on both China/American and Taiwan/American affairs. It had been helpful to have had occasional informal access to the knowledge and perspective of the number two American diplomat in Taiwan.[38]

That evening, Andrew Hsieh, one of my closest Taiwanese colleagues and friends, came for a reunion at our hotel. I had not seen Andrew since his visit to Hong Kong in 1975. We hugged and shed tears of joy that I had been allowed back into Taiwan and that we could see each other again. We talked late into the night, reminiscing about our days in student work together, catching up on family news, and assessing the current situation in both church and society in Taiwan. He reported that the political struggle with the KMT continued, but that the Taiwanese were inexorably gaining ground, and that their spirits were high.

Consultation and Colleagues

The five-day Christian Conference of Asia Consultation was convened the next day on the campus of the PCT's Hsinchu Bible School. There we were greeted by many friends and Taiwanese colleagues, including the Presbyterian Church's retired general secretary, C.M. Kao and his wife, Ruth. "C.M." had given me my Chinese name, we had worked as colleagues during the White Terror, and we had become good friends and stayed in touch over the years.

I had been asked by Godwin Singh, the CCA's secretary for mission and evangelism, to record the proceedings of the consultation so that he could produce a written report for later publication. As in all CCA gatherings, English was used as the common communication medium. That made tape recordings essential, since some participants struggled to express themselves in English or spoke with a hard-to-decipher accent. There were a few other Western missionaries there, and we rightly took a back seat and let our Asian brothers and sisters do most of the talking.

---

[37] See Club, Edmond, *20th Century China* (New York: Columbia Univ. Press, 1964).

[38] Glysteen never realized his ambition to become the United States' first ambassador to China, but he did serve as the American ambassador to South Korea from 1978-1981.

CCA conference
participants
(Renske front left,
author rear left)

Singh gave a keynote address, "The Mission of God ("Missio Dei") from an Asian Perspective." Other speakers addressed the issue of ecumenical solidarity, particularly in parts of Asia where the church was under pressure from hostile regimes and/or aggressive indigenous faiths. Papers were presented by Presbyterian participants on the political, social, economic, and spiritual contexts within which the church had been conducting God's mission in Taiwan. They stressed the importance of the ecumenical solidarity and support that had enabled them to carry out this mission in the face of great obstacles. The inspiring worship services employed Asian art and musical forms.

Following the consultation, Renske and I boarded a train and set off for the city of Tainan in the south. The change in the landscape was amazing. Gone were the quaint little country villages with their beautiful sloped Chinese roofs. In their place were towns with forests of new buildings designed in a plethora of European styles. Gone were the farmer's shacks and haystacks. In their place were modern white metal buildings that jarred with, rather than accommodated, the landscape. Gone were the water buffaloes plowing the rice paddies, guided by bare-footed farmers in banana-leaf hats. In their place were modern paddy tractors run by men and women dressed in Western garb. Gone were the narrow and twisting two-lane roads with their hundreds of buffalo-drawn carts, motor bikes, bicycles, and little Asian cars. In their place were modern expressways jammed with the latest model trucks, buses, and cars. Gone were the hovels and shacks and the hordes of poorly dressed people. In their place were newly built homes and crowds of well-fed and well-dressed folks. Taiwan had been transformed from a rather shabby place in the seventies into an obviously prosperous place in the nineties.

Arriving in Taiwan's former capital, we headed straight for the campus of Tainan Theological Seminary. Although a few new buildings had been constructed, the shaded campus with its historic buildings was as lovely as I remembered. I pointed out the house where Rowland

and Judy Van Es and their family had once lived, as well as the houses that Hsiao Cheng-feng, Dan Beeby, Han Tan, and Ong Heng-ti and their families had used to call home. These were all homes in which our family had been welcome guests. Now these friends were scattered all over the world. We did pay a visit to one who was still there, and with whom I had kept in close contact over the years—John Ji-giok Tin.

John had developed a lay academy at the seminary and had been a fervent supporter of all things Taiwanese, especially the preservation of the Taiwanese language. He had been an equally fervent and outspoken supporter of all things anti-KMT. He had done his Ph.D. work at Tubingen University in Germany and had stopped in Hong Kong to visit us on his way to and from Europe. Now he was in his seventies but still going strong. His study, as always, was jammed with books and papers, and he was as enthusiastic as ever about the Taiwanese cause. He repeated his famous phrase to us, "Taiwan-lang, chhut thau ti^n." ("Taiwanese, lift up your heads!")

Then it was on to dinner with two young faculty members who had been seminary students during my time in Taiwan—Tan Lam-chhiu and Ng Pek-ho. After his graduation, Lam-chhiu had become one of our most effective student workers and an ardent supporter of the Taiwanese cause. I had met Pek-ho in Hong Kong the year before, when he had given an impressive paper at a Hong Kong Christian Council symposium.[39] I was thrilled that these two rising stars had been appointed to the Tainan Seminary faculty. They were bright scholars who bode well for the future of the PCT and for the advancement of its struggle for democracy and human rights. We had a lot of catching up to do, and the evening went by before we knew it.

The next day, we took another train for the short ride to Kaohsiung and a rendezvous with Reformed Church missionaries Dave and Char Alexander and their children. Char was teaching English in a medical college, while Dave was involved in a church plant in the city. Since the next day was Sunday, we worshiped with the small congregation that Dave had painstakingly built up over a number of years. Dave's Taiwanese was impressive. He conducted the entire service in the local language, colloquialisms and all, without missing a beat. I was envious, considering my rusty skills in Taiwanese, but these eight days in Taiwan had proven to be a "must speak" refresher course, and much of the rust had worn off during our travels.

---

[39] Lam Pek-ho would go on to become the president of Tainan Theological Seminary and serve as such until 2007.

Dave Alexander in the pulpit at his Kaohsiung church plant

As we boarded our plane back to Hong Kong, I was still pinching myself. It had been like a dream to be back in this beloved place after an absence of nineteen years. When we could not return to Taiwan in 1973, I had left half my heart there. At last there had been a kind of closure, and I was most grateful.[40]

Ministry and Memories

In June 1997, since Renske had never had an opportunity to experience the full beauty of "Ilha Formosa," we decided to spend a week's vacation touring the island by train. We visited most of Taiwan's magnificent national parks and historical sites (including the remains of the three forts that our Dutch ancestors had once occupied when they ruled the island). We also enjoyed celebrating Sam and Lucy Noordhoff's seventieth birthdays with them in Taipei and having a dinner out with another Reformed Church missionary, Judy Estell, in Hualien on the other side of the island. It was always an inspiration to be with Judy. A widow for seven years, Judy had chosen to remain in Taiwan after the death of her husband, Bill, and remained active teaching English at the Yushan Bible College and conducting a very successful ministry in a local prison.

This trip offered another good opportunity to speak Taiwanese, but it was also frustrating in that the younger generation had begun to speak a garble of Taiwanese and Mandarin Chinese. Whenever I would ask young people to please speak Taiwanese, they would reply in perfect Taiwanese, "I *am* speaking Taiwanese," but a few sentences later they would unconsciously lapse back into their "Taidarin." The older

---

[40]   For a subsequent report on this journey, see Karsen, Wendell, "Taiwan after Nineteen Years," *News & Views*, June 1992, 3.

generation still spoke clear Taiwanese, and I especially enjoyed talking with a taxi driver on a long ride to the southern tip of Taiwan. We covered the political scene, the economic scene, the religious scene, and a lot more. At the end of the journey, he exclaimed that he had never met a foreigner with whom he could converse about such things in his own language and proceeded to open his trunk and insist on giving us a large bag of delicious mangos.

Our entry into Taiwan had gone very smoothly, and it was obvious that the political climate had improved dramatically. The Democratic People's Party had continued to gain ground in its struggle against the powerful Nationalist regime (the KMT). The DPP was mounting a serious attempt to win the next round of elections in 2000, when President Lee Teng-hui would be stepping down. The DPP's leader was a lawyer named Chen Shui-bian, who had dared to defend those falsely accused and jailed after the Kaohsiung incident. Chan looked like he might have a chance to become Taiwan's next president, since the Nationalists (KMT) were at each other's throats to the point of splitting into two factions and dividing their vote.

Many of the Presbyterian Church in Taiwan's pastors and lay leaders were in the thick of the political process and were praying that the DPP would eventually emerge victorious. By this time, they could more freely voice their suggestions for moving the country forward to reach the Taiwanese people's goal of achieving a free and democratic society after their long struggle against the repressive Nationalist regime.

Just one year later (June 1998), Renske and I were back in Taiwan. Since our ministry at Union Church Hong Kong would be concluding in the fall, and since our new assignment in Indonesia would not begin until mid-November, I had offered my services as an interim pastor for a small expatriate congregation in the southern city of Kaohsiung. We were there to meet the leaders of the Kaohsiung Christian Fellowship and to make arrangements for our impending ministry in Taiwan's second largest city. I was thrilled to be able to serve once again as a Reformed Church missionary on the island from which I had been so painfully expelled twenty-five years before. Renske and I were equally happy to have an opportunity to help this congregation that had been without a regular pastor for some time. We were also glad for another opportunity to reconnect with Dave and Char Alexander and their children, who were members of the congregation.

During our week on the island, we made a number of fruitful contacts with both PCT and RCA colleagues and friends. While staying

l-r: William Loh, the Karsens, Mrs. Loh, and the Kaos

at Tainan Seminary, Dr. Loh I-do and his wife invited us to visit them in their lovely home on the seminary campus. Loh was a famous Asian musicologist who was now the president of the seminary, while Mrs. Loh was a well-known Christian educator. We had a lot to cover during the visit and subsequent dinner, and it was wonderful once again to be among colleagues whom I had known so many years before.

Then it was on to Taipei and a visit to the PCT Church Office, where we were warmly received by old and new friends alike. The general secretary, the Reverend William Loh, and his wife graciously invited us to dinner in their home along with the former general secretary, C.M. Kao, and his wife, Ruth. We had a delightful evening reminiscing and getting updates on the latest developments in the church and in the political scene. Taiwan's president, Lee Teng-hui, a Presbyterian layman and good friend of the Lohs and the Kaos, was playing a key role in the country's peaceful transition to democracy and was one of the main topics of discussion. He, along with the PCT, was still very active in quietly promoting independence for Taiwan and in working to develop and strengthen the still fragile democracy. He faced an uphill battle, since the KMT hardliners were still hell-bent on demolishing all that he had so painstakingly built. Taiwan's hoped-for re-entry into the United Nations as an independent country was also a topic of discussion.

We next journeyed to Hualien to pay another visit to Judy Estell and to the Yushan Bible College where she had taught for many years. This visit produced two very poignant moments. One was a visit to the tiny cemetery on a hill within the campus where her husband, Bill, and his first wife, Eileen, were buried. My mind flashed back to the day, some twenty-seven years before, when, in the presence of Bill, his four boys, and a number of RCA and Yushan colleagues, I had helped lay Eileen to rest there after she had lost her battle with cancer.[41] The

---

[41] Bill Estell died of a sudden heart attack in 1990 at age sixty.

Author giving
benediction at funeral
for Eileen Estell

second moment was an emotional reunion with the Reverend Bob Hung. Bob had been a very effective campus minister in Taichung and had become a professor at Yushan. He had also been active in the Presbyterian Church's struggle against the KMT regime, and we both shed more than a few tears as he related all he and his colleagues had gone through during those White Terror years.

In September, Renske and I arrived in Kaohsiung to begin our ministry at the Kaohsiung Christian Fellowship. We lived with a delightful couple named Bob and MaryAnn Walters. Bob was the principal at the Morrison Academy campus in Kaohsiung. The job of being in charge of a school in a cross-cultural setting carried heavy responsibilities. He was also spearheading the development of a new campus. It was helpful for him to share his challenges with "his pastor," particularly those having to do with personnel problems. For example, one young male teacher, who was new to the school, had developed a serious case of spinal meningitis for which he was hospitalized. Renske and I accompanied Bob to the hospital one night to be with this teacher while he was undergoing a spinal tap, and then we made further calls on our own until he was able to return home after his fortunate recovery.[42] However, he did not want to heed Bob and his doctor's calls to delay his return to teaching until he had had sufficient time to recover fully. Together, Bob and I were able to persuade the young man to follow his doctor's orders. Our ministry to this fellowship was very fulfilling, and

---

[42] We did not have a car in Kaohsiung and made every hospital call and other calls by local bus and (as the Chinese liked to say) "the number 11 bus," i.e. using one's two legs to walk. Since Kaohsiung was a large city, some of these visits would take most of a morning or an afternoon to complete.

our six weeks there seemed to speed by all too quickly.

During this period in Taiwan, we traveled by train to Taipei to visit old haunts and old friends. A visit to MacKay Hospital confirmed that it had continued to develop at an impressive pace since our visit six years earlier. We talked over lunch with my former student work colleague, Susan Chang, and were impressed with her active involvement in the Presbyterian Church and in political and social issues. It was good to hear her perspective.

While in Taipei, we stayed at a Baptist guest house that was located only one block from the spot where my student work coordinator's office and The Way Student Center used to be. The Lutheran Student Center had been just down the lane and still was. We stopped in on the spur of the moment and found that a former student work colleague, Lutheran pastor Wendell Friest, was still there. The two gray-haired Wendells then enjoyed a chat about the "good old days" before bidding one another farewell once again.

Our student centers had been located close to the campus of the National Taiwan University, the premier university in Taiwan. However, security had been so tight at the time of my ministry there that I had never been allowed to set foot beyond the huge gates that led into the campus, since there had been no official reason to do so. Now those gates were wide open and anybody could walk in and saunter around the campus. It was a strange feeling to be wandering about at will in that place, and it confirmed how much things truly had changed.

The last lap around memory lane occurred just before we were due to wind up our ministry at the Kaohsiung Christian Fellowship. The annual meeting of the PCT Mission Council was to be held at a beautiful mountain retreat near Tainan, and we were invited to attend. This was, in effect, an annual gathering of missionaries working under the PCT to enjoy fellowship, discuss church policies and programs, provide updates on various ministries, make suggestions to the Presbyterian leadership, and worship and study together. We had always enjoyed these gatherings, and this one was even sweeter, since we not only met new PCT missionaries but also reconnected with colleagues we had not seen in decades, like Joy Randall and Jack Geddes.

The former associate general secretary and good friend, Ed Senner, had retired recently but had been invited to return to Taiwan for this gathering. Ed and I had first met in Hualien on the East Coast, when he was in community development work and I was in student work. There was also an opportunity to spend time with Rowland and Judy Van Es (who had returned to Taiwan to teach at Tainan Seminary), Dave and Char Alexandar (who were still teaching and pastoring in

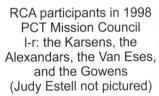

RCA participants in 1998
PCT Mission Council
l-r: the Karsens, the
Alexandars, the Van Eses,
and the Gowens
(Judy Estell not pictured)

Kaohsiung), Jeff and Kristen Gowen (who were teaching English in Tainan), and Judy Estell (who was still teaching at YuShan and in the prison in Hualien).

Before we knew it, it was time to bid farewell to our congregation and to the island and people that would always hold a special place in our hearts and move on to our new ministry in Indonesia. We thought it would be our last farewell to our PCT colleagues and friends, but we were mistaken.

Return and Reward

Democracy and Human Rights

When we were in Taiwan in 1969, it seemed as though the Nationalist KMT regime's iron grip on the island could never be broken and that the period of the White Terror would go on forever. However, a long list of brave Taiwanese, including many within the Presbyterian Church in Taiwan, never gave up on the pursuit of their ideal. They were determined to do whatever it took to break that grip, to make whatever sacrifice they must to overcome that terror, and to struggle to give birth to a new democratic era in Taiwan. For thousands, this meant taking great personal risks; for some, this meant decades in prison; for not a few, this meant torture and death (not to mention the thousands who had been slaughtered in 1947).

By the early years of the twenty-first century, what had only been dreamed about more than three decades before had become a reality. Those who had been imprisoned for their ideals were free—some of them serving at the highest levels of government (including Chen Shui-bian as president and Annette Lu as vice president). What could only have been whispered in dark corners in the past could be shouted in the public square. The dismantling of the vestiges of the KMT regime's repressive practices and injustices was in full swing. The crimes of the regime and the sacrifices of those who suffered at its hands were being documented in museums and inscribed on monuments. Political prisons like the infamous one on Green Island were a thing of the past. Statues of Chiang Kai-shek had been taken down and memorials to Taiwanese victims erected. An official apology for the 1947 massacre had been made and a memorial museum had been opened in a downtown park in Taipei to document that terrible crime. The infamous Taiwan Garrison Command Headquarters building had been closed, and people were increasingly willing and able to relate the horrible things that had happened to them and their families during the KMT's rule. Much remained to be done to consolidate Taiwan's democratic gains and to ensure that those who had perpetrated the travesties of the White Terror, or their successors, would not again come to power, but the political and human rights atmosphere on the island had dramatically changed.[43]

Remembrance and Appreciation

Nothing could have demonstrated this more than the December 6–12, 2003, event sponsored by the Taiwan Foundation for Democracy (TFD). In September of that year, I received an invitation to attend an event that would demonstrate dramatically how the values of the kingdom of God—truth, justice, love, and service—could overcome the "gates of hell." The TFD, a quasigovernment-funded nonpartisan body, modeled after its counterpart in the United States, was dedicated to the development of democracy and human rights in Taiwan and around the world. The event, "A Journey of Remembrance and Appreciation," was centered around the contributions of international friends who played a role in the development of democracy and human rights in Taiwan, particularly those who had been placed on the KMT regime's blacklist as a result of their activities. Thirty-six of us, including long-time colleagues Rowland and Judy Van Es, were invited to return to the island as honored guests of the foundation, along with our spouses. The goals of the gathering were:

1. to document the contributions of international friends (many of them done in secret and not publicly known) to the development of human rights and democracy in Taiwan;
2. to reflect on the ongoing struggle of the people of Taiwan to consolidate their gains in the areas of democratic values and human rights; and

[43]   *History,* 76-77, 89.

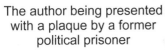

The author being presented with a plaque by a former political prisoner

3. to thank international friends for the contributions they made and the consequences they suffered.[44]

The week opened with Dr. Peng Ming-min hosting a luncheon for those who had taken great risks to help him escape from Taiwan in January 1970. Although we had not been directly involved in his escape, we were included because of my meeting with him in his home in Ann Arbor in 1974. Peng, now a senior advisor to the president, Chen Shuibian, was visibly moved as he thanked us for our efforts on his behalf and on behalf of the Taiwanese people over the years. Most of us in the room hadn't seen each other since we had been expelled or blacklisted decades before.

The first official TFD function was a welcome banquet where each international guest was awarded a beautiful framed plaque. Mine read, "This is to express our deep appreciation to Rev. Wendell Karsen for your contribution to the people of Taiwan, and for your unfailing devotion to the democracy and human rights development of this land." This was a particularly moving moment, since each of the thirty-six plaques was presented by a Taiwanese who had been an active dissident in the struggle. Most of them had been imprisoned for twenty or thirty years, with some still bearing the visible marks of their severe torture at the hands of the regime.

Murder and Redemption

The next day, we went as a group to the East Coast City of Ilan. There, the five-storied Tsunah Education and Cultural Center housed

---

44   *A Journey of Remembrance and Appreciation: International Friends and Taiwan's Democracy and Human Rights*, program booklet (Taipei: Taiwan Foundation for Democracy, Dec. 2003), 3-12.

The Lins and
the Karsens

a museum documenting the Taiwanese people's century-long struggle for democracy and human rights, first under the Japanese (1895–1945) and then under the Chinese Nationalists (1945–2000). The Lins were important figures in that struggle. The murderers of Mr. Lin's mother and their twins had never been brought to justice. Mr. Lin had been released from prison and had resumed his law practice. He and his wife had dedicated their lives to advancing the cause of democracy and human rights in Taiwan and had created the Tsunah Foundation for this purpose.

The Lins thanked us personally for our involvement in the human rights movement. They then introduced the Tsunah Foundation and its many educational and cultural programs and presented us with beautiful books detailing the struggle of the Taiwanese people to live in freedom and determine their own future. Our group's overwhelming feeling was that our small contributions in support of democracy and human rights in Taiwan paled in significance next to the great sacrifices that the Lin family had made.[45]

Presentations and Politicians

The next two days were taken up with a major human rights seminar held at the Taipei International Convention Center. Peng Ming-min delivered a keynote address, "The Development and Outlook of Taiwan's Democracy and Human Rights." Major sessions were devoted to the following topics: "Self-Determination and the Peng Ming-min Saga"; "The Religious Role: Taiwanization and Human

[45] Poignantly and proudly, the Lins told us that their surviving daughter, Judy, had married a North American and had borne them three lovely granddaughters.

Rights Enlightenment"; "Asians and Taiwan's Human Rights Issues"; "The Meh-li Tau Incident"; "Social Movements and Democratization under Martial Law"; "The Role of the International Press"; and "Martial law and Its Dismantling: Chiang Ching-kuo's Role in Taiwan's Democratization."

Each international guest appeared on an appropriate panel and had an opportunity to tell briefly about his or her involvement. During the seminar, each was videotaped in a studio for an hour as part of an oral history project. Documents that we had brought were collected and given to Taiwan's Academia Sinica for microfilming.[46] The foundation also printed each of our testimonies in an official publication,[47] and a number of us were interviewed by the press. Foundation leaders stressed how essential it was to document our contributions accurately, before those who had participated in the struggle would begin to die. It was important to publicize our stories so that the somewhat jaded young people of today's free and prosperous Taiwan would become more aware of the sacrifices made by so many Taiwanese and international friends alike for the freedoms they enjoyed.

After the first day's session, we were driven to the presidential palace for a meeting with President Chen. He thanked each of us individually for our contributions and then addressed us on the importance of continuing to guard the newly won freedoms enjoyed by the people of Taiwan. He also stressed the work still needing to be done to make those freedoms more secure, not only within Taiwan, but also internationally, particularly vis-à-vis the People's Republic of China and the United States. I was then privileged to represent the group in presenting him with a historically valuable Hokkien-English Romanized Dictionary. With knees knocking, I managed to do it in Taiwanese—a rather harrowing but rewarding experience.

The president had impressive credentials. As a young lawyer, he had risked his career by daring to defend those arrested after the Kaohsiung "incident" in 1979. He had later served two years in prison for actively participating in the human rights struggle against the regime. His wife had been in a wheelchair for years, permanently paralyzed from the waist down due to an attempt by the regime to silence him. Having narrowly lost an election in his hometown of Tainan in 1992, he and his wife had been walking along the streets,

---

[46] I had brought around two hundred documents.

[47] *A Journey of Remembrance and Appreciation: International Friends and Taiwan's Democracy and Human Rights* (Taipei: Taiwan Foundation for Democracy, Dec. 2003).

President Chen with missionaries that were honored (Karsens to Chen's left)

thanking their supporters, when a truck had suddenly come roaring around the corner. Chen had jumped out of the way, but the truck had knocked his wife down, stopped, backed up, ran over her again, stopped again, went forward and ran over her for a third time. The driver had been arrested but had been acquitted when he had told the judge that he had simply lost control of his truck. To everyone but the KMT judge, it had been obvious that the regime had hired the man to kill the Chens and make it look like an accident—a classic example of how the regime operated in those days.[48]

We then had photos taken and toured the large palace with its interesting displays and its museum highlighting the history of the struggle for democracy. It was humbling to think that we, who for so long had seen this building as the bastion of a repressive regime, would be welcomed within its walls by the president of a free Taiwan. One of my favorite sayings came to mind: "The power of weakness will overcome the weakness of power."

Following the tour, we were escorted to the state dining room where Vice President Lu had graciously invited us to a dinner in her honor. She was presented with an alumna of the year award by her old alma mater, the University of Illinois College of Law—a long way from the jail cell that she had occupied for six years as a Taiwanese dissident not too many years before. Both she and the president, who also spoke, included words of gratitude for our part in helping make a free Taiwan possible.

At the conclusion of the second day of the seminar, we were driven to a large outdoor amphitheater in a park on the grounds of

---

[48] Chen and his running mate would nearly be assassinated in Tainan in March 2004 on the day before their re-election, but the would-be assassin only managed to inflict surface wounds. Many thought the KMT was behind the attempt.

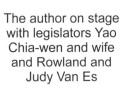

The author on stage with legislators Yao Chia-wen and wife and Rowland and Judy Van Es

the National Taiwan University, a few blocks from where my campus ministry office had once been. This nationally televised DPP rally was being held to honor us. A number of former political prisoners, now legislators, spoke. A few of our people delighted the crowd by bringing them greetings in Taiwanese. President Chen then delivered a major address centered on the struggles of the past, how we had participated in them, and why the people of Taiwan should remember and be grateful. At the climax of the rally, we all were invited to join the president on stage and given heartwarming applause.[49] The most impressive thing about the rally was that most of the people there were ordinary folks who were obviously rejoicing in their newfound freedoms. Many of them came up to us afterwards to grasp our hands and say thank you in Taiwanese. I was moved and humbled by their presence and gratitude.

Commemoration and Conversation

The next morning, December 10, we were flown to Tainan, the historical hub of Taiwanese life and culture. There we toured the Tainan Theological Seminary's campus, which had been a hotbed of activity on behalf of democratic and human rights through the years. There were reunions with Dr. and Mrs. C.M. Kao and old friends like Dr. Ng Pek-ho, then president of the seminary, who addressed our group in the seminary chapel. One of the most moving moments of the entire week occurred when, at the conclusion of the gathering, everyone stood spontaneously, held hands, and sang "We Shall Overcome!" We also toured the old Dutch Fort, Fort Providentia, which had been carefully restored by the Taiwanese. A large sculpture depicting the surrender of

---

49   See photo and article (in Chinese) in the December 10, 2003, *China Times.* Karsen, pr.p.

the Dutch to Koxenga stood in a prominent place in front of the fort, with the tall long-nosed Dutch commander on bended knee before the Chinese conqueror. We had a good laugh as the six "Dutchmen" in our group had our picture taken on bended knee in front of the statue.

Then it was off to Kaohsiung by bus and a Human Rights Day reception in a public park by city officials. After speeches and refreshments, we were bused to a beautifully decorated outdoor venue on the banks of the Love River for an evening gala to commemorate the Kaohsiung "incident," which had occurred there on Human Rights Day in 1979, exactly twenty-four years before. A large lighted pictorial historical exhibition had been erected, and laser beam displays were flashed on the walls of adjoining buildings.

A double line of uniformed schoolgirls welcomed each of us to the event with a red rose—the symbol for the evening. Guests sat at candlelit tables ready to eat a delicious Chinese buffet. The program featured speeches by retired veteran dissidents and their grown children who were now in office or in other professions. Mayor Frank Hsieh also spoke, introduced us to the crowd, and thanked us for our contributions to the demise of the regime and the emergence of human rights in Taiwan. Members of the mayor's office (including the mayor himself) supplied the entertainment, along with aboriginal dancers. The contrast with life under the old regime could not have been starker. Those days could be compared to living under a suffocating blanket. The atmosphere at the commemorative gala was like a breath of fresh air.

The time came to reflect on what had happened in Kaohsiung in 1979 and the resultant sacrifices that so many had made in the cause of freedom there. All were asked to come forward and "plant" their roses in a large green Styrofoam field surrounding a huge white raised image of the island of Taiwan. The emotional effect was electric.

However, the greatest illustration of the "new" Taiwan still awaited us. After checking into our hotel at the conclusion of the program, Renske and I decided to take a walk along the banks of the Love River, just a few blocks away. Bridges and fountains were lit by hundreds of colored lights, and festive tea stalls lined the walk. As we approached one of them, we ran right into a prominent couple who had played a key role in the Kaohsiung incident. Now members of the Legislative Yuen, they were walking along talking to the people and handing out popcorn. Then we came across Mayor Hsieh and the deputy secretary-general of the DPP Party, Lee Ying-yuan, and their friends who were sitting at tables drinking Kaohsiung's famous flower

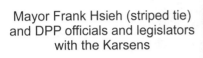

Mayor Frank Hsieh (striped tie) and DPP officials and legislators with the Karsens

tea. When they spotted us, still with our nametags on, they insisted that we sit down and have some tea and popcorn.

When we complemented the mayor on his performance on his small clay flute at the gala, he fished it out of his pocket and showed us that it was shaped like the island of Taiwan. After further conversation in Taiwanese, Lee, pointing to Hsieh, said, "You are talking to the future president of Taiwan," and they all laughed as the mayor humbly demurred. When we excused ourselves, the mayor stood up and said in English, "Just call me Frank. If you are ever in town again, please look me up." The contrast to the people who used to run things in Taiwan was overwhelming.[50]

The next evening, we saw "our friend Frank" on television, right at Chen Shui-Bian's elbow when the DPP Party announced that Chen would be its candidate for re-election in the March 2004 presidential election.[51] One reason why Hsieh was elected mayor of Taiwan's second largest city was because, as a young lawyer, he had also had the courage to defend the Kaohsiung "incident" prisoners of conscience in court, the kind of courage Taiwanese don't soon forget.

The next day we rode a special train to Taitang to visit a newly opened Aboriginal Museum. The museum was housed in a large and impressive structure on beautiful grounds. The history and continuing culture of nine of Taiwan's aboriginal tribes were represented (a tenth tribe having been "lost" by absorption into the other tribes). The displays were lavishly and beautifully presented. It was obvious that Taiwanese society had become wealthy enough to spend money on such projects. It was also obvious that it was making a concerted effort to celebrate and promote the interests of the tribal peoples who made up

[50] Hsieh would go on to become the DPP's 2008 presidential candidate. Unfortunately, he would lose the election.

[51] Photo and story (in Chinese) in the *Liberty Times*, December 11, 2003, Karsen, pr.p.

Thornberrys (with
daughter) and Karsens
being interviewed on TTV

2 percent of the island's population and were its original inhabitants.
After seeing the museum, we were flown back to Taipei.

Broadcast and Benediction

The next day, Renske and I were driven to the Taiwan Television
(TTV) studios, where we and Milo and Judith Thornberry were
interviewed for an hour on a popular talk show concerning our human
rights activities in Taiwan. The program was to be aired on Christmas
Day, which gave us a wonderful opportunity to explain why Jesus came
to earth—to give his life that we might have life, to "set the captives
free."

Then it was off to a restaurant for a reunion with Loh I-jian and
his wife Lucy. Our family's friendship with the Lohs went back more
than thirty years to our days in Taiwan and then in Hong Kong, where
our children were also good friends. I-jian had been a professor at the
Taiwan Theological College, had then served as chief Chinese translator
for the United Bible Societies in Hong Kong, and had concluded his
distinguished career by serving the Taiwan Bible Society. Although
elderly and frail, the Lohs were delighted to see us, and we them, our
first meeting since they had left Hong Kong some ten years before.

In the afternoon there was an afternoon reception at the
Presbyterian Church of Taiwan's General Assembly office for the
missionaries in our group who had served the PCT while in Taiwan.
It was a joyful time of reunion with old colleagues, and each of us who
had served with that church made a few remarks in Taiwanese. General
Secretary William Lo presented beautiful mementoes and thanked us
for our service to the PCT and to the Taiwanese people. He also gave an
encouraging report on how the church had developed over the decades
since we had been there, and how it continued to be a powerful witness
for Christ among the people of Taiwan. It was also holding steadfast

in advocating independence and membership in the United Nations for Taiwan. That evening, the PCT hosted a farewell banquet, at which we sang several of the Reverend John Tin's Taiwanese patriotic songs, a fitting conclusion to our journey. The church had bravely borne its cross in the past, and now its sorrow had been turned to joy.

Following the banquet, Edwin and Claudia Keh, from Hong Kong SWAP days, paid us a visit at our hotel with their three boys. Edwin was in charge of the Asian operations for Payless Shoes. We talked furiously during the short time we had together, catching up on family and ministry news. I had served as their marriage counselor, and then as Claudia's "father" at their wedding in Hong Kong more than twenty years before. They had stayed on in Asia to work and minister there.[52]

Our journey of remembrance and appreciation had come to an end, but it would always live in our memories as a remarkable, generous, and inspiring experience.[53] There had been great empathy and solidarity among our group of old vets who were thrilled to see and experience *together* the fruition of seeds planted and deeds done so long ago, often in comparative isolation.[54] However, the greatest thrill had been to see those who had suffered much and risked all now realizing their long cherished dream of living in a free and democratic society. As a Christian missionary, I was honored to have had the privilege of serving alongside those brave men and women in their just cause, and to have been given an opportunity to play a small part in helping them realize that dream.[55]

Rights and Referendum

Exactly four years later, I was back in Taiwan, this time to participate in the International Conference on Human Rights at the invitation of the Presbyterian Church in Taiwan. After landing in Taipei

[52] On Christmas morning, Edwin's secretary, whom we had met at his office, called him and told him to turn on the television. "The Karsens are on!" she said. True to their promise, the program we had recorded was aired by TTV on that day.

[53] For a brief synopsis of this event with photo, see Gerrit and Mei-chin van der Wees, eds., *Taiwan Communique*, "A Journey of Remembrance and Appreciation: International Friends Return to Taiwan," January 2004, 20-22.

[54] See brief sketches of all participants in *A Journey of Remembrance and Appreciation*, prog. booklet, 3-12.

[55] Mortenson, Pete, "Mission Possible," *Holland Sentinel*, January 3, 2004, A8. See also, "Missionary Honored for Human Rights Work in Taiwan," *RCA Today*, Vol. 17, No. 2, Feb. 2004.

I joined the other participants and boarded a bus to the Conference site in Hsinchu. As the towns and fields flashed by the bus window, it was amazing to see how much Taiwan had continued to prosper and develop since 2003.

The conference was convened on the premises of the Hsinchu Bible School, which had also undergone impressive development since the days when it had served as one of the Summer English Program sites. Returning to this campus after so many years brought back many memories of my student work days. One incident remained seared into my mind. While standing on a dormitory balcony on a hill overlooking a propane gas factory in the summer of 1972, a sudden explosion had triggered a series of explosions among scores of tanks stored in the factory yard. The blasts had shaken the building in which I was standing, and I could feel the rushes of hot air released after each explosion. The Summer English Program students had been frightened out of their wits, and it had taken everything I could muster to calm them down and to assure them that the school building would not be blown to bits. Later, the incident had led to a soul-searching discussion about the life to come and where we would have ended up had we all *been* blown to bits.

The Presbyterian Church in Taiwan had organized the December 6–9, 2007, conference to commemorate the thirtieth anniversary of the issuing of the PCT's 1977 Statement on Human Rights. That statement called on the then repressive Nationalist government to take effective measures "whereby Taiwan may become a new and independent country," and to appeal to the nations of the world to support the admission of Taiwan to the United Nations as a free and independent country.

By 2007, the island nation, equal in size to the Netherlands, had a population of 23 million and had become the second most densely populated country in the world. It was twenty-first in the world in GDP, sixteenth in the world in trade, and had built up cash reserves of US$242 billion. In this it ranked ahead of the majority of countries that currently made up the United Nations.[56]

The Democratic Progressive People's Party's Chen Shui-bian had been re-elected as Taiwan's president in 2004 with a majority of the vote. He had been steadily dismantling the remains of the Nationalist's oppressive policies and institutions and promoting an elusive quest for Taiwan's independence. For example, the name "Taiwan" had been

---

[56] "Taiwan," *Wikipedia*, Sept., 10, 2008, http://en.wikipedia.org/wiki/Taiwan, Sept., 10, 2009.

Conference
participants

substituted for "The Republic of China" on official buildings and in government-related organizations. The remaining statues of Chiang Kai-shek had been pulled down all over the island and replaced with memorials to the victims of the 1947 massacre. The Taipei airport was no longer named after Chiang, and during the week of the conference I witnessed his calligraphy being removed from the ceremonial arch leading to the massive Chiang Kai-shek Memorial Hall in the center of Taipei.

However, eradicating past wrongs was not the main focus of the Democrats or of the now 220,000-strong Presbyterian Church in Taiwan. Their major concern had to do with Taiwan's future. Critical elections for the national legislature were coming up in January, and the Nationalist remnant was trying to make a political comeback. The next presidential election, including a referendum on whether or not Taiwan should apply for membership in the UN as a nation in its own right, was to be held in March. According to a poll taken shortly before the time of the conference, 70 percent of Taiwan's people identified themselves as "Taiwanese" and not "Chinese." Whether they would have the courage to risk retaining the independence-minded DPP in power and vote "yes" to UN membership (tantamount to endorsing an effort to change Taiwan's status from a *de facto* to a *de jure* state) remained to be seen. At this critical moment in the young democracy's life, the Presbyterian Church had gathered 97 representatives from its partner churches around the world, along with 138 participants from within the PCT. It had also lined up ten experts in various aspects of Taiwan's history, international law, and theological rationale for three major presentations: "Introduction to the Background and documentation of the PCT Declaration on Human Rights"; "National Name Rectification of Taiwan as a Theological Task and a Way to Promote International Justice"; and "Taiwan Independence—from *de facto* to *de jure*."[57] The point of the conference was to rally worldwide

[57] *International Conference Program Manuel* (Taipei: Presbyterian Church in Taiwan, 2007), v-vi, 159-69.

support for the Presbyterian Church and the people of Taiwan in their quest for independence and UN membership.

Independence and Inclusion

As conference speakers pointed out, the Taiwanese were fighting an uphill battle in pursuing these goals. First, China had vehemently opposed such a move. The People's Republic of China (PRC) had declared consistently that Taiwan was an inalienable part of China. Just two years before, the National People's Congress had passed an "Anti-secession Law," which declared that should Taiwan declare independence, China reserved the right to use force to compel the island to submit to its rule. To back up that threat, China had over a thousand ballistic missiles aimed at Taiwan and had beefed up its land and naval forces opposite the island.

Second, the United States had also strongly opposed such a move. Economically, the annual U.S.-China trade had been massive, with enormous and growing deficits in China's favor. The United States did not want to support anything that would irritate China, since it was now in debt to the PRC to the tune of more than a trillion dollars. Suppose China should suddenly cash in all those IOUs! Politically, ever since the issuing of the Shanghai Communiqué at the conclusion of President Nixon's 1972 breakthrough visit to China, the position of the United States had been to promote a vague status quo between the two "sides" in China's as of yet unconcluded civil war. It had "taken note" of the PRC's claim to Taiwan, but had insisted that any future rapprochement between the PRC and the ROC should be achieved through peaceful means. Militarily, although the United States had recognized the PRC as the "sole government of the whole of China" in 1978, it had, through the Taiwan Relations Act, committed itself to the defense of Taiwan should it be attacked. However, the United States in 2007 was so strapped militarily in Iraq and Afghanistan that the last thing the Pentagon wanted was a face-off over Taiwan with an increasingly powerful China. Diplomatically, the United States' power position in the world had declined to the point where it needed a friendly China to acquiesce to its Iraq policy, to help contain Iran and North Korea, and to cooperate on world affairs as a now permanent member of the UN Security Council. Therefore, in the view of the United States, Taiwan should "cooperate," not do anything to "upset the status quo" (like change its name, its flag, its constitution or its UN status) and move towards some kind of peaceful rapprochement with the PRC.

Third, any adverse change in the Taiwan/China standoff could well have endangered the enormous trade relationship that had developed across the Taiwan Straits. Despite the strident rhetoric, by 2007 there were hundreds of thousands of Taiwanese businesspeople living and working in the People's Republic. One of the wealthiest "countries" in the world, from 1991–2007, Taiwan's entrepreneurs had officially invested over US$65 billion (or more than half of Taiwan's total overseas investments) in China's skyrocketing economic development. Unofficially, the totals were much higher.[58] Were relations between the island and China to deteriorate, that huge investment could be lost. For example, if sufficiently irked, China could have simply nationalized all joint venture projects and sent their Taiwanese entrepreneurs packing without so much as a penny of compensation in their briefcases. These business people were also very nervous about any move that would upset the status quo.

As conference speakers also pointed out, the leadership of the DPP and the PCT saw things very differently, and these leaders were increasingly confident that they represented the majority of the people of Taiwan. First, they rejected China's claim to Taiwan, both legally and historically, and with good reason.[59] Up to World War II, Taiwan had not even been listed as one of China's "lost territories" by either the Communists or the Nationalists until Chiang Kai-shek belatedly laid claim to it at the Cairo Conference in 1943. In fact, prior to that, both Mao and Chiang are on record as actually having favored encouraging the Taiwanese to revolt against Japan and declare independence.[60] Further, at the conclusion of World War II, Chiang was only asked to take the surrender of the Japanese forces on Taiwan and administer Japan's former colony on behalf of the Allied forces "until such time as the future status of the island can be determined." That status had still not been determined.

Second, conference speakers deplored the position of the United States vis-à-vis Taiwan. Like scores of other colonially occupied territories that gained their independence after World War II, they believed that Taiwan should also have been allowed to determine its own destiny rather than having had one imposed on it. The 1972 Shanghai Communiqué stated that "all Chinese on both sides of the Straits

---

[58] "Table – Taiwan 2007 Investments in China," *Reuters: India*, Jan. 21, 2008, http://in.reuters.com/article/idINTP26278020080121, Sept. 10, 2009.

[59] See pp. 41-43.

[60] See Snow, Edgar, *Red Star over China* (Middlesex, Eng.: Harmondsworth), 128-29 and Liu Xiaoyun, *A Partnership for Disorder: China, the United States, and Their Policies for the Postwar Disposition of the Japanese Empire, 1941-1945* (Cambridge: Cambridge Univ. Press, 2002), 64-65.

agree that there is but one China and that Taiwan is a part of China." However, the speakers contended that this "all" did not, and would not, include the great majority of the people on the island—the Taiwanese, who had never been consulted or allowed to exercise their God-given right to self-determination. Instead, after losing the Chinese civil war, Chiang Kai-shek had been allowed to occupy Taiwan illegally and turn it into a bastion from which he had forlornly hoped to reconquer the mainland and wrest it from the Communists. As a result, the Taiwanese had been caught in the middle of the Communist/Nationalist struggle as well as subjected to the White Terror. They had never agreed that Taiwan was part of China or even that there were "two Chinas."

When it came to Taiwan, they said, the United States had used a double standard. On the one hand, it had for decades preached democracy and human rights for all people of the world (including those in Iraq), but in the case of Taiwan, it had practiced "real politick" at the expense of the Taiwanese people. Those people had, at great cost and at great odds, struggled to free themselves from the Nationalist tyranny and had developed one of the freest democratic and prosperous societies in all of Asia. Denying them their own destiny for economic, political, military, and diplomatic reasons might be pragmatic, but, they said, such pragmatism was immoral.

Third, conference speakers acknowledged that Taiwanese entre-preneurs had invested a huge amount in the burgeoning Chinese market, but they did not believe this meant they necessarily supported an outdated "one China" policy or even the status quo. Business was business and patriotism was patriotism. Neither the DPP nor the PCT wanted Taiwan and China to be enemies. They welcomed increased trade and increased contacts between China and Taiwan and between the churches of China and the churches of Taiwan. They wished China well, and the churches of China well, and were glad that huge changes for the better had taken place there since the end of Mao's disastrous rule. However, they did not want China to prosper at the expense of Taiwan, and they reminded us that China was still, after all, a one-party state under autocratic rule. They hoped and prayed that in the future, the two neighbors could live peacefully side by side as one China and one Taiwan. They also hoped and prayed that China would evolve politically to the point where its people might one day enjoy the same freedoms and the same democratic processes that they enjoyed.

The speakers deplored the unfortunate fact that China had not seen things that way. They charged that China's policy towards Taiwan was to alternate between the carrot and the stick. As for the carrot,

President Hu had recently offered Taiwan a high degree of autonomy economically, politically, and even militarily for the foreseeable future—as long as Taiwan acknowledged that there was but one China and that Taiwan was an integral part of it. The Taiwanese could agree to the former, but not to the latter. To do so would be to surrender their unique identity and ultimately to surrender their hard-won freedom. As for the stick, in 2005 China had also passed the "Anti-secession Law," beefed up its missiles and its military, and made the kind of bellicose statements that had even concerned the United States. The speakers pointed out that such bullying had backfired in the past and predicted that it would continue to backfire in the future. It had driven China and Taiwan even farther apart than they had been ten years before. The more China had threatened, the more strongly the people of Taiwan had identified with their island. Such threats had certainly changed the status quo. Should China not have earned rebukes from the United States like those given to Taiwan's "authorities" every time they had been perceived to have upset the status quo? To the contrary, while the United States had felt free continually to criticize and restrict its longtime trading partner—and now free and democratic ally—its criticism of China had been strangely muted.

Again, conference speakers accused the United States of using a double standard. For example, the U.S. Congress had recently conferred its highest civilian medal on the Dalai Lama of China-occupied Tibet, a medal that had been presented by President Bush himself. China had howled its displeasure, but that had not seemed to matter.[61] Why was it then, the speakers wondered, that whenever China had howled about Taiwan, the United States had "kowtowed to the emperor?" For example, far from inviting the president of Taiwan to come to Washington to receive a medal, recently the United States had not even allowed his plane to be refueled on U.S. soil.

Conference speakers also lamented the double standard employed by overseas partner churches and the Christian ecumenical bodies to which the Presbyterian Church in Taiwan belonged. These partners and bodies had supported the people of Taiwan under their harsh Nationalist masters, affirming their right to self-determination. However, since China's rise on the world stage and the readmission of the China Christian Council to the World Council of Churches (WCC), these bodies had become strangely reticent to support the quest of the Taiwanese people to become a nation in their own right. They had been understandably keen to support the dramatic resurrection of the

---

[61] See "Bush Confers Medal on Dalai Lama," *Seattle Times*, October 18, 2007.

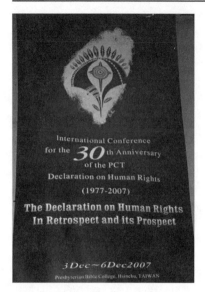

Banner proclaiming the theme
of the conference

Christian Church in China and to respond to new opportunities for
joint ventures there, such as providing resources for increased Bible
publication. However, in order to do so, they had not wanted to do or
say anything to offend their Chinese Christian brothers and sisters or
the more moderate Chinese Communist government that had allowed
China's Christians once again to worship, work, and witness in the open.
It was noted that, despite invitations having been issued to the leaders
of PCT partner churches, none had sent an official representative to the
conference. Perhaps that would have been politically incorrect.[62]

The irony, for example, of the World Council of Churches
having convened an International Ecumenical Consultation "towards
protection of human rights and human dignity amidst conflicts" in
Geneva on practically identical dates to that of the PCT conference had
not been lost on the conference delegates. The WCC consultation had
been called to prepare for the coming sixtieth anniversary of the UN
Universal Declaration of Human Rights in 2008. "This will be a fantastic
opportunity for churches to reconnect with the endeavor of protecting
and promoting human dignity and human rights," spokesman Peter
Prove had told the delegates.[63] However, if past precedence was any

---

[62] In fairness, it must be said that planning for the conference had not been
the most efficient and that invitations to church and ecumenical leaders
had been sent out quite late.

[63] "The Universal Declaration of Human Rights' 60th Anniversary Makes
2008 an Opportunity for Passionate Church Advocacy," *Oikoumene*,
December 7, 2007.

indication, the Presbyterian Church's call for support for the right of the people of Taiwan to determine their own future would never make it onto the WCC's agenda. Again, this did not mean that the Presbyterian Church in Taiwan did not fully support and rejoice in the renewed opportunities that Christians had to flourish once again in China. It simply meant that Taiwanese Christians were imploring their ecumenical brothers and sisters to be consistent and to follow an even-handed approach to churches on both sides of the Taiwan Straits.

The Conference on Human Rights demonstrated that the Taiwanese in general, and the membership of the Presbyterian Church in particular, were moving closer to a "now or never" position no matter what China, the United States, or the Christian ecumenical community might say. In this spirit, they concluded the conference by issuing a new "Declaration on the Right of Taiwan to Join the United Nations," in which they briefly summed up the essence of what had been discussed.

> Since the end of World War II in 1945, colonized peoples of the world have been exercising the basic human right of self-determination, thus becoming independent nations. The twenty-three million people of Taiwan remain the exception in that their inalienable right to statehood has been ignored or even actively opposed by member states of the United Nations. Clearly, the spirit of the Universal Declaration of Human Rights has not been implemented worldwide. This overt neglect is an injustice and an outright violation of the human rights of the Taiwanese people.
>
> Though the Taiwanese people had been successively ruled by foreign colonial powers, in 1996 they were able for the first time to directly elect a president in a democratic procedure that achieved a bloodless and peaceful revolution. Moreover they were even able to complete a peaceful transfer of power in 2000. A native Taiwanese administration led by the Democratic Progressive Party replaced the Chinese Nationalist (KMT) regime that had implemented their colonial rule over Taiwan for several decades by means of martial law. As a result of this change, the Taiwanese people today express a strong demand to join the United Nations using the name "Taiwan."
>
> However, China, the superpower to the west of Taiwan, has repeatedly exerted its emerging influence on the international community to violate, suppress, and isolate Taiwan in a way that has brutally oppressed the Taiwanese people and their fundamental rights. Despite being grieved and incensed by

Banner urging UN membership hanging on Taipei railway station

this degradation, we stand on the belief that human rights are ordained by God and that Taiwan has the right to membership in the United Nations so that the dignity of the Taiwanese people will be upheld by the international community.

Therefore we solemnly make this appeal to the world. We urge all to courageously support the Taiwanese people, who have been left on the outside, and open the door to United Nations membership so that hand in hand together we can promote justice and peace throughout the world.[64]

Dilemma and Direction

I left the conference feeling caught between a rock and a hard place—like the denomination I represented. On the one hand, the Reformed Church in America had been a partner in mission with the Presbyterian Church in Taiwan for more than half a century (1957–2007) and had sent scores of missionaries to assist the Taiwanese church in medical, educational, and evangelistic endeavors. It had for decades supported the PCT's struggle to rid Taiwan of the oppressive Nationalist regime and had consistently endorsed the right of the people of Taiwan to determine their own future. More recently, it had celebrated the development of a free and democratic society in Taiwan and the Presbyterian Church's continued growth and vibrant ministry there.

On the other hand, the Reformed Church had long historical ties to China, having been in mission in the Amoy area for more than a century (1842–1951). Beginning in 1977 with my first trip to China, the RCA had rejoiced over the transformation of China's leadership from a religion-bashing regime to one that promoted religious tolerance,

---

[64] For the full text of the declaration, see "The Presbyterian Church of Taiwan Goes on Record for Taiwan and the UN," *Jerome F. Keating's Writings*, Dec. 28, 2007, http://zen.sandiego.edu:8080/Jerome/1196920787/index_html, Sept. 9, 2009.

albeit imperfectly. It had celebrated the unbelievable resurrection and rapid growth of the Christian church there. Over the last fifteen years, it had entered into a new partnership with the China Christian Council and the Amity Foundation to provide support and personnel for university and seminary education. In 2006, it had been able to launch the "Xiamen Project" to provide support for church reconstruction and lay and evangelist training in the Amoy area through renewed ties with churches that traced their roots back to RCA mission endeavors.

The dilemma was that the Reformed Church related to partner churches on both sides of the Taiwan Straits, partners that saw the Taiwan/China issue from very different perspectives. The China Christian Council supported China's position that Taiwan was an inalienable part of China and should be returned to the motherland even through force, should all other means fail. The Presbyterian Church in Taiwan was adamant that the people of Taiwan had a right to determine their own future and that Taiwan had a right to become an independent country and take its rightful place among the family of nations. If the Reformed Church were to lean towards the Chinese view, it risked damaging relations with an old and treasured partner that would feel betrayed and abandoned. If it were to lean towards the Taiwanese view, it would risk jeopardizing its newfound relationships with China's resurging churches.

Pondering this conundrum, I came to the view that the direction in which we needed to move to resolve this impasse was to pay attention to Christian theology and not be swayed by political pragmatism. What did our theology demand? It demanded that we support the principle that all peoples of the world are created in God's image and have been given the right to live in dignity, freedom, and peace. While endeavoring to strengthen our relationship with the China Christian Council, we at the same time needed to encourage it to advocate greater freedom, human rights, and democratic processes within the People's Republic of China and to urge the Chinese government to adopt a peaceful rather than a threatening stance towards Taiwan. As for the Presbyterian Church in Taiwan, we needed to continue to support the right of the people of Taiwan to decide their own future (even if that decision turned out to be a declaration of independence). At the same time, we also needed to help the PCT's leaders see that their perennial question, "Can *anything* good come out of China?" could increasingly be answered yes. The only way forward would be for Christians on all sides of this seeming impasse to work and pray together and to encourage the leaders of both China and Taiwan to work out a future that would

Front l-r: David Gelzer, teacher,
C.M. and Ruth Kao, John Tin,
Rowland and Judy Van Es.
(Author rear right)

eventually produce a close and peaceful neighborly relationship between the two peoples. Both China and Taiwan needed to let bygones be bygones and to let people freely decide who they wanted to be.

We also needed to facilitate bridge building between the China Christian Council and the Presbyterian Church in Taiwan, encouraging Christians on both sides of the straits to advocate a peaceful and just resolution to the "Taiwan question." It should be made clear that one church's interests should not be sacrificed to the other church's interests, but that we wanted to relate to both churches in an even-handed way.

The conference offered much food for thought, but it was also a welcome opportunity to connect with Presbyterian colleagues and friends again—like C.M. Kao, Rowland and Judy Van Es, David Gelzer, Tan Lam-chhiu, C.S. Song, John Tin, Leonard Lin, Carlys Humphries, and others—and to make new friends like the new general secretary, Andrew Chang, and the general assembly moderator, James Pan.

Memorials and Memories

Following the conference, I spent several days on my own in Taipei. Being an avid collector of Chinese stamps, the first place I visited was the Post Office, where a large poster hung, advertising a future stamp issue featuring heroes of Taiwan's struggle for democracy and human rights. In the middle of the poster was the face of my old friend, Kuo Yu-shin, the onetime leader of the Taiwan Provincial Assembly, for whom I had once set up an escape plan. He had died some years before and had come to be hailed as one of four key political leaders who had stood up to the KMT regime. Needless to say, I ordered a first day of issue cover and a block of four of the stamps.

Next came a stroll through what used to be the Taipei New Park, but which had been renamed the 2–28 Peace Park. The park was a quiet

The 2-28 memorial

oasis in the midst of the noisy city that had not changed much. Old men were still "airing" their birds, while others with wispy beards were playing Chinese chess under weeping willow trees or softly playing their erhus (Chinese violins) and flutes. The park housed an impressive National Taiwan Museum (previously named the Taiwan *Provincial* Museum), built by the Japanese in 1908. However, the purpose of my visit was to see a large memorial that stood at one side of the park. The impressive 2-28 monument soared into the sky in memory of the tens of thousands of innocent Taiwanese who had been slaughtered by the Nationalist regime in 1947. I stood there in silence for a long time, close to tears. There was not a Taiwanese family that I knew that had not lost somebody in that euphemistically named "incident." Finally, sixty years later, their stories could be told openly. Linda Arrigo, a long-time democracy advocate, had compiled a thick file that documented many of those stories, along with the stories of thousands of others who had subsequently been imprisoned, tortured, and even executed over the years.[65] Exhibits in the park's 2-28 Museum told the story of this horrible massacre and its fifty-year aftermath in graphic detail. C.M. Kao's trial and imprisonment and the involvement of the Presbyterian Church in the struggle for democracy and human rights were also highlighted.

The next day was Sunday, so I headed for our old church, the PCT's Tiong-san Kau-hoe. The classic church building had been

[65]   See Arrigo, Linda, "Victims of the Kuomintang Regime" file, Karsen, pr.p.

dwarfed by modern structures, but it still stood in all its steepled glory as a prominent Christian witness. The structure had recently been declared a national treasure, and the congregation had just finished a complete renovation of the building inside and out.

Then it was on to our old neighborhood, which had changed beyond recognition. Not only had our old house disappeared, but even the lane in which it had once stood was occupied by a towering office building. The only recognizable feature was the campus of the old, dingy primary school that used to be around the corner, which had been filled with fancy new structures. The empty lot opposite the school, where our kids used to hunt for "buried treasure" and from which they had once attempted to launch a "rocket" had been transformed into a beautiful pocket park. I managed to find a few people who had lived in the lane long enough to remember what it was like when we were there. Even though they did not know me, they were delighted that I had returned to pay the old neighborhood a visit.

I next rode a bus out to the symbol of Taiwan's status as one of the world's wealthiest countries—the "101" building. Its name referred to the fact that, at 101 stories, it had until recently been the tallest building in the world. Located in an area that used to be truck farms, the building was surrounded by an impressive array of gleaming shopping malls, bank towers, and office complexes. Inside the building were floors and floors of glitzy shops, offices, and malls, with breathtaking atriums and impressive displays. Taiwan had come a long way since the days of banana hats and bicycles. The express elevator to the top provided a breathtaking view of the once dingy but now impressive city, set in a valley against a mountainous backdrop.

The last stop of the day was at a place that I had often passed but never entered—the complex that sheltered the home of Generalisimo and Madame Chiang Kai-shek. In those days, I had on a few occasions seen a line of black limousines emerge from the narrow road leading into the heavily guarded and secluded grounds of the presidential residence. The "G-mo's" car had not been identifiable, and the limousine lineup had never been the same. Like his counterpart across the Taiwan Straits, Chiang had been obsessed with security. He had seldom appeared in public, and when he had, elaborate security arrangements had been in place.

On this particular day, the place was mobbed. The elaborate grounds had been turned into a public park and, on that weekend, was the venue for the annual chrysanthemum flower show. I had not come to see the flowers but the home of the Taiwanese people's former

The Taipei "101" building

nemesis. To my disappointment, the remote house was still off limits and could only be viewed from behind a fence.

However, there was another building of interest open to the public—the former private chapel where the Chiangs had piously "worshiped the Lord" while their regime carried out a reign of terror on the island. Interestingly enough, it was called "Victory Chapel." The chapel was a replica of an identical one that the Chiangs had erected for their private use in Nanjing after the victory over the Japanese in World War II. A number of famous people had worshiped in this chapel as guests of the Chiangs, and their pictures adorned the walls.

This chapel was of particular interest because I had become personally acquainted with the Reverend Chou Lin-hua during our years in Taiwan. Chou had been the Chiangs' private chaplain and had for years conducted worship in this building for the presidential couple and their guests. This gifted Baptist preacher and scholar had once confided that he often agonized over his role as the Chiangs' chaplain. On the one hand, he believed that he had a unique opportunity to try to hold up Christ's ideals and goals before the country's leader. On the other hand, he was well aware that not all was well with the regime's policies and practices. However, he knew his limits. He could only say so much. He had decided that it was better to have an opportunity to say something than to speak his mind and lose his opportunity to say anything. These were the kinds of tragic moral choices that Taiwan's Christian leaders had been forced to make during the Nationalist era. Some, like Chou, had attempted to be "wise as serpents and innocent

Victory Chapel

as doves" and discreetly persevere without incurring the wrath of the regime. Others, like C.M. Kao, had chosen to confront those in power by "speaking the truth in love" and had paid the price for doing so.

That evening provided the privilege of reconnecting with human rights advocate Linda Arrigo and journalist Jerome Keating. Linda had been in the thick of the Kaohsiung protests in 1979 and had been documenting the abuses of the Nationalist regime ever since. She brought Jerome, an American journalist friend, to interview me at the YMCA where I was staying. Jerome had lived in Taiwan for a long time and had chronicled the transition from the Nationalist White Terror days to the new democratic society under the DPP. He was keen to record my memories of the Nationalist days and impressions of the new situation and to publish them on his Web site.[66] Linda and another veteran Taiwan watcher, Lynn Miles, were in the process of publishing a book on the contributions foreigners had made to the struggle for human rights and democracy in Taiwan.[67]

My last visitor of the evening was Syd Goldsmith, who had been one of my contacts at the American Embassy in Taipei. Syd was married to a Taiwanese woman and had lived in Taipei with his family for decades. He was still contributing analytical articles about Taiwan and China to papers like the *Christian Science Monitor*[68] and had recently published a novel about Taiwan entitled, *The Jade Phoenix*.[69] Our last

---

[66] For the resulting article based on this interview, see "Freedom, Taiwan's Presbyterian Church, China, and Religion," *Jerome F. Keating's Writings*, Dec. 5, 2007, http://zen.sandiego.edu:8080/Jerome/1196920787/index_html, Sept. 9, 2009.

[67] See Arrigo, Linda and Miles, Lynn, *A Borrowed Voice: Taiwan Human Rights Through International Networks, 1960-80*, (Taipei: Hanyao Color Printing, 2008).

[68] For example, see "For China and Taiwan, a Welcome Thaw," *Christian Science Monitor*, November 25, 2008, 9.

[69] (Lincoln, Neb.: Universe Books, 2006).

contact with each other had been during the Journey of Remembrance and Appreciation event in 2003. We spent the time reminiscing and talking about the current state of affairs in both China and Taiwan.

During the weekend, I had become aware of a controversy that was playing itself out on the wide avenue in front of Chiang Kai-shek's impressive Memorial Hall (architecturally inspired by the design and scope of Beijing's Temple of Heaven). The memorial was near downtown, where I was staying. TV news reports indicated that the DPP Administration was preparing to send a crew to the large Chinese arched gate in front of the memorial. They would be taking down the three Chinese characters over the central arch that contained Chang's calligraphy and substituting new ones that reflected the new name that had been given to the area—"Freedom Square." Memorial Hall had also been given a new moniker—the National Taiwan Democracy Memorial Hall. This development had provoked outrage among KMT stalwarts, and hundreds of them had gathered in front of the huge gate waving Nationalist flags, chanting slogans, and vowing to prevent the removal of the original characters. Crowds of DPP supporters had gathered in response, waving their flags and supporting the change in name. There had been some scuffles and even some casualties when a fanatical KMT supporter had driven a truck into the DPP crowd and injured a number of people severely.

On Monday morning I stood at a discrete distance from the memorial, watching the chaotic scene. The two groups were continuing to shout at each other and to wave their flags—separated by long lines of riot police blocking direct access to the gate area. I walked over to a regular policeman, explained who I was in Taiwanese, and asked to go through the police lines to take photographs of the demonstration. To my surprise, he agreed, and I got some great shots of democracy in action. Such demonstrations used to be unheard of in Taiwan. In the end, work trucks showed up, took down the old characters, and substituted the new, protected from the wrath of the KMT supporters and cheered on by their DPP counterparts. The result was televised around the island and the significance of this symbolic act was not lost on the people. A problem remained, however. What should be done with the immense memorial originally erected to glorify a now disgraced dictator? Ironically enough, Taiwan's Communist cousins across the straits were stuck with the same dilemma. How could they get rid of "the Great Helmsman's" portrait hanging above the gate of the Forbidden City and the memorial hall housing his embalmed remains in the middle of Tian An-men Square without having to

KMT demonstrators in front of gate to Chiang Kai-shek Memorial

acknowledge that he had turned out to be an even worse tyrant than the one he replaced?

Taiwan was again at an important crossroads, and I left wishing I could turn the clock back and serve there once again. However, I was grateful for the privilege of standing in solidarity with my Taiwanese colleagues and friends once again. As my plane took off, I wondered, with a lump in my throat, whether this might be my final farewell to Taiwan and to my treasured friends and colleagues there. Then again, who knows?[70]

Keeping in Touch

In January, back in the United States, we received the disappointing news that the Democratic Progressive Party had suffered a major defeat in elections for the Legislative Yuan. In the end, the Nationalists (KMT) and their allies won eighty-six seats to the DPP's twenty-seven. The Presbyterian Church in Taiwan still held out hope that the DPP could win the presidential election in March, but that also was not to be. Our friend Frank Hsieh garnered only 42 percent of the vote to the Nationalist's Ma Ying-jeou's 58 percent.[71]

---

[70] Upon my return to Michigan, I wrote an article laying out the case for the right of the people of Taiwan to pursue their own destiny. See Karsen, Wendell, "Taiwan: A Call for Justice," *Holland Sentinel*, February 2, 2008, A7.

[71] Lai, Jonathan, "Opposition sweep to victory in Taiwan," *Jonathan Lai, CNN. com*, January 12, 2008, http://www.cnn.com/2008/WORLD/asiapcf/01/12/taiwan.election/index.html, September 9, 2009, and "Opposition Wins Taiwan presidential vote," *Peter Enav, Democratic Undergroung.com*, January 12, 2008, http://www.democraticunderground.com/discuss/duboard.php?az=view_all&address=389x3046736, September 9, 2009.

Why had the DPP done so poorly? Why would the Taiwanese welcome back into power a party with such a sordid past; a party under which they had suffered so much in years gone by? The answer was fourfold. The DPP had splintered into factions that had sapped its vision, its performance, and its mission. The DPP had gotten too comfortable in office and was involved in a number of corruption scandals that even involved the president's family. The DPP, under Chen Shui-bian, had provoked China with its call for independence to the point where the powerful Taiwanese business elite were afraid that their enormous investments in China were under threat. To continue on this course would risk economic disaster and perhaps even war. And finally, in recent years, the Taiwanese economy had declined to the point that the common people were feeling the pinch in their pockets.

Ma, of course, promised to ease these fears. He would root out corruption. He would fix the economy. He would mend relations with China to the point where a joint peace agreement could finally be worked out and cross-straits transportation, postal, and shipping links could be forged. However, the PCT and many Taiwanese remained skeptical about such promises based on past experience and fearful, despite Ma's denials to the contrary, that the KMT might end up working out a deal with China behind the backs of the Taiwanese people.

True to his word, Ma invited Chen Yun-lin, chairman of China's Association for Relations Across the Taiwan Straits, to Taiwan for a five-day visit in November 2008. Chen was the highest-ranking official to visit the island since Chiang Kai-shek had fled the mainland in 1949. During his stay, four China-Taiwan agreements were worked out providing for direct air, shipping, and postal links and instituting food safety provisions. Ma also accepted a pair of "peace pandas" from the People's Republic. Meanwhile, thousands of Taiwanese demonstrated against Chen's visit. In the process, the old authoritarian instincts of the KMT came into play in the way the police clamped down on dissent. Protesters were manhandled and blocked from having any contact with Chen.[72]

In the aftermath, the Presbyterian Church in Taiwan asked its partner churches around the world to pray for Taiwan and for the church, since it feared that the hard-fought struggle for freedom, human rights, and democracy might once again be endangered.

---

[72] "Cross-straits Relations" and "Direct Links," "Ma Ying-jeou," *Wikipedia*, Sept. 9, 2009, http://en.wikipedia.org/wiki/Ma_Ying-jeou, Sept. 10, 2009.

PART TWO

The Cross of Colonialism:

Mission in Hong Kong, 1974-1984, 1990-1998

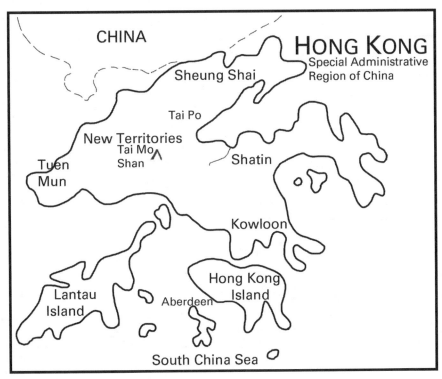

Map of Hong Kong drawn by Renske Karsen

CHAPTER 7

Crown Colony

Pearl of the Orient

Our plane slowly descended towards Hong Kong. It was June 1971, and our family was on the way to visit Reformed Church missionary colleagues Walter and Harriet DeVelder. The approach to Hong Kong's Kai Tak airport was one of the more breathtaking descents in the world. As we neared the ground, the high rise apartment blocks of Kowloon flashed by on our right. The plane suddenly dipped and made a 90-degree turn before it straightened out and gently touched down on what at first appeared to be the middle of the harbor. Because there was so little space, in 1958 the Hong Kong government had leveled a whole mountain, dumped it into the harbor, and created an airport.

It was a sunny day, but the mood in Hong Kong was anything but sunny. The colony had been lashed by typhoon Rose just before our arrival. As Walter drove us to our lodging at the Salisbury YMCA, we could see the evidence of Rose's fury. Trees were down, roads were closed, windows and signs were smashed, and ships were cast up on the shore like so many toys. Walter's sobering news was that more than

Hong Kong from
the air in 1971

250 people had been killed and many others injured. On the Hong Kong Island side of the harbor, a four-story apartment block had been dislodged by a landslide, slid down a rugged slope, and smashed into a twenty-five-story block of flats killing 125 people. On the Kowloon side, another 125 had been killed when a huge mud slide had gone right through the windows of three floors of a resettlement estate.

Despite the carnage, we could see why Hong Kong was called the "Pearl of the Orient."[1] Although in those days it was still something of a sleepy colonial backwater, Hong Kong boasted one of the great natural deep-water harbors in the world. Half of the city was vertical, rising eighteen hundred feet from the Central District on Hong Kong Island to Victoria Peak in less than a mile. A few days later Walter drove us to the top of Victoria Peak, which provided a spectacular view of the harbor. Ships were anchored as far as the eye could see. The buildings of downtown Victoria, many of them built on land reclaimed from the harbor, gleamed in the sun. The tip of Kowloon Peninsula[2]—covered with hotels, department stores, and crowded tenements—was clearly discernible on the Kowloon side of the harbor. Beyond it loomed the New Territories, the mountains and the border that separated the British Crown Colony from the People's Republic of China.

A Barren Rock

It was hard to believe that just 130 years before, Hong Kong had been described as a barren rock. The year was 1842. The British had just

[1]   "Hong Kong" means "fragrant harbor" in Chinese. Historians believe the "fragrant" part comes from a reference to a perfumed tree sap once produced and exported in Aberdeen, an ancient fishing village on the back side of Hong Kong island. Local wags joke that it refers to the stench that comes from a harbor that is rapidly turning into a huge polluted sewer.

[2]   "Kowloon" literally means "nine dragons" and refers to the original nine hills that dotted the landscape before most of them were leveled to build the airport and provide land for housing estates.

Hong Kong Island
ca. 1860

defeated the Chinese decisively in the first "opium war" (1839–42). The British naval commander, Captain Charles Elliot, demanded the cession of Hong Kong Island in perpetuity as a spoil of war, and the Chinese had no choice but to sign the 1843 Treaty of Nanking that formalized the arrangement. Some members of Parliament were astounded that Elliot had settled for a fifty-square-mile "barren rock with nary a house upon it," but the astute Elliot had foreseen the strategic potential of one of the great natural harbors of the world. In addition, the Chinese were forced to open five "treaty ports" along the southeastern coast of China for foreign trade.[3]

The war had actually been fought over an imbalance in trade. The British wanted what the Chinese had—tea, silk, cotton, ceramics, rice, etc.—while the self-sufficient Chinese wanted little of what the British had to offer in return. Consequently, much of Britain's silver reserves were slowly but steadily draining into Chinese coffers. The British solution to this problem was to export opium from British India and turn China into a nation of drug addicts. The British could grow the opium for practically nothing in India and sell it to the Chinese for astounding profits. The Chinese government naturally resisted, partly out of a concern that opium was bad for its people, and partly out of a concern that the trade imbalance would be reversed. However, Chinese leaders did not realize how far their dominance as Asia's "Central Kingdom"[4] had been eroded by modern military power, and they proved to be no match for the British Empire with its mighty fleet.

---

[3] Ningpo (Ningbo), Amoy (Xiamen), Shanghai, Canton (Guangzhou), and Foochow (Fuzhou).

[4] The name "China" (or Jung-gwo) literally means "Central Kingdom" and reflects the belief that China was at the center of the world, ruled by the "Son of Heaven" (the emperor), to whom all other "barbarians" should pay homage.

Opium continued to erode Chinese society to the point where, in 1860, the emperor sent a tough Mandarin named Lin to attempt to throw the British and their opium out of China's chief port of entry—Canton (Guangzhou) in southern China. Lin raided the British warehouses and ships and pulled off the equivalent of the Boston Tea Party. This led to a second "opium war," which the Chinese again lost handily. The opium "trade" was resumed, and the British forced the Chinese to cede the Kowloon Peninsula—a three and one-quarter square-mile tip of the mainland opposite Hong Kong Island—in perpetuity. This deal was formalized in the 1860 Convention of Peking. As a result, the British controlled both sides of its increasingly important port of entry into China. China was also forced to open five additional treaty ports along the coast at strategic points.[5] These two moves guaranteed the British a monopoly on the China trade.

British military leaders continued to be concerned about the defense of Hong Kong and to put pressure on the British government to acquire additional land for that purpose. At the same time, British speculators were also clamoring for more land for development in the crowded colony. In 1898, the British government pressured China into leasing an additional 397 square miles of land and islands to them that became known as the "New Territories." The lease, signed in a second Convention of Peking, was for ninety-nine years and would come due in 1997. The British assumed that the lease would be renewable, and in effect it integrated these territories into the Crown Colony of Hong Kong. As such, Hong Kong as a whole comprised 440 square miles of territory at the southern tip of the Chinese mainland. It was roughly forty miles wide and thirty miles deep and was situated forty miles east of the Portuguese enclave of Macao and ninety miles southeast of Guangzhou (Canton), the capital of China's Guangdong Province.

The Other Side of the Postcard

Although impressed by the splendid scenery of Hong Kong, once we began roaming its streets we ran into what could be described as "the other side of the postcard." People were packed into the place like sardines. Since much of the colony was made up of mountains, uninhabitable small islands, and rural mini-farms, 75 percent of its then four million people were crammed into approximately forty-five square miles of urban areas. The population density in the Sham Shui

---

5   Nanking (Nanjing), Hankow, Swatow (Shantou), Tientsin (Tianjin), and Niuzhung.

Po district of Kowloon, for example, was 425,000 per square mile—eighteen times as crowded as New York City.

Shortage of space meant that everything towered skyward. Downtown banks, hotels, and department stores soared twenty to thirty stories above street level. Although a small percentage of the very wealthy lived in houses, most of the well-off were housed in high rise apartment blocks. The majority of the population lived in blocks of eight-story "resettlement estates" with 5,500 people crammed into every block. Other thousands lived in huts scattered all over the hillsides in "squatter areas," while still other thousands lived on small boats moored in typhoon shelters. Factories were six to eight stories high. Although the downtown areas on both sides of the harbor had a few tree-lined boulevards with fancy stores and shops, most of the streets were narrow, crooked, and crammed with a colorful (and sometimes fragrant) conglomeration of Chinese markets, small shops, family businesses, tea houses, and restaurants.

We soon learned that "Hong Kongers" were a friendly but tough crowd. Ninety-eight percent of them were Chinese, with the other two percent being made up of British and Americans, along with a smattering of other nationalities. Although the vast majority of the Chinese were Cantonese, there were people from almost every province of China who spoke a myriad of Chinese dialects. Two-thirds of Hong Kong's inhabitants were refugees who had fled there after the Communist takeover of the Chinese mainland in 1949. They had come with practically nothing, but through hard work and ingenuity, they had learned how to survive, and some even thrived.

Hong Kongers had been toughened by weathering a number of natural, political, and economic storms. In 1894, an epidemic of bubonic plague spread to the colony from China and devastated the population over the next thirty years. At its height, the epidemic killed a hundred people a day. Although the disease was a great detriment to trade and brought about the temporary exodus of a hundred thousand Chinese from the colony, the majority persevered and the colony survived.[6]

In 1941, after a fierce battle, the Japanese conquered Hong Kong and instituted a harsh rule there until they were ousted in 1945. Again, the people hunkered down and emerged from their time of trial to rebuild Hong Kong and its economy. In 1950, upon the outbreak of

---

[6] "History of Hong Kong," Wikipedia, http://en.wikipedia.org/wiki/Hong_Kong#History, Sept. 30, 2009.

Japanese victory
parade through
Hong Kong

the Korean War, much of Hong Kong's entrepot trade with China was halted because of UN and U.S. embargoes. Despite handicaps like a scarcity of minerals, power sources, usable land, and fresh water, Hong Kong capitalized on its abundant supply of cheap labor, shifted into light manufacturing, and survived. When Communist-inspired riots and strikes almost paralyzed the colony in 1967 during China's Cultural Revolution, Hong Kong hung tough and broke the back of the strikes and the Communist network in the colony. These traits would continue to stand Hong Kongers in good stead as they approached the trials that awaited them in the decades ahead.

Tranquility and Typhoons

One day during our visit, Walter took us for a drive in the tranquil New Territories. What a contrast to the crowded city! We emerged on the other side of the Lion Rock Tunnel (which bored through the mountain range to the north of the city) to discover quaint villages with serene farm fields worked by Hakka women in their distinctive black-draped Asian hats. Because of its mountainous and rocky terrain, only about six percent of Hong Kong's land is arable. Rice and a variety of fruits and vegetables were grown, and pigs and chickens were raised, but, even at that time, most food was imported from mainland China. We also saw the big pipe through which 30 percent of Hong Kong's water was piped into the colony, the rest of its water being supplied by reservoirs and desalination plants constructed by the Hong Kong government. Fishponds also dotted the landscape. (Later, we would see large fleets of fishing vessels parked in island harbors, fishing being an important industry in Hong Kong).

We eventually came to Lok Ma Chau, a lookout point at the top of a hill from which we could look out over the border with "Red China" and beyond. We could see rice fields in the distance, with barefooted farmers in Asian hats plowing their fields with water buffalo as they had been doing for centuries. A few peasants were moving through a checkpoint on the narrow dusty road that traversed the border. The only other link with China proper at that time was the Kowloon Canton Railway line. However, all foreigners like us, except for a few British and other European businessmen and diplomats with special passports, could not go beyond the stop *before* the border town of Lou-Wu. For all practical purposes, China was a million miles away.

On the coastal road leading back towards Kowloon, we went through a forested area and stopped to see the Rhesus monkeys that were frolicking in the trees. Walter told us (and my naturalist son, Steve, would later confirm it) that, besides the monkeys, there were still barking deer, scaly anteaters, ferret badgers, civets, porcupines, shrews, bats, wild boar, mongoose, and a host of reptiles, amphibians, and birds in the New Territories where tigers once used to roam. We then proceeded to the ferry terminal to board a vehicular ferry for the fifteen-minute trip across the harbor to Hong Kong Island where the DeVelders lived.[7]

As for weather, we understood why the Cantonese were so slim. You sweat off the fat! Apart from a mild, damp "winter" from January through April, Hong Kong usually boasts temperatures in the nineties, with 90 percent humidity. It has a subtropical climate with plenty of rain during most months of the year, except for the drier and more pleasant months of October through December. Consequently, the place is abloom with all kinds of tropical flowers, trees, and shrubs. June through October constitutes the typhoon season, with three or four typhoons a season being the norm. Some typhoons are wind storms, some are rainstorms, and most are a combination of both. They can range from the killer type, of which we had just witnessed the aftermath, to milder storms that dump much needed water into the reservoirs. Adequate water supply was a constant concern in Hong Kong. If the typhoons didn't cooperate, water rationing would go into effect. During times of drought, the taps would only be turned on four hours a day. If there was a prolonged drought, they might only be turned on every other day.

---

[7]   In those days, there were no tunnels under the harbor, no bridges linking the islands, no super highways and no traffic jams—just two-lane roads and car ferries that carried a comparative trickle of cars, taxis, lorries, rickshaws, trams, and double-decker buses.

Chopsticks and Cheung Chau

Hong Kong was a British colony. The traffic moved on the left and cricket was played in Central.[8] However, it was a distinctly Chinese place. Western dress and Western modernity had been adopted by a majority of the people, but underneath, the Chinese were still very much Chinese. They did business in thousands of shops and out on the sidewalks in much the same way their ancestors had done. Coolie-pulled rickshaws still plied Hong Kong's back streets and alleyways. The Chinese liked their food fresh, and traditional markets, with their wondrous variety of live creatures, Chinese delicacies, and smells, were scattered throughout the colony. Hong Kong was the chopsticks capital of the Asian world. Dishes from a variety of its neighbors and from every province of China were served up in hundreds of restaurants and stalls. Chinese traditional medical treatments, like acupuncture, were widely practiced, and a plethora of traditional herbs and medicines were readily available.[9] The inhabited parts of the colony were crowded and noisy, which didn't seem to bother the Chinese one bit.[10] Hong Kong's "flags" consisted of thousands of bamboo poles jutting out of the sides of resettlement estates strung with wash hung out to dry.

Chinese temples nestled incongruously between tall buildings, while religious shrines were placed conspicuously in apartment hallways and shop interiors, complete with food offerings and smoking joss sticks. Mirrors adorned the sides of soaring apartment blocks in the direction of approaching roads and driveways in the belief that evil spirits would be warded off by seeing their own scary images. Walter told us that no new building in Hong Kong, even those designed and constructed by the best British architects and engineers, could be planned without consulting Taoist priests about *feng-shui*, or

---

[8]   The official name for the downtown area on Hong Kong Island was Victoria City, but it was invariably referred to as Central by the locals.

[9]   Before undergoing a knee replacement as a last resort in 1996, I tried Chinese acupuncture. It was an interesting experience, but it did not enable me to throw my cane away. However, I know many people who have been helped greatly by this and other traditional Chinese medical practices and medicines, although the exorbitant claims to cure everything from broken bones to constipation on some labels leave one greatly amused and more than a bit skeptical.

[10]   One of my colleagues, David Lin, retired and went to live with his son in beautiful Vancouver, Canada. He was back after a year, complaining that the place was too quiet.

Hong Kong resettlement estates in 1971

"topped out" without a Taoist ceremony on the roof.[11] Even Christian young people felt pressured into participating in their non-Christian grandparents' and parents' Buddhist funerals, complete with offerings to the ancestors and the burning of paper images depicting the necessities, and even luxuries, the deceased would need in the world of the spirits. Even the numbering of the floors in modern high rise buildings reflected Chinese superstitions. There was never a fourth floor, since no Chinese would live or work on one because the Chinese word for "four" sounds like the word for "death."

The DeVelders told us that British holidays simply brought Hong Kongers a respite from work, but Chinese holidays and festivals were observed with joyous abandon. The Mid-autumn Lantern Festival found parks and temples adorned with thousands of beautifully designed paper lanterns. Grave Sweeping Day brought families to cemeteries to beautify grave sites and pay their respects to the ancestors. During the Hungry Ghost Festival, hundreds of small fires were lit in the streets beside food and wine offerings to placate the spirits of any discontented souls. The major festival, however, was the four-day Lunar New Year celebration. All debts had to be paid by the eve of the New Year. (The years of the Chinese zodiac are made up of twelve animals and are known as the year of the monkey, dog, rooster, etc.). All houses had to be cleaned. All doorways had to be framed with red banners proclaiming propitious wishes for the New Year.[12] Everybody had to be

[11] One of the more humorous sights in Hong Kong was to see British *taipans* (company executives), architects and engineers in hard hats on the top of a construction project, joss sticks in hand, participating in a *feng-shui* "topping out" ceremony.

[12] These remained until they were replaced the following New Year, no matter how dirty or faded they might become. To remove them would bring bad luck.

dressed in the new clothes in which they would go to visit relatives and friends. Peach blossoms, symbolizing long life, and miniature orange trees, symbolizing wealth, decorated every home.

We took a ferry to one of the outlying islands, named Cheung Chau. Its mini-harbor was crammed with fishing vessels, which also served as homes to fishing families. There were no vehicles on the island. A few narrow crowded streets filled with Chinese shops, restaurants, and markets lined the western shore. People dressed in traditional Chinese garb and coolie hats filled the streets. It was as though we had been transported back to the China of a century before. The contrast with the city that we had left behind just an hour before was unbelievable. So was the contrast between the Chinese junks in Hong Kong's harbor, some of them battered hulks flying the PRC flag, and the gleaming rows of modern buildings that stretched along both sides as far as the eye could see. Hong Kong in 1971 could have been described as one of the great modern cities in Asia, but if you scratched its surface, you came up with one gigantic "Chinatown."

An Economic Powerhouse

In 1971, Hong Kong was already a free port, a bustling trade center, and a shipping and banking emporium—one of the greatest trading and transshipment centers in East Asia. Just five years before, the colony's external trade had already passed the US$2 billion mark. It had a booming textile and garment industry and was rapidly developing the capacity to manufacture plastics, electrical and electronic equipment, appliances, metal products, rubber products, chemicals, watches, jewelry, toys, and furniture. It had nascent shipbuilding, machine tooling, and other heavy industries. Tourism, motion-picture production, insurance, and publishing were also being developed. It was the fastest freight-handling port in the Far East, with most of the cargo being loaded and unloaded by lighters (small barges). There were more than 20,000 manufacturing establishments with a labor force of 500,000, figures that did not include unregistered "factories," the hundreds of family concerns, or the hundreds of job-working units to which the big firms farmed out garment-finishing and other rush work.[13]

Hong Kong was built on a free-trade philosophy and an uncompromising dedication to *lassie-faire* capitalism. It developed an establishment that in effect united government with big business.

---

[13] "Appendix 12," *Hong Kong 1972* (Hong Kong: Government Information Office, 1972).

Hong Kong
in the 1970s

Local wags said that power in Hong Kong resided in the Jockey Club, Jardine & Matheson Co. (the oldest big "hong," or company), the Hong Kong & Shanghai Bank (the colony's unofficial central bank), and the governor—in that order. The ideals were low taxes, no controls, quick profits, and hard work. Its economy was based on exports rather than on the domestic market. Most capital expenditure came out of current revenue. It was expected that investments would be recouped in five to seven years, and bank loans were made accordingly. An economic setback was seen as an "opportunity for adjustment," and a "recession" meant "a profit of only 100 percent."

British constitutional law, the maintenance of a level playing field, and a currency tied to the British pound sterling coupled with Chinese ingenuity, industry, and networking had built Hong Kong into a formidable economic bastion. The British were veteran hard-headed business operators who placed great stock in drive, individualism, rivalry, enterprise, secrecy, and venture. The Chinese were versatile experimenters, hard workers, technically skilled (or quickly teachable), and resilient, and were endowed with an innate gambler's instinct. Together they built a thriving economy that could absorb adversity, capitalize on opportunity, and leave competitors in the dust. However, these positive characteristics also had their built-in liabilities. Hong Kong's fiercely competitive atmosphere and its obsession with the bottom line resulted in the development of a "survival of the fittest" society living in a "concrete jungle" whose principle god was the Hong Kong dollar.

Our 1971 visit to Hong Kong had been both exhilarating and disturbing. We had enjoyed our stay and learned a lot, but we had also become aware of obvious inequities and blatant inequalities. We would become keenly aware of these conflicting feelings just three short years later, when the Pearl of the Orient became our home and our new mission challenge.

Hong Kong, Here We Come!

May 1974 found us repeating the breathtaking landing at Hong Kong's Kai Tak airport, only this time we were landing there to stay. Smiling representatives of the Church of Christ in China, to which the Reformed Church had seconded us, met us at the airport. They took us to the Ann Black Centre, a YWCA facility in Kowloon that would be our temporary home. We immediately registered the children at the Hong Kong International School on Hong Kong Island, run by the Missouri Synod Lutheran Church, and made arrangements for them to be bused there.[14] While they were at school, Joyce and I began flat hunting. Since we had made the cross-cultural adjustment in Taiwan, had visited Hong Kong several times, and were in the midst of a population in which the majority of the people could speak at least some English, we could function quite independently from the start. The children's school was on "the island," so we determined that it would be best for us to live on that side of the harbor. After three weeks of hunting, we succeeded in finding a decent flat to rent in what was called the "Mid-levels."[15] By U.S. standards it was expensive, but by Hong Kong standards it was cheap because it was on the ground floor of an old eight-story building.[16]

Then it was on to unpacking the shipment of our household goods, getting settled, and buying a small Toyota car. We also had to decide on a church. Since the English-speaking Union Church Hong Kong was just a few streets down from where we lived, we assumed

[14] By this time, a two-mile-long cross-harbor tunnel had been opened linking Kowloon to Hong Kong Island.

[15] At the edge of the harbor on the north side of mountainous Hong Kong Island was "Central" (the business district), which was comprised of a few blocks of reclaimed land along the harbor and a few more blocks of streets carved out of the steeply rising foot of Victoria Peak. Steep roads, a funicular tram, and flights of steps ascended the mountain to a series of terraced roads that traversed the "Mid-levels." Circular roads ascended ever higher until they reached "the Peak," or the top of Victoria Mountain, overlooking the harbor. Schools, churches, restaurants, shops, clubs, and hundreds of apartment blocks were built along this network of streets that ascended the mountain. Private homes for the extremely wealthy were scattered here and there, but were mostly concentrated near the Peak.

[16] In Hong Kong, the newer the building and the higher the floor, the more expensive the rent, particularly if there was even a glimpse of the harbor to be had.

Kowloon Union
Church retreat

that we would feel at home there. However, during our first visit we discovered that our cultural assumption that all English-speaking people in Hong Kong would be pretty much the same was wrong. The relatively conservative British, who made up 100 percent of the congregation, made no move to welcome us or even to speak to us. Many people in the congregation were part of the British colonial establishment, and it became readily apparent that this would not be a good fit for us American "democrats." The church did not have any program for children and young people. The multinational Kowloon Union Church (including both Chinese and British), which we had attended while living temporarily on the Kowloon side, offered a stark contrast in both warmth and program. We opted to drive through the newly opened and convenient cross-harbor tunnel and become part of that congregation. Kowloon Union Church proved to be a wonderful spiritual home to our family for the next decade.[17]

We were to work with many British colleagues and make many dear friends among our English, Scottish, Welsh, Irish, Australian, New Zealand, and Canadian "cousins." Nevertheless, these English-speaking peoples each had distinct cultural traits and were different from Americans. This is not to say that one culture or dialect was better or worse than another. They were just different. For one, the language was *not* the same. There were significant differences in vocabulary, spelling, usage, and nuance. There were different sayings, proverbs, and puns. What one considered funny or friendly, the other didn't. Americans tended to be very informal and outgoing, while the British tended to be more formal and conservative. Americans tended to share feelings

[17] Little could we have guessed then that twenty-five years later I would accept a call to become the pastor of a much-changed Union Church Hong Kong.

readily, often with complete strangers. The British tended to restrain their feelings and were more reserved. An American weakness was to brag about accomplishments, money, and size, while a British weakness was to display an air of superiority.

This attitude could become accentuated in a colonial setting like Hong Kong to the point of racial prejudice. Some "Brits" who would be considered quite ordinary back home tended to become arrogant colonialists when "out in the empire." They made little effort to acclimatize and acculturate but instead attempted to recreate little Englands abroad where they, for the most part, lived in isolated and segregated splendor apart from the "natives." At any rate, we discovered that we were in for a *double* culture shock in Hong Kong in trying to adjust to both the British and the Cantonese ways of being, thinking, and doing.

We had also assumed that a Chinese is a Chinese is a Chinese but found out that that too is a myth. There were Chinese from every province of China living in Hong Kong, the vast majority of them Cantonese. It only took us a few weeks to discover that we were dealing with a Chinese multicultural mix that spoke a myriad of different dialects, ate a plethora of different cuisines, and had a definite pecking order. Most Pekingese thought they were superior in language, size, and power to all others. Most Shanghaiese thought they were more urbane and sophisticated than all others. Most Cantonese thought they were more clever and feisty than all others. They all thought that Chiew-Chow people were drug addicts and crooks and that Taiwan people were ignorant and uncouth. Having lived among the Taiwanese for four years, we were put off about the latter and quite doubtful about the former. So we learned to relate to our new Chinese neighbors, colleagues, and friends the same way we had learned to relate to people elsewhere—as individuals with different characteristics. Many did not match their stereotypes, and most were delightful.

Tones, Tenses, and Tests

Although the official language of Hong Kong was English, we had also assumed that since the people were originally from the mainland, they would all speak the national language of China—Mandarin Chinese. Wrong again! Since the vast majority of the people were Cantonese, Cantonese was Hong Kong's practical lingua franca. In fact, because of Cantonese antipathy to the Communists and the northerners, it was considered something of a sellout to use the national language. Although I did use the Taiwanese we had learned in Taiwan to preach in the few Amoy-speaking churches in Hong Kong from time to time, it proved to be of little practical use there. The plan had been to study Mandarin and thus be able to converse with all Chinese in Hong Kong and perhaps someday in China proper. However, when we discovered that hardly anybody in Hong Kong used Mandarin, we decided that unless we wanted to be considered perpetual tourists and outsiders, we would have to learn Cantonese instead.

Our Taiwanese, however, was not wasted. Although the Taiwanese and the Cantonese could not understand one another, there were enough commonalities in grammar, tones, characters, and vocabulary in their languages to enable us to compress two years of Cantonese study into one. Also, having learned one Chinese dialect, learning a second did not seem quite so impossible. It was also helpful that just a few years before, our Hong Kong Language Institute director, Janey Chen, had Romanized our Cantonese textbooks, which meant that we did not have to spend an inordinate amount of time dealing with complicated written characters while learning the dialect. However, one had to be a disciplined student and throw caution to the winds in order not to succumb to the temptation to try to get along on English in a British colony. For example, when visiting the bank, I usually addressed the Chinese clerks in Cantonese while they usually addressed me in English. They were afraid that I might make a mistake in the numbers. Or when I learned to ask the fruit lady at the bottom of our stairs, "How much is it?" in respectable Cantonese, she might answer, "One dollah." When these things happened, one had to be a bit philosophical about language study. Especially at first, we were tempted to think, "Why bother?" However, our conviction proved to be correct that an ability to speak the local language would, in the end, be indispensable for meaningful mission in Hong Kong.

The Cantonese language also taught us something about the Cantonese people. For example, they spoke with gusto—so much so that if one didn't know better, one would often think they were arguing. One of the more deafening experiences in Hong Kong was to eat the famous Cantonese Dim Sum lunch in a restaurant seating a thousand people. The Cantonese were also southerners who wore their feelings on their sleeves. As a result, like the Italians, they had a number of suffixes that did not convey any specific meaning, but that did convey emotion. The more the discussion heated up, the more "aaaaaaaaaaaaaaaaaa"s were added to the endings of words. Or when the hero in a Cantonese sword movie made a spectacular move, a great "Waaaaaaaaaaaaaa!" resounded around the theater. Bargaining was taken to new heights in Hong Kong. Gestures, proverbs, tones, and body language all combined with words to turn making a deal into an art form. The Cantonese were also enthusiastic gamblers. The din of slamming Mahjong tiles onto table tops, along with appropriate comments, throughout the crowded resettlement estates on a Sunday afternoon was part of the Hong Kong symphony. The Cantonese also jammed the two world-class race courses built on Hong Kong's scarce land and employed all the fine points of the language in urging their favorites on to victory. Learning a language is essential for communication, but it also opens doors into the understanding of a people's culture, characteristics, and concerns.

Councils and Churches

The day after we landed in Hong Kong, I received a call from the general secretary of the Church of Christ in China (CCC), to whom we had been seconded by the Reformed Church in America. He was about to leave for an "open day" at a technical school run by the CCC. Would I care to come along? An hour later I was being whisked through the New Territories to an industrial area called Kun-Tong. Along the way, the no-nonsense general secretary, Dr. Peter Wong, gave me a running introduction to Hong Kong and to the CCC. Upon our arrival at the school, he cut the ribbon for the open day celebration, and we listened to the program offered by the students and inspected the exhibits. After he introduced me in English to the teachers and pastors who were there, we headed back to the YWCA and he laid out my mission as he conceived it. The CCC by that time was running a network of twenty-six primary and secondary schools in Hong Kong. My job would be to coordinate the religious education of that network in general, and to train and nurture the teachers that taught "Biblical Knowledge" classes and sponsored the Christian youth groups in the schools in particular. I would be given an office at CCC headquarters on the Kowloon side of the harbor, and the sooner I could begin my work, the better.

The Church of Christ in China had been born in Shanghai in 1927. Up to that point, a plethora of western mission agencies had been at work in China, each for the most part doing its own thing. However, this had not been the case in the Xiamen (Amoy) area on the southern coast of China, opposite Taiwan. There, beginning in 1842, Reformed Church in America, English Presbyterian, and London Missionary Society missionaries had together planted a united indigenous church based on what today has become known as the "three self" principle—self-government, self-propagation, and self-support.[18] They brought

---

[18] The RCA General Synod at first instructed its China missionaries to work independently to establish a Reformed Church in China. A seven-year struggle ensued, during which the China missionaries threatened to resign

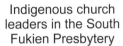

Indigenous church leaders in the South Fukien Presbytery

into being a South Fukien Presbytery based on these principles. Eventually, other mission agencies, following this example, became willing to join them in bringing about a united indigenous church in China. These efforts came to fruition in Shanghai in 1927. Although not every mission agency joined the Church of Christ in China, the great majority of mainland denominational groups, from the English Baptists to the American Methodists, did (with the notable exception of the Lutherans and the Anglicans).[19]

After its founding, and despite the major upheavals brought about by Chinese civil wars and then the war with Japan (1931–1945), the Church of Christ in China continued to grow stronger. By 1950, it had over 1,000 organized churches with 200,000 communicant members, 500 ordained ministers, and almost 1,500 evangelists, including a section called the Hong Kong Council.[20] After the Communist victory in 1949–50 and the expulsion of all foreign missionaries from China by the end of 1951, hundreds of missionaries and thousands of Chinese Christians fled to Hong Kong. Overnight, the Hong Kong Council

---

en masse unless they were given the freedom to work with like-minded ecumenical partners to establish a united indigenous Chinese church. The missionaries won the struggle and thus established the principles that continue to undergird RCA mission efforts to this day. For a comprehensive discussion of this issue and survey of the RCA's 150-year mission effort in the Amoy area, see De Jong, Gerald, *The Reformed Church in China 1842-1951*, Historical Series of the Reformed Church in America, no. 22 (Grand Rapids: Eerdmans, 1992).

[19] RCA Amoy missionary, A.J. Warnshuis, was a leading figure in this movement. Beginning in 1914, he served as the National Evangelistic Secretary for the China Continuation Committee, the precursor that eventually became the CCC in 1927 (see Merwin, Wallace, *Adventure in Unity* (Grand Rapids: Eerdmans, 1974), 27.

[20] Ibid., 223.

of the CCC burgeoned in numbers, and former leaders from Kwong-Tung Province and elsewhere, like Peter Wong, were given leadership and pastoral posts. Mission bodies like the RCA reassigned China missionaries to serve under the Church of Christ in China, Hong Kong Council (CCCHKC).

As thousands of refugees continued to pour into Hong Kong during the fifties, humanitarian needs mushroomed and churches, including the CCCHKC, responded. Noodle factories were opened to help feed the refugees. Rooftop schools were improvised to educate their children. The churches persuaded the government to provide temporary shelter and other services for them. People were assisted in finding some type of employment, however humble. In all of this, a great opportunity for evangelism presented itself as destitute and fearful refugees looked for inner strength to survive and a purpose for which to live.

Meanwhile, in China, the noose around the churches' necks was slowly being tightened. All denominations were forced to merge. Even though the creation of a national indigenous church had been the goal of the Church of Christ in China, the Chinese government considered it merely another western-oriented denomination and forced it to merge with the others. "Three-Self Patriotic Movements" were created by the Communist Government's Religious Affairs Bureau, both to rid China of the vestiges of missionary influence and western imperialism within the Protestant and Roman Catholic churches, and to control the future life and witness of those churches. After the advent of the Korean War in 1952 and China's eventual participation in it, all contact with and support from western churches, missions, and Christian organizations was cut off. This isolated the Hong Kong Council of the CCC, and it became in effect the sole vestigial remnant of the Church of Christ in China. As a result of these peculiar circumstances, the CCCHKC had grown rapidly, both in number of congregations and in the development of a network of primary and secondary schools. It had also participated in the establishment of the United Christian Hospital in Kwuntong in 1973 and in the development of other social services.

In 1954, faced with so many challenges, the churches in Hong Kong, including the CCCHKC, had agreed to come together to form the Hong Kong Christian Council (HKCC). The premise underlying this ecumenical development was that the churches could undertake the large tasks they were being called on to undertake more successfully together than they could separately. The council was to promote joint Christian action in Hong Kong by developing ecumenical relations

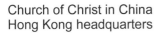
Church of Christ in China
Hong Kong headquarters

and by carrying out the social ministry agenda of the churches. (For example, in 1978, in place of a plethora of denominational social service agencies and projects, the HKCC would launch Hong Kong Christian Service—a large-scale multifaceted social service arm that enabled it to tackle large needs with large resources.) Since the emergency needs in Hong Kong were so great during the refugee years, the CCCHKC and the HKCC both continued to receive financial and personnel assistance from abroad and to retain and develop their ecumenical links with churches around the world.

The roots of the twenty-three Protestant churches affiliated with the council date back to 1844, when Union Church Hong Kong was established by Scottish missionary scholar the Reverend James Legge. By the time of our arrival in 1974, the Protestants had evolved into 50 denominations and groups with 600 congregations and 210,000 adherents. The Baptists formed the largest denomination, followed by the Lutherans. Other major denominations were the Adventists, the Anglicans, the Christian and Missionary Alliance, the Church of Christ in China (representing the Presbyterian and Congregational traditions), the Methodists, and the Pentecostals. Due to an emphasis on youth work (particularly through schools), over half of the congregations were made up of young people. Protestant churches and organizations operated a number of theological seminaries and Bible institutes, three post-secondary colleges, 130 secondary schools and 250 primary schools. In addition, they operated a plethora of kindergartens, Christian publishing houses, two weekly newspapers, Christian bookstores, hospitals and clinics, social service agencies, and guest hotels (managed by the YMCA and the YWCA). Six parachurch

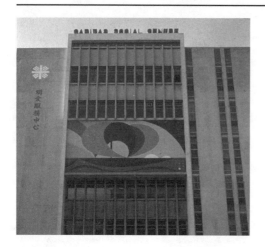

Roman Catholic
Caritas Center

agencies and a number of Christian action groups operated alongside the churches.[21]

As for the Roman Catholic Church, it was first planted in Hong Kong in 1841. By 1974, it had grown to 53 parishes with 260,000 members served by 340 priests and 900 religious brothers and sisters from 36 religious orders and congregations. The Catholics operated a seminary and 201 secondary and primary schools. In addition, they operated 6 hospitals with over 3,000 beds, 27 clinics, and 52 social service organizations.[22]

A large percentage of Hong Kong's population was Buddhist and Taoist. This was evidenced by the more than 360 Buddhist and Taoist temples scattered around the colony. Hong Kong's 50,000 Muslims also made their presence felt as they thronged to their three mosques for prayers each day. A Hindu temple in Happy Valley served as a focal point for Hong Kong's 10,000 Hindus. There were also small minorities of Jews, Sikhs, Zoroastrians, Mormons, Christian Scientists, and Jehovah's Witnesses, along with their synagogues, temples, reading rooms, and meeting places. Muslims ran a few secondary schools for Muslims, Buddhists for Buddhists, Confucians for Confucianists, etc.[23]

Although the Christian churches faced a formidable evangelistic task in this kind of religious environment, they had a distinct advantage

[21] "Report for the Year 1974," *Hong Kong 1975* (Hong Kong: Government Information Service, 1975), 165-66.

[22] Ibid., 166-67.

[23] "Report for the Year 1984," *Hong Kong 1985* (Hong Kong: Government Information Service, 1985), 251-52, 254-55.

in that Hong Kong was ruled by a "Christian" nation whose officials were by and large members of Christian churches. Thus, when the churches offered assistance in education, social services, communications, and moral education, the government saw them as natural partners. This did not mean that Hong Kong's government did not make an effort to be fair to people and groups of all religious persuasions. It simply meant that even though Christians only made up around 10 percent of the population, Christian bodies had more influence in high places than did their counterparts of other faiths.

CHAPTER 8

Benevolent Dictatorship

Governors and Rickshaws

As we have seen, the British took most of Hong Kong from China at the point of a gun and forced it to lease them the rest. At that time, Great Britain truly was great. It was the most powerful nation on earth and could boast that the sun never set on the British Empire. Although the British were the first to develop a social, economic, judicial, and political system based on Christian morals, fair trade, common law, and democratic principles at home, they tended to ignore these ideals when establishing colonies abroad. In this, they were unduly influenced by venture capitalists like those of the British East Asia Company, who promoted the establishment of empire on the twin pillars of power and profit. The goal was to promote the interests of the companies and the home country, which too often meant ignoring the interests of the peoples that happened to live in the conquered or annexed territories. Britain, like other colonial powers, by and large ruled as conquerors, exploiters, and cultural imperialists, while thinking they were improving the lot of those over whom they ruled by introducing them to Christianity, commerce, and "civilization."

British flag flying over
Hong Kong

To be fair, when compared with other colonial powers of the time, the British did much more for their colonial subjects. They had a strong commitment to law and to fairness. Their Christian heritage and Victorian culture restrained them from installing or tolerating cruel and oppressive regimes. They allowed a certain amount of criticism and introduced reforms to correct flagrant abuse. They developed educational, medical, and social institutions in their colonies. They brought economic prosperity and opportunity to many. After the Japanese broke the back of the European colonial empires during World War II, the British were more successful at preparing their colonies for independence than were France, Belgium, Spain, Portugal, Germany, Italy, the Netherlands, and even the United States. However, none of this can ameliorate the fact that wherever the British ruled, they did *rule*, and they ruled over *subjects* who too often felt like—and were treated like—objects.

Why were the British able to rule over so many for so long against their will? First, because the British built up the greatest navy the world had ever seen. This enabled them to project their power around the world. It gave them the mobility to move troops and military equipment rapidly wherever it was needed to back up their national interests. Whenever a crisis loomed in Hong Kong, for example, the resident naval squadron and local garrison were beefed up to meet the threat.

Second, the British had style. Even though they could not maintain real power simultaneously everywhere in their far-flung empire, they gave the *impression* that they could. They were masters of the art of the bluff. Their huge monuments, impressive government buildings, and imperial pageantry created a sense of awe in the peoples over whom they ruled. In Hong Kong, for example, Government House, the imposing residence of the governor, stood high above the city and left no doubt in anybody's mind as to who was in control. This impression was reinforced by the governor's resplendent uniform, complete with ostrich-plumed hat, and his colorful retinue whenever he appeared at any official function. The locals joked that the hierarchy of power in Hong Kong was as follows: the governor, the head of the Hong Kong & Shanghai Bank, the Taipan of the Jardine & Mattheson Company, and God—in that order.

Third, the British employed a system of using some colonial subjects to control others, and in so doing created a buffer between themselves and their subjects. In Hong Kong, for example, Sikhs from British India (known for their honesty, size, and toughness) were sprinkled throughout the local Chinese police force, while Gurkha regiments from British-controlled Nepal (known to be the toughest fighters in the world) were stationed in the New Territories. British officers in both the police force and the military knew that in an emergency they could count on these non-Chinese forces to put down any local uprising.

Fourth, they educated and employed a compradore class whose personal interests became tied to British colonial interests.[1] These made up the backbone of the civil service and the managers in business, in institutions, and even in the church. In Hong Kong, for example, the aristocratic British believed in educating only 15 percent of "the best of the best" to serve in these capacities. They viewed universal education as being detrimental to their interests. The more educated and liberated local minds they had to contend with, the greater would be the threat to their control.

Fifth, the British made the rules that governed political, social, and economic life in their colonies. Although they had a great respect for law and for fair play, they were adept at tilting the colonial boards in favor of their business and national interests. In Hong Kong, for example, they created a banking cartel that controlled monetary policy, set interest rates, and even printed Hong Kong's currency. Collusion to promote the interests of the big capitalists, rather than competition to safeguard the interests of the masses, ruled the day.

---

[1] A compradore was a Chinese agent engaged by a foreign establishment in China to be in charge of its Chinese employees and to act as an intermediary in business affairs.

Sixth, English was the sole official language in all British colonies.[2] If one wanted to get anywhere in life, one was compelled to learn the language of the masters. Very few British officials bothered to learn the local language. In Hong Kong, for example, court procedures, meetings at all levels of government, and meetings in most public organizations were conducted in English and translated. Except for a small percentage of the highly educated, locals struggled to understand and to express themselves in an alien tongue, often, in Hong Kong's case, lapsing into "Chinglish"—a mixture of Chinese and English. Since language equals power, the rulers always had a distinct advantage over the ruled.

By the time we arrived in Hong Kong in 1974, colonialism was a spent force. At the conclusion of World War II, a great movement for independence had swept through the remnants of the great empires, including Japan's. The creation of the United Nations in 1945 helped promote the ideals of liberal democracy and independence for the oppressed peoples of the world. The great majority of the colonies of the former empires had been given their independence. Hong Kong, for a number of reasons, was a glaring exception. Like some nineteenth-century anachronism, the Union Jack still flew over what the British described as "the last jewel in the imperial crown." The lease on the New Territories would not be up for another twenty-three years. It was assumed that China would sign another one and that Britain would go on ruling Hong Kong for the foreseeable future. Hardly anybody talked about the lease or about what would happen if China would *not* agree to extend it. Meanwhile, life went on in colonial Hong Kong pretty much the way it had gone on for most of the thirteen decades the British had ruled there. Even the coolie-pulled rickshaws had not yet been phased out.

The governor, as the appointed personal representative of the Queen, was invested with full powers to rule the crown colony. As such, he was equivalent to a benevolent dictator. There was a Legislative Council, but the governor appointed the council's entire membership. Some prominent Chinese businessmen and professionals were appointed as "unofficial" members, but the majority of the members were British colonial ministers and civil servants that were appointed as "official" members. The council was thus engineered in such a way that on any issue that it really cared about, the colonial government could never lose a vote. This rendered the supposed representative body

---

[2]   Chinese was not recognized as an additional official language in Hong Kong until 1974.

Statue of King George VI
in Hong Kong's
Botanical Garden

of the people a rubber stamp on two counts: it would always support government policy, and its unofficial representatives could always be counted on to support legislation that favored the interests of big business.

The governor also appointed an Executive Council to advise him. The council was composed of five ex-officio high-ranking government and military officials, one official member, and eight unofficial members who were all trustworthy members of the local oligarchy. Technically, policy decisions or legislative initiatives would be made by the "governor-in-council," but power actually rested in the governor himself, since he could ignore the advice of his councilors if he so wished.[3]

There was also an Urban Council whose "powers" were limited to decisions concerning parks, garbage collection, and the like. As a sop to those who were making noises about the lack of representation in government, a system was devised whereby half of its members were appointed by the governor and half elected by a carefully chosen segment of the population. Although this was at least a feeble step towards some form of democratic representation, the Urban Council had no real power.

There had been one short-lived attempt at political reform in Hong Kong in 1945 following Britain's resumption of control after

[3]   See Governor Christopher Patten's similar assessment in *East and West: China, Power and the Future of Asia* (New York: Times Books, Random House, 1998), 16–17.

the end of the Japanese occupation. Sir Mark Young, who had been governor at the time of Hong Kong's capitulation to Japan in 1941, and who had been interned by the Japanese during the war, resumed his office after Japan's capitulation. He was convinced that the only way to maintain British rule in the colony was to introduce democratic reforms. His ideas were opposed both by the British Foreign Office in London and by the "Taipans" and "Mandarins" (British and Chinese business tycoons) in Hong Kong. Sir Mark was replaced after a year with a new governor who would not brook any more nonsense about democratic reforms.[4]

Why did the Hong Kong Chinese not rebel against their British overlords and take charge of their own destiny? The answer to this question lies in an analysis of modern Chinese history. The vast majority of Hong Kong's people were refugees. The Chinese mainland had been in turmoil for more than a century. The disintegration of the Ching Dynasty, the chaotic period of the warlords, the disastrous war with Japan, and the equally disastrous civil war between the Nationalists and the Communists had all proved to be a nightmare for the people of China. Untold millions had been killed or had starved to death. Thousands had fled to the relative safety and economic security of British Hong Kong. The Japanese conquest of Hong Kong and subsequent harsh rule there from 1941–1945 had proven to be instructive as well. Compared to the Japanese, the British colonial rulers came across as gentlemen and scholars. Then the Communist terrors of the Hundred Flowers Campaign, the Great Leap Forward, and the Great Proletariat Cultural Revolution had convulsed China yet again. Thousands more had fled to Hong Kong. The British might be "foreign devils," but the Communists by comparison were the devil incarnate. In the end, it was not that Hong Kongers liked the British or their colonial administration, but that they settled for the lesser of two evils. After reaching such a conclusion, one did not rock the boat by which one had been rescued.

Threats and Warnings

In 1962, the power structure in Hong Kong was rudely reminded that, as one wag put it, Hong Kong was merely "a pimple on the belly of China." Before the Chinese Communists had come to power, people had been able to pass freely back and forth between the mainland and the colony. However, following 1949, it became obvious to both the

---

4   Ibid., 15.

Entrance to
Bank of China,
unofficial headquarters
for Chinese Communist
affairs in Hong Kong

Chinese and Hong Kong governments that the border could not be left open. As far as the Chinese Communists were concerned, the less contact between the "contaminated" people of Hong Kong and the Chinese on the mainland the better. Nor did they want malcontents to escape to Hong Kong and tell tales of the terrors that were happening on their side of the border. A network of pill boxes and armed guards was set up on the People's Republic side, and anyone who tried to cross the border illegally was ruthlessly gunned down.

As for the British, on the one hand they were concerned lest yet another horde of refugees descend on the already overcrowded colony and swamp the place.[5] On the other hand, they were sensitive to Western opinion, which took a dim view of the British turning back refugees trying to escape from Communist China at the risk of their lives. They decided on a middle course. They negotiated with the Chinese, and it was agreed that the border would be closed except for the Lok Ma Chau and Lou Wu checkpoints. It was also agreed that up to two thousand Chinese per month who already had relatives in Hong Kong would be allowed to enter the colony legally. Illegals who dared to swim across the shark-infested waters of Mirs Bay or to sneak through the border defenses, if caught, would be repatriated to China without reprisal.[6] The Hong Kong government built a twelve-foot high

---

[5]   In 1962, the population of the colony was 3.2 million, who were rationed to four hours of water a day.

[6]   However, it was the unwritten rule of the colony that if an illegal made it to a central registration office undetected she or he would be allowed to stay. This was called the "touch base" policy.

barbed wire fence along the entire length of the thirteen-mile border, reinforced by police and Gurkha troops. Even then, by 1962 the leakage of illegals that made it to registration centers had been averaging seven thousand per month.

Suddenly, in April, the Chinese withdrew their border guards and allowed a mass of the mostly hungry, elderly, ill, handicapped, and other "useless mouths" from southern China to sweep across the border, tear down the Hong Kong fence, and stream into the colony. The Hong Kong government announced that it could not permit the unrestricted reception of illegal migrants. Its agents frantically rounded them up and tried to repatriate them, only to have them turn around and make another attempt. During the next twenty-four days, seventy thousand refugees poured across the porous border. These reported that many others who were even worse off had lagged behind along China's roads, and that many had died.

The British government finally protested formally to the Chinese government. As suddenly as the mass exodus had begun, it was forcibly ended. The Chinese border guards returned and reinstated their shoot to kill policy. The Hong Kong government rebuilt the fence, and things returned to normal. It remained a mystery as to who had ordered the exodus and why. Was it because the Chinese government had in desperation decided on an extensive thinning-out operation involving the compulsory movement of hundreds of thousands of people in order to ease congestion in the cities and relieve pressure in food-scarce areas? Was it a message to the British that China could drive them out of Hong Kong any time it wished simply by opening the refugee floodgates and turning off the water supply? Nobody knew. However, the lesson was not lost on the British government or its underlings in the colony. For the first time, it began to dawn on them that Hong Kong was vulnerable and that, whatever the Chinese should decide to do, British rulers were essentially powerless to stop them.[7]

What happened in 1962 had been a warning. What happened in 1967 was nothing less than a threat. Mao Tse Tung had just launched the Great Proletariat Cultural Revolution that was rapidly enveloping China in the kind of chaos that would, in some places, eventually result in the outbreak of mini civil wars. Upheavals in China usually meant crises in Hong Kong, and this one proved to be no exception. China had, of course, attempted continually to infiltrate its agents into Hong

---

[7]   Hughes, Richard, *Borrowed Place on Borrowed Time* (Hong Kong: Andre Deutsch, 1968), 142–52.

Kong to report on the situation there and to win as many friends for the Communists as possible. The Special Branch (the British secret service organization) had been fairly successful in infiltrating Communist cells and in keeping China's agents under surveillance. However, these agents were particularly successful in enlisting the support of local Chinese who were more anti-British than they were pro-Communist. The agents played on their feelings of nationalism and their pride in the Chinese race. Not knowing the full extent of the dire conditions in the secretive and deceptive People's Republic, they believed the propaganda they were fed. The arrogant and out-of-touch colonial government did not help matters by the way they dealt with labor issues in the colony.

However, thinking they would steal a page out of Mao's book, the Hong Kong Communist leaders seized on the outbreak of the Cultural Revolution to launch a revolution of their own in Hong Kong, with the goal of driving the British from the colony. Enlisting the help of the triads,[8] frustrated young people, and a miscellany of thugs and hoodlums, they took to the streets and demanded the end of "British fascism, imperialism and tyranny." Hong Kong had experienced its share of uprisings of discontent, labor brawls between strikers and police, and triad wars over the years. In 1956, for example, mobs in Kowloon had taken over the streets with stones, knives, fire, and iron. They had caused many deaths and widespread destruction until the government had declared martial law, suspended traffic between Hong Kong and Kowloon, made thousands of arrests, and broken the back of the uprising.[9] In 1966, stone throwing mobs had gone on a rampage for days after the ferry companies had announced they were going to raise fares by ten cents. Obviously, this meager fare raise had simply been the means of venting the pent-up steam of multiple frustrations. The police had only been able to bring things back under control when the government announced that the fare raise would be rescinded.[10]

However, these riots were child's play compared to what happened next. Over a period of three months, the Communists exploited a few minor strikes, browbeat students and workers in leftist-run schools and factories, paid killers to plant and throw bombs, and imported young, trained activists from Macao and Canton. Aping the fanatical mobs

---

[8] Triads were secret societies that were formed in imperial China to promote nationalism. In Hong Kong, they had metamorphosed into criminal secret societies that were akin to the Mafia.

[9] Hughes, *Borrowed Place*, 38–39.

[10] Cameron, Nigel, *An Illustrated History of Hong Kong* (Hong Kong: Oxford, 1991), 308–10.

Rioters terrorize Hong Kong

shouting the praises of Mao and brandishing the "little red book" of his infallible thoughts in China, they rampaged through the streets and terrorized the colony. Their attempt not only failed, it backfired. It failed because they were confronted by a strong and calm governor,[11] a restrained and wise police force, and firm action that had the full backing of the British government. It backfired because the very Hong Kong Chinese who were being incited to throw the British out were so revolted by the Communist excesses and so worried by the reports coming out of China that they rallied to the support of the colonial government.[12]

The reaction in Beijing was swift. The local cadres were ordered to cancel the revolt. Who had ordered them to begin it in the first place? Had they done it on their own initiative? Hardly. Perhaps authorities in Canton had incited them to act.[13] Whoever was behind it, the PRC regime realized that there had been a grave miscalculation. Not only had Hong Kong's population been turned against them rather than being won over, but the economic goose that laid China's golden eggs had also come to the brink of being done in. The British government

---

[11]   Sir David Trench, who served from 1964 to 1971.

[12]   Cameron, *Illustrated History*, 310–12.

[13]   These same authorities had authorized a similar revolt in Portuguese Macao a few months before that had been quite successful. Although the Portuguese administration had been left in place for practical purposes, the real power had passed to the Communist cadres in what the Portuguese referred to as an overseas province. Perhaps the Cantonese authorities were then emboldened to think that they could achieve a similar outcome in Hong Kong.

and the Hong Kong power structure learned two lessons from the 1967 riots. First, they learned that in order to hold the newly won allegiance of the Hong Kong Chinese, they were going to have to do more than they had done in the past to earn it. Gross shortcomings in housing, education, labor, and social services were going to have to be addressed. Second, Beijing had removed this threat only because Hong Kong had been useful to China as an economic generator and as a channel to the outside world. The British would only be allowed to continue to administer the colony if, and so long as, it remained useful.[14]

The Chinese Nationalists on Taiwan were another element that the Hong Kong government had to worry about. The Nationalists had many supporters in the colony. Remnants of their defeated army had made it across the border at the end of the Chinese civil war, and many were settled in shacks in a squatter area known as Rennie's Mill and elsewhere. A good number of the civilian refugees who had poured into the colony in the fifties were at the least anti-Communist, and at the most pro-Nationalist. The tension in the colony between the pro-Communists and the pro-Nationalists was palpable. Every year they would fight what came to be known as "the flag wars." On the People's Republic of China's national day on October 1, Communist flags and slogans would appear all over the city. Nine days later, on the Republic of China's national day, nationalist flags and slogans would take their places.

Like the Communists, the Nationalists on Taiwan were unofficially represented in the colony. They also tried to use Hong Kong as a staging point from which their agents could cross the border and carry out espionage and even sabotage on the mainland. The British knew that if Communist China thought for one minute that Hong Kong was being used as a subversive base to support Nationalist Chinese designs for a return to the mainland, they would attempt to take the place over without a second thought. Therefore, the Hong Kong government adopted a position of strict neutrality. Both sides were allowed to celebrate their national days and display their propaganda, but neither side was allowed to subvert the colony or to use the colony to subvert one another. The Special Branch routinely rounded up groups of Nationalist subversives and their stockpiles of lethal equipment and shipped them back to Taiwan.[15]

The British had returned after World War II and reclaimed their Crown Colony. They had rebuilt a shattered Hong Kong and

[14]   Hughes, *Borrowed Place*, 39–40.
[15]   Ibid., 33–34.

Chinese Communist
flag flying
in New Territories
village

were confident that they would continue to rule the last jewel in the imperial crown as they had always done. However, by 1974, they were just beginning to realize that they were ruling a borrowed place on borrowed time. Their hold on the colony was becoming increasingly precarious. They would continue to rule only as long as they could navigate successfully all the political, social, and economic currents that were swirling beneath their feet. They could no longer practice their old imperial ways and maintain an unbending allegiance to the ideas of Adam Smith. Some things, at least, would have to change.

Nevertheless, when we arrived in 1974, not a whole lot had changed. The locals were as frustrated as ever, but their fear of what was happening on the other side of the border in China was even greater. Most Hong Kongers believed that the British establishment continued to turn a blind eye on gross inequities in their society. They also believed that they had no more say about what was happening in Hong Kong in 1974 than they did in 1956. However, they also knew they were a blessed lot compared to their brothers and sisters in the People's Republic of China. Then too, a new dynamic governor, Sir Murray MacLehose, had arrived in 1971, and reform was in the air. Perhaps their concerns would be heard at last.

CHAPTER 9

A Compradore Church, 1945–1974

The 1956 riot had nothing to do with ideology but everything to do with frustration. Much of that frustration could be attributed to social and economic inequities, but at least some of it reflected the humiliation of living under the heel of an alien establishment, however benevolent that establishment might be. Some colonial types reacted with surprise: "They don't like us." The more enlightened responded with frankness: "Why should they?" Why should they, indeed.

On the political front in 1974, and for two decades to come, the local population would have no say in the decisions that affected their lives. After Governor Mark Young's squashed attempt to introduce democratic reforms in Hong Kong following World War II, subsequent British administrations, backed by the business community, ruled out elections in any form. All officials would continue to be appointed by the governor, and it could safely be assumed that those appointed would support the status quo. In theory, the people would be consulted on major policy decisions through the issuing of "green" and "white" papers on which they were free to comment. However, in the end, public officials would make final decisions as they saw fit and could not be held accountable by the people for those decisions.[1]

On the economic front following World War II, Hong Kong faced a number of economic crises. First, the colony had to be rebuilt. Second, after China's intervention in the Korean War the UN placed an embargo on goods bound for China, and much of the entrepot traffic through Hong Kong dried up. The colony survived because its resourceful citizens reinvented the economy through innovation and diversification, and because it was the chief beneficiary of a massive influx of capital from wealthy Chinese fleeing the mainland. Third, after the Communist takeover, Hong Kong was inundated with a host of refugees from mainland China. On the one hand, this migration caused severe strains in the areas of housing, education, medical services, food, water, and social services. On the other hand, it supplied a mass of cheap labor for Hong Kong's exploding factories, wharves, and enterprises. Once the crises of the fifties had been surmounted, however, Hong Kong went on to develop into a virtual gold mine. Unfortunately, most of the gold went into the pockets of a relative few.[2] There were a number of reasons for this.

First, Hong Kong's workers were virtually defenseless. Their wages, for the most part, were insufficient to support a family or to keep up with inflation, and their working conditions were deplorable. Second, government policies and budgets were heavily weighted in favor of industrialists and entrepreneurs. Third, corporate taxes were well below those in comparable countries while profits were extremely high. Hong Kong companies considered it a bad year if they did not show at least a 25 percent increase in profit over the previous year. Fourth, the government allowed a banking cartel to control banking services and interest rates. In effect, the wealthy banks colluded to deprive Hong Kong's people of a fair return on their savings. Chinese are great savers, but they earned negative interest rates in Hong Kong banks (i.e., the rate of return did not keep up with inflation). Fifth, the government had a hands-off policy vis-à-vis the raw, laissez-faire capitalism practiced in Hong Kong *until* the interests of the moneyed class were involved. Then it would intervene to restore a favorable balance for the chosen few, sometimes even to the point of making massive interventions in the Hong Kong stock market.

---

[1]   Patten, *East and West*, 16–17.
[2]   Hughes, *Borrowed Place*, 46–48.

Hong Kong workers securing a hillside

Sixth, all land in Hong Kong, some of the most valuable real estate in the world, belonged to the British Crown. No one could buy it; one could only lease it for a fixed period of time. Developers would bid huge sums for these leases at government-run land auctions, and most of the massive proceeds would be salted away in the Hong Kong Reserves. Between a fixed income tax rate of 15 percent and a variety of other taxes levied on the populace, further millions were collected. The Hong Kong government almost never ran a deficit. Rather, it continued to add to its reserves year by year until it eventually held the largest reserves in the world. They were banked in Britain and were rumored to be one of the key props that held up the British pound sterling. The public reason given for amassing such huge reserves was that the government was prudently saving for the eventuality of an economic "rainy day" in Hong Kong. Most Hong Kongers believed that they would never live to see it "rain." Even if an economic crisis were to hit, it would mean government belt tightening, not the provision of an economic umbrella. Meanwhile, a comparative pittance was spent on education, housing, and social welfare year after year. As Richard Hughes, the famous British author of *Hong Kong: Borrowed Place on Borrowed Time*, put it, "The British, one hopes, will progress to a swifter and more equitable sharing of the colony's income."[3]

On the labor front, although most companies were making massive profits, the average Hong Kong worker did not earn enough to

[3]   P. 41 (see also 17–21).

sustain a family. This meant that both parents, and often an older child, had to work in order for the family to make ends meet. Children aged fourteen and older could legally work, but informal child labor was still common. Workers worked long hours, most of them six days a week, with only public holidays as vacation time. Many were not paid more for required overtime work. Many others worked on a per piece basis that required high output under pressure in order to earn a decent wage. Workers could be fired or locked out with no advance notice. It was not uncommon for a company to announce closure by posting a sign on a locked gate that confronted workers upon their arrival in the morning. In such cases, compensation often would not be paid. If a worker was injured or died, little compensation would be paid to his family. There was no such thing as maternity leave. There was no workman's compensation for workers temporarily out of work. There was no social security plan to help provide for workers upon their retirement. People often worked under ill lit and cramped conditions, and safety standards for equipment and premises were frequently insufficient, resulting in a high incidence of industrial accidents. If workers tried to organize unions to gain some defensive collective bargaining power, they faced the prospect of being sacked without reason. It is true that even in those days the people of Hong Kong enjoyed a higher standard of living than people in most other Asian countries. However, when comparing profit levels, it is apparent that the average Hong Konger was getting a very small piece of the pie. As Hughes put it, "Life here for most workers is hard....There is no real middle class in Hong Kong....In the depths, there is a horrible combination of slum living, grinding labor, and charity."[4]

For the most part, Hong Kong's churches had considered the macro-structures of politics, economics, and labor to be beyond the pale of what they understood the life and mission of the church to be. Politicians were responsible for government, economists for the economy, and industrialists for the welfare of the workforce. The church existed for evangelizing, developing Christian communities, and tending the sores of society.

Housing, Social Services, and Education

On the housing front, after the massive influx of refugees from China poured across the border during the fifties, Hong Kong faced an acute housing shortage. The refugees spread out into the hills surrounding the city, constructing squatter shacks by the thousands

4   Ibid., 48 (see also 45–47).

Squatter huts
in Hong Kong

out of whatever they could find. They had no direct access to clean water, no electricity, no roads, no postal delivery, and no protection from typhoons and fire. At first, the Hong Kong government figured the refugees' presence was a temporary phenomenon and that they would eventually return to China. However, after a decade had gone by, and a disastrous 1953 Christmas Day fire had burned out fifty thousand people overnight, it became clear that something had to be done.[5] The "something" was the hasty construction of three-story blocks of concrete "resettlement estates," which were designed in the shape of an H. Rows of 250-square-foot flats lined both sides of each wing of the H. The middle section connecting the two wings housed communal toilets and bathing facilities consisting of a hose at the top of a cubicle that shot out cold water. There were no kitchens. Enterprising residents built wooden cabinets to store cooking utensils and used the communal balconies running around the blocks as makeshift outdoor kitchens. Each flat had one set of windows facing the balcony. However, there were no openings in the joint side or rear walls to let any air through. The results were ovens in the summer and igloos in the winter. The lack of privacy in the communal toilets and showers was a nightmare, especially for the women. Entire three-generation families of six to eight people were jammed into 250 square feet like so many sardines, 24 square feet per person being the officially allotted

---

[5]   During our early years in Hong Kong, a number of other massive squatter hut fires occurred, the worst one being the Aldrich Bay fire in 1983, which burned out thousands of people overnight.

space. The government recouped much of the expense by charging rent. The rent was cheap, but when taken as a percentage of the wages of an average family, it was not that cheap.[6]

Since China refugees continued to swell Hong Kong's population year after year, more and more resettlement blocks continued to be built, and a housing authority was eventually set up in 1973. The later models were somewhat improved, the initial models were eventually renovated, and the size of the flats were doubled, but supply always ran well behind demand. New arrivals would still have to live in makeshift huts in squatter villages with their names placed on a waiting list.[7] When your turn came, you could "move up" to a rented space in a "re-site area." This meant that you were provided with a concrete floor space with posts and a roof, but you had to supply the rest. You still did not have electricity or plumbing, and you lived cheek by jowl with a host of neighbors in conditions that were barely above squalid. If you were lucky, you would finally make it into a resettlement estate some eight years after your arrival. However, the estate to which you were assigned might be a long way from where you were employed, and you would suddenly be thrust into a new building housing five thousand people, none of whom you knew.[8] On the one hand, the government was to be commended for initiating a massive construction program to house Hong Kong's multiplying masses. On the other hand, more resources should have and could have been invested and more units constructed to cut down the waiting list, and more social research should have and could have been done to make people's living quarters more humane. However, it was difficult to line up enough developers and contractors for these projects. There was a lot more money to be made in the construction of private flats for the well to do.[9]

Then there were the boat people. Thousands of fishing families lived on their fishing boats. At least these were sturdy and kept in good repair. However, still other thousands worked on land but lived

---

[6] Hughes, 43–45. See also Cameron, *Illustrated History*, 282–84.

[7] With the continuous influx of China refugees over the years, squatter huts continued to be a common sight. By 1988, there would still be over 430,000 people living in squatter huts (*News & Views*, March 1988, 9–11).

[8] By 1990, half of the entire population of Hong Kong was housed in public housing estates.

[9] For a comprehensive report on housing problems and subsequent initiatives by residents, see Hans Lutz's comprehensive article, "The Hong Kong People's Council on Public Housing Policy," in the June 1983 issue of *News & Views*, Hong Kong Christian Council, 5.

Early resettlement estates with markets between blocks

on rickety old sampans and leaking fishing boats jammed into the Yaumatei and Causeway Bay typhoon shelters. They had no amenities and had to tie their small children to the boats in order to keep them from falling overboard and drowning in the stinking water. These people wanted to move into resettlement estates but were not allowed to since they already had "homes."

At the other end of the scale, property developers were in fact speculators whose sole goal was to push rents and sales for privately constructed flats as high as the traffic could bear.[10] This was in the government's best interest, since the higher the rents and sales, the higher the price of land. And the higher the price of land, the more money from land sales would go into the government's coffers. A public outcry eventually led to a modicum of rent controls, but they were short lived.

On the social services front, although government coffers overflowed each year and record profits continued to be made by Hong Kong's commercial sector, only a fraction of that income was invested in the well being of the people who produced the wealth. Social services for families were minimal. The amount of public assistance provided for the destitute hardly kept them alive. Beggars abounded on Hong Kong's streets, some of them blind, others displaying open sores. Two thousand elderly people languished in hospital beds, abandoned by their relatives, while six thousand lived in abysmal conditions waiting for access to senior housing. Hundreds of single male day laborers who earned subsistence wages were known as "cage men" because they

---

[10]   Hong Kong's real estate values eventually passed Tokyo's and became the highest in the world.

lived in literal cages in flophouse apartments like so many animals in a zoo. Psychiatric care was extremely limited, and more than a thousand deranged people roamed downtown streets in filthy, tattered clothes, scavenged in garbage cans, and slept in cardboard boxes under road overpasses. Mentally retarded children and youths were chained to beds or locked in closets while desperate parents worked two jobs to keep the family afloat because there were no public services available.[11]

Little attention was paid to the special needs of handicapped people, who found Hong Kong's streets, buildings, and public transport almost impossible to navigate. Triad societies actively recruited bored young people who had no opportunity to continue their education past the ninth grade and who were provided with no youth centers or positive development programs. An ever-growing population of drug addicts found little help for rehabilitation. Hundreds of hawkers tried to eke out a living by peddling goods on city streets, offering payoffs to corrupt police for the public space they illegally occupied. The one bright spot was the universal medical care system imported from the United Kingdom. However, even that system was tarnished by long waits, swamped facilities, and crass treatment. In fact, the inadequacies of the public medical system was one factor that led to the expansion of the private high quality medical and dental care offered by Christian hospitals that mainly catered to those who could afford to pay for it.[12]

"This," I used to tell visitors, "is the other side of Hong Kong's postcard."

During the crisis days of the fifties, the Christian churches had been of great help to the Hong Kong government in meeting many of Hong Kong's emergency social needs. However, once the colony regained its feet, rather than the government setting aside a fair share of public revenue to shoulder its social responsibilities, it continued to rely on churches and other philanthropic organizations to bandage Hong Kong's social sores. This saved it a large amount of money. Further, it insulated the government and the commercial sector from having to face and deal with the systemic *causes* of those sores. Thus the churches, eager to evangelize and to "offer the cup of cold water" to hurting people, contributed unwittingly to the retention of the exploitation, oppression, and paternalism of the colonial regime.

[11]   Hughes, 18. (See also the author's editorials in the Hong Kong Christian Council's *News & Views*: "No Room in the Inn," Dec. 1991, 2; "Let Them Eat Congee!" March 1993, 3–4; and "Rags and Riches," Sept. 1995, 3.)

[12]   See my editorial, "Dreams and Nightmares" in *News & Views*, June 1993, 3.

On the education front, the British philosophy of concentrating most of the education budget on providing the best for the best prevailed. In that view, 15 percent of the most gifted of the population would rise to the top through a withering set of examination hoops to become a compradore elite that would assist them in running the government, the economy, the social infrastructure, and even the church. This approach resulted in an anxiety-laden, elitist educational system that began with high-pressure private kindergartens. Kindergarten exams weeded out underachievers and identified ultra-achievers. The ultra-achievers were funneled to the best primary schools, while the underachievers were sent to the ordinary ones. An exam at the end of the sixth grade had the same effect, with the best students advancing from feeder primary schools into the elite high schools with which they were affiliated. Three years later, a Certificate of Education exam served the same purpose, only this time, the majority of the children that had entered the educational competition in the first grade would be eliminated altogether. Since these children could not legally work until they were sixteen years of age, this exam, in effect, sentenced tens of thousands of fourteen-year-old children to two years in limbo. Those who survived the "Cert" exam were, at the young age of fourteen, "streamed" into liberal arts, science, or history tracks, which would determine their future careers. Two years later, the chosen few would become fewer still through sitting an "Ordinary Level" exam for entrance into the Chinese University of Hong Kong, or an "Advanced Level" exam for entrance into the prestigious University of Hong Kong. In all, they competed for three thousand tertiary places, with the thousands who did not succeed being consigned to the work force at the tender age of sixteen.

As late as 1970, even primary education was neither free nor compulsory. Thousands of primary aged children were still being educated in makeshift "rooftop schools," which were shacks on the flat roofs of resettlement estates, and staffed by missionaries and other philanthropists. Still other thousands were in no schools at all, since they lived on fishing boats or their parents could not afford the modest school fees, textbooks, and school uniforms, or the family could not lose the income the children earned by making plastic flowers or other simple wares.[13]

Ironically, for evangelistic, philanthropic, and sometimes even financial reasons, the churches were the biggest players in this elitist educational sweepstakes. They were running 24 percent of the

---

[13] Cameron, *Illustrated History*, 288–92.

Primary school
children in class in
Hong Kong

kindergartens, 30 percent of the primary schools, 55 percent of the high schools, and three tertiary institutions. This suited the government well, since it saved a lot of government money. In exchange for the privilege of running schools, the churches were required to recruit school staff, administer their schools, and provide 10 percent of the capital costs for the construction of school facilities.[14]

A Compradore Class

These were still the conditions that prevailed in Hong Kong upon our arrival in 1974. We were disturbed to discover that up to that time, despite all of these political and social inequities, Hong Kong's churches had, for the most part, been more closely identified with the establishment than with the masses. One reason for this, as we have seen, is that they held a privileged position. The British had brought their Christian assumptions, ideas, and traditions with them. Although other perspectives on the Christian faith had come to be tolerated in the United Kingdom, the British had never adopted the concept of the separation of church and state. The Anglican Church had been the British state church for four centuries, first in England and then throughout the realm. All official state functions at every level were infused with Christian symbols and ceremonies. The idea of a Christian civilization underlay the whole of British culture and life. The key markers in life were all celebrated in the church, whether one was an active participant in church life or not. The mark of a truly civilized gentleman was that he had some knowledge of and practiced Christian

[14] Karsen, Wendell, "The Church and Education in Hong Kong" in Evans, Rob, and Tosh Arai, *The Church and Education in Asia* (Singapore: Christian Conference of Asia, 1980), 23–35.

St. John's Anglican
Cathedral

virtues. Courses in the Christian faith were considered an essential element in the curricula of both public and private schools. Public radio stations were expected to include religious programming in their broadcast schedules as a matter of course. The export of the Christian faith abroad by Christian missionaries was viewed as a desirable and noble undertaking.

It was only natural, therefore, that in a British-run colony like Hong Kong, the Christian church would have been planted and developed as an integral part of colonial society, with the Anglican Church enjoying a position of preeminence among its peers.[15] It was always a bit incongruous, for example, to witness the annual swearing in of the judiciary. Chinese judges dressed, along with their British counterparts, in British robes and wigs, would attend a public Christian service in St. John's Anglican Cathedral as a part of the proceedings,

---

[15] This is not what had been intended by the first British missionary to Hong Kong—a Scott named James Legge. He had founded the Union Church in 1854 with the intention that all Protestant Christians, whatever their denominational stripe in the countries from which they came, would worship, work, and witness together. In a federated arrangement, Chinese Christians worshiped in Chinese, while European Christians worshiped in English. This ideal did not last long. Queen Victoria demanded that a proper Anglican cathedral be constructed, and that an Anglican communion be separately constituted as the established church in the colony. Her youngest son, the Duke of Edinburgh, journeyed to Hong Kong in 1869 to lay the cornerstone of what was to become St. John's Cathedral. From that point on, the scourge of European and American denominationalism spread, until today Hong Kong is plagued with the presence of more than fifty different churches and Christian movements of one kind or another—a confusing detriment to its witness to the Chinese population.

whatever their private religious persuasions. It was also incongruous to see the Anglican bishop's name listed as number four on the list of those who would assume power in a time of emergency. Christians were quite happy to be, in a sense, part of a privileged class in the colony. This is not to say that the British were intolerant of other faiths. As we have seen, Buddhists, Hindus, Muslims, Zoroastrians, Taoists, Jews, and others were allowed to worship freely in their own traditions and to build their own temples, mosques, and synagogues in Hong Kong, but they did so within a definite Christian ethos.

A second reason why the churches were closely aligned with the establishment was that they were enjoying unprecedented security. Since the introduction of Christianity into China by the Nestorians in the seventh century,[16] Christians had undergone a series of persecutions that had threatened them with extinction at various points in China's history. Under Mao's atheistic Communists, they were facing another onslaught. In the fifties, many Christians had fled to Hong Kong when Mao's minions made it clear that one of their goals was to eradicate religion, "the opiate of the people," from Chinese life—and particularly Christianity, the religion most closely associated with Western imperialism. Hong Kong's Christians were grateful for a new home where they could practice their faith freely and take advantage of new opportunities. True, they were ruled by foreigners and lived in a society that was fraught with inequities, but at the time that did not seem so important.

A third reason why Christians were not interested in rocking the colonial boat during the fifties and sixties was that they had their minds on other things. They were concentrating on obtaining financial security, on procuring a decent education for their children, on building up their churches and schools, and on evangelizing non-Christian refugees. The Christians who fled from China had brought whatever assets they could manage and were helped to rebuild their lives by the Christians in Hong Kong. The churches also reached out to assist thousands of non-Christian refugees as well, many of them arriving with only the shirts on their backs. Their desperate situation, their spiritual poverty, and the practical Christian love shown to them combined to win many converts to the faith. Ideological and political concerns took a back seat to the practical tasks of reestablishing their

---

[16] A Syrian Nestorian monk named Alopen arrived in Chang-an (Xian), the capital of Tang China, in the year 635 A.D. He was given an audience by the emperor and allowed to stay in China to propagate Nestorian Christianity.

Entrance to
United Christian
Hospital

lives in Hong Kong. Established Christians there were generally quite well off. The newcomers, with the same kind of high motivation, support, frugal living, and wise investment soon became so as well. The more Christians learned how to thrive within the system, the less willing they were to risk upsetting that system.

A fourth reason why at least some Christians had little interest in dealing with Hong Kong's fundamental inequities was because they had been taught by fundamentalist missionaries that Christians should not get involved in public affairs, particularly not in political affairs. These things were "of the world" and were to be left to the world. Christians were to concentrate on the inner life, on church life, on helping the poor, on evangelizing the "lost," and on the life to come. God would in his own time take care of redressing wrongs in the macro-structures of society. Christians could be salt, leaven, and light in society by their example of holy living. The best way to bring about changes for the good was to convert as many people as possible to the Christian faith and to encourage them to live Christlike lives in the world.

For these reasons, Christians by and large made up a significant component of the compradore class in Hong Kong's colonial society. They had been natural partners for the British in developing a society within the colony that was built on the pillars of power and profit. They had been glad for government-granted opportunities to carry out their traditional roles of feeding the hungry, clothing the naked, tending the sick, and teaching the young, and they saw these endeavors as golden opportunities to evangelize. However, in so doing, they had tended to overlook the bigger picture. In applying Band-Aids to social sores, they had by and large ignored the unjust, oppressive, and exploitative systemic roots of those sores. In opting for privilege, security, and prosperity, they had too often been blind to the evils of the colonial system that had produced them. In joining an establishment that was by and large based on imperialism, greed, and raw capitalism, Christians tended to aid what they should have opposed, or at least tried to ameliorate.[17] In sum, instead of identifying and challenging the evils of colonialism, they had ignored them, and in so doing had contributed to making the cross of colonialism even heavier to bear for the people of Hong Kong.

[17] For an incisive analysis of this situation, see Raymond Fung's "The Corporation and the Contractor" in *News & Views*, March 1980, 7–9.

CHAPTER 10

An Awakening Church, 1974–1980

Shortly after our family's arrival in Hong Kong in 1974, a seismic shift began that would eventually lead to dramatic changes in the colony and in the life and witness of the Christian church there. There were three reasons for this. First, a dynamic new governor had arrived on the scene in 1971. After sizing up the situation, Sir Murray MacLehose launched a series of reforms over the next ten years that would have a far-reaching impact on all aspects of life in Hong Kong. The people of Hong Kong responded to these reforms very positively. For the first time, they, and especially their children, began to leave their China refugee mentality behind and to identify with Hong Kong as their place, a place in which they began to believe they might have a stake.

Second, although nobody was yet saying anything about it out loud, both the rulers and the ruled were beginning to think about 1997—the year when Britain's lease on the New Territories would expire. At the time, twenty-three years seemed a long way off. However, not a few people began to have forebodings about what might happen to the colony when that fateful day arrived. "Business" was most likely not going to go on as usual. What would need to be done in order to prepare the people of Hong Kong for a future that would arrive before they knew it?

Third, a new generation of Christian activists came to the fore that was not satisfied with the status quo in Hong Kong or with the church's complicity in that status quo. They not only dared to question the way things were, but they engaged in fresh theological thinking that eventually drove them to launch programs and movements that addressed the Hong Kong situation directly. The Reverend Kwok Nai-wang and Rose Wu energized a Church of Christ in China congregation in the poor Sam Shui-po district to focus its mission on the social justice issues that gripped that community. A Methodist physician, L.K. Ding, and a Baptist layman, Raymond Fung, launched a Christian Industrial Committee (CIC) to deal with labor issues. A newly arrived Christian refugee from China, Lau Chin Shek, soon joined them. Tso Kwok-ming began a Society for Community Organization (SOCO), which organized people living in resettlement estates to push for better housing. The Reverend William Tung, a Methodist pastor, became general secretary of the Hong Kong Christian Council and acted as a catalyst to encourage member denominations to get more involved in dealing with Hong Kong's problems. The Reverend Lo Lung-kwong, a young Methodist pastor, began to stimulate Christians to take up their responsibilities in the political arena and personally demonstrated the way to do so. The Reverend Lee Ching-chee, a chaplain at the CCC's Ying Wa Girl's School, became a progressive voice in the educational arena. Philip Lam, a layman with a heart for Christian social concerns, became an executive secretary of the Hong Kong Christian Council and began to lay the foundation for a more activist stance by the council in the social arena. Church of Christ in China pastor Archie Lee returned from graduate school as a biblical scholar who challenged the church to apply biblical paradigms in fresh ways to meet its wider responsibilities to the community. Ng Chung-meng formed the Education Action Group to push for educational reforms from a Christian perspective. And there were more.

Some would go on to become legislators and prominent activists in Hong Kong. Others would eventually contribute to the world church by accepting posts at the World Council of Churches in Geneva. Still others would form more Christian action organizations that would continue to be leading lights in Hong Kong in the decades ahead. A significant change in perspective would not come to the churches themselves until the next decade, but these young committed leaders

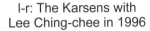

l-r: The Karsens with Lee Ching-chee in 1996

who had a love for the Lord and for Hong Kong were the sparks that would set it off. They and veteran missionaries like the Reverend Hans Lutz of the Basel Mission, the Reverend Ewing and Millie Carroll and the Reverend Tom Lung of the United Methodist Church, Doris Caldwell of the United Presbyterian Church USA, Father Harold Naylor of the Jesuit Order, and Rex King from the Presbyterian Church of New Zealand, who worked alongside them, became the colleagues with whom I was privileged to work for more than twenty years.

Precipitating Labor Reforms

The first significant step Hong Kong's Christians had taken to nudge the church out of its comprador role was the formation in 1967 of a Christian Industrial Committee (CIC) under the umbrella of the Hong Kong Christian Council. The CIC began largely as an industrial chaplaincy program—visiting factories, getting to know the people and their problems, and then providing personal counseling. Sometimes this took the form of seminars for every type of person involved in industry. The assumption was that if all the elements in modern industry—owners, workers, managers, government officials, educators, clergy, etc.—could be brought together in good will, something good would emerge that could overcome hostility in industrial relations. In sum, the CIC at first tried to play the role of middleman.

Eventually, Raymond Fung and his staff began to realize that it would be impossible for the Christian Industrial Committee to continue to take a neutral stance in the Hong Kong context. With employers and capitalists holding all the power, to be "neutral" meant that, in the end, the workers perceived the CIC as being on the side of the wealthy. Not to be on the side of the poor was to be on the side of the exploiter. This led to a bold change of policy in the 1970s that made more than a few member churches of the Hong Kong Christian Council nervous.[1] The CIC would cease being a consultant and take a pro-worker stance. As the chairman, L.K. Ding, put it: "We did so for two reasons: 1) there is no escaping the fact that in Hong Kong a wealthy minority continuously dominates and exploits the working majority; 2) our understanding of the Christian faith tells us that the place of the Christian is on the side of the poor and the oppressed."[2]

The CIC published a newsletter, the *Worker's Weekly*, describing its new stance and providing working class people an opportunity to tell their stories from their own perspectives. The committee also began a system of labor education among workers in which it explained tools of analysis to recognize the forces of exploitation, tools of understanding to strip the exploiters of their mystique, and tools of organization to empower the poor to unite and fight back. This soon led to dispute counseling in which workers were advised of their rights, the options of law and of bargaining, and the probable consequences. "Together we analyzed the situation, identified weak spots for the application of pressures, and formulated feasible demands. Then the workers decided what to do."[3]

Through these activities the CIC eventually attracted a large working-class constituency, which led to the formation of networks of worker groups in every industrial area. These networks, in turn, planned and carried out labor education, dispute counseling, and mobilization under the tutelage of the CIC. The CIC found that its clear pro-worker stance, based on principles of the Christian faith, rather than isolating it actually opened many doors in the community, in big business and in government. "Because of our community with workers, our voice is heard, our views are studied and our action...is consequential," said Ding.[4] By 1980, for example, the CIC could claim major credit for legislation providing for four rest days per month for all Hong Kong workers, the provision of public assistance benefits to single unemployed workers, paid maternity leave, and workman's compensation. It set the goal, did the research, spearheaded the lobbying effort, and organized the pressure for these bills. It also exerted pressure to modify government bills regarding severance payment, the labor tribunal, and annual paid leave.

---

[1]   Two denominations ended up withdrawing their memberships in and support for the CIC because of this change of stance.
[2]   Ding, L.K., "The Hong Kong Christian Industrial Committee's Imperatives in the '80's," *News & Views*, 1980, 6.
[3]   Ibid.
[4]   Ibid., 7.

As for the CIC's stance on the Hong Kong government, Ding declared, "We hold to a basic belief that a colonial government, by its very nature, is untrustworthy and therefore must be watched, scrutinized and criticized until, on specific issues, it demonstrates to the people otherwise....We are open to cooperation with Government on specific issues....We are, however, always ready to challenge it."[5] This applied also to the committee's relationship with employers.

> We are firm in our belief that as long as a situation of power imbalance is maintained in Hong Kong, CIC has no place except on the side of labor. We are also firm in our desire for dialogue and reconciliation, but both in the life of Jesus Christ and in the daily reality of Hong Kong, we know that there is no dialogue and no reconciliation without confrontation. It is the employer who almost always sparks off the disputes and it is the employer who refuses to come to the negotiating table. It is the employer who defies the law, and when he can't get away from it, shows contempt for the law. It is the employer who creates conflict, and it is the employer who does not care for industrial peace.[6]

And what about *Christian* employers? Ding's frank assessment stung the churches. "It saddens me to say that Christian employers are no exception. Christian employers were among those who opposed the Sunday rest legislation and the paid annual leave—fortunately to no avail. And today, Christian employers are also among those who want to create the means which would force woman workers to work night shifts."[7]

Christian critics of the CIC's stance were quick to ask, "What about the initial 'C' in the CIC's name? It is all well and good to try to better workers' conditions, but what about their spiritual lives?" The critics should have known better. The more the CIC helped Hong Kong's workers fight for more humane working conditions, the more effective they were in evangelism. Workers who would not have dreamed of darkening the door of a Christian church became interested in the faith that motivated the CIC to help them with their burdens. This was particularly true after the CIC launched a drive in 1979 to cut down on industrial accidents by pushing the government to improve safety standards in the workplace. CIC personnel also began visiting and assisting injured workers and their families. The workers' reaction to such concrete expressions of concern led them to ask what motivated

[5]   Ibid.
[6]   Ibid.
[7]   Ibid.

Hong Kong industrial workers

the committee to do this. The gospel was shared, study opportunities were offered, and many workers and their families committed their lives to Christ. As Ding put it, "We are devoting our efforts towards proclaiming the Good News of Jesus Christ among the working class. We are now working together with five congregations on labor education and evangelism in their own context. We have witnessed many worker conversions."[8]

Tragically, when these low-income converts were referred to local churches, they felt out of place within fellowships that consisted mostly of middle- and upper-class people. So the CIC formed "workers' churches" and launched a "missionary movement among the poor." This in turn provided a model for local churches, whose mission vision had become blurred. Much effort was being poured into "church growth" efforts—large evangelistic crusades featuring famous Western evangelists like Billy Graham and Luis Palau—but the churches were not growing. Said Ding,

> I believe that, in the long run, what we stand for is going to carry the day. Not necessarily because of the persuasiveness of our theology, but simply because of the fact that despite all the evangelistic activism of the conservative churches, the churches in Hong Kong are not growing. And the majority of Hong Kong's people, the 80 percent who make up the working class, are not touched. It is up to the CIC to show the way. Already, we have demonstrated that being a Christian and being a worker are not mutually exclusive; that the fight for justice and knowing God are not separate processes. The CIC's relationship with the

---

[8]   Ibid.

church will remain ambivalent, given the latter's middle class constituency and mentality. We should not see that as a threat, but as a continued opportunity.[9]

Precipitating Educational Reforms

A second step that Hong Kong's Christians took to nudge the church out of its compradore role was to begin to urge the churches to put their educational houses in order and to push the government for significant educational reforms. Until the mid-1970s, the churches by and large had been involved in the educational sphere for two reasons: to provide desperately needed school seats for the hordes of children that did not have any, and to use education as a golden opportunity for evangelism. The Church of Christ in China had invited me to work in the area of education in its rapidly expanding secondary school system. This included developing programs for students and conducting teacher-training programs, particularly for teachers who taught "Biblical Knowledge" classes.

Personal Development Retreat

One of my initial projects brought me into contact with a man who was to be a key colleague and a lifetime friend—Hudson Soo. Hudson's family had become Christians through the ministry of the Reformed Church's Amoy mission and had fled to Hong Kong in 1950. At the urging of Reformed Church missionaries Walter and Harriet DeVelder, Hudson had gone on to graduate from Hope College and attend Western Theological Seminary in Holland, Michigan. At the time I met him in Hong Kong, he was a lecturer in psychology at the Chinese University and an up-and-coming leader in the Church of Christ in China. We teamed up to plan and carry out a week-long CCC Senior Student Personal Development Retreat in the spring of 1975, a program that would continue for more than a decade. A staff of fifteen CCC college students and young teachers and pastors were recruited and trained to carry out this pioneer program. The aim was to bring together a mix of more than a hundred Christian and non-Christian

---

[9]   Ibid., 8. L.K. Ding was both a visionary and a warm person with a great sense of humor. "L.K." and I began a long friendship when we roomed together at the Fifth Assembly of the East Asia Christian Conference in Singapore in 1973. Our friendship deepened when my family was transferred to Hong Kong in 1974, and, for the next twenty-five years, he served as an inspiring mentor on questions of the church's involvement in the quest for justice in the public realm.

Hudson Soo with the
author in 1998

high school senior representatives from CCC high schools for an intensive week in a rural retreat center in the New Territories to wrestle with personal and social issues from a Christian perspective.

The theme of the retreat was "Living Life Fully" (John 10:10). The daily themes were "Understanding Myself," "Successfully Relating to Others," "Taking Responsibility for the Needs of Society," and "Having Clear and Worthwhile Goals in Life." Each theme was processed through an entire day of physical exercises, inspirational talks, lectures, workshops, discussion groups, recreational activities, sharing groups, situation games, and an evening of enjoyable activities with a point. Guest speakers, like Lau Chin-shek, director of the Christian Industrial Committee (who would later go on to become an elected member of the Legislative Council), challenged participants to not only think about their personal needs, but also about social and justice issues in Hong Kong. Non-Christians were encouraged to consider the Christian faith seriously, while Christian students were challenged to deepen their faith.

Besides personal faith and growth issues, the social and political realities of Hong Kong life were explored graphically through a variety of simulation games that I designed. For example, one evening was spent in "the town of Double Happiness." The staff set up and manned the "town," serving in roles such as shopkeepers, policemen, judge, jailer, and social welfare officer. As they entered the town, each student was given a name tag and an envelope containing "double happiness money." The goal was to use the next thirty minutes to buy materials and create a beautiful poster that would be entered into a contest to determine which twenty-five lucky students would be accepted as citizens of the town of Double Happiness. When the thirty minutes were up a whistle blew, and the participants were asked to sit on the floor with the staff seated on chairs before them. Each student then stood to display a poster, while the staff loudly cheered some and welcomed those students to sit with them as citizens of the town—no matter how ugly the posters. They booed others equally loudly and rudely told them to sit down again—no matter how beautiful their posters. The tension kept building until the rejected students became quite angry, some to the point of tears, while the accepted students would become embarrassed because they knew their posters were sub-par. Everybody sensed that some kind of inequity was going on, but no one was quite sure why and how.

The "contest" was then stopped and students were asked what was going on. Some brave student would always angrily guess that the staff was in some way persecuting a minority group and somehow could tell who the members of that group were. What the students did not know, of course, was that a certain colored name tag was the clue. When the "contest" began, students with this tag received an envelope that only contained half the money that the envelopes of the other students contained. They were charged double the price for poster materials. They were harassed by the "police" and unfairly judged and jailed by the authorities. When they ran out of funds and applied for social welfare, they had to stand in long lines, fill out long forms, and then were told they had made some insignificant error and had to start the process all over again.

These secrets were revealed to the students, and a discussion would then ensue. Students were asked to compare their experiences in the game with their real experiences in Hong Kong. Their feelings came pouring out. They told how it felt to be colonial subjects, stigmatized because they were poor, powerless to protect themselves from unjust harassment from the police, living in cramped quarters with families who were struggling to survive, and much more. They were then asked what could be done about these unjust circumstances, and their ideas came pouring out—some practical, some wildly idealistic. The discussion then shifted to how one might live a meaningful life in the *midst* of these circumstances, leading to comments about the way in which Christ and his followers have dealt with similar difficulties through the ages.

The honest interaction promoted between the participants in this very concentrated week touched the lives of some twelve hundred students over the years. Christians were challenged to deepen their faith, while "not yet Christians" were invited to follow the way of Christ.

This kind of approach was new in Hong Kong, and its materials and methods began to spread, spawning similar programs among other organizations. For example, the student union of the University of Hong Kong (Hong Kong's top university) asked if it could have permission to use some of these ideas in its activities. My permission was coupled with prayers that the Christian emphasis that permeated

First senior student
personal development
retreat

these materials and methods would also be perceived by those who used them elsewhere.

A Christian Philosophy of Education

During the first year we were in Hong Kong, I visited schools, interviewed head masters and teachers, and taught a biblical knowledge class at the CCC's Ying Wa College in order to assess needs and opportunities. It soon became apparent that much of the CCC's energy and resources, both material and human, had been poured into the pragmatic concerns of increasing the quantity of education that was being offered at the expense of its quality. This was true of other denominational schools as well. For the most part, the education being offered in church-sponsored schools was not all that different from what was being offered in government-run schools or in secular private schools. The religious trappings were there in terms of Christian names over the doors, chapel services, Bible classes, Christian clubs, and religious emphasis weeks, but there was no particular Christian philosophy of education that had ever been articulated to give purpose, direction, and shape to the churches' educational enterprises. In that sense, what were commonly labeled "Christian" schools could have better been labeled "church-related" schools.[10]

It was my privilege to work with a small education committee of the CCC whose members were very open to examining and assessing the educational scene in Hong Kong in general, and that of the CCC school system in particular. Dr. Franklin Woo, chaplain of Chung Chi College at the Chinese University, and the Reverend Lee Ching-chee, chaplain of the Ying-Wa Girl's School, joined me in working out a new initiative. Our goal was "to work out a position on all aspects

[10] I spelled this out in the paper, "Christian Schools in Hong Kong; Why Have Them?" which was translated into Chinese and published in several publications, including *Happy Children Magazine*, Hong Kong, January 1977, 3–7.

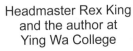

Headmaster Rex King
and the author at
Ying Wa College

of education in Hong Kong from a Christian perspective, calling for reform, innovation, abolition, extension, or whatever is needed to bring about what we conceive to be an ideal education for young people in Hong Kong."[11] We first worked through the presuppositions, goals, scope, and democratic nature of education from a Christian perspective and then applied these both to the Hong Kong educational scene in general and to the CCC system in particular, exposing weaknesses and advocating reforms.[12] We then set out what we considered to be the ideal perspective (philosophy), approach (methodology), and viewpoint (strategy) of an effective ministry through church-operated schools and made twenty-one specific recommendations as to how this kind of ministry could be developed.[13]

During this stimulating process, Rex King, a member of the CCC's Executive Committee and headmaster of Ying Wa College, convinced me that my best contribution to the furtherance of these goals was to get out of the church office and into the school trenches. There, together with other teachers and administrators, I could struggle to work out at least some of these recommendations on the ground and demonstrate that they could be done. Rex more or less gave me a blank check at Ying Wa to work out a whole new approach to religious studies, pioneer a counseling program, develop creative approaches to chapel services, offer values clarification courses to senior students, and promote a Christian philosophy of education among the teaching staff. The

---

[11] For the author's contribution to the paper, see "Some Tentative Thoughts," Karsen, pr.p, 1.
[12] Ibid., 2–4.
[13] Ibid, 1.

foundations for my approach were spelled out in the paper, "Thoughts on a Philosophy of Education from a Christian Perspective."[14] The paper contained a critique of Hong Kong's traditional approach to education and then dealt with the goal, presupposition, scope, and opportunity of a new approach based on the Christian perspective. This paper gained a wide circulation among educational circles in Hong Kong and elsewhere and led to a deeper involvement in the push for educational reforms in the colony.

Religious Studies

Ninety percent of the twelve hundred boys at Ying Wa College came from non-Christian backgrounds. The biblical knowledge courses to which they had been subjected previously were based on the British model of communicating the facts of the Bible and the teachings of the Christian faith as one of the various educational components that would produce well-rounded and knowledgeable "civilized gentlemen." The government examination system included biblical knowledge examinations. Students were expected to memorize and then regurgitate the information disseminated in these classes. I discovered that, due to a shortage of trained Christian personnel in church-related schools, non-Christian teachers, who were merely expected to pass on information, were teaching many of these courses.

My aim was to shift the emphasis in these courses from the memorization of biblical data to a life-centered interaction with the message of the Bible and with its central figure, Jesus Christ. My conviction was that such courses needed to deal with the problems and possibilities with which students were coping, particularly the 90 percent who were "not yet" Christians. I renamed the courses "Faith and Life" and broadened the curriculum to deal with all aspects of life, including a Christian's responsibilities in the social, economic, and political realms. I also dispensed with factual examinations and substituted open-book, open answer essay questions. Students no longer had to deal with questions such as, "Did Jesus ride into Jerusalem on a donkey, a horse, or a camel?" Instead, they were encouraged to express their opinions on life-related issues raised by the Christian faith. Students were allowed access to the Bible and other resources, thus removing the necessity for the rote memorization of reams of data. This eventually resulted in the removal of this required subject as

[14] *Christian Conference of Asia Christian Education Newsletter,* July 1978, no. 7, 8–12.

The author teaching a religious studies class
at Ying Wa College

a graded course on report cards altogether, since I had long contended that students should not be graded on a subject having to do with their beliefs and convictions.

At first there were many skeptics. How could students be motivated to study without the threat of examinations hanging over their heads? My answer was to make Faith and Life classes so relevant and so interesting that they would *want* to study and participate. The former was accomplished through the development of Bible-rooted, but life-related materials. The latter was accomplished through the use of student-centered participatory methods. This approach was vindicated and the skeptics silenced when, three years later, for the first time in Ying Wa's history, a significant number of third-year students selected what would eventually become known as "religious studies" as an elective for their senior schedules.

Curing and Counseling

In 1975, even the churches had not yet acknowledged the need for the provision of personal counseling by trained counselors in Hong Kong's secondary schools. However, Rex King encouraged me to begin a pilot counseling program at Ying Wa. The only place available for my office was the "medical room," which was located on the ground floor right off the busy, noisy playground. The room had a wash basin and a cot against the back wall, but, Rex assured me, it was hardly ever used. We would put a divider curtain up between my desk and chairs and the cot just in case a sick boy had to use it from time to time. Although I had no medical training, it did not take long before a fairly steady stream of sick or constipated or injured boys came to see "Dr. Karsen," as the younger students respectfully called me. As all good sick or injured Chinese do, they loved to smear pungent "green oil" on their foreheads for its supposed medicinal purposes, no matter what the malady. Pretty soon, my office and I began to smell like green oil.

At first, I did not make the connection between my "medical ministry" and my counseling ministry. Then one day, shortly before I was to speak in chapel, a young boy came in and proceeded to vomit all over himself and all over my office. As I was kneeling down, mopping him and the floor with wet towels, I said to myself, "I didn't come here to do this! I came here to teach, to write materials, to do counseling, to speak in chapel, to..." Then I looked at the towel in my hand, and in a second my mind flashed back to the picture of Jesus kneeling before his disciples and washing their feet. This *was* the reason I was here—to *serve*, no matter what the need might be or how messy it might get.

Before long, another connection became apparent. Having come to me with their physical problems, more and more boys felt free to come to me with their inner problems. And there were plenty of those. I began to learn about their turmoil, their difficult family situations, their fear of failure in such a competitive educational system, and the strains that many from poorer families felt as their parents struggled to make it in Hong Kong's concrete jungle. I learned about the pressures they were under from triad gangs, drugs, and pornography and how difficult it was to resist those things. I discovered the ambivalence they felt growing up in a traditional Chinese society while being exposed to Western cultural norms. I listened to them wonder about how to relate to girls while being part of an all boys school, worry about their academic struggles, and wish they had more faith in such an uncertain world.

As a staff member, I was required to make home visits to assess the financial condition of families applying for financial aid for books, school uniforms, and tuition. These were eye openers to the physical and social conditions under which more than half of Hong Kong's population lived. Three generations crammed into stark 250-square-foot flats with no private kitchens, toilets, or showers. Both parents working, with kids letting themselves in after school. Some kids bored out of their skins with nothing to do because there were no school places for them and they were not yet old enough to work. Families forced to place all their bets on one child that seemed to be the brightest, with that child feeling a tremendous pressure to succeed. In my assessment, I had to note whether a family had such "luxuries" as a telephone, a fan, a TV, or a table-top fridge. These exposures not only stirred me deeply, motivating me to support the struggle of the underclass in such a wealthy, greedy, and stingy colony, they also helped me understand where "my boys" were coming from.

Worship and Witness

We held chapel at Ying Wa every day. Imagine yourself addressing twelve hundred boys, 90 percent of them non-Christian, jammed into a huge hall. How do you get them interested and keep them interested? How do you make these services relevant to them? How do you tell the "old story" in new ways? Again, Rex was very supportive of my chapel experiments, although at times I would detect a raised eyebrow that revealed his inner anxiety about what this slightly crazy American missionary was going to come up with next. One Christmas, I wrote a script entitled, "The Six Disasters of Christmas," with students taking the parts in a drama that unfolded weekly during the six-week season that stretched from Advent through Epiphany. The final scene involved student "firemen" running down the aisles with fire hoses to put out a burning "Christmas tree" on stage that the students had constructed. Rex was off-stage with a big fire extinguisher just in case anything went wrong. Nothing did, except that in the excitement, he tripped over the fire extinguisher and set it off. Were the students interested? Yes!

I hung frames at the front of every classroom and in hallways all over the building. Students serving detentions helped insert a series of posters with thought-provoking messages into the frames every week. I would then select a related scripture passage and address one of these poster subjects in chapel. Holidays offered special opportunities to write and perform plays involving many students. Once in awhile, I would get tripped up culturally. Where I thought students would laugh, they didn't. Where I thought things would be dead serious, they would laugh.

I am a philatelist. One of my collections is a topical collection featuring the Christian faith on the stamps of the world. I served as the sponsor of the Stamp Club at Ying Wa, another bridge to students. I asked a friend of mine named Tom Simon to help with the project. Since he was a hospital pathologist, he had a suitable high-powered slide camera to photograph two series of stamps—one on Christmas and one on Easter. When these series were shown, students accompanied them with appropriate readings and music. These and other approaches demonstrated that worship could be interesting and enjoyable while still being challenging.

The author with
a sample wall poster

The stamp project took on a life of its own. I was asked to present a stamp program on the life of Christ at the Kowloon Union Church. The general secretary of the Hong Kong Bible Society, Heyward Wong, was in attendance. He was fascinated with this approach and authorized the publication of a forty-five-page, bilingual, full-color minibook entitled, *Stamps, Famous Paintings and the Good News.*[15] Key biblical passages were strung together in the book to present a simplified life of Christ that was illustrated by the stamps. The book was printed in two versions—one using the traditional Chinese script for distribution in Hong Kong, Taiwan, Singapore, and elsewhere, and the other using the simplified script for distribution in the People's Republic of China. The Bible society also distributed a beautiful full-color minicalendar using the same concept.

Upon our return to the United States on home assignment in 1982, I intended to upgrade the program with more stamps and add a sound track in both English and Cantonese so that it could be multiplied and used in schools and churches in Hong Kong and elsewhere. I called a graphics company named PhotoSix out of the blue to enquire if such a project could be done and how much it would cost. It turned out that the owner of the company, Jim Canon, was an ardent Christian and fellow stamp collector. After viewing the prototype, Jim became an enthusiastic backer of the project. In the end, the original stamps were rephotographed, more stamps were added, and a new sound track was recorded—all at no charge. Upon our return to Hong Kong, the HKCC's Communications Department recorded the Cantonese version and duplicated the program in both English

---

[15]   (Hong Kong: Hong Kong Bible Society, 1982).

Cover for
*Man On a Mission:
the Life & Work of
Jesus the Christ*

and Cantonese for wide distribution to schools, churches, and other organizations in Hong Kong and as far afield as Finland.

The Reformed Church's Division of World Mission picked up on the stamp theme and used a whole page of my stamps in the *Church Herald* to illustrate how the Christian gospel was making an impact in countries around the world.[16] Hundreds of these stamps subsequently appeared in a series of religious education textbooks that I wrote for use in Hong Kong's high schools. It was thrilling to see how God could take a hobby and multiply it as an effective tool to communicate his timeless message.

Teacher Training

Strangely enough, in terms of Chinese tradition, teachers were not held in high regard in Hong Kong society, because they did not make a lot of money. Except for the unusually dedicated, people only chose the teaching profession as a last resort if they could not become doctors, lawyers, or go into business. There were a few government teacher-training colleges, but they were not known for imaginative approaches to curriculum development and pedagogy. At the same time, teaching was a demanding profession that not only included instruction in the classroom, with all of its preparation and follow-up, but sponsorship of extracurricular activities, playground supervision, staff meetings, and attendance at all special school functions. Classrooms were jammed with forty-two students per class, facilities were usually crowded and noisy, and equipment was often inadequate.[17] Overall, schoolteacher morale was not high.

[16]   See back cover, *Church Herald*, December 21, 1984.
[17]   In well-to-do Kowloon Tong, for example, there were six schools with twelve hundred pupils each jammed into half a square mile. These were directly under the flight path approach to Kai Tak Airport, which meant

The author lecturing at a Religious Education Teachers Association workshop

Ying Wa College was a highly rated school with a long tradition,[18] and its teaching staff was quite skilled and quite well motivated. Even there, however, and in other church-related schools as well, teachers tended to look at their involvement as a necessary job that produced a dependable paycheck rather than as a mission opportunity to develop young lives. Traditionally, Chinese teachers were viewed as authorities that used authoritarian methods. It was therefore difficult for Hong Kong teachers to envision themselves as both teachers and friends to their students. For the most part, they believed they were there to dispense information and that their students' personal problems, for example, were their own affair. Over the years, I would have many opportunities to work at helping raise teacher morale, provide them with better materials, and encourage especially the Christian teachers to see their vocation not simply as a job but as a mission—a mission to be involved in all aspects of their students' lives.

The first opportunity to do this came shortly after I began teaching at Ying Wa. Several prominent religious education teachers were forming a new Religious Education Teachers Association, and I was invited to join them. I was active in the association for the next

that under certain conditions, one would have to stop teaching for several minutes while a plane passed overhead, this being repeated as many as eight times in one session!

18   Ying Wa (English-Chinese) College was founded in Malacca (in today's Malaysia) by Robert Morrison, the first Protestant missionary to China, in 1818. It was the world's first Anglo-Chinese school and was moved to Hong Kong in 1843.

ten years, serving on its steering committee, conducting seminars and workshops, and writing for its journal. The purpose of the association was to provide a forum where teachers could share new religious education methods and materials, have their biblical and theological understanding of education from a Christian perspective strengthened, and be encouraged and inspired by their common concerns and spiritual insights. The association grew rapidly, and members were keenly interested in my experiments in religious education, counseling, and worship at Ying Wa. As I had been putting everything down on paper, I could share my materials in the rough and demonstrate my methods. Eventually, a growing number of teachers began to use these materials and methods in both Protestant and Roman Catholic schools.

A second opportunity to encourage teachers came in the summer of 1977. William Tung, the general secretary of the Hong Kong Christian Council, urged me to become the council's education secretary. He wanted me to share what I had been doing in the CCC, at Ying Wa, and through the teachers association with the wider church (including my underlying philosophy of education from a Christian perspective). It was a difficult decision to make. I loved my work "in the trenches" at Ying Wa, but I also felt a responsibility to share what had been tested there with the wider church, and, in the end, I accepted. Beginning in 1978, my major assignments at the council were to develop youth education programs, produce religious education materials, initiate and edit an English quarterly, and serve as the staff person for the Educational Concerns Committee.

Summer with a Purpose

In the summer of 1978, in addition to continuing the CCC's Senior Students Personal Development Retreat, I launched another program, called "Summer with a Purpose" (SWAP), a program which was to have a twenty-three-year run. The purpose of this program was to give senior secondary school students an intense opportunity to grow in every aspect of their personhood—mentally, physically, spiritually, emotionally, socially, culturally, and philanthropically. The program ran for five weeks, with participants living at a campsite on remote Lantau Island and returning home on weekends. Mentally, participants were challenged to improve their English. Physically, they ran through an exercise routine every morning and enjoyed recreational activities. Spiritually, they participated in morning meditation and in a daily "Faith and Life" class that included discussions about social and justice issues. Emotionally, they were refreshed by the rural atmosphere

The author with
1983 SWAP staff

and relaxed pace away from the concrete jungle and the high-pressure school scene. Socially, they bonded with peers and staff in a deeper way than most of them had experienced before. Culturally, they swapped traditions and customs with the American staff and vice versa. Philanthropically, they participated in a practical social service project one day a week. The underlying philosophy of this approach was to help students grow in an integrated and healthy way by stimulating them with an interesting holistic program and loving environment, and then giving them the freedom to explore and evaluate and embrace or eschew.[19]

The SWAP cross-cultural staff was made up of volunteer American RCA and local Chinese college seniors and graduates. They were run through a rigorous ten-day orientation and training program in which they learned how to live and work together, assimilate the materials, and conduct the program. The program was advertised throughout the Hong Kong secondary school system, and students were urged to apply. Personal interviews were conducted with all applicants, and selections were based on potential for growth, spiritual orientation, and level of English skills. We deliberately accepted a mix of 65 percent non-Christian and 35 percent Christian applicants with the idea that non-Christians would be exposed to the faith within a unique loving and accepting community, while Christians would be challenged to grow.

When the summer was over, SWAP would go on. An RCA "Intern in Mission" stayed on for the year to follow up with the participants. "SWAP Clubs" were organized for English practice and Bible study, and periodic activities for site gatherings were also carried out. A SWAP Planning Committee was eventually organized among SWAP alumni

[19]   See Karsen, Wendell, "Summer with a Purpose," *News & Views*, June 1980, 12–13, and Karsen pr.p., "From Hudsonville to Hong Kong," unpub. ms., August 1982.

who, under the leadership of Rex King, eventually took over most of the responsibility for planning and running the program.

There was, of course, a welter of other summer camps and activities organized by churches, voluntary organizations, and government departments. However, most were of short duration and offered programs that were either fun, but without depth, or serious, but without much appeal. Skeptics said that a long-term, intensive program like the one we offered would never work in Hong Kong. However, applications from students and teachers who had heard about SWAP grew to the point that we were hard pressed to accommodate even half of them. The first year we had twenty-one participants from six schools and six staff at one site. By the fifth year, we had grown to seventy-two participants from twenty-one schools and twelve staff at two sites. SWAP's concepts and methods spread and were used by other groups in Hong Kong. Hudson Soo, who by that time had served as the headmaster of several CCC secondary schools for several decades, eventually set up a similar program for the Church of Christ in China using Canadian volunteers.

The relationships that developed and the personal growth achieved among the fifteen hundred students who went through the SWAP program over the years were so intense that students spontaneously organized annual reunions at their sites, engaged in correspondence with each other for years, and kept in touch with their teachers as well. Many of them went on to make significant contributions to church and society in Hong Kong and elsewhere. SWAP also enhanced cross-cultural understanding, stimulated spiritual growth, and developed leadership skills among the 250 staff members who participated. A goodly number went on to become pastors, missionaries, social workers, immigrant language teachers, or volunteers.

The Faith and Life Curriculum

The Hong Kong Christian Council hoped that the religious studies material that I had produced and shared while at Ying Wa College could be expanded into a full-blown, first-of-its-kind locally contextualized curriculum for Hong Kong's secondary schools. I spent a considerable amount of time during 1978 working out a plan for an extensive five year "Faith and Life" curriculum, which included students' books, teachers' manuals, study Bibles, and audiovisual resources. Council officials approached the publisher of a local Christian publishing house that was a member of the council. However, the project required a considerable outlay of advance cash with no guarantee that the investment could be fully recouped. It was a great disappointment to us all when the publisher declined to underwrite and publish the series. However, just when it looked as though the project might be stillborn, a representative of Arnold Publications, one of the leading publishers in the UK, walked into my office one day. He said he had heard about this project, had seen samples of my work, and was there to make an offer from Arnold to underwrite and publish the entire curriculum through its local subsidiary, Federal Publications. ("The Lord works in mysterious ways his wonders to perform!") The council was delighted to sign a contract that in time would bring it royalties of over US$100,000 to invest in carrying out its mission in Hong Kong, and that would provide it with an opportunity to spread the Christian gospel to tens of thousands of secondary school students.

Outlining a plan is one thing; putting flesh on the bones is another. For the next three years I spent one day in the office attending to other responsibilities and four days a week secluded like a monk in a cloister in Rex King's apartment researching and writing. Only Rex, my wife, my secretary Peony Wong, and the general secretary knew where I was. When the three years were finished, 1,200 pages worth of students' books, 250 pages worth of teachers' manuals, and five resource tapes had been produced. In addition, an agreement was signed with Dennis Mulder, a colleague from Taiwan days then director of the USA's World Home Bible League, to provide free specially designed Bibles in the Today's Chinese Version or the Today's English Version for all students using the curriculum.

Book I, *A Book, A People, A Mission*, introduced students to the Bible, the church, and the Christian mission (including justice issues) in Hong Kong and around the world. Book II, *Me and My World*, dealt with personal, family, and social issues in the Hong Kong context from a Christian perspective. Book III, *People of Faith*, surveyed salvation history within the context of world history, particularly Chinese history. Book IV, *The Lifestyle of Jesus*, exposed students to the ethics of the kingdom of God as demonstrated by Jesus Christ. Book V, *Christianity under the Microscope*, dealt with Christian apologetics.

Religious education teachers were delighted with the teachers' manuals. Before, although not trained how to do so, they had been required to take the Education Department's bare bones biblical knowledge syllabus, put flesh on the bones themselves, and invent their own methods of instruction. Now, for the first time, they had it all laid out for them, along with audiovisual resources and periodic teacher training workshops that the publisher asked me to conduct. They were

Faith and Life books

also delighted to have these materials and the students' books in their own language. The publisher had wanted first to publish the series in English to cater to the elite schools that used English as the medium of instruction, religious studies included. Backed by the council, I held out for Chinese first, since that was the heart language of the entire student population and the curriculum's pedagogy called for a lot of participation. The publisher agreed, and, while I was writing, a team of translators was employed to translate the entire project into Chinese. Each book was published upon its completion, and the entire Chinese series was in the schools for use by the end of 1982. It was an immediate success, with over 100,000 students a year using the series at its height.

Over the next ten years the series underwent numerous reprintings. I revised Book I substantially, and by 1986 Books I and II were published in English. In 1990, I began revising the first three books for Federal Publications. This task was completed by 1993 and gave the series a second life.[20] Meanwhile, led by Rex King (by then the officer in charge of the religious studies section of the Hong Kong government's Religious Studies Examinations Unit), the Education Department had initiated the sweeping reforms that we had been advocating through our Religious Education Teachers Association and the council's Educational Concerns Committee. This development led to my embarking on another major curriculum development project for the senior secondary students who would sit the newly designed "open book, open answer" religious studies exams—the "Faith for Today" series. By 1996, three years and eight hundred pages later, the

[20] Some still used these books as late as 2000, when I retired. By that time the Anglicans, the Lutherans, the Roman Catholics, and a youth organization called Breakthrough had all produced excellent series of local religious studies textbooks that featured a similar biblically rooted but relevant religious approach.

Chinese Christian Literature Council had published this three-volume series in English.[21] Book I, *Man On a Mission*, covered the four gospels and was essentially a life of Christ. Book II, *Living Life Fully*, dealt with personal and social issues in the Hong Kong context from a Christian perspective. Book III, *People Who Knew God*, was a greatly expanded version of Book III in the Faith and Life Series, which had never been published in English. The council took over where the World Home Bible League left off and published a special edition of the Today's Chinese Version Students' Bible for distribution with this series.[22]

These two series made an impact for Christ not only on the thousands of students who used them, but also on the people who taught them and who worked to produce them, including several publishers and a number of editors. Except for a gifted illustrator by the name of Jonah Tse, none of the Federal Publications people were Christians, and I became involved in long conversations explaining Christian beliefs, practices, social ministries, and political involvement. For example, the Buddhist head of Federal Publications, Tom Ng, and I spent more hours than our work required discussing these things at his request. One editor in particular, Grace Cheung, showed more and more interest in the Christian perspective as time went on. She also came from a Buddhist background but, over the course of several years, gradually came to the conviction that only through Christ could she experience the full life that God intends for all of us. Then she took a lucrative position with another company and I lost contact with her. Three years later, I attended Jonah Tse's wedding, and there was Grace! She sat down next to me and whispered, "I'm so excited to see you! I have a surprise to tell you after the ceremony is over." The surprise turned out to be that she was going to be married to a Christian man shortly and she was going to be baptized in three weeks time. I thanked God for his persistence in the life of this gifted young woman.[23]

By the time we left Hong Kong in 1998, it was gratifying to see how far religious education reforms had come in the colony's unique educational setting since I had begun my initial experiments at Ying Wa College. Subjects like sex education and social and justice issues

---

[21] Books I and II were revised and reprinted in 1996. Book I was also translated and published in Chinese by the CCLC in 1998. These books were still in use in Hong Kong at the time of writing.

[22] For a full rationale for and introduction to this series, see Karsen, Wendell, "A Rationale for a New Religious Studies Series for Senior Secondary Students," *Hong Kong Journal of Religious Education*, Vol. 6, Dec. 1994, 57–63.

[23] See Karsen, pr.p., "Aiming at Students, Hitting an Editor."

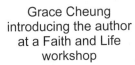

Grace Cheung introducing the author at a Faith and Life workshop

had been recognized as relevant parts of a student's religious education. Examination objectives and practices had been altered radically to take into account the large numbers of non-Christian students in church-related schools. And religious education teachers had at last been given decent tools with which to introduce students to the Christian faith in an interesting, relevant, and effective manner.

Public Education Reforms

At the Hong Kong Christian Council, my educational ministry took on a broader aspect. As the council's education secretary, it was my responsibility to work with its Educational Concerns Committee. Our mandate included not only church-related schools and religious education, but the entire educational enterprise in Hong Kong. In essence, the council became a pressure group for overall reforms in the education system in general, and in church-related schools in particular. Although the Roman Catholic Church was not an official member of the council, it did agree to participate in some aspects of the council's work where there was a common ecumenical interest, the Educational Concerns Committee being one of them. Father Joe Foley, a prominent Roman Catholic educator; the Reverend David Vikner, a leading Lutheran educator; and the Church of Christ in China's Hudson Soo and Rex King were key members of the committee for a number of years. We, together with others, addressed some of the pressing educational needs in Hong Kong.

Based upon a theological rationale and a Christian philosophy of education, we urged the Hong Kong government to provide nine years of free, compulsory education for all children and to develop secondary technical schools for those not academically inclined. When this became a reality, we then advocated the abolition of "weeding out" exams and the provision of enough places for all students to have a full, free, twelve-year education. We encouraged the use of Chinese as the basic language of instruction, with English taught as a second language. We favored the abolition of private profit-making schools, the provision of enough facilities to end bisessionalism,[24] and an end to the "streaming" of fourteen-year-old children into vocational tracks that determined their fate so early in life. We advocated the provision of trained counselors for all secondary schools and the development of technical colleges and expansion of university places so that all that were gifted to do so, and that wished to do so, could have a tertiary education. We urged the inclusion of modern Chinese history, Hong Kong history, and civic education in the curriculum.[25] The committee joined other groups in scrutinizing and commenting on government-issued reports and "green papers" and "white papers" on education.[26]

By the time we departed from Hong Kong in 1998, quite a bit of what the committee had advocated in earlier years had come to pass. Much of this had to do with the initiatives of a dynamic governor, Sir Murray MacLehose, who arrived in Hong Kong in 1971. Upon assessing Hong Kong's stark inequities, MacLehose developed a passion for social and educational reforms. He cajoled the business community into harnessing much more of Hong Kong's substantial wealth to finance reforms that would benefit the people who had been producing that wealth. He surrounded himself with competent aides who helped him draft visionary plans for tackling Hong Kong's massive social and educational needs. His administration was more responsive to the issues raised by organizations like the Hong Kong Christian Council and its

[24]   A concept whereby two schools operated bare-bones, shortened programs using the same facility—one in the morning and one in the afternoon.

[25]   Until that time, for political reasons, the Hong Kong government did not allow any discussion of the Chinese Communist revolution and subsequent takeover of China after 1949, fearing that this might stir nationalist sentiment among young people and influence them towards communism. It did not include civic studies in the curriculum, fearing the development of any political base that would threaten the colonial authority.

[26]   "Green papers" were papers issued by the government to express its intended policy in a given area and to solicit public comment. "White papers" were then issued as policy documents to be implemented. However, if the public outcry was strong enough, a white paper could be withdrawn and amended.

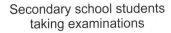

Secondary school students
taking examinations

allies than other administrations had been. He was no democrat, but he did have a big heart for the people's welfare. By the time he left in 1981, the foundations had been laid for what would eventually be a great leap forward in educational and social programs. The palpable success of MacLehose's early reforms paved the political and economic road for successive governors, so that by the time Hong Kong approached its 1997 handover date with China, it had developed some of the best educational and social welfare systems in Asia. This did not, of course, happen overnight. It took many skirmishes with government officials and departments and the continued application of public pressure to reach these goals.

The committee also addressed reforms in church-sponsored public education. The churches were urged to press for the democratization of public education and to forsake the kind of partnership with government that furthered an elitist system that mostly benefited a privileged and gifted minority and neglected the needs of the deprived and underprivileged majority. Church groups were encouraged to reassess their philosophy of education from a Christian perspective and to concentrate more on quality than on quantity. They were asked to reassess their approach to evangelism in schools where, on average, 90 percent of the students were non-Christian. They were urged to recruit and train a new cadre of committed Christian teachers who would be capable of integrating their faith and their fields. They were, in short, encouraged to revitalize their approach to education in a way that would make their contribution significantly different from that of purely secular schools. They too would go on to make significant improvements in a number of these areas during the 1980s and 90s.

The Education Department, at the urging of the churches, proclaimed the first Sunday before the opening of the school year as

Education Sunday poster

"Education Sunday." This gave our committee an excellent vehicle through which it could disseminate its views. Each year, it adopted a theme (like "Education produces caring people" or "To be a parent means to be a teacher") and prepared a packet of bilingual materials for the churches, both Catholic and Protestant, for special teacher dedication services, and for mass distribution based on the theme. The Hong Kong education system was built around rote memorization, theoretical ideas, and passive students. One year we created an acrostic using the letters of the word *education* to suggest more creative ways of doing things: "**E**xperiencing, **D**iscovering, **U**nderstanding, **C**reating, **A**nalyzing, **T**hinking, **I**ntegrating, **O**bserving, **N**urturing."

The council also began producing materials to aid teachers and students in the area of civic education. A monthly bulletin, called "Education and Public Affairs," was published for use in all schools. Periodic civic education workshops were conducted for teachers. Christians were beginning to respond to the call for reform.

Precipitating Social Reforms

It has been mentioned that Governor MacLehose was primarily responsible for beginning to change the selfish, laissez-faire mind-set of Hong Kong's ruling political and business elite into one that was more amenable to its social responsibilities. Before he came to power, nongovernmental organizations, especially the churches, had been relied upon to deal with the most apparent social sores in the community. Parsimonious funding had been made available to assist them, but, by and large, the powers that be had turned a blind eye to the systemic causes of those sores. In 1971, that began to change. As with education, MacLehose laid the foundation for launching massive programs to deal with Hong Kong's pressing social problems. Over the next two decades, huge housing estate developments were undertaken, until over half of Hong Kong's population would be housed in them. New towns with modern amenities were constructed in the New Territories. The social safety net for the elderly and the destitute was strengthened significantly. New hospitals and clinics were built or funded. A massive school construction program was launched at every level, and teacher-training programs were expanded greatly. Youth centers were constructed and staffed, and drug rehabilitation programs were launched. Increased funding became available for organizations that created services for those that most needed them. Again, this did not happen overnight, and it did not happen without a struggle between visionary leaders of church and other nongovernmental organizations and the colonial government apparatus, but it did happen.

Ministry to the Mentally Challenged

One such needy segment of society that had been almost completely ignored was that of the severely mentally challenged, particularly children and young people. When we arrived in Hong Kong in 1974, there were no programs of any sort to meet the needs of these obviously hurting people. To be mentally challenged was a great social stigma in Hong Kong. Parents of severely mentally and/or physically challenged children tried to hide them from the public and to deal with them as best they could completely on their own. Such children and young people were difficult to raise in the tiny spaces in hillside shacks, re-site areas, and resettlement estate flats in which the majority of Hong Kong's people lived. Even when grandparents were available, they were hard pressed to know what to do to help. Since the majority of families could only make ends meet if father, mother, and older siblings all worked, parents would leave such a child locked in a room or chained to a bed while they were away. Some in desperation would be driven to the point of abandoning their children on the streets. At that time, it was estimated that there were 2,400 severely mentally challenged people in Hong Kong living under these conditions.[27]

---

[27] *Annual Report, 25th Anniversary Commemorative Issue* (Hong Kong: Wai Ji Christian Service, Dec., 2004), 41.

A young physical therapist named Bernie Ng, who attended Kowloon Union Church with us, became very moved by the plight of the severely mentally challenged, particularly the children and young people. Shortly after we joined the church, he proposed that it do something to reach out to these desperately needy people. A number of people were interested in his proposal, including Joyce. However, almost nobody in the whole colony had any experience in undertaking this kind of ministry. By the time a committee was formed, inquiries made, and preliminary plans laid, Bernie Ng was dead of cancer at the young age of thirty-seven. However, Joyce and colleagues from the church, particularly Marie Murphy, Paul Webb, and the pastor, Bill McLoed, were committed to carrying out Bernie's vision. They presented that vision to the church council and the government's Social Welfare Department and secured their backing and funding. They found Bonnie Chan, one of the few social workers in Hong Kong who had gone abroad for training in this area, and hired her to be the director of what they called "The Wai Ji Center for the Mentally Handicapped,"[28] along with support staff. They continued to read everything they could find on servicing severely mentally challenged people, and Joyce and Marie eventually even went on a sixteen-day trip to New Zealand and Australia to study advanced programs there, courtesy of Hong Kong's Cathay Pacific Airlines. Their mission statement read: "The mission of Wai Ji is to reflect God's love for people with disabilities by offering them support, encouraging their efforts to integrate into society, defending their rights and liberties and empowering them to make contributions to the community at large."[29]

The center opened in 1979 in the small fellowship hall of Kowloon Union Church with a half-day program for six clients. Bonnie was extremely gifted, and it was amazing to see the progress these young people made in self-care, socialization, and the arts after only six months of training. Their parents were amazed too, which led to an immediate expansion of the program—a support outreach for parents. Parents were relieved to find other parents who had children with similar needs and with whom they could share their burdens and compare notes. They were also encouraged that something could be done to help their children. It was moving to see the change that came over them after they became involved in parent support efforts. At first depressed, worried, and worn, they were transformed into enthusiastic and hopeful team members and supporters.

[28] "Handicapped" was the term for physically or mentally challenged people in general use at the time.

[29] Wai Ji Christian Service, *2003–2004 Annual Report*, 15.

Joyce Karsen with
Wai Ji client in 1988

Several years later, with the program firmly established and growing, Bonnie Chan moved on to another position and a dynamic new director was hired by the name of Silva Yeung. Over the next twenty-five years, Silva expanded and developed the program beyond the founders' wildest dreams. In almost every one of those years, Wai Ji pioneered some new aspect of care for the severely mentally and/or physically challenged. The Social Welfare Department recognized the groundbreaking work that the center was doing and responded by providing ever-increasing funding and larger buildings. A new full-day center was opened on new premises in a resettlement estate. More staff were hired and trained. The number of clients continued to grow. A second center was opened that had residential facilities. Then a sheltered workshop came into being, and work opportunities for able clients were solicited among local companies. Annual sports days and other innovative programs were introduced. Home-based training services, respite care services, occupational services, and clinical psychological services eventually came into being. Public education efforts about those with mental and physical disabilities were also begun. Day excursions were carried out that enabled clients to mix with the general population, learn how to function in society, and enjoy Hong Kong's parks and other attractions.

After Joyce's death in 1989 and my return to Hong Kong in 1990, I was asked to be a member of the Wai Ji board and eventually chaired it during the years when a major expansion of its programs and facilities took place. By 1998, Wai Ji had 250 staff members and was serving 1,200 clients through eleven separate programs in seven major facilities.[30] Annual "walkathons" were launched that both raised funds

---

[30]   By 2004, it had expanded to 300 staff serving 1,800 clients through twenty separate services in eight major facilities. Wai Ji Christian Service, *Annual Report, 25th Anniversary Commemorative Issue*, Hong Kong, December 2004, 12.

Director Silva Yeung and author with others opening the 1998 Wai Ji Christian Service Walkathon

and highlighted the needs and achievements of the mentally challenged and the increased services that were being provided for them. It was also during this time that its board was expanded to include social service experts and parent representatives and that its name was changed to Wai Ji Christian Service.

Each year, Renske and I had the privilege of walking among tables and greeting the several thousand clients and family supporters gathered for our annual Christmas celebration in one of Hong Kong's largest banquet facilities.[31] As I brought greetings on behalf of the board and looked out over the large crowd, I would get a lump in my throat remembering Wai Ji's humble beginnings and the courage of its founders in tackling such a big challenge with so little experience in the name of Christ. God had taken the early seeds that were sown and developed them into a virtual miracle. Not only had Wai Ji taken great strides, but, as *the* pioneer program in developing services for the severely mentally challenged, it had stimulated the Social Welfare Department to develop and fund large scale services based on Wai Ji's model for the entire colony. As Rose Goodstadt, senior social welfare officer in charge of the government's rehabilitation program, would later put it: "Wai Ji never lost its first vision of helping the most difficult cases out of Christian love....I would like to take this opportunity to thank Wai Ji Christian Service for their willingness to accept a very difficult challenge, for their tremendous contribution to Hong Kong in the past 25 years and for their unfailing efforts to put their Christian faith and love into practice."[32]

Social Service Pioneers

There were other areas where Christians began to make an

---

[31]   The owners of the establishment provided the premises and a sumptuous Chinese feast gratis.

[32]   Wai Ji, *25th Anniversary*, 42.

impact on government policy regarding pressing social needs. Some developed pioneer programs that drew such public attention to a social sore that it could no longer be ignored. Penny Lawton, an Anglican lay woman, was so moved by the plight of street sleepers that she singlehandedly began the Barnabas Society, a group devoted to ministering to those desperately needy people. Eventually the Social Welfare Department provided her group with a center for their work. Two single British women, Wendy Blackmur and Valerie Courtney, rented an old building and began caring for severely disabled children who had been abandoned. Naming their center "The Home of Loving Faithfulness," they operated on the principle that God would provide funding. When the mortgage came due on the premises and they did not have enough money to pay, the hard-nosed board members of the Hong Kong and Shanghai Bank were too embarrassed to foreclose and deeded the property over to them. God certainly *had* provided. Through the publicity this action generated, funds began flowing in, including some from the Social Welfare Department, and the Home of Loving Faithfulness was eventually able to have a modern care facility constructed on the site.

A British single woman, Jackie Pullenger, "invaded" the infamous "walled city" district in Kowloon and began a very successful ministry to drug addicts, many of them members of the triad gangs.[33] John Paul Chen, a Baptist pastor, began a similar ministry with equal success at a rural site in the New Territories. These efforts goaded the government into increasing its recognition of and treatment programs for drug addiction, a major problem in Hong Kong. The HKCC's service arm, Hong Kong Christian Service, provided early models for the care of

---

[33] The 1898 treaty extending British rule over the New Territories excluded the Walled City, with a population of roughly seven hundred. The enclave, once a Chinese fort, remained part of Chinese territory despite the turbulent events of the early twentieth century. During its World War II occupation of Hong Kong, Japan evicted people from the city and then demolished much of it, including the wall. After the war, the now unwalled "city" became a haven for crime and drugs, as the Hong Kong police had no right to enter the "city" and China refused to take care of it. Triad gangs took it over until the British finally moved to restore some semblance of order in 1974. Most residents were not involved in crime and lived peacefully within its boundaries. However, by the early 1980s, the "city's" population had grown to thirty-five thousand, and the enclave was notorious for its excess of brothels, casinos, opium dens, cocaine parlors, and secret factories. In 1987, the Chinese finally agreed to let the British demolish the place, resettle the population, and redevelop the site into a large public park.

Children on boat in typhoon shelter

mentally disabled children through its Sunnyside Hostel, care of the elderly through its Wah Hong and Kwai Fong Hostels, and youth services through its School Social Work Service. The Social Welfare Department eventually helped subsidize these programs, and then it emulated them. The Kowloon Union Church and Union Church Hong Kong opened hostels for abused female migrant workers.

The Christian Industrial Committee's Hans Lutz took up the cause of Hong Kong's boat people. Seven hundred families living on defunct fishing boats in the Yaumatei typhoon shelter under abysmal conditions had been pressing the government to consider their plight for two years. On January 7, 1979, both Protestant and Roman Catholic Christians and clergy joined seventy-six of them in peacefully protesting the government's apathetic attitude towards their plight and petitioning the governor to grant them access to decent public housing on land. Their buses were stopped and they were arrested for unlawful assembly. This raised the twin questions of the humane right to adequate housing and the human right to freedom of peaceful assembly. Lutz joined the protest, challenged the church to act, and wrote a brilliant theological rationale for such action.[34] The Housing Authority eventually resettled all of the nonfishing boat population in Hong Kong on land.

The Vietnamese Refugee Crisis

Then there was the church's response to the crisis of the Vietnamese boat people. Upon the collapse of the South Vietnamese

---

[34]   Lutz, Hans, "Justice in Yaumatei," *News & Views*, June 1979, 6-8.

government and the end of the United States' military intervention in Indochina in 1975, thousands of Vietnamese of Chinese descent were forced out of the country in rickety fishing boats, rusting freighters, and anything else that would float. They headed for Malaysia, Thailand, the Philippine Islands, Indonesia, and Hong Kong. In May of that year, the freighter *Clara Maersk* arrived in Hong Kong with 3,743 Vietnamese refugees on board. By November 1978, 13,516 refugees had been allowed into Hong Kong for permanent resettlement and an average of 100 more were arriving every day. When our family took a ferry to Macau, a Portuguese enclave on the coast of China forty miles across the Pearl River estuary, we saw scores of small derelict boats crammed with men, women, and children as far as the eye could see. Tragically, it was estimated that over half of those who set out from Viet Nam drowned on the way.

Like other Asian peoples, after World War II, the Vietnamese had risen up against their former colonial masters and defeated the French in the northern part of the country. However, as a part of its anti-Communist campaign, the United States had picked up the French "colonial burden" in Vietnam by propping up an anti-Communist regime in the south, while undermining the regime in the north. The South Vietnam regime was corrupt and did not have the support of the local people. The more the regime in the north tried to reunite the country under the leadership of Ho Chi-minh, the more the United States was sucked into the conflict in support of the ever-weakening regime in the south.[35] And the more it was sucked in, the more this ill-advised war fought for ill-advised reasons lost the support of the American people. Ironically, the conflict that ultimately proved to be a disaster came to a jarring end on the eve of the celebration of the two hundredth anniversary of America's declaration of independence.

I had been opposed to the U.S. intervention in Viet Nam from the beginning, but the debacle was brought home to us in a very personal way in the person of Pastor Nhon Le Thanh. Thanh was a YMCA worker based in Saigon who had come to Hong Kong in the fall of 1974 to participate in a year-long training course at the YMCA Institute, where I was teaching the course, "Christian Values in a Changing World." The young pastor, along with YMCA workers from all over Asia, was one of my students. Through interaction in the class, social events in our home, and worship at Kowloon Union Church, our family got to

---

[35]   Renske and I "met" Ho Chi-minh once—lying in a glass coffin in his mausoleum in Hanoi.

l-r: Philip, Pastor Thanh, author, Rachel, and Stephen

know these students, especially Thanh, very well. He proudly showed us pictures of his wife and seven children who, of course, he missed very much.

On April 30, 1975, Thanh sat in our living room with anxiety etched all over his face. The morning papers had trumpeted the devastating news: "SAIGON FALLS TO VIET CONG. THOUSANDS OF REFUGEES FLEE ON AMERICAN ARMADA!" Thanh had not heard from his family recently and had no idea what their fate might be. Neither had he heard from the YMCA headquarters in Saigon, which had sponsored his participation in the course, and had no idea what his future held. We assured him of our support, the support of the Hong Kong YMCA, and the support of our church. [36]

I was moved by these events to write an article for the *Church Herald* entitled, "Where Have All the Revolutionaries Gone?" It was one of only a few articles out of scores that I submitted to the magazine over the years that was never published. The article began by drawing a parallel between the ideals and goals of the American revolutionaries against the British Empire and those of the peoples of Asia, particularly the Vietnamese, who were also trying to throw off colonial shackles of imperialism, exploitation, and oppression. It asked what motivated

---

[36] Thanh learned eventually that his family was safe, but that the Saigon YMCA had ceased to function. It was therefore not possible for him to return to Vietnam. With the financial support of Kowloon Union Church, the Hong Kong YMCA, and friends, he continued in the YMCA course and began trying to get his family out of Vietnam. Finally, six months after finishing his course, his family was able to come to Hong Kong when his wife's family paid a large sum to Vietnamese authorities to enable them to leave the country. The Thanh family subsequently applied for and was granted asylum in the United States and immigrated to Texas, where they eventually settled and where he began a ministry to Vietnamese refugees in the area.

those early American men, women, and children, including Christian pastors, to make grave sacrifices, to brave divisions within their families and to risk their fortunes, their careers, and their very lives in support of what seemed like a hopeless cause against a mighty power. The answer included: "No taxation without representation!" "Give me liberty or give me death!" and "I regret that I only have one life to give for my country." The article then pointed out that the peoples of Asia had heard those statements and had read Franklin Roosevelt's subsequent call for an end to colonialism through a universal declaration of human rights.

> They had high hopes that the descendants of the revolutionaries would encourage them in their struggle to throw out the exploiters and their puppets and usher in a new era of justice, equality, dignity, and sharing of the wealth for the masses of Asia. They had dared to hope that modern Americans, like the Americans of old, would be willing to sacrifice self-interest for the sake of justice and to risk security for the sake of what is right in human affairs—only this time in Asia.

The article went on to tell Thanh's story and to characterize the recent events in Saigon as the ruinous culmination of a series of military blunders and political misjudgments that had contradicted our revolutionary principles and our stated national ideals. It continued,

> The editorial pages in Asia are full of analyses of what has happened and why. Contrary to what some Americans might expect, they are not for the most part bewailing the advance of communism, but are instead hoping aloud that perhaps America has finally learned her lesson in Asia. It comes as a shock to Americans to hear themselves referred to as imperialists and neocolonialists. In response, we all ask, "What went wrong? Why have we gotten burned so often in Asia when we meant well?"
>
> The answer lies somewhere along the road between Lexington and Saigon. Somewhere, somehow, the fire that burned so brightly in the hearts of the revolutionaries of long ago has almost flickered out in their descendants. Somewhere, somehow, we have changed from a nation obsessed by principles to a nation obsessed by security. Somehow, somewhere, we have crossed out the words sacrifice, risk, and frugality in our moral dictionaries and written in their place the words comfort, safety, and squander.

Nowhere has this been more evident than in our post-World War II policy in Asia. Rather than identifying with the masses in their desperate struggle to rid themselves of the exploiters and the oppressors, we all too often aligned ourselves with and propped up those very exploiters and oppressors. One only has to think of Chiang in China, Rhee in Korea, Lon Nol in Cambodia, Thieu in Vietnam, and Kttikachorn in Thailand in the past, or of a new Chiang in Taiwan, Park in Korea, Marcos in the Philippines, and Lee in Singapore in the present. Rather than enabling the masses of the poor and powerless to realize their rising expectations, our policies for the most part have helped the rich to stay rich and get richer and the poor to stay poor and get poorer. One only has to think of the huge profits made by American companies in Asia where labor is cheap and the worker defenseless.

As a result, the Asians who know better have long ago realized that what they hoped for and expected from America after World War II has turned into an illusion. Rather than seeing us as fellow revolutionaries in the fight for justice, dignity, and an equal share of the wealth for the common man, they have come to see us more and more as the enemy of the masses and upholder of the status quo in the name of security and profit. The ultimate outcome has been the loss of our moral power in Asia and the abandonment of the masses to those who *will* sacrifice, risk, and face deprivation to help them win their revolution. One wonders whether even the present leaders of China and Indochina would be our enemies today, and not be so doctrinaire in their ideology, if they had found us years ago ready to support a new day for the common man in Asia, a day that was consistent with the principles of our own revolution. Instead, they have been confronted with the likes of John Foster Dulles and Henry Kissinger, the arch *counter*-revolutionaries of our time, whose main concern was and is to work for stability in the region and security for the United States at all costs—to others!

Where has the church been in all of this? Unfortunately, except for a few unheeded voices in the wilderness, it too has found and finds itself, for the most part, paralyzed by the powers that be. It has, for the most part, supported (either actively or by inaction) the status quo, not wanting to take the risk of fearlessly announcing the implications of the gospel for all of life or denouncing the exploiters and oppressors of those whom

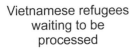

Vietnamese refugees
waiting to be
processed

Jesus came to set free in spirit and in body. Americans have played a large part in bringing the Asian church into being. But the descendants of the pastors who involved themselves in the American revolutionary struggle have also lost something on the road between Lexington and Saigon. They have taught the church in Asia to concentrate on applying Band-aids to the sores of individuals while ignoring the cancerous social and political structures that are the source of the sores. Thus, rather than being at the forefront of the forces that championed the cause of the masses in China and Indochina, the church (rightly or wrongly) was judged by those forces to be part and parcel of the structures that had oppressed and exploited the masses and was rejected outright. Surely the story would have been different if the church and its missionary advisors had been different....

I received a letter the other day asking whether the debacle in Vietnam would affect our work here in Hong Kong. My only answer is that it is pretty tough to be an American working with the church in Asia today and continually face the question in the eyes, if not on the lips, of young Asians who know what the score is: "Where have all the revolutionaries gone?" Let's hope we as Americans, and as churchmen, will have, and demonstrate the answer to, that question at home and in Asia before our bicentennial is over.[37]

The Hong Kong government at first set up makeshift camps to allow new refugees to stay temporarily and worked with the UN Commission on Refugees to resettle them in other countries, a process that would take eighteen months on average. However, in December,

---

[37]   Karsen, pr.p., April, 1975.

a large ship, the *S.S. Huey Fong*, entered Hong Kong's harbor jammed with another 3,400 refugees. This presented the government with a dilemma. Hong Kong was already greatly overcrowded. In 1978 alone, it had accepted 71,571 legal and an estimated 30,000 illegal immigrants from China. At the time, Hong Kong had neither the land nor the financial resources to provide additional thousands of people with accommodation, jobs, and social services. If the *Huey Fong* refugees were allowed to land, local resentment would build and other refugees would be encouraged to head for Hong Kong. In the hope that the ship would go elsewhere, the government decided to give the refugees food and medicine, but not allow them to land. In an article published in the *YMCA Bulletin*, I addressed the legitimate worries of Hong Kong's people, but then pointed out that, as in the story of Jesus feeding of the five thousand, we could either see these refugees as a big problem and send them away, or we could see their plight as a huge opportunity to sacrificially meet their needs.[38]

The conditions on board ship grew worse by the day until, on December 28, the Hong Kong Christian Council and the Roman Catholic Church dared to take an unpopular stance and issue a joint statement urging the government to allow the refugees to land, which it did.[39] Boat refugees continued to pour in at the rate of a hundred a day. A week later, the *S.S. Skyluck* arrived crammed with 2,700 more.

A potential catastrophe was upon us. Ten expatriate clergy published a public appeal to the governments and councils of churches in our home countries to receive additional refugees, to speed up their procedures for screening and selecting, and to contribute material and personnel resources to assist the refugees in resettling.[40] We received six immediate replies promising greater efforts.

The extent of the crisis was reflected in a report that I wrote for the council's English quarterly, *News & Views*, six months later.

> At the moment, there are over 35,000 Vietnamese refugees in Hong Kong. Of these, 4,000 are afloat in small boats in the government dock area and 2,700 are entering their fourth month jammed aboard the *Skyluck*, an aging freighter. In addition, 982 are aboard the British freighter *Sibonga* anchored outside the international limit pending the settlement of an argument over whether Britain will agree to take responsibility for them. Two

[38] "Boat Opportunities," *YMCA Bulletin*, August 1979, 4-5.
[39] "Vietnamese Refugee Update," *News & Views*, March 1979, 14.
[40] Ibid, 15.

more freighters with refugees aboard are reported to be heading towards Hong Kong. Over 10,000 refugees are jammed into the government dockyard and are living under the most primitive conditions. Other thousands are living in various refugee camps, old prisons, and the like.

To date, more than 35,000 Vietnamese refugees have poured into Hong Kong since January 1, with some 15,000 having arrived in the month of May alone! Of the 1979 arrivals, only 3,357 have been resettled to other countries so far....A far more serious problem, however, are the immigrants from China, since once they arrive in Hong Kong, they stay permanently. 48,000 legal immigrants have arrived so far this year, while an estimated 75,000 "illegals" have slipped in one way or another. An additional 31,000 "illegals" have been apprehended during that period and repatriated to China. If the daily average of 191 "legals" and 500 "illegals" continues, the projection is that Hong Kong's population of almost 5 million, living on 400 square miles (much of which is uninhabitable) will have been swollen by another 250–300,000 by the end of the year—a development that will have serious implications for the solving of already serious long-term social needs....The clear message is that nations that are much better endowed with space and/or wealth than Hong Kong is, must come forward with massive help quickly, or Hong Kong will become an ever more deeply troubled and tense community facing an ever more bleak future.[41]

Over the next four years, boat people by the thousands continued to pour into Hong Kong. In all, nine special camps were set up to house them temporarily. One of those camps, at Shum Shui-po and housing 9,000 people, was entirely run by the council's Hong Kong Christian Service. Caritas, the Roman Catholic service arm, also ran a camp. The churches contributed volunteers and material to conduct educational and social programs in government-run camps, among them our own SWAP interns Edwin Keh and Claudia Burroughs. Edwin published the camp newspaper, *Hope*, while Claudia set up an English teaching program. Among other things, the volunteers distributed snacks and sweatshirts to new arrivals and ran two refugee clinics.[42] Some refugees languished in the camps for years before finally being resettled abroad.

41   "Vietnamese Refugee Update," *News & Views*, June 1979, 8.
42   See my article, "Interns in Mission," *Church Herald*, Aug. 8, 1980, 10-11, for an account of life and ministry in this camp. See also "A Ministry to Vietnamese Refugees," *News & Views*, Dec. 1979, 3.

Vietnamese
refugee camp

By 1983, the Vietnamese refugee crisis seemed to have wound down. Arrivals were down to a trickle, and resettlement and repatriation totals had risen. By then, the Hong Kong government had spent over US$15 million tax dollars on the refugee crisis, while voluntary organizations, including the church, had spent over US$5.6 million in donated funds.[43]

It was years, however, before the remaining refugees were resettled and the refugee camps closed. A second wave of mostly economic refugees began arriving in 1983.[44] By 1990, there would still be more than 52,000 refugees languishing in camps awaiting resettlement in other countries or repatriation to Vietnam, some of them for more than seven years.[45] Christian organizations continued to provide services of various kinds. Only after the British worked out a repatriation agreement with the Vietnamese government did the refugee flow cease. By 1997, the last camp was closed and all refugees were resettled or repatriated. The church could be proud of its record. It had taken a courageous leadership role in helping the community do the right thing, and it had sacrificed to put its money and personnel where its mouth was.

---

[43] "The Vietnamese Refuge Situation in Hong Kong," *News & Views*, June 1983, 19.
[44] Ibid, 19.
[45] "Vietnamese Refugee Update," *News & Views*, March 1991, 20-21.

Ministry to Migrant Workers

Other Christians developed social services but also acted as pressure groups to cajole a reluctant government into enacting humane legislation or providing funding for much needed social programs. Elsie Elliot, a British Plymouth Brethren missionary who first served in China, arrived in Hong Kong in 1951 and was appalled by the conditions she found. She immediately went to work starting schools and a clinic, and she began acting as an unofficial ombudsman for the poor and the powerless. Through her mushrooming popular support, she soon became a formidable force that every department of the government had to reckon with.

Another group, the Society for Community Organization, organized people living in unsafe shanties, abysmal re-site areas, and cramped resettlement estates into effective lobbying groups. They eventually wrung renovations and expedited access to better accommodations and more humane resettlement policies out of the Housing Authority.

The Mission to Migrant Workers was given accommodation in one of St. John's Cathedral outbuildings and became the chief advocate for the ever-increasing thousands of the mostly Filippina domestic maids.[46] Initially, the maids were almost unprotected. Recruited by agencies that promised high-paying jobs in Hong Kong for a high fee, many maids found themselves in debt, underpaid, overworked, and physically abused. The mission sponsored hostels for abused maids who were thrown out on the street by unscrupulous employers and were then under the threat of imminent deportation. It also hired a lawyer to advise maids of their meager rights and to produce materials for mass distribution.

When I left the council in 1996 to pastor the Union Church Hong Kong, Renske and I got directly involved in the domestic worker's plight on three separate occasions. I was once preaching at a weekly service that Union Church held for these women when it was announced that a maid named Connie Hernandez, who had been undergoing treatment for breast cancer, had been thrown out by her employers for fear she would bring bad luck to the household. She had no place to go. We invited her to live with us for six months until she was strong enough to return to the Philippines. Another maid, Elvie Vergara, had

---

[46] By the time we left in 1998, there were 120,000 foreign domestic maids working in Hong Kong.

The Karsens with
Elvie Vergara
at Union Church

been severely physically abused. Through the mission, she had brought charges against her employers. Her case had gone all the way up to the Privy Council in London before she lost. Terrified to live with another employer, she asked if she could work part time for us. We did not really need a maid but knew that this would be the right thing to do, even though it bent the law slightly.

A third maid, an Indonesian named Kadek Wijaya, had been virtually imprisoned for months by her employers in their apartment. She was only paid half the salary promised, given no days off, frequently beaten, and forbidden to go outside except briefly to empty the garbage. A woman in our church befriended her at the garbage can one day, and together they made a plan for her escape. The nervous women asked me to accompany them to the Labor Department for a confrontation with her employers for back wages, and then to escort them to the Indonesian Consulate to arrange for her trip back home. Like these three, hundreds of women found themselves in similar dire circumstances. The mission, through a publicity campaign, lobbying, and legal initiatives, gradually succeeded in pressuring the Labor Department into amending the laws until foreign domestic workers had gained better protection.

Ministry to Children

In November 1978, I was asked to serve as a commissioner on the Hong Kong International Year of the Child Commission. United Nations' annual themes gave churches around the world a golden opportunity to assess what they and their societies were doing or not doing for families, children, women, the disabled, the elderly, etc. I joined a number of people involved in ministries to children of all ages to give reports on conditions that children faced in Hong Kong, and on what was being done by governments, nongovernmental organizations, civic organizations, and especially churches to meet their needs and to protect them from abuse. Although conditions for children in Hong Kong were better than those in most other Asian countries in terms of child labor, lack of educational and vocational opportunities, parental neglect, sexual abuse, and poverty, there was still plenty to be done. In an editorial in *News & Views*, I listed some of the challenges that Hong Kong's children were facing:

1. The children of 130,000 families still live in squatter huts.
2. The children among 10,000 people burned out of their huts in October's fires experienced a good deal of anxiety when their parents had to resort to public demonstrations to force the Housing Authority to relocate them within a reasonable distance of jobs and schools.
3. The children of thousands of Hong Kong boat families still live in cramped, unsanitary, and dangerous conditions in Yaumati and other typhoon shelters.
4. 11,000 young children living on Hong Kong's fishing boats do not go to school.
5. Only 685 out of the 3,000 children in the Sham Shui Po Vietnamese Refugee Camp are being given any education, and then for only 3 hours per day.
6. The construction of 12 new secondary schools has been delayed indefinitely.
7. Despite claims to the contrary, child labor is still wide-spread enough to gain the attention of the outside world.
8. The great majority of some 190,000 kindergarten children are subjected to a harmful regimen by the untrained staff of profit-making institutions.
9. Most films shown at public cinemas (and an increasing number on television) are "unsuitable for children."[47]

At the year's conclusion, the Hong Kong International Year of the Child Commission published a book, *The Child in Hong Kong*, which included my essay, "The Concern of the Church for the Children of Hong Kong."[48] Another of my articles, "The Child in Hong Kong,"

---

[47] Karsen, Wendell, "Lest We Forget," *News & Views*, Dec. 1979, 2. This article was also published in the *South China Morning Post*, Dec. 15, 1979, 8.
[48] Pp. 198-205.

The Child in Hong Kong

was published by *Yu Chun Keung Memorial College Magazine.*[49] As a result of the commission's efforts, the government and private agencies, including the churches, renewed their efforts to ameliorate a number of the challenges faced by the children of the territory. The opportunity of serving on the commission gave me valuable insights into the needs and difficulties faced by Hong Kong's families and particularly Hong Kong's children as well as to learn more about what the churches were doing to minister to them.

Precipitating Political Reforms

On the surface, Hong Kong looked like a free and open place. However, beneath the surface, it was tightly controlled. Hong Kong's section of Britain's Special Branch oversaw security. Externally, it had an understandably tough job contending with attempts at infiltration and espionage by both the Chinese Communists and the Chinese Nationalists. Internally, backed by the British military and the Hong Kong police (both officered by British personnel), it enforced the authority of the colonial regime. The regime enforced its control over the population through draconian security laws. Every organization had to register with the police. Any public activity involving more than three people had to have police permission. Every person had to have a photo ID card and could be stopped and questioned by police without

---

[49] No. 4, 1978-1979.

pretext. Permanent stay visas for people like us were granted on a "behave yourself" basis. An initial three-month visa could be extended to six months and then to one year if you did not cause any "trouble." Only after you had been a cooperative resident for more than three years would you be granted the privilege of obtaining a three-year visa, and that could always be revoked.

The media were self-censored. They could offer mild criticism of government policies and departments, but no editor or broadcaster could call the colonial system into question or advocate the creation of a representative form of government. For example, the Reverend Bill McCloed, pastor of Kowloon Union Church, once preached a sermon that included criticism of the evils of the colonial system. The service was being broadcast, and Governor McLehose happened to be listening. The next day, McCloed, an Australian citizen, was called in by the director of broadcasting and told in no uncertain terms that if he ever advocated such ideas again publicly, he would be summarily deported, citizen of a British Commonwealth country or not. If expatriate residents received such treatment, one could easily understand local Chinese reticence to get publicly involved in sensitive issues, a reticence that was often cited by the authorities as evidence that they were perfectly happy with things the way they were.

However, as the sons and daughters of the refugee generation came of age, that reticence began to melt. They began to perceive Hong Kong not simply as a secure economic and political haven, but as their place, and therefore as a place where they wanted at least some say in the decisions that affected their lives. This was especially true among emerging Christian leaders like Lau Chin-sek, Martin Lee, Lo Lung-kwong, Kwok Nai-wang, Rose Wu, and Raymond Fung.

A Courageous Crusader

And then there was Elsie Elliot. I met Elsie in 1976 at a meeting of forty local Chinese and expatriate residents to organize a movement for representation in government. On the surface, she looked like a typical pith helmet and tennis shoes type of missionary. However, under that surface, she was a courageous, crusading ball of fire. Outraged by the conditions and inequities she found upon her arrival in Hong Kong in 1951, she had not only done something practical to ameliorate those conditions, but she had also taken on the powers that had created and sustained those inequities. Interviewed by *Asiaweek* magazine in 1996, Elsie said:

I witnessed widespread corruption and brutality by the authorities very soon after my arrival in Hong Kong. I lived with the very poor in squatter areas where the living conditions were terrible. The people had to pay a considerable part of their meager earnings to the police so their shanties wouldn't be torn down. I also saw Chinese and sometimes British policemen beating up the people. Once I gave something to a friend. Later the police arrested him and said he had stolen it from me. The people didn't have a chance against the authorities. It was outrageous. That fired me up to speak out. The Hong Kong government does not care for the people, just the business....

The Housing Department is just as bad [as the police], if not worse; also the Public Works Department and many others. The whole bureaucracy is inefficient, corrupt, and indifferent. The government is a sinister conglomerate of dishonest international businessmen. There are exceptions...like the present governor, Sir Murray MacLehose, who, unlike his predecessors, is not part of the gang....I thought I could at least find some of the British democratic principles and fair rule here in Hong Kong. I soon learned that this was not the case. A representative government, members of the legislature, should be elected, not appointed. The people must have representation to make labor, health, education, housing, and social welfare laws. Otherwise, how can their rights and interests be protected? [Hong Kong's peculiar geographical and political situation]...are not reasons for sustaining a bad government. All these are excuses—that Chinese tradition has a place for corruption; that the people like what it is here; that it is better not to rock the boat. The local ruling clique has been using all kinds of excuses to justify its non-action....Some of my Chinese friends tried to speak out, but they were effectively silenced.[50]

How could Elsie get away with such a frontal assault on the "ruling clique"? First, she was a British citizen and had come to Hong Kong as a Christian missionary. Had she been deported, there would have been a huge stink in Britain. Second, she had won the hearts and support of the common people and the respect of many leaders in the community. Had she been deported, there would have been a loud outcry in Hong Kong. Third, she had just been awarded the prestigious $10,000 Magsaysay Award for Government Service by the Philippine government. Had she been deported, there would have been a fuss in

[50]   "'Yeh Sik-yin' Fights On," *Asiaweek*, 1976, No. 36: 3.

Elsie Elliot

the international community. Fourth, she had the courage to speak the unvarnished truth and had firsthand knowledge to back up her claims. Had she been deported, there would have been an investigation in the United Kingdom. There *had* been a plot to get rid of her in 1966. She was summoned before a commission of inquiry that was set up to investigate the cause of the 1966 riots and accused of having instigated the riots. Corrupt police forced some of the young people who had been arrested to lie and say that she had paid them to throw rocks. However, in the end, it was proved that the *police* were lying, and she was acquitted. No action was taken against the police.[51]

Seated next to me at the meeting, Elsie told me that her conservative Plymouth Brethern Mission had not approved of her public crusading activities and had cut off her support. "So," she said, "I am no longer a missionary." "Elsie," I replied, "In my book, you are one of the most effective missionaries the Christian church has ever had." The movement we were meeting to organize was thwarted and eventually fizzled out, but Elsie went on to become one of the first elected officials of the first partially elected body in Hong Kong's history—the Urban Council. The council only had power to oversee things like garbage collection and public parks, but it was the first step on the long road to democratic reforms in Hong Kong. Elsie did not waste the opportunity. She used her public position as a bully pulpit to continue her crusade over the next two decades.

[51]   Cameron, *Illustrated History*, 308-10.

Lines of mourners
waiting to pay their
respects to Mao
at the Bank of China

Through the actions of individual Christians, pioneering Christian organizations, and courageous pressure groups, the church in Hong Kong began to awaken to its wider social and political responsibilities. The emphasis of the churches rightly continued to be on nurturing the Christian community, evangelizing the wider community, and carrying out their traditional teaching, healing, and helping ministries. However, church leaders and their congregations were beginning to see that the Christian mission includes *all* aspects of life, including the public domain and the political arena.

Death of a Demigod

On October 18, 1976, the Chinese government announced that Mao Tse-tung, who had been a dominating force in China's history for more than fifty years, had died. The whole Chinese nation went into shock. We watched on television as more than two billion people stood in silence across China during his funeral, many with tears streaming down their faces. Mao had so dominated events since 1949 that the Chinese reacted as though they had lost their father and teacher. "The Great Helmsman" was no longer at the tiller, and many wondered how the country could get along without him. Memorial wreaths were piled five feet deep around the entire block on which the Bank of China stood in Hong Kong—a bank from which his visage had stared down on the colonial capitalist enclave for decades. Huge lines of the Communist faithful and their sympathizers lined up for blocks for days on end to enter the bank and pay their respects before a large portrait of the man who had been revered like a god. There was a palpable feeling that an old era had passed and that the future looked uncertain.

But there was another Mao to remember—the megalomaniac monster who had ruled the country like a tyrant. He had both mesmerized and terrified the population—the former in public, the latter in private. In the process, he had forged a personality cult that would have put Hitler and Stalin to shame. He had ramrodded China into the modern world in pursuit of a reckless utopian vision, but at an enormous price. Contrary to the myth that he had so successfully marketed both at home and abroad, he had ruled China for decades as a hypocritical demigod, and the people of China had suffered accordingly, some 700 million of them dying in the process.[52]

Within six months of Mao's death, the PRC government declared an official end to Mao's last bizarre campaign, a ten-year movement to regain total political control that had practically ruined the country and brought it to the brink of civil war—The Great Proletarian Cultural Revolution. Huge changes would be swift to follow, but at that point, no one was sure what would happen. Meanwhile, life in Hong Kong, particularly for the churches, resumed its normal ebb and flow. There was relief that Mao had at last passed from the scene and hope that his successors would prove to be less radical Communists than their mentor had been.

[52] For a thoroughly documented account of Mao's misrule, see Jung Chang and Jon Halliday's *Mao: the Unknown Story* (New York: Knopf, 2005). See also Xhi-sui Li, *The Private Life of Chairman Mao: The Inside Story of the Man who Made Modern China* (London: Chatto & Windus, 1994).

CHAPTER 11

A Challenging Church, 1980–1998

The Church Finds its Voice

When I became an executive secretary at the Hong Kong Christian Council in 1978, in addition to my education responsibilities I was asked to serve as director of the council's Communications Centre from 1982–1984 and to function as coordinator and producer for the HKCC-affiliated Ecumenical Radio Broadcasting and Television Advisory Committee from 1990–1996. Besides its ongoing provision of audiovisual resources for the life, ministry, and outreach of the churches, the Communications Centre contributed to the church's growing involvement in public affairs by producing resources for mass media education and civic education. The Advisory Committee was responsible for twelve Christian radio programs per week, all of them broadcast over the government station—Radio Television Hong Kong—as well as two one-hour telecasts for Christmas and Easter on a commercial channel. Most of the broadcasts were devotional, but on occasion sensitive public issues were addressed as well.[1]

---

[1] For a comprehensive overview of this ministry, see Karsen, Wendell,

HKCC Communications
Centre staff in 1982

My main communications task, however, was to produce a
printed English quarterly that could be a voice for the council in Hong
Kong and a conduit of information to our ecumenical partners abroad.
It was launched in December of 1978 and named *News & Views*—"news"
because it would be a vehicle for the dissemination of information, and
"views" because it would be a forum for the expression of local opinion
and ideas. I served as its editor from 1978–1984 and again from 1990–
1996.[2] With this responsibility came an opportunity to participate in
the church's challenge to the colonial establishment.

News & Views became the main English outlet for Christian
reform advocates and church leaders to express themselves on public
issues during the crucial decades leading up to 1997, the year when
Hong Kong would be returned to China. Raymond Fung set the tone in
the very first issue.

> There have been a number of exchanges recently about
> Government responsiveness to the Hong Kong community. As I
> see it, the question is not so much whether or not the Government
> serves the people. Anyone, even a colonial government, can build
> a case on any issue...to show that its policy serves the people's
> interest. The real question is, to whom does Government
> consider itself accountable, or more simply, to whom does
> Government speak?...For example, the first words of the new anti-
> corruption Chief were that the Independent Commission Against

"Religious Broadcasting in Hong Kong," *RTHK Magazine: FM Fine Music*,
October 1996, 10.

2   *News & Views* was still being published by the HKCC at the time of
writing.

HKCC English quarterly
News & Views

Corruption[3] would actively cooperate with the police—to him, a diplomatic and technically correct thing to say. But to every factory worker I talked to, it was either a joke or a sellout. I think there are only two possible explanations. Either the Hong Kong Government really does not give a hoot about the feelings of the people, or it is incredibly stupid. On second thought, I think it is a little bit of both.[4]

During those decades, as the church gradually became more involved in public issues, it gained confidence that it was doing the right thing for the right theological reasons. This involvement and this confidence were reflected in the pages of *News & Views* and also in the public press. For example, in 1978, the secretary for the environment (of all people) laid out his vision for the Hong Kong of the future in which he contemplated various development scenarios that would make it possible eventually to pack twelve million people into the territory. In protest, I wrote a letter to the *South China Morning Post* that raised the alarm about such a hare-brained scheme and that was cosigned by my colleagues Raymond Fung and Philip Lam. After introducing the subject, I wrote,

---

3   Governor MacLehose created the Independent Commission Against Corruption (ICAC) in 1974 to root out what was at that time endemic corruption in all departments of government, but most prominently in the police force. The resultant crunch came when the police in effect mutinied against the governor in 1977. However, backed by the military, he stood his ground, the ICAC made arrests, and, over the next decade, through vigorous prosecution in all departments and at all levels, corruption was greatly diminished as a major evil in the colonial establishment of Hong Kong. See Cameron, *Illustrated History*, 314–19.

4   "Opinion Page," *News & Views*, Dec. 1978, 10.

Before these proposals become policy in whole or in part, may we ask the Secretary for the Environment to answer these questions?

Is not the SFE supposed to be dedicated to the preservation of Hong Kong's environment? It seems to us that these proposals will do the exact reverse—destroy our environment.

Does the Secretary envision an eventual concrete maze with cubicles for all in which people will need to wear gas masks, ear muffs, and elbow pads, drink bottled water, swim in natural septic tanks, and visit nature museums to view grass and trees?

Air, noise, water, land, and people pollution are getting out of hand now with a population of six million. Does the Secretary have some as of yet secret pollution cure-all as a part of his scenario for the future?

Does not the Secretary's "vision" contradict the Governor's rationale for the recent almost draconian measures taken to halt the flow of immigrants from China? We were told, and we believe, that the territory is already severely overcrowded, that the quality of existing social services is strained, that our transport problems are serious, and that the well-being and standard of living of Hong Kong's residents is threatened. Can the Secretary explain how he is magically going to double the population without exacerbating what are already serious problems?

Has the Secretary calculated the social consequences of these "development" scenarios? He advocates packing people as tightly together in urban areas as possible because it is cheaper and more efficient. What happens to human beings when they get crowded together?...There is a direct connection between overcrowding and an increase in anti-social behavior....There is also a direct connection between people's mental and emotional wholeness and their proximity to the natural environment. The more human nature is alienated from nature, the less "human" it becomes.

Has the SFE figured out the following facts when contemplating his scenarios? Hong Kong's present "official" population of five million people lives on 11,416,360 square feet. This means that each person has an average of 2.2 square feet to stand on. In Mr. Jones' favored urban areas, however, where 80 percent of the population live, the density is far worse....Two people share an average of one square foot, and in high density areas...the density averages out to some 12 people per square foot.

If Mr. Jones' 12 million people ever materialize, each person will have to stand on an average of less than 11 square inches, and the place will sink!

What is the SFE's goal for Hong Kong? What is his objective for our community? Surely it must be to improve the quality of life for the existing population. And surely planning to provide for a dramatic increase in the population in the name of development is the surest way to defeat that goal....

Why then would the Secretary float such scenarios in public? Is it because he lives in a low density area where every person has an average of 11.6 square feet to romp around in and just doesn't realize what it is like to live in Mongkok or Wong Tai Sin?

That would be too simple an explanation. The more likely one is that such "development" plans in the long run will produce land worth trillions in Government coffers, deals worth billions to land developers, and business worth millions to the hongs and their subsidiaries. All it will produce for the vast majority of Hong Kong's population in our view, however, is further tension and hardship....[5]

A New Definition of Mission

In November 1980, the Hong Kong Christian Council convened a four-day church consultation on the mission of the church in Hong Kong in the 1980s. This proved to be a seminal event in the church's involvement in public affairs. One hundred twenty official delegates from member churches and organizations, along with fraternal representatives from the Roman Catholic diocese and conservative evangelical groups, participated. Major addresses were given by the right Reverend Gilbert Baker, bishop of the Anglican Diocese of Hong Kong and Macau; Peter Wong, general secretary of the Church of Christ in China (and then chair of the HKCC's Executive Committee); and Cardinal John Wu, head of the Roman Catholic Diocese of Hong Kong, along with others. A series of thought-provoking Bible expositions were given by Drs. Archie Lee, Richard Deutsch, and James Pan, all faculty members of Chung Chi College's Theology Division, the leading ecumenical seminary in Hong Kong. Five working groups were convened to deal separately with five major issues: "Good News for the

[5] "Environment Chief Drops a Bomb," letter, South *China Morning Post*, November 15, 1978, 6.

THE MISSION OF THE CHURCH IN HONG KONG IN THE 80'S

(Excerpts from an Official Report of the November 17-20, 1980
Consultation convened by the Hong Kong Christian Council - Part II*)

PARTICIPATION IN PUBLIC POLICIES

A third area of consensus had to do with Christian participation in
making public policies. The Consultation affirmed such participation
as part of Christian mission. This is nothing new. What is new is its
ty. The Working Group on the subject specifically pointed out the inadequacy of
's consultative process of making public policies. It stated: "There is consi-
imitation in the present consultative system. As things stand, the power of
aking rests entirely with a small number of Government bureaucrats and business

News & Views report
of 1980 Consultation

Poor," "Ministry among Students," "Concern for Christians in China," "Participation in Public Policies," and "Influencing Mass Values." For the first time, major church leaders issued clear calls to the church to stand up and challenge the Hong Kong government in the areas of government policy, justice, and the plight of the poor. As reported in *News & Views*:

> By most accounts, it was an amazing Consultation. Everybody was pleasantly shocked by the amount of consensus on major issues. The leaders of the Anglican Church and the Church of Christ in China wasted no time in calling for the churches to be prophetic. Bishop Baker announced, "There are times when it is necessary to speak out plainly perhaps in criticism of Government or of some particular policy—according to the trends and dangers which we may perceive in society." Dr. Peter Wong specifically pointed out that the poor should be the number one mission priority for the churches in the 80s....A theological and strategical assessment of the church's mission to the poor was spelled out by Dr. Peter Lee and Mr. Raymond Fung....Rev. Canon Alan Chan, in his address on the local church envisioned the local church in low-income housing estates as a rallying point for community action, justice and caring....Church leaders urged continued cooperation with Government, but not conformity. They called on church social work agencies and schools to keep free of Government intervention even at the risk of losing Government support. It was recognized that there were good historical reasons for a close Church-state relationship in the past. However, there are also good reasons arising out of present Hong Kong realities to reverse the trend.
>
> Was this simply another church consultation of well-meaning statements and no action? [Two] things suggest otherwise. One: towards the end, the Consultation voted

to oppose the 100 percent fare increase sought by the bus monopolies. That was on November 20. Today, the church has taken action, lodged a formal protest to the authorities and initiated a citywide coalition of people's organizations.[6] Two: between November 17 and now, the Christian church has become news, and not on the religious page only. The Consultation papers have been given much space on the business, cultural and editorial pages of the city's many Chinese newspapers because the Consultation, representing most major denominations, showed serious interest in Hong Kong's coming decade."[7]

My December 1980 editorial also addressed this theme:

There is a Christmas carol which goes like this: "When the song of the angels is stilled, when the star in the sky is gone, when the kings and the shepherds have found their way home, the work of Christmas is begun." So it is with the Consultation. Now that the celebration is over, it is time for us to get down to serious work. The needs of people in Hong Kong are pressing in all around us. We must leave the old ways and quirks and jealousies and power struggles and middle class image of the 70s behind us. We must open ourselves to creative change, risk and sacrifice in the decade that lies before us. If our churches are not united in both name and spirit by the end of this decade, we will have forfeited the legitimacy of our call to people to live in love, peace and unity. If we continue by and large to remain aloof from the masses in the 80s, we will have muted Jesus' announcement that his coming means good news for the poor. If we do not simplify our lifestyle during these 10 years, we will have little to say to Hong Kong (or to China) in terms of a reassessment of values. If we cannot overcome our innate conservatism before 1990, we will find ourselves slaves of Government policy rather than participants

[6]   By January 1981, the HKCC had mobilized three hundred organizations in a coalition to protest a fare increase that would have been devastating to Hong Kong's low-income majority. The private owners of Hong Kong utility and public service monopolies were powerful elites who had undue influence on government officials and supervising bodies. As a result of the coalition's pressure, the government's Transport Advisory Committee recommended a 20–30 percent increase, more stringent monitoring of one of the major bus companies, and new financing structures that would take into account the considerable property assets and government subsidies and loan guarantees. See "HKCC News," *News & Views*, March 1981, 2.

[7]   "HKCC News," *News & Views*, Dec. 1980, 1–2.

Author writing
News & Views editorial

in the shaping of it. If young people do not perceive us as Jesus' joyful revolutionaries in the 80s, we will have laid the foundation for an ecclesiastical gerontocracy in the 90s.

Our task is formidable, Hong Kong's needs are great and the time is short. We will be tempted by fear to let this Consultation become a report on the shelf rather than a catalyst for change. But the Christmas angel calls loudly to us: "Don't be afraid! I am here with good news for you, which will bring great joy to all the people." If the Consultation did anything at all, it underlined the words "fear," "good news," "joy," and "all the people" in this message. We were called to wrestle with the powers that oppress as joyful followers of Jesus, not as disgruntled cynics. We were urged to be a church that warmly embraces all of the people, not just some of the people. Like the shepherds of old then, let us get over our fear and get on with our task of together sharing the good news in a way that will bring true joy to the lives of all the people of Hong Kong in the 80s.[8]

An immediate result of the consultation was the appointment by the Hong Kong Christian Council of a Commission on Public Issues to "give voice to matters of public concern." Four key activists were appointed: lecturer Joseph Kuang, Chung Chi professor Kwok Pui-lan, Methodist pastor Lo Lung-kwong, and Church of Christ in China leader Rose Wu. They swung into action on five fronts. They issued a statement advocating an increase in personal tax allowance for low-income people. They scheduled a meeting with legislative councilors

---

[8]   "Christmas and the Consultation," *News & Views*, Dec. 1980, 3.

to lobby for an increase in social expenditure in the new budget. They organized a theological forum, "The Future of Hong Kong and the Church in Hong Kong." They joined fifteen other religious and social organizations in initiating a joint committee on monitoring public enterprises. And they laid plans to study and get involved in a new local administration scheme by organizing a major seminar, called "The Local Church and Local Administration." This scheme, which involved electing district councilors with limited powers for the running of district affairs, was the first feeble step taken by the government toward allowing very limited local participation in government.[9]

Mission in the Public Arena

The Hong Kong church continued to act on its new understanding of mission with increasing involvement in public issues in the colony over the next two decades, including political issues. For example, in January 1981, the council's Commission on Public Policy became an active member of the Coalition for Monitoring Public Utilities through a campaign that called on the public to delay monthly payments of electricity bills until final warning notices were received. This action was taken to protest the total disregard of public opinion by the two privately owned power companies (as expressed through 500,000 petition signatures) and to pressure the companies into changing their disclosure and profit policies.

In March, the Educational Concerns Committee set up a textbook review project in which it reviewed secondary school textbooks to identify key deficiencies in critical subject areas. These were Chinese language, Chinese literature, Chinese history, world history, economics and public affairs, religious studies, the English language, and English literature. The committee held a series of forums, published its findings, and called for major revisions. For example, it advocated the inclusion of modern Chinese history after 1949, civic education, and the use of Chinese as the major medium of instruction in all schools. The committee also published an extensive critique of a government-sponsored comprehensive review of the entire Hong Kong educational system by an outside panel of experts from the United Kingdom.[10] The critique spelled out basic assumptions about education in Hong Kong,

9   "HKCC News," *News & Views*, March 1981, 2.
10   *1983 Report by a Visiting Panel on the Hong Kong Education System*, otherwise known as the Llewellyn Report (after the panel's chair) (Hong Kong Government Press).

Public policy rally

delineated a Christian philosophy of education, and made fourteen specific and comprehensive proposals for educational reforms.[11]

The council's general secretary, the Reverend Kwok Nai-wang, put it well:

> Education should be a vehicle to harmonize social relations and to narrow the gap between the rich and the poor. It is, therefore, necessary for Christian schools to desist from following elitism as the norm and to adopt an egalitarian outlook on education....It is high time for us to give due attention to the overriding purpose of education, namely enabling young people to acquire the abilities to analyze, reflect and make decisions....We must make them aware that the meaning of life lies not in receiving and possessing, but in giving and contributing, and that the fullness of life is not determined by material well-being, but by harmonious relationships with God, nature and our fellow humans....The students must learn the meaning and importance of democracy, election and accountability and be able to differentiate common good from special interests. The origins and theories of capitalism and communism, their insights and deficiencies, must be discussed in economics and public affairs lessons....Furthermore, the Chinese language and Chinese history must be accorded top priority in the new curriculum, for it is our responsibility to help the younger generations recover their cultural roots and reaffirm their identity as Chinese....we must produce a new crop of dedicated leaders who possess not only the expertise to run a modern sophisticated metropolis with a population of six million, but also the political craftsmanship to

[11]   Most of these proposals were adopted over the next two decades.

take on the historically unprecedented task of working with over one billion of our compatriots north of the border.[12]

In May, the Hong Kong Christian Council asked me to set up an alternative tours program for expatriates living in Hong Kong and for travelers who wanted to have a deeper experience of the territory than merely shopping or visiting tourist attractions. It was surprising how many people who had been living in Hong Kong for years had never attempted to learn a word of Cantonese, had never visited a Chinese market or temple, had never been to a resettlement estate, or had never made any Chinese friends. They were perpetual tourists living in a cocoon with likeminded people. Unfortunately, this mindset could also be found among at least some of the members of Hong Kong's expatriate English-speaking congregations, even when it came to being exposed to the many Christian ministries going on in the territory. Through Alternative Tours, we provided a bus and a knowledgeable guide and offered people opportunities to visit various Christian ministries and cultural sites around the city. The program was well received and helped raise public awareness of the challenges that Hong Kong's people faced and the ways in which the churches were reaching out to the community.[13]

In December, the council sponsored a poll on the government's proposed district administration scheme that for the first time would introduce the principle of universal suffrage in Hong Kong, albeit on a very narrow basis. It interviewed 480 church members and 40 ministers about what this scheme would need to include to motivate ordinary people to register and to vote. The results were published in the December 1981 issue of *News & Views*. The overwhelming majority indicated that they would only participate in the voting if the District Board had sufficient power to act as a watchdog, and if elected board members formed the majority,[14] which, in the end, was the way it turned out.

That same year, the Christian Industrial Committee joined eighty-one other labor organizations to petition the governor for more labor reforms. They asked that price increases by the profit-bloated private

12 "Some Thoughts on the Future Prospect of Education in Hong Kong," *News & Views*, June 1984, 21.

13 For a more comprehensive introduction to this program, see Karsen, Wendell, "Tourists or Pilgrims?" *St. John's Review*, vol. 50, no. 9 (Sept., 1983), 1.

14 "HKCC Poll on the Government's Proposed District Administration Scheme," *News & Views*, Dec. 1981, 2–3.

Author conducting
an Alternative Tour

utility monopolies be halted and that the people be represented in monitoring them. They requested that real wages be protected against inflation and that a comprehensive social security system be established that would include unemployment benefits, old age pensions, and improved compensation for accident victims and the sick. They called for legislation on unfair dismissal, the recognition of unions, and the right to bargain by employees. They further suggested a wage security fund to offset unscrupulous employers and that Labor Day be declared a statutory holiday.[15]

In March 1983, L.K. Ding, Methodist chair of the Christian Industrial Committee, was the first Christian leader to call publicly for major democratic reforms in Hong Kong. In his speech at the committee's annual general meeting he said:

> We have come to the conclusion that social progress is no longer possible under the present style of Government. The much vaunted government by consensus and consultation is dead....In order to achieve further progress and to solve future problems, the whole process of governing Hong Kong needs to be challenged....The majority of those who are—by necessity or by choice—committed to Hong Kong needs to be brought into the governing process....We do not accept Government's point of view that reforms in Government administration will have been completed with the District Board and Urban Council elections. To us these elections are but a step to opening up the process of government....

[15] "HKCC News," *News & Views*, June 1983, 2. Many of these reforms were adopted eventually.

All members of the District Boards and Urban Council should be elected. There must be elected members on both the Legislative and Executive Councils. Elections to District Boards and the Urban Council are mere window dressing unless the election process is extended to the bodies that really matter. Government has repeatedly dismissed the idea of election to these two bodies because, we suspect, elected representatives cannot be controlled....People must be able to participate effectively in the governing process. This is a basic human right. As a Christian, I believe in people having the right to shape their own destiny."[16]

The extent of the growing involvement of Christians in every aspect of public life in Hong Kong can be measured by the results of the "Mid-decade Consultation on the Mission of the Church," sponsored by the Hong Kong Christian Council in January 1986. A planning group involving fifty church leaders from many denominations and fields was convened in August 1985 to set the agenda and generate resource material. Situation reports and chronologies of council-related actions were presented in five major areas: "Evangelism among the Low-incomed," "Ministry to Students," "Relationship with the Church in China," "Influencing Social Values," and "Participation in the Shaping of Public Policy." The chronology under the last topic records thirty-seven specific actions or campaigns over a five-year period.[17] When the consultation was convened, the following mission priorities for the next five years were set: development of a representative government in Hong Kong; a full-scale push on civic education; concern for the livelihood of the masses; renewal of local congregations; and strengthening of interchurch cooperation.[18]

Chernobyl and Daya Bay

In April 1986, Hong Kong, a compact city with a population of almost six million with nowhere to flee, woke up to the fact that a nuclear disaster could happen on its doorstep. In that month, the world watched in horror as a major nuclear disaster unfolded in Chernobyl, in the USSR. In 1980, an announcement that China and the Hong Kong-based China Light and Power Company were going to build a nuclear

16   "Christian Industrial Committee News," *News & Views*, Dec. 1981, 2–3, 11.
17   "Mid-decade Consultation on the Mission of the Church," *News & Views*, Sept. 1985, 6–19.
18   "Report on the Mid-decade Consultation on the Mission of the Church," *News & Views*, March 1986, 4.

The Rev. Ho Tin-hau
registering for
Mid-decade
Consultation

power plant jointly in Daya Bay, just fifty kilometers from Hong Kong's border, had gone almost unnoticed. It had not, however, gone unnoticed by some in the Christian community who were concerned about nuclear weapons and the effects of peaceful nuclear energy production on the environment. The December 1983 issue of *News & Views* carried an article by John McLean, "N-plant to Make Hong Kong a Bomb Target,"[19] a full-page poster captioned, "Could Nuclear Power Make Hong Kong a Ghost Town?" and an article by Fr. Harold Naylor entitled, "Nuclear Power and Hong Kong."

The crisis in Chernobyl woke up the public to the fact that China and the local power monopoly were about to begin building the Daya Bay nuclear plant that had been quietly announced in 1980. In light of the Chernobyl disaster, China's sloppy technological methods, its legendary lack of concern for the environment, and its crass view of the value of human life weighed on the public consciousness. A public outcry ensued that lasted for months. An Anglican Priest, the Reverend Fung Chi Wood, organized the "Joint Coalition for the Shelving of the Daya Bay Nuclear Power Plant." One million signatures were gathered on a petition to the Hong Kong and Chinese governments asking that the project be halted. Polls showed that 70 percent of Hong Kong's population opposed the venture. *News & Views* ran ten pages of articles supporting the outcry and the anti-Daya Bay plant campaign from a Christian perspective.[20] Outrage was expressed over the British, Chinese, and French (who were selling the technology) governments' failure to consult the people of Hong Kong on such a vital local issue.

In the end, the business community and the three governments overrode local outrage, and plant construction went ahead.[21] However,

[19]   Pp. 16–18.
[20]   "The Daya Bay Fiasco," *News & Views*, Sept., 1986, 2–11.
[21]   The people's concerns were not unfounded. The project was plagued

The Rev. Kwok Nai-wang

for the first time, the people of Hong Kong had stood up en masse, made it clear that they deeply cared about "their" place, and demanded to have a say in what happened to it and to them. And they noted that when the chips were down, the Christian church had stood with them and helped articulate their concerns.

The Hong Kong Christian Institute and the Hong Kong Christian Council

1988 saw the birth of the Hong Kong Christian Institute (HKCI). Backed by 120 Christian activist leaders, the Reverend Kowk Nai-wang, a former colleague and general secretary of the Hong Kong Christian Council, launched the institute and became its first director. In introducing the institute, Kwok said:

> For the past forty years the church has been playing an important role in Hong Kong as a social service provider, serving those in need. This work has been much appreciated by the wider community. As Hong Kong is now facing radical changes in the coming years, it requires fresh responses to its many new needs. As the churches in Hong Kong carry many institutional burdens, they are not free enough to take on these new challenges....The institute is seeking new ways to serve and to renew the churches in Hong Kong so that they may bear an ever more effective witness to God's love and justice in our society.[22]

with technical and safety problems and the plant did not become fully operational until the year 2000. Meanwhile, the Chinese foreign minister dismissed the polls and signature campaign by sniffing, "We are not going to let a few misguided people stand in the way of such a major project."

22 "Introducing the Hong Kong Christian Institute," *News & Views*, March 1992, 4.

Kwok gathered a gifted and visionary staff to carry out the institute's programs, including Raymond Fung.[23] The institute set itself six goals, two of them being "to be a sign of a continuing quest for human rights, democracy and justice," and "to be a think tank that searches for directions in mission for churches and Christians and to develop a contextual theology in Hong Kong." Over the next few years the institute cooperated with a significant number of local organizations to further its agenda, and it also launched its own programs and publications. It became an increasingly significant catalyst for enabling Christians in Hong Kong to be involved in efforts to influence public policy.

After my return to Hong Kong in 1990 to, among other things, resume the editorship of *News & Views*, the Hong Kong Christian Council, representing the major denominations in Hong Kong, continued to lead the way in coordinating efforts in mission, evangelism, church unity, education, and social services. However, as the calendar moved ever nearer the fateful year of 1997, its major concern became rallying the churches to face the coming realities and challenging them to become more involved in influencing public policy from a Christian perspective. That this was more necessary than ever was evident upon returning after an absence of six years:

> My third impression is that the Church in Hong Kong has become more isolated, fragmented and weak. More isolated in the sense that the gap between the by and large middle class Christians and the mass of the population most affected by 1997 concerns continues to grow wider. More fragmented in the sense that the pressures of 1997 have polarized Christians into various camps that hold widely divergent views of how the Church should deal with preparations for Hong Kong's future. More weak in the sense that increasing numbers of church members and even pastors are emigrating to other countries. On the brighter side, there are a good number of committed, gifted people who are dedicated to rallying the Church "for such a time as this." They are convinced that opportunities for ministry in this place have never been greater, and that the Church will rise to the challenge. I believe they are right.[24]

---

[23] Fung eventually became executive secretary of the World Council of Churches' Commission on World Mission and Evangelism.

[24] Karsen, Wendell, "First Impressions," *News & Views*, Dec. 1990, 3.

The Rev. Dr. Tso Man-king

Shortly after my return, the council's new general secretary, Dr. Tso Man-king, took office. He proved to be a strong leader who helped the Hong Kong church through a difficult decade. The path down which he would lead the council was defined in a consultation on the mission of the church in Hong Kong in the nineties that was convened April 17–23, 1990, just months before his arrival. One hundred thirty-six participants—forty-three from denominations and independent churches, fifteen from parachurch organizations, eleven from seminaries, and forty-two academics and observers—spent a whole week deliberating the future mission of the church. Presentations on solidarity and unity among churches during the political transitional period, the strategy for communicating the gospel under circumstances of rapid change, and the work of the church in society at large during the transitional period set the tone for the consultation. These, together with the input from preconsultation meetings, the results of a youth consultation held two months prior, plus other research references especially collected for this purpose, constituted the main resource material for the week. Ten working groups were set up to discuss ten topics suggested by the preparatory committee:

1. The pursuit of solidarity and unity among the churches during this time of social change.
2. The stimulation of mutual concern and cooperation with overseas churches and churches in China during this crucial period.
3. The development of ways in which to spread the Good News among Hong Kong's populace during this transitional period.
4. The definition of the roles of parachurch organizations and various other Christian groups in supplementing and enhancing the work of the church in this unique era.

5. The strengthening of theological training to face the challenges of this age.
6. The development of pastoral work in the congregations during this period of rapid change.
7. The strengthening of the social service work of the church during this time of transition.
8. The enhancement of educational work during this preparatory period.
9. The encouragement of Christians to become involved in building a democratic government during these changing times.
10. The implementation of the concept of the "priesthood of all believers" in the life and work of the church in this era of change.

The week concluded with a plenary session to review the work of the consultation and to adopt a ten-point statement, "Manifesto on the Mission of the Church in Hong Kong in the '90s." Among other things, the manifesto, signed by the four hundred people present, declared:

> The 1990s will be a determinative period for the world, for China and for Hong Kong. The world is in rapid change. China is at a critical juncture in history. Hong Kong is experiencing a crisis of confidence and is full of anxiety about its change in status. The churches of Hong Kong will face a severe test in this coming decade....In order to manifest their life in Christ, the churches must first of all be one, lovingly melding in one body their various gifts and ideas....We sorrowfully repent of the divisions caused by denominationalism and the prejudices of sectarian-mindedness, of the tension between the congregations and church organizations, of the cleavage between the clergy and the laity....It is our intention that henceforth we will bind ourselves closer together, support one another, and build up the body of Christ in love.
>
> To live the life of Christ is to identify with the people; to share their trials and tribulations, even to the point of giving up one's life. To this end, Hong Kong's churches must identify themselves with the broad masses and be with them in their suffering, doubts and struggles....Whereas on the one hand Hong Kong's churches should value their fine tradition of engagement in social service and involvement in educational work, they must on the other hand wake up to their mistakes and shortcomings in

these areas of ministry. In repentance, they must seek a ministry of service which is humble in spirit and is done for the sake of others. They must mobilize their educational resources. By doing this, they can help to mold character and nurture the democratic spirit....

At this period of political transition, responding to God's demands for justice, the churches must work with the people of Hong Kong to seek a political structure which provides a high degree of self-government and upholds human rights, freedom, democracy and the rule of law....We recognize that the churches must henceforth make a greater effort to better equip their believers and to better train their pastors, to the end that the whole Church will be transformed into well-conditioned soldiers for Christ who will fulfill the responsibilities entrusted to them.[25]

At the conclusion of the consultation, Philemon Choi, director of Breakthrough Ministries, challenged the consultation by declaring that Christians must be ready to bear the cross of Christ during the next decade for the good of the future of the people of Hong Kong. It was obvious that as Hong Kong's 1997 date of destiny with China drew inexorably closer, the church was determined to end its isolation, heal its fragmentation, and overcome its weakness. It had found its voice, was ready to shoulder its cross, and was prepared to stand up.

---

[25] "Consultation on the Mission of the Church in Hong Kong in the Nineties," *News & Views*, Hong Kong Christian Council, December 1990, pp. 8–10.

CHAPTER 12

Change Is Coming!

As we have seen, the British gained the island of Hong Kong in 1848 as a spoil of the first opium war, and the Kowloon Peninsula in 1860 as a spoil of the second opium war. These territories were signed over to the British "in perpetuity." The subsequent arrangement for the acquisition of additional territory north of Kowloon was different. In 1898, China agreed to lease an additional 350 square miles of land to the British called the "New Territories." The lease was to run for ninety-nine years, which meant that it would come due in 1997. At that time, 1997 not only seemed a long way off, but the British assumed that there would be no problem in renewing the lease. After all, they represented the dominant power in the world at the time, and China had proven to be no match for Britain's military might.

The Beginning of the End

The power equation in the Far East changed during World War II. Japan "liberated" many territories that had been subject to western colonial powers, and Asians suddenly realized that those powers were not invincible. Asians also became aware of declarations

l-r: Chiang Kai-shek, Franklin Roosevelt and Winston Churchill at the 1943 Cairo Conference

by the United States calling for an end to the colonial system and for self-determination for the peoples who had been under colonial domination. However, when Japan was defeated in 1945 and expelled from the territories it had "liberated," France, the Netherlands, Britain, Belgium, and Portugal all rushed back to reassert their authority over "their" colonies. However, local patriots emerged in territory after territory that fanned nationalist sentiment into flames of rebellion and called for independence. Within the next ten years, most of the colonial masters had been forced to relinquish their hold on their overseas possessions, and a flock of new independent nations had come into being. One of the glaring exceptions to this trend was the British Crown Colony of Hong Kong—the last jewel in the crown of the formerly far-flung British Empire.

During the war, over Churchill's objection, Roosevelt insisted that China's Chiang Kai-shek be accepted as one of the "big four" leaders representing the major allied powers that were conducting the war. Chiang pushed his allies to revoke what the Chinese called the "unequal treaties"[1]—treaties that had been forced on China by the Western colonial powers during the nineteenth century at the point of a gun. The allies agreed, and the treaties were revoked in 1943 after the Cairo Conference.[2] He also demanded that Japan be forced to give back Taiwan and the Pescadores and all former German concessions in China that had been awarded to them at the end of World War I. Again

---

[1] The Chinese viewed the nineteenth-century treaties made between them and the western powers as "unequal" because the terms were dictated to China following humiliating military defeats. In many cases China was forced to pay large reparations, open up ports for trade, cede or lease territories, allow enclaves that were governed by foreign nationals and their troops, and grant "extraterritorial" rights wherein western nationals were given special protection from local Chinese laws and courts.

[2] Payne, Robert, *Chiang Kai-shek* (New York: Weybright & Talley, 1969), 246–47.

they agreed. He further demanded that the British hand back Hong Kong, which had been wrested from China during the opium wars. Roosevelt was in favor and pressed Churchill to agree. However, after two years of protracted negotiations involving a number of possible scenarios, Churchill and the British refused to give up their last main vestige of empire in Southeast Asia.[3]

The war suddenly ended in September 1945 as a result of atomic bomb attacks on Japan. Chiang had every intention of sending troops into Hong Kong from adjoining Guangdong Province and reclaiming sovereignty over the territory before the British could get there. However, he was prevented from doing so by several developments. A strong Chinese Communist drive to take Manchuria over from the Japanese demanded that he use all of his military resources to counter this move, including his southern army in Guangdong.[4] Furthermore, the British were steaming towards Hong Kong with a strong force and had every intention of resuming sovereignty after the departure of the Japanese. They had been one of China's major allies during the war. To confront them militarily over Hong Kong would deprive him of a strong supporter in his struggle with the Communists for control of China after the war. In the end, the British won the race by default. However, notice had been served that the Chinese regarded the British as *temporary* custodians of *their* territory—so-called treaties or no treaties.

Hong Kong's New Neighbors

With the victory of the Chinese Communists over the Chinese Nationalists in 1949, the situation changed dramatically. The Communists owed nothing to Britain and were not dependent on Britain. They viewed Hong Kong as a British pimple on the body of the Chinese nation—to be endured temporarily for practical reasons until the time would be ripe for its incision. Meanwhile, the balance of power was changing. Britain, bleeding from the thousand cuts of World War II and shorn of the economic and strategic advantages of empire, was declining rapidly as a world power. China, on the other hand, had stood up under the Communists, had fought the United States to a stalemate in Korea, and was gaining in stature in the world, both diplomatically

---

[3]   Tsang, Steve, *Hong Kong: An Appointment with China* (London: I.B. Tauris, 1997), 33–51.

[4]   A futile effort, as it turned out, due to Chiang's bungling and mismanagement of his forces and equipment.

and militarily. The Chinese knew that time was on their side and that they held all the cards. The British "emperor" no longer had any clothes! Nor did the British people have any further delusions about maintaining an empire. In fact, many were embarrassed that after the world had bid farewell to the colonial era, they were still ruling over a colony abroad containing millions of people who had no say in the decisions that determined their lives.

The Chinese strategy, especially during the first three decades following the war, was to harass the British steadily enough and long enough that when their lease on the New Territories came to an end, they would have neither the choice nor the stomach to remain. Meanwhile, British Hong Kong had become more and more dependent on China. As its population had swelled over the years, it had been forced to look to China to supply more and more of its food, water, and other needs. All China needed to do was to turn off the water tap or to withhold the food cornucopia, and the colony could be brought to its knees in a hurry. Or, as in 1967, China could simply choose to inundate the tiny territory with hordes of refugees and swamp it. Furthermore, Hong Kong was practically indefensible. This had been shown at the beginning of World War II, when the Japanese had overrun the place in a matter of weeks. A weakened Britain would be hard put to stand up to a determined China from a tiny redoubt on its coast, especially since 98 percent of the colony's inhabitants were Chinese who might not love the Communists, but who did not exactly like the British either. Furthermore, as time wore on, the New Territories had become more and more integrated with Kowloon and Hong Kong Island. At first a rural backwater, slowly but surely, under the press of increased population, towns, industry, infrastructure, and even a new airport would be built there. This process developed to the point where, by the 1990s, it was impossible to physically separate the New Territories from the rest of the colony should China refuse to renew the lease.

All this slowly dawned on the British as the lease clock ticked along toward 1997. *Slowly* dawned on the British in the sense that, even as late as 1984, they more or less naively assumed that China would agree to renew their lease and let them stay. Or even if China refused to renew the lease, they would at least have the *right* to remain in Kowloon and Hong Kong Island by international treaty. When our family arrived in Hong Kong in 1974, for example, nobody ever mentioned the lease or 1997 or uncertainty over the future. After all, 1997 was still twenty-three years off, and a lot could happen before then, including the possibility that the Communist regime might be thrown into the

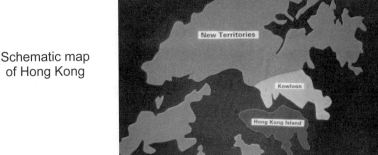

Schematic map
of Hong Kong

dustbin of history. The churches were busy with the "now" of their evangelistic, educational, and social ministries, and gave no thought whatsoever to the "then" of "What if the lease is not renewed?" Like the colonial government, the churches assumed, and at first even hoped, that the lease would be extended and that the British would continue to supply a stable, prosperous, safe haven for them in which to carry on their ministry.

The MacLehose Gambit

After Mao's death in 1976, great changes took place in the People's Republic of China (PRC). The government launched a "Four Modernizations" program,[5] relaxed social controls on the population, and opened up to the outside world. As a result, it came to view Hong Kong as a key asset in the internal development of China, and the British as a key ally in the development of its external relations with the West. In this new climate, then governor Murray MacLehose, a career British diplomat, sought to move relations between the two governments from confrontation to cooperation. For the first time, he gave his public blessing to the presence of the Xinhua "News" Agency, Beijing's de-facto headquarters in Hong Kong. In 1978, he attended the local celebration of the PRC's national day.

In 1979, MacLehose was invited to Beijing to discuss future economic cooperation between China and Hong Kong. He seized this opportunity to put out a feeler as to the PRC government's long-term intentions concerning the future of Hong Kong. All land leases that had been granted by the Hong Kong government were due to expire when the New Territories lease expired in 1997. MacLeHose hoped that

---

[5]   These were the modernization of industry, agriculture, science, and defense.

he could persuade the Chinese government to do something to blur the 1997 deadline so as to sustain confidence in Hong Kong and, in return, enable Hong Kong to help in China's modernization. With such tacit approval, the British could then amend the Royal Order in Council of 1898 and, in effect, remove the terminal date of the New Territories lease without ever having had to raise the question of the lease per se. The assumption was that so long as nobody on either side officially raised the question, the future of Hong Kong would remain in limbo and the British could go on assuming their assumptions and not be considered a lame duck administration. They knew that if they did raise the question directly, the Chinese of necessity would be provoked into taking a nationalistic stand and insist on its termination.

However, MacLehose made what is now regarded by many as a strategic blunder. By raising a question about lease matters, even indirectly, he in essence invited the Chinese to put their cards about Hong Kong's long-term future on the table. Deng Xiao-ping seized this opportunity to tell MacLehose in no uncertain terms, "A negotiated settlement of the Hong Kong question in the future should be based on the premise that the territory is part of China. However, we will treat Hong Kong as a special region. For a considerable length of time, Hong Kong may continue to practice its capitalist system while we practice our socialist system."[6] This was the first public mention of the "one country, two systems" formula that would eventually prevail. By raising the matter of the lease in the way he had, MacLehose had unwittingly implied to the Chinese that the British were willing to compromise over the future of Hong Kong. In 1981, in response to this British "initiative," the Communist Party Politburo decided to recover sovereignty over Hong Kong in 1997, ensure that Hong Kong would continue to serve the PRC's economic and political interests, and devise an appropriate arrangement to achieve those two goals.[7]

Whither the Church?

I first broached the subject of 1997 in *News & Views* in March 1980 in the editorial, "Whither the Church in Hong Kong?" Mine proved to be a lone voice in the wilderness, since even at the Hong Kong Christian Council's progressive-minded November 1980 consultation, nary a word would be said about 1997. The editorial read:

[6]   Tsang, *Hong Kong*, 88.
[7]   Ibid., 92.

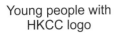

Young people with
HKCC logo

Since the leadership turnover in China in late 1976, people have been asking, "Wither Hong Kong?" It has become fairly clear, for a number of reasons, that Hong Kong's days as a British colony are probably numbered.

1. The border with China has become increasingly porous with the former trickle of capital, immigrants and technology now taking on flood proportions. One wonders how long it will be before crossing it will be like crossing a state line in the United States.

2. The revolutionary change in China's direction from the pursuit of dogmatic socialist ideals to the quest for pragmatic rapid modernization has transformed practical, materialistic Hong Kong from a fly in China's ointment to an active working partner.

3. The moderation of the new Chinese leadership and the deep-seated yearning of particularly the young of Hong Kong to have a place and a people has stirred a tangible and growing sense of identity with the "Motherland" among Hong Kong's people.

4. China continues to literally "buy up" Hong Kong. The PRC's investments here are growing while for the first time some of the British "Hongs" are facing the potential prospect of being taken over by PRC-backed consortiums.

5. Even the British don't see themselves as more than temporary administrators of Hong Kong. Britain does not dispute China's claim that Hong Kong is Chinese territory, and even the word "colony" has quietly been buried in favor of "dependent territory."

So it is probably no longer a question of "if," but of "when"—a question whose answer is anybody's guess at this point, but which some think might be answered more quickly than most imagine.

What does this future prospect that will more and more influence Hong Kong's present, say to the Church about its own present and future here? It says that unless we change rapidly and decisively in the present, we will find ourselves without much of a future in Hong Kong. There are a number of reasons for this.

1. Our comfortably middle-class Church generally finds itself too out of touch with the majority of Hong Kong's population that will figure larger in her future—the workers and "peasants." Unless we are not only ready to reach out to them and welcome them, but also to see things from their standpoint and stand with them in their struggle for a just and meaningful life, we will remain out of touch with them and mortgage our future—for the "last" *will* someday be "first."

2. Our comfortably establishment Church finds itself too much in touch with the minority of Hong Kong's population that will figure smaller in her future—the powerful and wealthy. Unless we adopt a more prophetic stance, more actively disassociate ourselves from the unjust macro-structures that inhibit a just distribution of power and wealth in our community, and more literally follow the politico-socio-economic implications of Jesus' good news, we will mortgage our principles and our future—for the "first" *will* someday be "last."

3. Our comfortably traditional Church finds itself being increasingly deserted or discounted by a key segment of Hong Kong's population that will dominate her future—the idealistic young. Unless we can convince them that our message supersedes barren ideology by better demonstrating to them that our "program" can meet the holistic needs of urban man, both individually and collectively, we will find them embracing other programs that promise more but in the long run produce less, and mortgage our credibility and our future—for "if the trumpet gives an uncertain sound, who will prepare for battle?"

4. Our comfortably Westernized Church still finds itself too dependent on external funds, personnel, materials, theology, liturgy, hymnology and the like, and too cut off from Chinese thought, culture, tradition, ideology and self-reliance. The experience of the Church in China teaches us that unless we get more in touch with ourselves, contextualize the good

news from our own perspective and more clearly declare our independence, we will not be deeply rooted enough in the soil of the real Hong Kong, and mortgage our future—for "the form of this era is passing away."

If the Church in Hong Kong is going to speak more effectively in the present and at all in the future, it is going to have to follow its prophets and reorder its priorities—not merely as a strategy for survival, but as an affirmation of its fundamental nature and faith.[8]

The *South China Morning Post* ran a condensed version of the article, which gave this point of view a much broader exposure.[9]

The British Must Go!

In 1982, Prime Minister Margaret Thatcher visited Beijing. High on her agenda were future arrangements for Hong Kong. Anxiety about the future was beginning to build. For example, Hong Kong's banks were faced with adjusting their usual fifteen-year mortgage terms to take into account their 1997 due date. Thatcher was under the illusion that both Britain's position in the world and her personal stature had been greatly enhanced by the British victory in the Falklands war. Her intention was to argue that Britain's sovereignty over Hong Kong Island and the Kowloon Peninsula was guaranteed by internationally recognized treaties, and that since these territories were no longer viable without the New Territories, the British should have the right to continue to administer the whole colony well into the future. Also, continuing British administration was necessary to maintain stability and ensure prosperity in Hong Kong. Only a stable and prosperous Hong Kong would be an asset in China's drive towards modernization. However, "paramount leader" Deng Xiao-ping made plain that the People's Republic was dealing with realities and not with illusions. He flatly reiterated that sovereignty over the whole of Hong Kong belonged to China and was not negotiable. During World War II, the Allied Powers had renounced the "unequal treaties" that China had once signed under duress, and the treaties concerning Hong Kong were no different. The lease on the New Territories would not be extended

---

[8]   Karsen, Wendell, "Whither the Church in Hong Kong?" *News & Views*, March 1980, 2.
[9]   See "Church Must Heed Wind of Change," *South China Morning Post*, March 31, 1980, 6.

Visa line alongside
U.S. Consulate
in Hong Kong
in 1982

under any circumstances. The only thing to be negotiated was the *way* in which Hong Kong was to be returned to China, not when. If the British were not prepared to hand over Hong Kong by 1997, China would proceed to take it over unilaterally and be ready to pay whatever price such a catastrophe would demand. He would allow a year or two for negotiations, but if these proved futile, China would announce a unilateral solution.[10]

When news of this development reached Hong Kong, panic set in. Within ten days of Thatcher's departure from Beijing, the Hang Seng Stock Market dropped 25 percent. Within a month, the Hong Kong dollar had lost 12 percent of its value, and within six months, the property market had dropped 50 percent. Some of the large British "Hongs," which had been linchpins of the Hong Kong economy since the founding of the colony, also began hedging their bets. For example, Jardine Matheson moved much of its resources to Bermuda, while the Hong Kong and Shanghai Bank also diversified overseas.

Those who could afford it began to make plans to leave—most heading to the United States and Canada, and some to Western Europe. Wives and children were sent abroad to establish residence and obtain green cards, while husbands (who came to be called "astronauts") continued to conduct business by commuting between Hong Kong and their homes away from home. Since Christians were by and large upwardly mobile people, the percentage that turned their eyes abroad

10   Dimbleby, Jonathan, *The Last Governor* (New York: Warner Books, 1997), 54–57.

was even greater than that of the population as a whole. Congregations were depleted as family after family established a home overseas where it could resettle or at least use as a base to wait and see how things would eventually turn out. Even a number of pastors began looking for Chinese churches abroad where they could serve.

On the one hand, the tug of Chinese nationalism and the dislike of colonialism were incentives to people to stay and participate in their motherland's future, no matter what that future might turn out to be. On the other hand, their revulsion at the atrocious human rights record and draconian socialist economic policies of the Chinese Communist regime, and the vested economic interests that they had built up in British-run Hong Kong, made them fear a PRC takeover. They knew that independence on the Singapore model was out of the question. However, they had hoped desperately that some agreement could have been worked out whereby even though China's ultimate sovereignty over Hong Kong would have been recognized, Hong Kong would have continued to be administered by Britain for the foreseeable future. However, the strong stance taken by Deng during Thatcher's visit had made it clear that this was not to be. Even so, things eventually began to settle down as most people hoped for a diplomatic miracle that would keep the Communists from taking over.

The first phase of negotiations lasted until June 1983. The Chinese demanded that the British clearly acknowledge Chinese sovereignty over the whole of what then constituted Hong Kong. When the British resisted this, China began leaking details of a twelve-point policy paper outlining its plans for the future of Hong Kong to the press—creating a "Special Administrative Region," the one country but two systems formula; Hong Kong people governing Hong Kong; etc. The British, alarmed that China was already positioning itself to call the shots, offered a compromise. Britain would relinquish its claims on Hong Kong if the people of Hong Kong accepted the outcome of the negotiations. The Chinese interpreted this gesture as a *de facto* recognition of their sovereignty, and, in July 1983, the talks moved into a second stage of working out matters of substance.[11]

Christians Speak Up

Although these negotiations had been the buzz of Hong Kong for almost two years, church leaders had said very little about it in public.

---

[11]   Segal, Gerald, *The Fate of Hong Kong* (London: Simon & Schuster, 1993), 37–40.

However, when the talks entered their second stage, some leaders began to speak up. A report from the Hong Kong Christian Council general secretary, Kwok Nai-wang, appeared in the March 1983 *News & Views*. It included the section, "The Future of Hong Kong," in which Kwok wrote:

> ...ministers from many churches have been holding serious discussions about the future of Hong Kong. During the past ten months, the Council has organized two forums, one for theological teachers and another for local church pastors. While we realize we are no experts on the highly complex, top-level negotiations being held between Beijing and London, we are very much concerned about the uncertain and insecure feelings of a large segment of the general public. Here we have a pastoral role to play! Whatever change takes place, we would hope that it will be in the direction of making Hong Kong a more just, participatory and sustainable society....In mid-March, the Executive Committee of the Council will have an informal session on "1997."[12]

Three articles and an editorial in that same issue focused on the church and 1997. Peter Lee, director of the Chinese Christian Study Centre, addressed "The Limit Set by 1997." He defined this "limit" as the wish of the privileged minority, who enjoyed freedom and prosperity in Hong Kong, to keep it that way. He went on to argue that even if Hong Kong were to revert to China, perhaps as a Special Administrative Region, the church would have a new opportunity to reorder Hong Kong's priorities and extend true freedom and prosperity to the masses rather than reserve them, as they had been reserved, for the rich and the powerful.[13]

The YWCA's K.C. Wong asked, "What Does the Church Want in 1997?" He pointed out that most discussion had thus far centered on how the church might adapt to a new political system by dealing with the psychological and theological aspects of adaptation. He went on to argue,

> Church people are still now in fact seeking a psychological outlet for their anxieties as well as a theological self justification for their position when encountering the issue, when, in fact, the issue is fundamentally a *political* one. Church people seldom ask themselves how the church is going to move and act before

[12] P. 2.
[13] Ibid., 21.

and after the critical year of 1997. What do we want in terms of relations between church and state?...What do we want in terms of our relations with the global ecumenical movement?...How are we going to dialogue with the Chinese church?...What do we want in terms of a just society in Hong Kong that is consistent with the witness of our Christian faith?...Why don't we stand up and say what we want so that people with power will put our wants into their negotiating agenda for serious consideration *before it is too late?*...Seeking ways to remove our anxieties about the future will only create more anxieties because this is a political issue rather than a psychological one. God does not ask us to make ourselves comfortable but to translate "thy Kingdom come" into concrete reality in our society. It is now time to face that reality and act![14]

This issue also contained my article, "The Church, the Schools and 1997," which began by saying, "The answer to the question as to what will happen to Hong Kong after 1997 has serious implications for every sector of society, the church included. And within the church's life and structure, the answer to that question is particularly relevant to the future of the schools operated by the churches, especially in light of what happened to such schools in China in the early '50s."

The article went on to spell out eight reasons why the churches needed to repent (read "change") concerning our educational enterprise in Hong Kong during the fourteen years remaining before 1997 and made practical suggestions as to how those changes might be brought about. The eight reasons were:

1. We have mainly served the government as a contractor rather than as a catalytic agent.
2. We have contributed to the de-culturalization (dehumanization) of the people in our schools.
3. We have weakened our influence on Hong Kong's educational scene through our divisions.
4. We have not sufficiently challenged the presuppositions underlying governmental educational philosophy and pushed for our own.
5. We have run schools that have too often been "Christian" at the periphery rather than at the core.
6. We have staffed our schools with a majority of people who do not share our Christian perspective as far as educational philosophy is concerned.

---

[14] Ibid., 19.

Teacher and students
in church-related
secondary school

7. We have helped to perpetuate an elitist educational system that is contrary to our Christian calling.

8. We have not been willing to make the sacrifices that are necessary to guarantee the Christian quality of the education we offer.

It concluded by saying,

A growing number of Christian educators are becoming more and more aware of these problems and their implications for the future. They see that if the Church is going to be a relevant and progressive force in education in Hong Kong, these problems are going to have to be squarely faced and courageously dealt with. If we maintain a "business as usual" attitude, the number of these reformers will inevitably decrease to the point where our running church-related schools will become increasingly pointless long before 1997 arrives. If, however, we take a fresh look at where we are and what we must do, and have the will to encourage them to do what needs to be done, we can move ahead with a new sense of purpose and mission that will be equal to the searching inquiries of today's young people and to the unknown challenges of an uncertain future."[15]

My editorial, "Nineteen Ninety-Seven...Again," also dealt with our date with destiny:

One thing we could contribute to the discussion [about 1997] would be a critical assessment of the values assumptions underlying the present public debate. China, Great Britain

---

[15] Ibid., 8–12.

and just about everybody else are saying that the chief end of all future arrangements for Hong Kong is to assure continued prosperity and security. (Looking around at the way most people are forced to live in Hong Kong, we could immediately ask the rich and powerful who are trumpeting these themes—security and prosperity *for whom* and to *do what*?—but even that would only be a secondary question). Many Christians by their silence on the subject seem to agree with these goals and the values assumptions underlying them. However, even a small boy well versed in the Westminster Confession would be able to tell us that the chief end of man is not to attain prosperity and security, but to glorify God and enjoy him forever. And anybody well versed in the Bible would be able to tell us that the kind of security and prosperity it talks about are very different from the kind that the negotiators of Hong Kong's future are talking about. Somehow, we Christians need to translate these ideas into terms that the secular world can understand and live them out in a way that will cause the secular world to take notice.

Another thing we Christians could contribute to these troubled times is a demonstration of calm commitment to our people and our place. At a time when people are rushing to buy property overseas, making investments abroad, planning to study in foreign parts never to return, preparing to abandon ship at the first sign of trouble, we Christians could be a stabilizing influence in our community by demonstrating with our feet and through our faith that our roots run deep, our commitment is strong and our mission is clear. Our Gospel reflects a tradition of believers standing firm in times of adversity, inwardly thriving while outwardly surviving. Hong Kong is watching to see if we are going to stand in that tradition. Unfortunately, there are some signs that point in the opposite direction. Not a few Christians are in the front of the line hoping to head for other shores. Some denominations are experiencing a shortage of experienced pastors, having lost them to Chinese congregations abroad....

A third thing we Christians could contribute would be to get serious about beginning what has been termed a new missionary movement to the poor. The poor make up the majority of the population here, and, as Jesus said, they will always be with us. They have nowhere to run to! They are stuck here for good or for ill and will have to make the best of it come what may. They are at present conspicuously absent from the majority of our congregations. We must reach out to them for their sakes and for our own sakes. They are likely to be the wave of the future in Hong Kong, and without them, the church here will perhaps have no future."[16]

The 1997 discussion pot was beginning to boil. Three more leading churchmen summed up the various viewpoints emerging among Hong Kong's Christians in the December 1983 issue of *News & Views*. Christopher Morris, a staff member of the Chinese Church Research Centre, voiced the fear that Hong Kong might

> "simply become a colony of China rather than of England." He made three predictions: "Nearly all the missionaries will leave.... Many Chinese Christians will also leave....But the majority of Chinese Christians will be staying and will experience life under a Communist regime, many for the second time in their lives." He argued that "the need for preparation now overshadows the old problems among Christians in Hong Kong, whether of deep denominational divisions, lack of theological knowledge, over-emphasis on institutions, or even lack of commitment in many Christians....For churches, responding to the urgency of the situation would mean strengthening individual and small group fellowship, exploring ways of informal friendship evangelism, starting leadership and theological training for small groups of laymen, and financially sponsoring seminary studies and missionary experiences for church members."

He concluded that the key to learning how to live with what was coming was to support China's Christians and to learn from their experience.[17]

Andrew Chiu, president of Concordia Theological Seminary, pointed out that five schools of thought had developed among Hong Kong's Christians concerning the 1997 hand-over. The school of optimism: When sovereignty is turned back to China, the church will change its wrong inclination and have a new opportunity to be concerned about the common people. The school of pessimism: The history of mainland China is an example of what will happen in the future. China's Christians tried to relate to the Three-Self Patriotic Movement but were persecuted in one way or another. The same will happen in Hong Kong when the sovereignty of Hong Kong reverts to

---

[16] Ibid., 3.
[17] Pp. 7–8.

China. The school of ostriches: Simply carry on as before and don't worry about it. Ignore the danger and it will go away. The school of Jonah: Run away from it. Escape overseas and save your skins. The school of responsibility-bearing: We have a responsibility to bear the past mistakes of the church, but also to bear the problems of the church in the future so that it will not fall into the same mistakes.

He went on to say, "The political atmosphere in Mainland China has changed very often, and our hope is always that it will change for the better; but, at the same time, we need to prepare for the worst." He then offered seven suggestions as to how the church should prepare for 1997.

1. We should not be building-centered, but believer-centered.
2. We should not be denomination-centered, but Christ-centered.
3. We should not be preacher-centered, but lay-centered.
4. We should not be missionary-centered, but indigenous-centered.
5. We should not be self-centered, but community-centered.
6. We should not be Hong Kongese, but Chinese.
7. We should not be naive idealists, but realistic pragmatists.

He concluded by saying,

After 1997, it is very possible that there will be much restriction on the coming in and the going out of foreign missionaries. It is also possible that the Government will have control of foreign exchange. Also, it may no longer be possible to send people from Hong Kong churches to other lands as missionaries. The opportunity to broadcast the Gospel and to publish religious books might not be so free as it is today. Present church organizations, such as schools and social centers, may be forced into a completely different mold or even eliminated. Questions like these need to be discussed in the Church and the necessary steps must be taken to arrange things for the future.[18]

Philip Lam, executive secretary for mission for the Hong Kong Christian Council, discussed 1997 and original sin.

Original sin is hereditary and destructive. 1997, a legacy of the past, is now proving destructive, and nobody in this Colony can

---

[18] Ibid., 7–11.

escape from it....Some people are experiencing a growing sense of hopelessness, pessimism and total frustration. Others are affected by a growing erosion of commitment. Socially, the sin of 1997 has proliferated into currency speculation, run-away inflation, the flight of capital and talented people and the bleeding of the city. Like original sin, 1997 is hurting everybody. But where is our grace, our forgiveness and hope? This is dependent on our repentance and renewed commitment. God's grace is present if we can reaffirm that Hong Kong has been built by the sweat and blood of the people of Hong Kong, and is not something that has been given to us from outside. We need to better this city, not only for us, but also for our sons and daughters, grandsons and granddaughters. God's grace is present if we can take up the responsibility which has been given to us by the historical process, and which, we believe, is in the hands of God, the Lord of history. The content of our responsibility to the future is to be our own master. God's grace is present if we can affirm our identity as Chinese—neither American-Chinese, nor British-Chinese but Chinese in a Chinese land. For Christians who can commit themselves and work for the future, 1997 is surely a good chance to root our faith in the Chinese soil, a good opportunity to get involved in the shaping of a new Hong Kong.

He concluded by using the example of the apostles staying in Jerusalem to minister in a tough context as a model for local Chinese ministers who were thinking of deserting the church to go abroad. He urged the church to focus on a mission to its Hong Kong compatriots rather than on a mission to the Chinese in the mainland. He called for a renewed commitment based on faith and hope rather than succumbing to a gospel of despair based on fear.[19]

In November 1983, Lo Lung-kwong, a Methodist pastor and seminary lecturer, wrote a major paper in which he set out twelve principles for a Christian approach to 1997 "that are derived from the viewpoints of Hong Kong Christians who have different denominational and theological backgrounds" and their implications for Hong Kong's reversion to China.

1. God is the Lord of history.
2. God entrusts people to rule.
3. The church is the body of Christ.

[19]   Ibid., 11–12, 21.

4. The "state" refers to a territory created by God as well as to the people living in it.

5. China is an Asian country whose territory was illegally trespassed upon by foreign powers. In returning those territories, the wishes of the people living there must be respected.

6. Hong Kong is a part of Chinese territory.

7. Hong Kong is a "free" society.

8. Hong Kong's political status will change.

9. Hong Kong's people should remain confident in Hong Kong's future.

10. Hong Kong's people should have the right to administer Hong Kong democratically.

11. The Chinese Communist authorities must prove themselves worthy of the trust of Hong Kong's people.

12. Whatever changes may come, the church must remain faithful to its priestly and prophetic calling.[20]

The British over the Barrel

By the time serious negotiations got under way in July 1983, another career diplomat, Edward Youde, had succeeded Murray MacLehose as governor of Hong Kong. China refused to allow him to participate in the talks as Hong Kong's representative. He could only be a member of the British delegation, since the talks were between China and Britain. There was to be no "three-legged stool." The Chinese said that since Hong Kong belonged to them, *they* would represent the people of Hong Kong. The British acquiesced, with the result that the people of Hong Kong had no representative and no say in the vital decisions concerning their future. Youde did brief and consult the unofficial members of the Executive Council (UMELCO) throughout the negotiations, but the people had not elected them. The British position was that it was willing to relinquish sovereignty in exchange for continuing to administer Hong Kong for as long as possible beyond 1997. The Chinese refused to separate sovereignty and administration. To them, this was merely replacing an old unequal treaty with a new one. China announced that it would recover *both* sovereignty *and* administration in 1997.

---

[20] "A Tentative Search for a Standpoint in Envisaging the Future of Hong Kong," *News & Views*, March 1984, 18–20.

Hong Kong reacted to this development with even greater panic. By the fall of 1983, the Hong Kong dollar had slid to 40 percent of its value, and local residents started to stock up on essentials. Confidence was restored only by the British taking the drastic action of cutting the Hong Kong dollar loose from the British pound sterling and pegging it to the U.S. dollar.

Meanwhile, the Chinese announced that unless agreement was reached within a year, they would impose a unilateral solution. Once again, the British gave ground, conceding that without PRC cooperation, they would be unable to administer the colony after 1997. Furthermore, they had now painted themselves into the corner of avoiding the breakdown of the talks at any price. In November 1983, they announced that Britain would relinquish all authority over Hong Kong in 1997. The British bottom line then shifted to "extracting concessions of substance from Peking and enshrining them in a binding agreement...within the Chinese timetable."[21] China, of course, did not want a detailed agreement. A compromise was reached with the two sides agreeing to a relatively brief statement with three annexes. The British worked hard to make suggestions and explain how Hong Kong worked in the hope that the Chinese would adopt their suggestions in the final agreement. This worked to an extent. Under pressure to meet its own announced deadline, China agreed to a number of these ideas, including ideas defining the scope of political developments in the period of transition and the basis for Hong Kong's future. In order to ensure a smooth transition, a Sino-British Joint Liaison Group was set up for mutual consultation during the thirteen years leading up to the handover and for the first three years following it. The central focus was on securing the territory's prosperity and stability.[22]

Dialogue in Beijing

So far, most of the public Christian comment on 1997 and its implications for the church had come from the ecumenical camp. However, the events of 1983–84 had finally stirred the evangelical camp to action. As the HKCC's Philip Lam put it:

> Though not totally monopolized by them, it is surely true that topics like human rights, democracy, freedom, social concerns, social involvement, etc. are the favorites of ecumenicals in their

21   Cradock, Percy, *Experiences of China*, 197.
22   Dimbleby, *Last Governor*, 58–62.

theological discussions. On the other hand, the favorite topics of evangelicals and fundamentalists are overseas missions, commitment, spiritual life, discipleship, evangelism, etc. But suddenly, with unthinkable speed, the evangelicals are changing topics. They have started to talk about human rights, democracy and social concerns in their devotional meetings and seminars, and to talk loudly.

The latest example was a Biblical Seminar sponsored by Christian Communications Limited, an Overseas Missionary Fellowship-related para-church agency in Hong Kong. The theme of the seminar was: "The Biblical Perspective on Human rights, Freedom, Democracy and the Legal System"....[This] lecture series is only one of the recent events that indicate a significant emerging phenomenon—the radical politicization of Hong Kong's evangelicals. Why have they suddenly become so socially conscious?...The obvious answer is the appearance of the ominous year of 1997 over the horizon and the threat that it poses to religious freedom. The Government of China has had a notorious record of having suppressed religious activities in China after 1949, and it is only in recent years that religious activities have been allowed to take place with limited freedom. This threat is in fact not only felt by evangelicals, but by all Christians in Hong Kong who have a similar anxiety...Christians in Hong Kong, facing the same destiny and the same anxiety, will surely have more and more in common to talk to each other about as time goes on.[23]

This was to put it mildly. By the end of August of that same year, the evangelical and ecumenical camps had issued a joint "Manifesto of the Protestant Churches in Hong Kong on Religious Freedom." More than one hundred Christians from different denominations and theological traditions had been consulted by the drafters over a six-month period of intense and prayerful dialogue (a first in Hong Kong's ecclesiastical history). One hundred well-known church leaders had signed an open appeal to Christian groups to support the manifesto. Within six weeks, twelve denominational bodies, two hundred churches, five theological seminaries, and forty-four Christian organizations and groups responded. On August 31, the manifesto and its list of supporters was sent to the Hong Kong representatives of the

[23] Lam, Philip, "Common Ground," *News & Views*, June 1984, 22.

Stationery of some
denominations that
endorsed the manifesto

Chinese and British governments with the message, "It is hoped that, in the drafting of the Basic Law and in carrying out the policy in regard to religion after 1997, consideration and respect will be given to religious freedom which all along has been enjoyed by the churches in Hong Kong for over a hundred years."[24]

The manifesto leaned heavily on the concept of human rights, with free religious expression as one of those God-given rights. It then spelled out in specific and practical terms how that right was expressed in Hong Kong with regard to the individual, the family, and the church. With regard to the church, the manifesto dealt with the right of assembly, evangelism and spiritual nurture, service and witness, the use of human and other resources, organization and management, and any other work related to the church. In its closing paragraphs, the manifesto declared,

> We earnestly hope that the church in Hong Kong will be able to enjoy and exercise these rights and freedoms after 1997. We believe that Christians should commit themselves to the keeping and development of a society that respects human rights. Christians in Hong Kong have the responsibility to make Hong Kong a place where people will continue to live in freedom, stability and prosperity even after its sovereignty reverts to China. They also have the duty to champion the cause of human rights and democracy, and thus to contribute to the future happiness of the Chinese people.[25]

---

[24] "Manifesto of the Protestant Churches in Hong Kong on Religious Freedom," *News & Views*, Oct. 1984, 1.

[25] Ibid., 1–3.

The reaction from Beijing was swift and surprisingly positive. A broadly representative delegation of twenty-two Protestant church leaders was invited to the capital by the Religious Affairs Bureau from September 6–8 to exchange views with Ji Peng-fei, head of the Hong Kong and Macau Office, and Madam Chow En-lai, chair of the National People's Congress. The talks centered on the future of Hong Kong in general and religious freedom after 1997 in particular. A carefully drafted position paper on the future of Hong Kong was presented during the consultation. This paper dealt with a much broader range of issues than the manifesto. The preamble stated, "Reversion of Hong Kong's sovereignty to China in 1997 is indisputable and reasonable. We believe that self-administration with a high degree of autonomy under the principle of 'one country, two systems' is the best solution for Hong Kong's future."[26] It then went on to discuss the delegation's views of Hong Kong:

1. Hong Kong's economic success has been made possible by the interplay of a free and open social climate, the rule of law, and the noninterventionist policy of the government.
2. The moral problems and social inequities of Hong Kong need to be rectified.
3. To ensure Hong Kong's future stability and prosperity, a government with credibility and authority needs to be set up. This government must be directly answerable to the people; strive to further Hong Kong's economic development without jeopardizing the interests of the silent majority; and preserve the independence of the legislative, judicial, and executive branches.
4. Hong Kong's current efficient government machinery can be gradually improved, but there should not be drastic and disruptive changes.
5. Hong Kong must continue to maintain and develop its international links. Its citizens should be free to travel and conduct business abroad.
6. The people of Hong Kong are entitled to participate in the process of drawing up and amending the Basic Law. This law should only be able to be amended by the Hong Kong government in consultation with the people. Its content must

[26] "Position Paper on the Future of Hong Kong," *News & Views*, Dec. 1984, 14–16.

Hong Kong
factory worker

be based on the principles of freedom, openness, rule of law, and respect for human rights.

7. The Hong Kong authorities must not overemphasize the interests of investors and professionals to the detriment of the rights and needs of workers. Workers should have freedom to choose their jobs, to have job security, to be protected against withheld wages and wanton dismissal, to strike, to organize and participate in trade unions, to bargain collectively, etc.

8. The public investment in education must under no circumstances be cut. Rather, it must be strengthened at all levels. The curriculum must be further diversified, Chinese must be adopted as the language of instruction, and moral education must be emphasized.

9. In the future, a comprehensive social security system must gradually be set up to provide all the people with the basic needs for their welfare.

10. Democratization of the political system on a gradual basis must begin immediately to prepare the people of Hong Kong for self-administration.

In addition to the manifesto previously presented to the Chinese and Hong Kong governments, the following views were expressed on the church:

1. The future Hong Kong administration will have to maintain its noninterventionist policy in the areas of freedom of thought, religion, and choice of life-style.

2. The religious freedoms and activities that the people of Hong Kong enjoy, as outlined in "A Manifesto on Religious Freedom," should be stated in detail in the Basic Law.

3. Hong Kong's churches should be able to continue to contribute

to the renewal of Hong Kong's social, moral, and spiritual life through their social, educational, and medical services that were initiated to provide what was not being adequately provided by the colonial government.

4. The government subsidization of these services should be continued in the future.

5. The links that Hong Kong's churches have with churches and Christians around the world from different denominational traditions should be maintained.

The document concluded, "As Christians in Hong Kong, we reaffirm our faith in God and our commitment to Hong Kong and the Church here. We identify ourselves as Chinese. We love our country and its people. We are with our compatriots in China for better or for worse...."[27]

What a remarkable document! If anybody had predicted five years earlier that a broad cross-section of Hong Kong's Christians would come together in this fashion and agree to speak so directly and boldly, not only about the church's internal concerns, but also about the community's social, economic, and even political needs, that person would have been considered a lunatic. Hong Kong's Christians had come a long way in understanding that gospel concerns include all aspects of life and society, and that the church, particularly in times of crisis, has a responsibility to be the voice of the people, whatever the risk.

The only fly in the ointment, as pointed out by a respected church leader, Dr. Timothy Chow, was that there was no mention of the relationship of the Hong Kong church to the church in China. What should that relationship be?[28] On the one hand, some feared that after the handover, the Hong Kong churches would be forced to come under the aegis of the Chinese Three-self Patriotic Movement. This conjured up disturbing memories of how Chinese Christians had been severely persecuted in the past, not only by the Chinese government, but also by some within the Three-self Movement, persecution that had only recently begun to ease. Would strict oversight of their lives and curtailment of their evangelistic and social service activities ensue if the Three-Self Patriotic Movement became their "big brother" after 1997? On the other hand, many Hong Kong Christians wanted to establish

27 Ibid.
28 Chou, Timothy, "Comments on the Position Paper," *News & Views*, Dec. 1984, 3.

The HKCCC's
Dr. Peter Wong
pouring tea for the
China CCC's
Bishop K. H. Ting
(right) in 1984

better contacts with, and give support and encouragement to, their Christian brothers and sisters on the mainland.

A good start had already been made in this regard. It had been an exciting day for all of us when a Chinese church delegation, led by K.H. Ting, had broken the ice with a very successful visit to the Hong Kong Christian Council and the Christian Conference of Asia in 1980.[29] Since that time, a number of visits and exchanges had taken place among pastors, church leaders, young people, and social service personnel, and relations between the newly formed China Christian Council[30] and the churches in Hong Kong had developed apace. But, despite assurances from our Chinese visitors, nobody yet knew exactly what the relationship would be between Hong Kong's churches and the church in China after 1997.

The Hong Kong delegation returned from Beijing encouraged by the results of their consultation. Assurances were given that the views expressed in the manifesto and in the position paper would be taken seriously and that religious freedom would be guaranteed.

Celebrating Christ

Meanwhile, in the United States, Reformed Church Women (the women's program of the Reformed Church in America) was planning to focus on Asia in 1984 and had asked if Joyce and I would be willing to produce a program introducing the Asian context and highlighting Reformed Church mission efforts there. They were particularly

---

[29]   See "HKCC News," *News & Views*, June 1981, 1, 14, for a detailed account of that visit. I had first met Bishop Ting and his colleagues in China in May 1980 as part of a Hong Kong Christian study group that spent more than two weeks visiting Chinese churches and church leaders. See Karsen, Wendell, "A New Chapter in Acts," *Church Herald*, Oct. 31, 1980, 4–15.

[30]   The China Christian Council was formed in October 1980.

interested in Taiwan, Hong Kong, Japan, India, and the Philippines. We accepted the challenge, pleased that there was active interest in the part of the world that had been our home and the focus of our mission for fourteen years.

The program we produced was entitled "Celebrating Christ in Asia Today." Its objectives were that participants would learn about the context and churches of the Asian nations where RCA personnel were at work; that they would learn something about the ministries of those churches and the role of RCA missionaries in those ministries; that they would celebrate the unity in diversity that Christians in Asia and North America shared; that their commitment to support the mission of Christ in Asia would increase; and that they would learn what American Christians could receive from their Asian brothers and sisters in terms of goals for mission and ministry.

The program included fact sheets for the five countries covered and an audio tape containing Asian music, hymns, prayers, scripture readings in indigenous languages, and interviews that Joyce conducted with five Asian women. Each meeting place was to be transformed into a jet plane cabin and the participants "flown" to Asia. They were then to be taken on "tours" of the five Asian countries by visiting five booths where they could sample food, obtain information, and meet "Asians" dressed in their national dress who would introduce them to their countries, cultures, churches, cuisines, and missionary characters. The experience would be capped by a worship service using the taped material.[31]

The Sino-British Joint Declaration

On September 26, 1984, China and Great Britain issued the Sino-British Joint Declaration that came into force in May 1985. The agreement stated that sovereignty over the whole of Hong Kong would be transferred to the People's Republic of China on July 1, 1997. During the transitional period, the British would be "responsible" for the administration of Hong Kong, to which the PRC would "give its cooperation." After 1997, Hong Kong would become a "Special Administrative Region" (SAR) of China and would "enjoy a high degree of autonomy, except in foreign and defense affairs." It would be "vested with executive, legislative, and independent judicial power, including that of final adjudication," where the "laws currently in

[31] See Karsen, "Celebrating Christ in Asia" correspondence and materials, pr.p., May–July, 1984.

Fate of Hong Kong decided
by Sino-British 1984
Joint Declaration

force in Hong Kong will remain basically unchanged." Its government would be "composed of local inhabitants" and its chief executive would be appointed by the Chinese government "on the basis of the results of elections or consultations to be held locally." The SAR's principal officials would be "nominated by the chief executive...for appointment by" the Chinese government. "Foreign nationals previously working in the public and police services in the government departments of Hong Kong" would "remain in employment." It would keep the current social and economic systems as well as the existing life-style, whereby "rights and freedom, including those of the person, of speech, of the press, of assembly, of association, of travel, of movement, and of correspondence, of strike, of choice of occupation, of academic research and of religious belief" would "be ensured by law."

Private property, ownership of enterprises, legitimate rights of inheritance, and foreign investments would also be protected by law. Hong Kong would remain "a free port and a separate customs territory." It would "retain the status of an international financial center, as well as its markets for foreign exchange, gold, securities, and futures." It would continue to enjoy the free flow of capital and a freely convertible currency. It would not be subject to taxation from China and would have independent finances. It would have the right to "establish mutually beneficial economic relations with the United Kingdom and other countries," and "conclude relevant agreements with states, regions, and relevant international organizations" for economic and cultural purposes. Its government would be able to "on its own issue documents for entry into and exit from Hong Kong" and would be responsible for maintaining public order there. These commitments would be implemented through the drafting of a "Basic Law" for the SAR to be promulgated by the National People's Congress, which would "remain unchanged for fifty years."[32]

When the declaration was announced, the people of Hong Kong, especially its Christians, heaved a collective sigh of relief. These were terms they could live with. A naive euphoria set in and confidence was restored. However, there were those who pointed out that the fulfillment of the commitments made in the joint declaration would ultimately depend on the PRC's goodwill and sincerity, and on its ability to interpret correctly the rather general terms of the declaration. The Communist track record in this regard had not exactly been encouraging. Furthermore, it had become obvious that the British government did not have the will or the power to try to enforce the agreement should the PRC not abide by it or deviate from it. Still, even if the declaration was not airtight, since the people of Hong Kong had no choice or voice in the matter, this agreement was much better than no agreement.

The entire December 1984 issue of *News & Views* was devoted to the Sino-British Joint Declaration and its implications for the church. Views were expressed by a representative plethora of church leaders: Paul Clasper, dean of St. John's Cathedral; Carl Smith, church historian at Chung Chi College; Lo Lung-kwong, Methodist pastor; Ken Anderson, pastor of the English-speaking Methodist church; Chung Yuk Sum, Student Christian Movement executive; Alan Chan, head of the Chung Chi College Theology Division; and Harold Naylor, ecumenical officer for the Roman Catholic Church, all highly respected colleagues and friends. The Hong Kong Christian Council's general secretary, Kwok Nai-wang, provided the most comprehensive and prescient coverage in a speech he delivered to the Hong Kong Clergy and Ministers Association.

Kwok gave three reasons why Hong Kong's Christians could accept the joint declaration:

1. Because it provides opportunities for the people in Hong Kong to be able to govern themselves through an elected government.

[32] "The Sino-British Joint Declaration on the Future of Hong Kong," *Hong Kong 1985*, Government Information Services, 1–15.

2. Because it provides for all the basic ingredients that have led to the success of Hong Kong for at least fifty years beyond 1997.

3. Because it provides for the rights and freedoms of religious belief (along with other crucial individual rights and freedoms), and for the right for the churches to continue to provide social services, foster international relationships, and relate to the church in China on the basis of mutual respect and independence.

However, Kwok was quick to note the considerable hurdles and pitfalls that remained before high-sounding principles could be turned into practical realities. Little did he realize at the time how prophetic his words would turn out to be.

1. The form and structure of the future government in Hong Kong needs to be spelled out in greater detail, in particular the power and authority of the chief executive and the process for his election.

2. The stationing of troops in Hong Kong by the Central People's government may be inevitable, but their accountability needs to be carefully spelled out.

3. No matter how well the Basic Law is worked out, there will always be points that require further clarification or interpretation. The agreement has not made clear where the final authority to interpret the Basic Law will rest and has not developed the process whereby it may be amended.

For each hurdle, he offered a number of specific suggestions.

He then laid out four implications of the agreement for the church.

1. The church must prepare its members well for the radical political changes in the coming years. It needs to draw ever closer to the people, understand their fears, be a source of strength to them, and when necessary, speak for the "voiceless."

2. The PRC has said that although the Basic Law will be implemented by the Central People's government, Hong Kong people will have ample opportunities to air their opinions as to how that law should be drafted. The church must seize this opportunity to give as much input as possible. This gives further opportunity for all Christians in Hong Kong to strengthen and build upon the unity that has already been established through the issuing of the manifesto and the position paper.

3. Since the goal is to have a fully elected legislature by 1994,

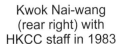

Kwok Nai-wang
(rear right) with
HKCC staff in 1983

the churches, through their congregations, seminaries, and educational institutions, should combat political apathy, nurture citizenship training, and encourage people to register to vote.

4. Hong Kong and China's stability and prosperity are inextricably linked. Christians need to encourage Hong Kong people to make significant contributions to the modernization and reform program in China. A process of Sinoization needs to begin in our language and culture in order to help us rediscover our cultural roots and heritage after having been cut off from China for so many years.

Kwok concluded by throwing out a ringing challenge to the church.

> Whether the "agreement" regarding the future of Hong Kong can be worked out or not depends on four major factors: the sincerity of the Chinese; the cooperation of the British and Hong Kong governments; acceptance by the international community; and the determination and commitment of the people of Hong Kong....the first three factors are there, but the most important factor is missing....The people of Hong Kong are in dire need of a guiding force. I believe the church, with its spiritual qualities and commitment to the people, can play this role. It is time for the church in Hong Kong to re-dedicate itself and take on that unenviable role—to guide the people of Hong Kong through 1997 and beyond.[33]

The Hong Kong church had become determined to make its voice heard in the public realm. It was not going to carry the colonial cross any longer, and it was serving notice that it did not intend to replace it with the cross of communism.

[33] Kwok, Nai-wang, "The Church and the Joint Declaration," *News & Views*, Dec. 1984, 1–4.

The people of Hong Kong—caught in the middle

Defining 'Democracy'

Democratic Britain was now in the ironic position of having to introduce democratic reforms in colonial Hong Kong to meet socialist China's "democratic" expectations. The British had wanted an agreement so badly that they had not insisted that the declaration spell out how, and how much, political power was to be handed over to the people of Hong Kong. In fact, British and Chinese assumptions about what this meant were inherently contradictory. This contradiction formed the center of the ensuing struggle of the people of Hong Kong for a true democracy, a struggle that continues to this day. The British were reluctant to give too much too soon for fear the Chinese would panic and break the agreement. The Chinese, in turn, looked at elections as a public exercise in which the outcome could be determined in advance. They also suspected that the British wanted to set up a political structure whose strings, and especially whose purse strings, they could continue to control from behind the scenes long after 1997.

Steve Tang sums it up succinctly.

> Britain set its role in the transitional period as that of a custodian of its own and Hong Kong's best interests. It also recognized the need to secure the blessings of the PRC for its policies there...the rationale behind Britain's Hong Kong policy was to withdraw with honor....If Britain mismanaged the transition and public confidence snapped, Hong Kong's economy would collapse. The British Treasury would then have to bail Hong Kong out until arrangements could be made for the PRC to take over ahead of the appointed date. An exodus from Hong Kong in a crisis would likewise create a huge problem of refugee relief for which Britain could not but play the leading role....Britain thought it had considerable latitude to continue to run the territory until

1997 through the Hong Kong Government in accordance with established practice...the transition was to ensure that the pieces would be in place for the Chinese takeover. Little would need to be done apart from a formal hand-over of sovereignty....the British did not recognize the signing of the Joint Declaration marked the beginning of the end of their preeminence in the politics of Hong Kong....Britain would not transfer power to the local people but would relinquish political authority to a new metropolitan power, the PRC. The PRC, in turn, would empower the people of Hong Kong, through the Basic Law, to establish a Special Administrative Region....[The British] proceeded on the assumption that they would have a free hand to reform Hong Kong's political system within the framework defined by the Joint Declaration. They attempted to introduce democratization.... The idea of democratizing Hong Kong's political system was important both to political and public opinion in Britain for accepting the retrocession of Hong Kong...the Chinese regime under Deng was a Communist Party state with a poor record in human rights....Britain would hand over about six million people to this regime. More than half of them were British nationals by birth and the rest had run away from this regime to seek the protection of the British flag.[34]

The Hong Kong government opened the first crack in the colonial political wall by allowing indirect elections for twenty-four of the Legislative Council's fifty-six members in 1985. Twelve were "elected" by an electoral college that was made up of the chairs of nineteen district boards, whose members had been directly elected by narrowly "qualified" voters within their districts. Twelve were "elected" by members of functional constituencies representing various professional, commercial, and industrial groups.[35]

Only six months after this first feeble step towards democratic government, the hopes of Hong Kong's people for a smooth transition to democracy were dashed. Alarmed at Britain's intention to carry out the terms of the declaration and its plans for democratic reforms literally, China's representative in Hong Kong, Xu Jia-tun, announced that political reforms in Hong Kong had to *converge* with the SAR's Basic Law (whose content, coincidentally, would be determined by China's interpretation of the terms of the declaration). The drafting of this law

[34]   Tsang, *Hong Kong*, 112–14.
[35]   Cameron, *Illustrated History*, 325.

The Legislative Council
Building

was only then in the beginning stages and would not be promulgated until five years later in 1990. By then, it would be too late for Britain to gradually implement full democratic reforms by 1997, as prescribed in the joint declaration, which provided for "an elected legislature by 1997 and an executive accountable to it."[36]

This move, in essence, was a Chinese veto of the British understanding of the terms of the joint declaration. The British, constantly fearing a unilateral move on the part of China if agreement could not be reached, caved in again. Despite their public promises to the people of Hong Kong, they secretly agreed not to introduce any major political reform until the Basic Law was promulgated in 1990, and then do nothing that would breach the Basic Law. Part of the rationale for this agreement was to introduce such reforms as could be introduced by 1995, and then let that legislature span the handover in order to ensure a smooth transition. This idea became known as the "through train." It set the stage for twelve years of tense maneuvering and tortuous negotiations between the two governments, with the people of Hong Kong caught in between.[37]

It was within this context that the drafting of the Basic Law (amounting to a miniconstitution for Hong Kong) commenced. The British viewed the law as simply an instrument whereby the terms of Annex I of the 1984 Sino-British Joint Declaration would be spelled out in appropriate legal form. The Chinese considered the law to be a subsidiary of their own constitution and were determined to make it serve their best interests. The people of Hong Kong regarded the law as a symbol of China's sincerity and as the instrument that would preserve their "system" and their way of life for at least fifty years.

36   "Sino-British Joint Declaration," 4.
37   Tsang, *Hong Kong*, 124–26.

Realizing that it had to win over the Hong Kong population, in July 1985, the PRC's National People's Congress decided to appoint 23 specially selected Hong Kong members to a 59-member Basic Law Drafting Committee (BLDC). It also appointed a 180-member Basic Law Consultative Committee (BLCC), composed of a variety of Hong Kong residents, to give advice and counsel. The BLDC was divided into five task groups: political system; PRC/SAR relations; SAR residents' rights; economic and finance; and education, science, technology, culture, sports, and religion. The design was to give Hong Kong people a *say* in the drafting process, while China retained *control* of the process. That process was to follow the classic Maoist methodology of the mass line and the united front. Local members were to conduct the initial drafting process with the invisible hand of the Communist Party guiding them. A draft was to be submitted to Beijing that was then to be sent back to Hong Kong for public consultation. Finally, local members were to complete the drafting work and resubmit the final product to Beijing for formal promulgation by the NPC. Beijing's basic approach was to allow maximum flexibility within a rigid framework. Its major concern was that its ultimate control not be undermined. Once it was assured of this, it was willing to consider the proposals and concerns expressed by Hong Kong's people.[38]

The Church Speaks Up

Taking these developments as a key opportunity to attempt to influence this whole process, Hong Kong church leaders, spearheaded by the Hong Kong Christian Council, sprang into action. They were not going to sit idly by and end up exchanging the cross of colonialism for the cross of communism. The council hired legal expert Iris Tsang as a full-time staff member to give the church legal advice concerning the drafting of the Basic Law.[39] A seminar on civic education was organized which declared, "To facilitate Hong Kong's political transition from a Crown Colony to a democratic self-governing SAR of the PRC in 1997, the promotion of civic education is absolutely essential."[40] Christian leaders formed a Committee of Christian Concern for the Basic Law. Its aim was to "continually reflect the wishes and opinions of Hong Kong people and to make appropriate responses."[41] The committee

---

[38]   Ibid., 149, 154.
[39]   Kwok, Nai-wang, "The Employment of a Lawyer," *News & Views*, June 1985, 6.
[40]   Ibid, 1.
[41]   "Christian Concern for the Basic Law," *News & Views*, Spring 1986, 7.

included eleven church leaders as advisors, an assembly of clergy, and work groups on political, legal, economic, and social issues; religious freedom; and human rights and personal freedom.

A forum was held that featured as guest speaker Lu Ping, secretary general of the PRC's Hong Kong and Macau Affairs Office and deputy secretary-general of the Basic Law Drafting Committee. Lu assured the large gathering of religious representatives that religious freedom would be written into the law, that the government would continue to subsidize schools, hospitals, and social work programs run by religious and other volunteer bodies, and that it would also provide free land for churches and temples.[42] The January 19–22, 1986, Mid-decade Consultation on the Mission of the Church in Hong Kong in the '80s featured 1997-related issues in all aspects of its deliberations, particularly the church's responsibility to help shape the new Basic Law. The preamble of its declaration stated, "The agenda for discussion reveals a deep tension and a rising sense of political awareness and responsibility for the Territory within the Church in general."[43] Two Hong Kong Christian Council staff members were sent on a democracy study tour to Britain and Sweden. Their incisive reports and applications to Hong Kong's situation, along with several other articles by people like Martin Lee, prominent Roman Catholic and a member of the Legislative Council, were featured in the September 1986 issue of *News & Views*.[44]

In November 1986, the government called for the public to make its views known on the future political structure of Hong Kong so that those views could be incorporated into the 1987 political review. In that same month, the Basic Law Drafting Committee decided to defer discussion on the SAR's future political system so that there would be more time to collect public views on the subject. Hot debate raged in Hong Kong, with proposals and counter proposals grabbing the headlines. Democrats not only found themselves contending with a reluctant China, but also with the well-healed Hong Kong business tycoons who wanted to keep things pretty much the way they were in Hong Kong and score points with Beijing in the process. Their representatives on the Basic Law Consultative Committee issued what became known as "the 57 proposal,"[45] a proposal that more or less

---

[42] "The Basic Law—Hong Kong's Blueprint for the Future," *News & Views*, Spring 1986, 8.

[43] "Hong Kong's Ecumenical Priorities," *News & Views*, 2, 7.

[44] "Hong Kong and Democracy," *News & Views*, Sept. 1986, 12–18.

[45] Named for its fifty-seven sponsors on the BLCC.

Democracy rally

advocated on-going rule by an oligarchy after 1997.

This prompted an immediate counter proposal, dubbed the "190 proposal,"[46] and also the first public mass rally in support of democracy for Hong Kong. The newly formed Joint Committee for the Promotion of Democratic Government organized the rally at Ko Shan. Half of the twelve speakers were prominent Christians, the HKCC's general secretary, Kwok Nai-wang, among them. Seventeen pages in the December 1986 issue of *News & Views* were filled with carefully worked out position papers and the expressed views of a wide variety of Christians. Iris Tsang wrote, "Ever since the publication of the Green paper on 'The Development of Representative Government' in July 1984, Christians in Hong Kong have been active in promoting democracy in Hong Kong. In a pragmatic society such as Hong Kong, the belief of Christians provides an ideological foundation for the cause of having a more open and democratic form of government. Man is born equal and should have equal political rights. It is this conviction and commitment to the well being of society that the Hong Kong Christian Council has in the past years abided by and held fast."[47]

Over the next year, the drafting of the Basic Law and the Hong Kong government's political review dominated the scene, both in Hong Kong at large and in the church. The April 1987 issue of *News & Views* was devoted to the Basic Law and religious freedom. It also reprinted a substantial essay by a PRC "front" man, San Wei-sze, which had appeared in the Chinese press and had sparked a public debate. San had argued that religious freedom did not mean freedom to "meddle in

---

[46] Named for its 190 prominent democratically minded sponsors, supported by 25 BLCC members.

[47] Tsang, Iris Y.L., "The Ko Shan Mass Rally," *News & Views*, Sept. 1986, 12–18.

politics." The Christian church in general and the Hong Kong Christian Council in particular should, he said, respect the separation of church and state and stay out of political and social issues. If they didn't, there could be "unpleasant consequences."

This essay touched a raw nerve in the church and was viewed as a warning shot across the bow. However, without hesitation, a well-crafted four-page editorial rebuttal by then *News & Views* editor, Richard Worssam, made it abundantly clear that, come what may, the Hong Kong church would not be cowed. "Being a believer in this world is to commit oneself to the whole destiny of mankind, and it is therefore right to be involved in politics in order to build a just, equal and caring society....As long as religious activities do not break the law, the government should not intervene. Whether Christians get involved in politics or not is an internal matter for the churches, and outsiders should not have the power to dictate the behavior of Christians as long as they remain within the law. Therefore, on this level there *should* be a separation between church and state."[48]

A Shameful Subterfuge

Having in 1984 announced their intention publicly to proceed with full democratic reforms in Hong Kong, the British now had to find a way to keep their secret commitment to the Chinese while not seeming to back down in the eyes of the people of Hong Kong. In 1987, the Hong Kong government published a green paper on political reforms for public comment that, instead of specific goals, laid out general obscure principles. This move did not fool anybody, especially Hong Kong's Christians. The July 1987 issue of *News & Views* dealt with the theme, "Is Democracy Dangerous?" and was aimed at debunking the myth of the commercial/industrial oligarchy that democracy would destabilize Hong Kong. It also carried extensive critical comment on the government's green paper: "The 1987 Review of Developments in Representative Government." The editor wrote,

> The Green Paper obscures [the issue of direct legislative elections in 1988] behind an almost impenetrable jungle of possible alternatives and minor issues in a publication of 42 pages and 170 paragraphs that hardly makes for bedtime reading....It offers no sense of direction or guidance...it reveals a bias in favor of the status quo....The way the Green Paper deals with [the substantive]

[48] "The Church and State Debate," *News & Views*, Dec. 1986, 4.

Man at democracy rally
trying to see over
the heads of the crowd

issues which it could not afford to leave out is to practice the art of obfuscation....It puts forward so many alternatives, and treats minor issues at such length, that it cannot effectively provide the framework for a public debate from which a true consensus and the views of the silent majority can emerge. And without any clear conclusion, the Government will be free to interpret opinion on the Green Paper as it sees fit."[49]

In August, more than 1,100 Christians turned out for a mass rally at the Hong Kong Baptist College organized by 80 Christian clergy, academics, and professionals. At the meeting, a declaration was issued in support of the partial introduction of direct elections to the Legislative Council in 1988 that was based on three principles: 1. All are equal before God, and power should be justly shared by all. 2. God loves all, and the political system should be open to all. 3. The sooner direct elections are introduced the better prepared Hong Kong will be for self-rule in 1997.[50] Hong Kong's Christians were standing up and being counted.

To give the appearance that the people of Hong Kong were being duly consulted, the government set up a Survey Office to collect and collate public responses on this question. In the end, by a cynical sleight of hand, the survey report distorted the results to make it appear that even though Hong Kong people had overwhelmingly supported such elections in 1984, they now did not really want them after all. The Survey Office reported receiving 125,833 individual submissions, of which 67 percent opposed such elections, even though the great majority supported direct elections in principle. Included were 69,557

[49] Worssam, Richard, "To Vote or Not to Vote," *News & Views*, July 1987, 5–6.
[50] "Local Church News," *News & Views*, Sept. 1987, 26.

form letters handed out to employees by the managers of PRC-owned banks and businesses in Hong Kong. However, *not* included were the results of twenty-one different signature campaigns in which 233,666 signatories supported and, only 295 opposed, direct elections in 1988. Through this kind of legerdemain, the conclusion was drawn that although the people of Hong Kong supported *eventual* direct elections to the Legislative Council in general, they did not support introducing them in 1988. The results of two government-sponsored surveys were also released purporting to back up the Survey Office report. These were directly contradicted by results garnered through a number of professionally conducted private polls showing that the people actually favored partial direct elections in 1988 by a two to one margin. Why this contradiction? Because the government-sponsored polls nowhere offered respondents a clear choice to support such elections. One will only get a clear answer if one asks a clear question. It was obvious that the authorities did not *want* a clear answer.[51]

The people of Hong Kong, particularly the Christian leaders among them, were not stupid. They easily saw through the thin veneer of the cynical public exercise that had just been conducted, and they were angry. Many reacted by giving up on Hong Kong altogether and making preparations to depart for other lands. The December 1987 *News & Views* headline said it all: "Emigration Hits Hong Kong."[52] Some, however, were galvanized into action.

The Joint Committee on the Promotion of Democratic Government (including twenty-four Christian groups) staged a rally in downtown Hong Kong Sunday, November 15, involving more than seven hundred people, to protest the government's actions. They handed a petition to the government secretariat asking the governor to give the 230,000 signatures from the signature campaigns and the results of the private polls in support of direct elections due weight. On Wednesday, November 18, they submitted a written protest to the Legislative Council on the day the report was debated. They also sent delegations to Beijing and to London to express their views.

The Christian groups within the joint committee issued a statement of response to the report of the Survey Office, in which they expressed clearly the frustration of the community as a whole. "Public opinion over the sensitive issue of direct elections [in 1998] has been seriously twisted and a wrong picture has been represented, which has

---

[51]   Tsang, *Hong Kong*, 127–28 and Patten, *East and West*, 26.
[52]   P. 1.

Government House,
home of British
governors

led inevitably to public frustration. We consider that if a government is to be trusted by her citizens, she must maintain absolute justice in handling public opinion....The confidence of citizens towards the future will receive a severe blow and the prestige of the Government will be at stake. The Government cannot underestimate and neglect the serious consequences posed by the outcome."[53]

In February 1988, the government published a white policy paper entitled, "The Development of Representative Government: The Way Forward." This paper of necessity had to spell out more specific objectives and conclude the matter. It stated that political reforms should continue to evolve to suit Hong Kong's special circumstances, but that they should be prudent and gradual. The reforms should have the widest possible support of the community and should permit a smooth transition in 1997 and a high degree of continuity thereafter. Therefore, the paper declared, there would be ten directly elected seats allowed in 1991 (out of a total of fifty-six).[54] Why ten, and why 1991? Because the British already knew that in order to placate the Hong Kong public, the Chinese intended to allow that number. Such a small number of seats would prove to be no threat to Chinese interests when it came to the ultimate control of Hong Kong. The British also knew that the PRC's basic policy was to let Hong Kong enjoy a level of autonomy after 1997, but only in a way that would benefit, not

[53] "Statement on a Christian Response to the Report of the Survey Office," *News & Views*, Dec. 1987, 27.
[54] Tsang, *Hong Kong*, 126–27.

potentially undermine, the interests of the Chinese Communist Party. They further knew that by 1991, it would be too late, procedurally, to advance down the road towards the full democratization of Hong Kong before the handover just seven years later. In the end, it became apparent that the Hong Kong government had conducted its public consultation subterfuge because it feared being exposed as a lame duck. It also feared that setting up democratic reforms that the Chinese government opposed would simply invite the government to dismantle them after 1997. However, the Hong Kong government never gave its people the right to decide for themselves whether or not they wanted to run that risk.[55]

The reaction of the community at large, and the Christian community in particular, was predictable. The Hong Kong Christian Council's Kowk Nai-wang spoke for many.

> We all recognize that the Hong Kong Government is trying to avoid the image of being a lame duck government. Actions speak louder than words. The Hong Kong Government stands to lose even more credibility as a result of this White Paper. No wonder almost all local newspaper editorials and all columnists gave poor ratings to [this] Paper. In many ways, this...Paper is not a step forward—as the tile suggests—but rather a step backward, at least when compared with the 1984 White Paper....In the 1988 Paper, the whole tone is on convergence with the Basic Law of the future S.A.R. government which is to be promulgated in 1990....
>
> The people of Hong Kong have a confidence crisis regarding the Territory's future (and hence their future as well)....The 1988 White Paper shows the Hong Kong Government is increasingly losing its grip on things, and its own confidence. This is perhaps the root problem Hong Kong is now facing. The sooner the Beijing and London governments realize this, the better.
>
> The people of Hong Kong...must not be afraid to speak up, to articulate their hopes and fears. Church leaders and concerned Christians must also become more vocal, for what is at stake is not so much their own existence, but the well-being of the entire community....
>
> Hong Kong has been developing [politically] very rapidly in recent years. To try to stop the process is suicidal. To maintain the status quo, to continue to allow the few elite to rule Hong Kong,

[55]   Ibid, 127–28.

Kwok Nai-wang (left)
with Philip and Marlene
Bauman

is no longer desirable or possible. Hong Kong must change. It does not need to be revolutionary. It can be evolutionary, prudent and gradual. But it must move ahead. Beijing and London must give Hong Kong a sufficiently free hand and full support."[56]

At that time Kwok, still unaware of the secret agreement between Britain and China, continued to be hopeful. "I would assume the ultimate goal of all these exercises is to develop a fully representative government in Hong Kong prior to 1997."[57] Richard Worssam read the tea leaves more realistically.

> The White Paper is largely a holding operation until the Basic Law is promulgated in 1990 It was forced upon the Government by the promises in the 1984 White Paper made during the heady days of the Sino-British negotiations when change and conviction were the catchwords. A growing political awareness fostered hopes for democracy in accordance with the Joint Declaration, which states that the legislature shall be constituted by elections. However, Beijing was not amused and the ingenuity of the Hong Kong Government was stretched to the limit in devising a political review which would trim these aspirations down to size, while still maintaining the appearance of taking the views of Hong Kong people into account....At the end of this pyretic process, the Government has emerged with its image rather the worse for wear, and Hong Kong citizens are now generally pessimistic of any significant proportion of Legco seats ever being returned by direct elections....
>
> The first draft of the Basic Law is due to be released at the

[56] "White Paper Reforms—'Far too Late, Far too Few,'" *News & Views*, March 1988, 23.

[57] Ibid, 22.

end of April this year and it is scheduled to be promulgated by the National People's Congress in 1990....The true way forward will be known once the Basic Law is finalized, and this will be very much under China's direction. The important task now is for Hong Kong citizens to make their views known once the first draft of the Basic Law is published in April."[58]

The Basic Law

When the first draft of the Basic Law came out, most people were pleased with the sections dealing with economic and cultural affairs, including religious affairs. It was obvious that a key concern of the People's Republic was to preserve the prosperity and stability of the goose that continued to lay the golden eggs that were underpinning China's "four modernizations." The wishes and expectations of the religious community had also largely been taken into account in the details spelled out in the Protestant manifesto and other statements that had been submitted to the Chinese and Hong Kong governments. The sticking point, however, continued to be the increasingly divergent views of the people of Hong Kong and the PRC in the areas of human rights and democratic development.

Christians continued to play an active part in the debate. Prominent lawyer, Martin Lee, and his political colleague, Szeto Wah, both members of the Basic Law Drafting Committee, published a detailed critique of the draft Basic Law in a booklet entitled, *The Basic Law: Some Basic Flaws*.[59] Sixty-three Hong Kong Christian leaders endorsed a carefully drafted and well thought out nine-page position paper drawn up by a Joint Conference of Christians on the Response to the Basic Law. In it, they spelled out their Christian presuppositions and made twenty specific recommendations to both the BLDC and the BLCC in the areas of human rights, religious freedom, the political system, and judicial guarantees.

As for human rights, the group demanded, "To protect human rights, we demand that all the provisions of the International Covenant on Civil and Political Rights applicable to Hong Kong with legal effect shall have legal effect in the HKSAR. Any law of the HKSAR shall be rendered invalid to the extent that its provisions are repugnant to the corresponding provisions in the International Covenant. The

---

[58]   Worssam, Richard, "White Paper Reforms—'Far too Late, Far too Few,'" *News & Views*, March 1988, 24–25.

[59]   Hong Kong: Kasper, 1988.

The Basic Law: Some Basic Flaws

International Covenant on Economic, Social and Cultural Rights shall apply to Hong Kong where applicable and be enforced in accordance with the laws of the HKSAR."[60]

As for the political system, the group proposed that as of 1997:

1. The Chief Executive must be nominated by no less than 10 percent of the members of the Legislative Council and elected by all the citizens of Hong Kong on the basis of a "one person, one vote" direct election.

2. Secretaries of departments, albeit appointed by the Chief Executive, are political appointments by nature, and they must be politically accountable for the making and execution of their policies.

3. At least half of the members of the Legislative Council must be directly elected. After 1997, the Legislative Council should gradually move along democratic lines towards direct election of all its [members].[61]

As for judicial guarantees, the group asked that Article 18 be amended to read, "The HKSAR is vested with independent judicial power, including that of final adjudication. Courts of the HKSAR

---

[60] "Position Paper by Hong Kong Protestant Church Workers Regarding the Draft Basic Law," *News & Views*, Sept. 1988, 10.

[61] Ibid., 13.

shall have jurisdiction over all cases in the Region, except that the restrictions of their jurisdiction imposed by Hong Kong's previous legal system shall be maintained....The Standing Committee of the National People's Congress should empower courts of the HKSAR to interpret all the provisions of the Basic Law [except in the areas of defense and foreign affairs.]"[62]

In the end, the final draft of the Basic Law was passed and promulgated by the PRC's National People's Congress on April 4, 1990. Overall, Hong Kong received about the best it could have hoped for under the circumstances, but there was "no joy in Mudville" when it was announced. Politically, a few more directly elected Legislative Council seats had been wrung out of China, but the prospects for true democracy had not been advanced substantially. Nor were people happy about a vague "subversion" clause that had been added. Steve Tsang summed it up, "By and large, the PRC commits itself in the Basic Law to recreate in the SAR a Chinese version of the British Crown Colony system of government that existed in Hong Kong in the 1980s."[63] In other words, the people of Hong Kong had exchanged one colonial master for another.

Massacre in Beijing—Fear in Hong Kong

Meanwhile, the church in Hong Kong had championed the cause of the people, but not without a price. The initial unity sparked by the fear of coming under Communist rule had begun to fray at the edges. Some believed that the church had more or less gained what it had sought in the area of religious freedom and that it should now leave the rest of the agenda to others. Others were tiring of the continuing tension and feared that to take an increasingly confrontational approach on behalf of democratic reforms risked bringing down China's wrath on the community in general and on the church in particular. Under these circumstances, the position of a leading Christian activist like Kwok Nai-wang became increasingly difficult. Increasing resistance by some member churches to the Hong Kong Christian Council's active role in the public struggle for democracy and human rights led Kwok to resign as general secretary in September of 1988 and to form the Hong Kong Christian Institute. The institute, he announced, had been formed as a voice for the Christian community on these specific issues.[64]

---

[62] Ibid., 15–16.
[63] Tsang, *Hong Kong*, 155.
[64] Kwok, Nai-wang, "Reflections on Ten Years as HKCC's General Secretary," *News & Views*, 3–8.

Then came the tumultuous events of the spring of 1989. Joyce and I joined millions of people around the world watching television screens in horror as Chinese troops massacred hundreds, perhaps thousands,[65] of their unarmed compatriots in cold blood on the streets of Beijing.[66] The people of Hong Kong were, of course, also watching. They had been closely following events in Beijing and other cities for months as students rose to denounce rampant corruption in the Communist Party, high unemployment due to economic reforms, a rapidly accelerating gap between rich and poor, and the failure of the party to add a "fifth modernization" (democracy) to the country's agenda. Simple protests had turned into mass demonstrations, especially in the capital's Tiananmen Square, on the doorstep of the government's seat of power. This had led to hunger strikes, a call for party leaders to step down, and an ever more strident demand for democracy. In the process, the general populace of Beijing had become more and more supportive of the students and so had the people of Hong Kong.

Hong Kong's people felt frustrated, betrayed, and helpless after discovering that the once promising terms of the 1984 joint declaration were going to be only partially carried out. They also believed that if democracy and human rights could not become a reality in China, then there was no way in which they could be protected after the handover in 1997. Consequently, like the people of Beijing, they became increasingly supportive of the Chinese student movement, even sending generous donations to help finance it. Their hopes became tied to the students' hopes. To them, the students were on the front lines fighting their democracy and human rights battle against the feared Communist regime. When Chinese Primer Li Peng imposed martial law in Beijing on May 20 and tried to quash the student movement, 500,000 Hong Kongers took to the streets in a mass sympathy demonstration. These were followed by further demonstrations on May 28 and June 4, with upwards of one million people participating (out of a population of six million). Steve Tsang aptly summed it up:

> On the night of 3-4 June...the People's Liberation Army executed the orders of the top communist leaders and carried out a

---

[65] To this day, the PRC government has never released casualty figures for this tragedy. Most informants on the scene, and subsequent analyses of the event, put the death toll anywhere from hundreds to thousands.

[66] This was the last thing Joyce did consciously before her death. Having given fifteen years of her life to ministry among the Chinese people, she had a great concern for them to the end.

Chinese troops near
Tiananmen Square

massacre. It used excessive and indiscriminate force to suppress
the Beijing protest movement centered on Tiananmen Square.
The communist leaders intended not only to disperse the
demonstrators, but also to teach them and the rest of the nation
a lesson. Their message was that the party-state had the might
to maintain power and the will to use it. It was a classic case of
applying the old Chinese proverb of "killing a cock to warn the
monkey." This public and bloody suppression was designed
to pre-empt any similar protest movement in the future...the
armored units were there for the rest of the nation to notice."[67]

The world may have been shocked, but the people of Hong Kong
were devastated. Their hopes for and trust in the Chinese government
were shattered. As I reported in the pages of the *Church Herald*,

> When news of the massacre in Beijing's Tiananmen Square came
> on June 4, the people of Hong Kong went into deep shock. Their
> first reaction was grief for the slain students and their smashed
> ideals. Their second was anger and revulsion at a leadership that
> would resort to such barbaric methods to maintain its grip on
> power. Their third was shame that the proud name of China, and
> therefore of all Chinese, would once again be so terribly tarnished
> in the eyes of the whole world. Their fourth was fear that once
> their motherland had turned on and devoured her own children,
> her stepchildren in Hong Kong might be next![68]

---

[67] Tsang, *Hong Kong*, 161–62.
[68] Karsen, Wendell, "Borrowed Place, Borrowed Time," *Church Herald*, Dec.
1989, 12–15. This article included a synopsis of the history of Hong Kong,
a discussion of freedom of religion there, and an analysis of the impact of
the massacre on Hong Kong and the role of the Hong Kong church in its
aftermath.

An immediate effect of the massacre was a great surge in the number of people emigrating from Hong Kong. They began going abroad at a rate that, had it continued, would have resulted in some half million people leaving the colony by 1996, leading to an estimated shortfall of 93,400 professionals, technical experts, and managers.[69] The Chinese Communist regime suddenly became a pariah in the world. It was isolated diplomatically and suffered arms embargoes, sanctions, and other practical expressions of political and economic disapproval. The giant demonstrations and subsequent emigration in Hong Kong had alarmed both the Chinese and the British governments. On the one hand, China knew that its four modernizations could not continue without an economically vibrant Hong Kong. On the other hand, the British knew that unless there were some dramatic gestures to offset the massive loss of confidence in Hong Kong, the place could become ungovernable and Britain would be stuck with a morass.

The British took a number of immediate measures to restore confidence. In October 1989, then governor David Wilson announced an enormous US$16 billion Port-Airport Development Strategy (PADS), with the new airport to be completed by 1997, and the whole project to be completed by 2006. In April 1990, Britain created an escape hatch for the cream of Hong Kong's society in case things went amok in the future. Having anticipated the possibility of a future mass exodus to Britain, in 1962 Parliament had passed a Nationality Act that in effect had taken away full British citizenship rights from the people of Hong Kong. Now it quickly passed a "Nationality Package" that restored those rights to 50,000 key Hong Kong households (limited to 225,000 persons).[70] In February 1990, Britain reached an understanding with the Chinese government and announced that the number of directly elected seats to the Legislative Council would be increased from ten to eighteen in 1991. In that same year, the Hong Kong government enacted a Bill of Rights "to incorporate provisions of the International Covenant on Civil and Political Rights as applied to Hong Kong and the laws of Hong Kong."[71]

---

[69]   The number was 62,000 in 1990, compared to 30,000 in 1987; 45,800 in 1988; and 42,000 in 1989. *News & Views*, Dec. 1990, 26.

[70]   Sympathetic Singapore offered to give entry visas good for ten years to an additional 250,000 people, while the United States doubled the quota for Hong Kong immigrants from 5,000 to 10,000 a year and extended entry visa validation to 2002.

[71]   Hong Kong Government, *An Introduction to Hong Kong Bill of Rights Ordinance* (Hong Kong, 1991), 3.

China's moves were mixed. Eager to mend relations with the western powers after the Tiananmen fiasco, it had secretly agreed to the British request to increase directly elected Legislative Council seats from ten to eighteen in 1991, twenty in 1997, twenty-four in 1999, and thirty (or half) in 2003. These moves would not threaten China's ultimate control and could be incorporated into the Basic Law in a way that would give China credit for them. It also eventually agreed, in June 1991, to allow the PADS project to move forward, a blessing that was necessary because the project straddled the handover. However, the PRC regime now felt very threatened. It had resorted to force to quell discontent at home. It had watched the collapse of the worldwide Communist movement, and the disintegration of its principle ally, the USSR, in 1989–90. It had witnessed the people of Hong Kong enthusiastically supporting what it regarded as a subversive movement that had challenged its authority. Its reaction was to tighten its negotiating stance vis-à-vis Hong Kong.

China nullified the British Nationality Package by saying that it would not honor the special passports issued for this purpose. It also said that the "Bill of Rights" had been passed without its consent and that it therefore would disregard it after 1997. It tried to pressure the Hong Kong government into banning the Alliance in Support of the Patriotic and Democratic Movement in China, founded by Martin Lee and Szeto Wah in support of the student demonstrations.[72] The government refused, citing legal grounds. China then called Lee and Wah subversives publicly and expelled them abruptly from the Basic Law Drafting Committee. This move backfired, however. In the eyes of the people of Hong Kong, the men's expulsion transformed them into champions of democracy and made them more popular than ever. China also insisted that the BLDC add a clause to the Basic Law "forbidding any subversive activities in Hong Kong."

The Tiananmen massacre also strengthened the determination of the people who remained in Hong Kong to stay, come what may, and those who spoke for them. Both China and Britain hoped that people would forget about Tiananmen, simmer down, and go back to what they liked to do best—make money. However, the opposite occurred. A citywide demonstration organized by the alliance and involving 200,000

---

[72] Martin Lee and Szeto Wah were both elected members of the Legislative Council. Martin, a Roman Catholic, founded the United Democrats Party and was very helpful in 1996 when I investigated the possibility of getting Union Church Hong Kong's charter amended in the legislature. Szeto Wah was head of the Hong Kong Teachers Union.

Mass candlelight vigil in Victoria Park

people took place on June 3, 1990, to commemorate the victims of the massacre—the "goddess of democracy" included. Another 200,000 turned out for a candlelight vigil on the evening of June 4. The massacre even brought the oligarchy's politicians together. Conservative, liberal, and moderate unofficial *appointed* members of the Legislative Council (UMELCO) agreed to ask for half of the council to be directly elected by 1997, all members to be directly elected by 2003, and the chief executive to be directly elected by that same year. Meanwhile, the democrats had united behind Martin Lee and Szeto Wah and formed the United Democrats party. These prodemocracy groups and their allies won a landslide victory in the 1991 Legislative Council elections, garnering fifteen of the eighteen seats and 58 percent of the votes. Even though the PRC used every united front, intimidation, and bribery trick in its bag, *every one* of the pro-PRC candidates lost, and by large margins. The people of Hong Kong had *not* forgotten Tiananmen, but they *had* demonstrated overwhelmingly that they were ready for democracy. The flip side of this victory was Beijing's resolution henceforth to drag its heels when it came to any proposal to quicken the pace of democratization in Hong Kong.

Christians Stand Together

The tumultuous events of 1989–91 once again jolted the church out of its creeping apathy and fostered a new sense of unity. Christian leaders and the people in their churches took an active part in the mass demonstrations protesting, and then commemorating, the June 4 massacre. Martin Lee, Kwok Nai-wang, Lo Lung-kwong, Raymond Fung, Lau Chin-sek, Tso Man-king, and others played key roles in challenging the church to become involved in the struggle for democracy and human rights. Christian leaders from different denominations and theological backgrounds founded the Hong Kong Christian Patriotic and Democratic Movement June 24, 1989. The movement organized many prayer meetings, lectures, seminars, and rallies to boost Christian morale and to provide both spiritual support and intellectual input on issues related to China and democracy. In September 1990, it sent a delegation of fourteen people to Poland and Czechoslovakia to study the church's involvement in the democratization process in those two countries. In October of that same year, it published a book entitled, *From East Europe to Hong Kong: The Communist Regime and the Church.*[73]

In April 1990, the Hong Kong Christian Council convened a week-long consultation on the mission of the church in Hong Kong in the nineties. One hundred thirty-six participants from various denominations, independent churches, parachurch organizations, educational institutions, and seminaries gathered to wrestle with the theme, "Serving the Millions in Unity." New approaches for a new era were discussed in the areas of evangelism, education, social service, pastoral work, lay leadership development, and theological education. Particular attention was paid to:

1. The pursuit of solidarity and unity among the churches during this time of social change.
2. The stimulation of mutual concern and cooperation with overseas churches and churches in China during this crucial period.
3. The encouragement of Christians to become involved in building a democratic government during these changing times.

Dr. Philemon Choi of Breakthrough Ministry addressed the closing assembly of four hundred people, urging Christians to be "ready to bear the cross of Christ during this decade for the good of the future of Hong Kong." At the conclusion of the consultation, all four hundred present signed "A Manifesto on the Mission of the Church in Hong Kong in the Nineties." It stated, "The churches of Hong Kong will face a severe test in this coming decade. In the midst of difficulties and doubts and in response to the challenge of the times, they will need to resolutely carry out the changeless mission entrusted to them by God. By doing this, the churches will be transforming a crisis into an opportunity." One of the manifesto's ten sections dealt with the role the church should play in the political struggle.

> At this period of political transition, responding to God's demands for justice, the churches must work with the people of Hong Kong to seek a political structure which provides a high degree of self-government, and upholds human rights, freedom,

---

[73] Kwong, Lo-lung, "Christian Concerns," *News & Views*, Dec. 1990, 28.

democracy and the rule of law. In their prophetic role, facing squarely the troubles of the times, the churches must speak out responsibly. Together with a broad spectrum of society, they must remind the governments of China and Britain to implement the promises of the Sino-British Joint Declaration, and to see to it that the Basic Law will uphold a society which respects human rights, practices justice and shows equality and benevolence.[74]

In 1990, I returned to Hong Kong to resume my work for the council in the areas of communications and education, taking my son Andrew with me.[75] In July of that year, a Methodist pastor, the Reverend Dr. Tso Man-king, was appointed as the new general secretary. It was clear from the beginning that he had the skills to restore unity of purpose among the churches that made up the council and to help them strengthen their life and outreach. However, it was also clear that he would not shrink from urging them to renew their commitment to work for a just, sustainable, and participatory society in Hong Kong. In his first article as general secretary, he called on the churches to learn from the example of Esther. She had become queen of Persia "for such a time as this." This had three implications for the church in Hong Kong. First, this was a time for "self-examination and repentance." Second, this was a time to "speak out, to take a stand, and to be counted." Third, this was a time for "commitment and dedication." He concluded, "At a time like this, Christians in crisis situations are challenged to make a commitment, even to the extent of sacrificing their own well-being. How much I admire Esther's response to Mordecai, 'I will go to the King, though it is against the law; and if I perish, I perish.' I hope our people in Hong Kong who plan to stay can respond to our crisis in the same manner by saying, 'I am going to stay, though it is against the trend of the time; and if I perish, I perish.'...At a time like this...it is the Church's responsibility to prepare her people for a high level of commitment, dedication and even sacrifice. This is what the Hong Kong Christian Council is committed to helping the churches of Hong Kong do."[76]

On Sunday, January 27, 1991, the council launched a major, year-long "We Love Hong Kong" campaign to strengthen the general public's

---

[74] "A Manifesto on the Mission of the Church in Hong Kong in the Nineties," *News & Views*, Dec. 1990, 8–10.

[75] See Karsen, Wendell, "Sharing the Word in Hong Kong," *Church Herald*, July/August 1991, for a description of this work.

[76] Tso, Man-king, "General Secretary's Column," *News & Views*, Dec. 1990, 13–14.

"We Love Hong Kong"
event

identity as "Hong Kongers," as well as their commitment to their place and people. Simultaneous kickoff ceremonies were held in three key downtown areas, each attended by over a thousand people. Thirty social service and church organizations were involved in planning the large campaign around the theme: "Creating a Caring Society...Building a Community of Hope...Shaping a Better Tomorrow." The campaign had four goals:

1. To redirect attention from those who are leaving Hong Kong (1,000+ per week) to those who are staying.
2. To stimulate people to appreciate and celebrate the industrious character of our people and to encourage them to carry on.
3. To stimulate people to express their concerns, love, and hope for Hong Kong.
4. To encourage people to have a sense of commitment to, and to take responsibility for, the future of Hong Kong, come what may, and to strengthen their values and develop a sense of mission.[77]

Ten additional major events were held throughout the year including a "We Love Hong Kong" academic forum, a "We Love Hong Kong" unity Sunday, a young people's voting simulation exercise, a "Hand in Hand Around Hong Kong" event, and the burying of an "Across '97" time capsule. Some of these events made a large impact on the public. More than 31,000 young people participated in the voting exercise. More than 11,000 people attended a mass choir event. Further thousands formed a human chain around the central areas of Hong Kong.

The campaign was climaxed by the lowering of the time capsule in Kowloon Park January 18, 1992. As I watched, two legislative councilors

[77] "HKCC News," *News & Views*, March 1991, 1.

The newlyweds
in Hong Kong with RCA
Asia secretary Elaine Tanis
and husband Elliot

and the chair of the Urban Council led a group of dignitaries in lowering the capsule into the ground amid a fanfare of flags and bands. One could only hope and pray that by the time the capsule would be dug up in 2002, the hopes and aspirations of Hong Kong's people would have been realized.

A Ray of Sunshine

Meanwhile, in June of that year, Andrew and I had been joined in Hong Kong by my second gift from God, my new bride, Renske Greve. Renske's family and my family were members of the Wheaton Christian Reformed Church in Wheaton, Illinois. Renske and I had become reacquainted when I spoke at the church in June 1990, just before Andrew and I were to return to Hong Kong. I say "reacquainted" with tongue in cheek since, when Renske's family immigrated from the Netherlands to Wheaton in 1957, she had been a six-year-old girl with a big white ribbon in her hair, while I had been a sophomore in college. Renske, a nurse, had remained single and was serving as an area manager for the Servicemaster Corporation.

Six months later, Andrew and I had returned to the States to visit our family during the Christmas and New Year holiday. I asked Renkse out for dinner on New Year's Eve, and we discovered that we had many things in common—bridges that immediately bound us together. A whirlwind romance followed, mostly carried on by phone and post. Renske came to visit Andrew and me for three weeks in March when we had marriage counseling with my good friend, Earl Westrick, and threw a big engagement party. Then it had been three more long months before we were married June 15, 1991, in the same Wheaton church where we had first encountered each other thirty-four years before. Renske joined the Reformed Church and became my missionary partner in Hong Kong, bringing a ray of sunshine into my life that dispelled the sorrow and loneliness that I had endured since Joyce's death two years before.

Appointment in Beijing

In the fall of 1991, the Hong Kong Christian Council had received an invitation from the PRC's Religious Affairs Bureau to send a high level Protestant church delegation to Beijing for another consultation. A nineteen-member, broadly representative ecumenical delegation arrived in Beijing November 16, 1991. During the next week, they met with Chen Zhi-ying, deputy director of the China State Department's Hong Kong and Macau Affairs Office; Ren Wu-zhi, director of the Religious Affairs Bureau; and Bishop K.H. Ting, president of the China Christian Council and head of the Three-self Protestant Patriotic Movement.[78] It was obvious that the purpose of the talks was to reassure the churches that nothing had changed after the "Beijing incident." The delegation presented a situation paper, entitled "A Reaffirmation of the Role of the Hong Kong Church," which expressed various opinions and included suggestions concerning Hong Kong's social concerns, the 1997 transition, the church's concerns, and China's situation. The group also raised the issues of democracy and human rights. The paper, which was presented to the Chinese authorities, was a remarkable and courageous document that not only dealt with the future life and witness of the Hong Kong church, but also with the thorny issues of democracy, human rights, and religious freedom in *both* China and Hong Kong. It stated,

> During this transition time, there have been certain subjects about which the people of Hong Kong and the people of China have held different points of view. The relationship between Hong Kong and China has also had to weather many problems which has led to a deterioration of confidence in the future of Hong Kong, and to an erosion of trust in the Chinese Government....Since 1989, the people of Hong Kong have also become more concerned about the issue of human rights, the role of law in government and the development of a more democratic political system. Last September, the first direct elections for the Legislative Council were held in Hong Kong. This proved that the people of Hong Kong, though still under colonial rule, are gradually learning to exercise their political rights. This is a huge step towards realizing the post-1997 goals set out in the Joint Declaration, namely of developing a "high level of self-government," and of enabling "Hong Kong to be governed by Hong Kong people."...

[78] "HKCC News," *News & Views*, Dec. 1991, 1.

Bishop Ting welcoming the
Hong Kong delegation

Hong Kong's people recognize that China, in her drive towards modernization, has to still overcome many difficulties....They will want to see gradual and stable developments in the areas of respect for human rights, the development of a democratic system, the evolution of an independent legal system and the correct and concrete implementation of the Constitution of the People's Republic of China. They will also want to see fair constitutional treatment given to people who use non-violent means to struggle for democracy....They will hope for great success in the area of economic reform that will enable China to remain open to the outside world and that will enhance the people's livelihood and improve the quality of their life....The Church in Hong Kong is also greatly concerned about the situation of the Church and of Christians in China. It is hoped that the 1979 policy of more freedom and openness for religious activities can be equally implemented and developed in all provinces and cities of China.[79]

Chen assured the delegation that everything that had been promised, and spelled out in the Basic Law, concerning religious freedom in post-1997 Hong Kong would remain unchanged. However, he declined to address directly the democracy and human rights concerns. Chen reiterated that neither the Religious Affairs Bureau, nor the church in China, nor the SAR government would interfere in the internal affairs of Hong Kong's churches or in any religious activities that did not violate SAR laws. Religious bodies in Hong Kong would be free to relate to religious organizations in China, and vice versa,

[79] "A Reaffirmation of the Role of the Hong Kong Church: a Position Paper of the 1991 Hong Kong Church Delegation to China," *News & Views*, Dec. 1991, 19.

according to the principles of nonsubordination, noninterference, and mutual respect. Ting stressed that there should be more exchanges between the churches in Hong Kong and the churches in China.[80] The delegation returned to Hong Kong quite satisfied with the reassurances given about religious freedom but quite dissatisfied with the reluctance it encountered about addressing the broader political and human rights issues.

---

[80] "China Reaffirms the Role of Hong Kong Churches Unchanged After 1997!" *News & Views*, June 1992, 17–19.

CHAPTER 13

The Struggle for Democracy and Human Rights

The Last Governor

Just seven months after the delegation's return from Beijing, another political bombshell exploded in Hong Kong in the person of its last British governor—Chris Patten. John Major had replaced Margaret Thatcher as Britain's prime minister in 1991. In reviewing Thatcher's policy vis-à-vis China and Hong Kong, Major believed that old China hands like David Wilson and Percy Cradock, with all their diplomatic experience and finesse, had managed to be outfoxed by the Chinese government for a decade at the expense of British interests and the interests of the people of Hong Kong. The People's Republic had been allowed to get away with ignoring key political commitments it had made in the 1984 joint declaration. Major was determined that, under his administration, Britain would stand up to the Chinese and not give any more ground. With that in mind, he retired Craddock, the chief Foreign Office architect of recent Hong Kong policy. He also summarily removed Sir David Wilson from the governorship in January

1992 and replaced him with a dynamic Conservative Party politician, Chris Patten.[1]

From his first day in Hong Kong, Patten broke all the molds. Unlike previous governors, who were mostly professional diplomats, he was a blunt democrat. His driving purpose in coming to Hong Kong was to gain the most that could be gained for Hong Kong's people during the five years remaining before the handover. Unlike too many other governors who were aloof "Mandarins" who reveled in their near dictatorial powers and colonial trappings, he was a man of the people who encouraged the sharing of power and eschewed all such trappings. He befriended democrats and refused to wear anything but a plain business suit at official functions. Unlike his predecessors, too many of which were "Christian gentlemen" who did not let their Christian principles interfere unduly with the execution of colonial rule, he was a devout Roman Catholic who strove to implement those principles in the public square. Unlike his immediate predecessors, who had believed they could out-nuance the Chinese Communists through compromise, he believed that Britain needed to stand for what was in the best interests of the United Kingdom and the people of Hong Kong, and let the chips fall where they may. He purposely did not accept the PRC's invitation to pay a "kow-tow" visit to Beijing on his way to Hong Kong.[2]

Renske and I met Chris Patten shortly after his arrival in Hong Kong in July 1992. He had been invited to the YMCA to address a gathering of church leaders and other prominent Christians in the community. He exuded warmth and sincerity as he laid out his concerns about and hopes for Hong Kong. His deep faith and commitment to Christian principles also came through loud and clear. On a personal level, he was down to earth and interested in us and in the other people with whom he conversed. I remember remarking to Renske on the way home, "At last we have a man of conviction who will stand up for the people and refuse to preside over a final sell out."[3]

For months before his arrival, the extremely able Patten had pored over historical documents, diplomatic and legal papers, and economic

---

[1]   Dimbleby, Jonathan, *The Last Governor* (London: Warner, 1997), 11–13.

[2]   Ibid., 2–5.

[3]   Patton was dressed in a business suit and was very approachable. Four years later, I would have met him again in the governor's mansion over a welcome dinner for the Archbishop of Canterbury to which I was invited. However, much to everyone's chagrin, the bishop of Hong Kong and Macau was suddenly summoned to a meeting in Beijing, and the archbishop's visit, and therefore the dinner, had to be cancelled, since the local bishop's presence was required for such a visit.

reports. He had consulted diplomats, former governors, academics, and businessmen about every aspect of the negotiations and about Hong Kong's governance and life. He had sought opinions about what the PRC would do if Britain granted democracy to Hong Kong. Patten had paid special attention to every detail of the new Basic Law. In so doing, he came to the conclusion that there was more room to develop democracy and ensure human rights *within* the parameters of the Basic Law than people had thought. He also concluded that his main emphasis should not be on further appeasing China but on securing the support of the people of Hong Kong by restoring credibility to the governorship and engendering confidence in the administration. The will of the people could then be used as leverage on China to secure concessions on the democratization of Hong Kong within the parameters of existing agreements. At the same time, recognizing the difficult task he faced, Major invested Patten with the power to make decisions almost independently of the Foreign Office.[4]

In October 1992, in his first policy address to the Legislative Council, Patten electrified Hong Kong and shocked China by laying out a political reform package of ten proposals that would give Hong Kong as much democratization as possible before 1997 without breaching the Basic Law. It was a master stroke of ingenuity in that it looked to the people of Hong Kong like a major step forward, while in reality it was only a modest step that was legally allowable within the parameters of the Basic Law. However, rather than seeing it as the modest step it really was, the PRC inflated the importance of the package and overreacted. It did so because the local PRC cadres misunderstood and misinterpreted how the complex plan would work, because Patten laid such stress on freedom and democracy, and because he had not consulted them in advance. Legality was not the issue. The Chinese went into convulsions because they thought they smelled a rat. Was this a subtle plot by the British to extend their influence beyond 1997? The Chinese had lost the political initiative to this brash British politician, and they meant to get it back even if it resulted in the derailing of the "through train."[5]

Patten was called every evil name in the Chinese Communist glossary. The aim was to discredit him in the eyes of the people of Hong Kong so that the British would remove him and return to the "convergence" policy that would leave China in control of the pace of democratization in Hong Kong. The strategy backfired. The British

---

[4]   Ibid., 14–16.
[5]   Patten, *East and West*, 45–52.

PRC emblem on Hsin-hwa News Agency,
China's de facto headquarters
in Hong Kong

closed ranks and stood behind Patten, and in the eyes of the people of Hong Kong (except for the nervous oligarchy), the more abuse the PRC heaped upon him, the greater champion of democracy their governor became. Beijing's abuse also turned Patten into an international hero.

When the Chinese realized that their campaign had backfired, they finally agreed to resume negotiations with the British in April 1993. The negotiations lasted for seven months and went through seventeen rounds, the Chinese all the while acting as though the governor was not involved, even though he was the key figure behind the scenes on the British side. The Chinese argued that Patten's plan violated the terms of the joint declaration, the Basic Law and "certain understandings" they thought had been reached after the Tiananmen "incident." They were incensed that the British had the temerity to disagree. Since the Basic Law was a piece of *Chinese* legislation, only *they* could be the final interpreters of what it *meant*, never mind what it said or didn't say.[6]

As negotiations continued, Patten's proposals were amended slightly in an endeavor to secure Chinese agreement, but with no result. In November 1993, with time running out, the British announced that Patten's original 1992 proposals would be submitted to the Legislative Council for approval. The PRC immediately broke off talks and announced that it would dismantle those proposals after 1997, should they be approved. Once the council turned the proposals into law in June 1994, the Chinese made it clear that the vaunted "through train" had been derailed. Had the British implemented such proposals before 1984, they may well have succeeded. Ten years later, regrettably, it was too little too late.[7]

When it was clear that the British were no longer going to adhere to what the Chinese understood as the policy of convergence, the Chinese government proceeded to set up what it called a "new kitchen" for

[6]   Ibid., 44–65.
[7]   Patten, *East and West*, 15.

Hong Kong. It established a fifty-seven-member Preliminary Working Committee as a precursor to the Preparatory Committee for the Hong Kong SAR which, under the terms of the Basic Law, was to come into being in 1996 to prepare the transition to Chinese rule in 1997. The Preliminary Working Committee was composed of twenty-seven cadres within the PRC establishment and thirty Hong Kong residents who had taken a pro-Beijing stance over the Patten reform proposals and who could be counted on to safeguard the PRC's interests. In effect, the committee functioned as a shadow government whose overall concern was to demolish Patten's political and human rights reforms and to lay the blame on him for derailing the "through train."[8]

Elections went ahead in September 1995 under the terms of the new arrangements. Martin Lee's United Democrats gained additional seats, but even under the new conditions, it would have been impossible for them to come to power. The PRC-backed candidates did poorly, gaining only sixteen of sixty seats, which hardened the determination of the PRC not to allow the kind of democracy in Hong Kong that could deprive it of retaining ultimate control. In January 1996, it set up the Preparatory Committee and gave it the task of establishing yet another committee—a Selection Committee. The Selection Committee, in turn, would be responsible for selecting a Provisional Legislature to govern Hong Kong through the transition until new elections could be held in 2000, and to select the first chief executive. Adding the selection of a Provisional Legislature to the tasks of the Selection Committee contradicted the terms of both the joint declaration and the Basic Law. However, the British were powerless to prevent it happening and could only hope that cooperation on practical matters would enable a relatively smooth handover.[9]

To Bless or Not to Bless?

This development created uproar in the church. Religious organizations, including the Hong Kong Christian Council, were invited to select a few representatives of the "religious sector" to sit on the Selection Committee as provided for in the Basic Law. Some Christians thought the church should respond positively and thereby have some say in the proceedings. Other Christians vehemently opposed such a move, arguing that a Provisional Legislature was an illegal entity created by China to disrupt Patten's political and human

[8]   Tsang, *Hong Kong*, 201–04.
[9]   Ibid., 204–05.

rights reforms and derail the agreed-upon "through train" for a smooth transition in 1997. By participating in such an illegal action as members of the committee, Christian representatives would, in effect, be blessing China's blatant disregard for the provisions of the Basic Law and setting a dangerous precedent for the future.

In April, the council convened an open forum to enable people to air various points of view. An Executive Committee meeting and an Extraordinary General Meeting followed the forum. At the general meeting it was decided to adopt a compromise. The council would send representatives, but they would only participate in the election of the chief executive (as stipulated in the Basic Law), but not in the formation of a Provisional Legislature. Following the principle of the separation of church and state, participants would participate as individuals, not as representatives of the council. The council would work with other church organizations to form a joint nominating committee to recommend members to the Selection Committee when that committee was formed. The Roman Catholic Church adopted the same compromise formula.

A few weeks later, on May 17, the Hong Kong Christian Institute, the council's own Christian Industrial Committee, and six other Protestant religious groups published a statement of opposition to the Selection Committee. It called for the church to boycott the Selection Committee altogether in order to make a clear statement to the authorities that it objected to the creation of a Provisional Legislature, and to what amounted to a regression in the democratization process of Hong Kong.[10]

The people of Hong Kong in general were not happy about the Provisional Legislature idea either. The Selection Committee tried to appease them by selecting thirty-three members of the sitting Legislative Council to also sit on the Provisional Legislature. However, *none* of the United Democrats was selected. "Seats were allocated both to reward groups closest to the PRC and to guarantee the PRC's ability to dominate the Council. Ten of those who campaigned (but were defeated) on pro-PRC platforms in the 1995 Legislative Council elections were appointed, and 85 per cent of all appointees were themselves members of the Selection Committee."[11]

In December, the Selection Committee also "elected" Tung Chee-hwa, a Hong Kong shipping magnate whose company depended

---

[10]   "Statement of Opposition to the Selection Committee," *News & Views*, June 1996, 1, 2, 6.

[11]   Tsang, *Hong Kong*, 206.

on trade with China, as the first chief executive of Hong Kong. Tung named his Executive Council in early 1997 and was slated to take office on July 1, 1997, the day of the handover. Twenty-one of his twenty-three nominees for senior government posts were officials who were already serving in the Hong Kong government. His selections again reflected China's policy: appease Hong Kong's people with safe local appointments, but safeguard China's interests with the appointment of proven loyalists. China's overriding concern would continue to be to ensure that Hong Kong "would not become a Western capitalist Trojan Horse handed over by the British to bring down its political system."[12] This paranoia was heightened by the knowledge of what had happened in the USSR and its satellites during the collapse of Communist regimes in Eastern Europe just five years earlier.

In Memory of Priscilla

In January of that year, Renske happily announced that she was pregnant. Since I was almost fifty-seven at the time, I felt like Zechariah—a bit dumb-struck, but eagerly looking forward to the big event. We kept the news to ourselves until she had passed the first trimester, and then enjoyed sharing it with friends and family. When a sonogram showed that it would be a girl, after considerable deliberation we chose the name Priscilla after the energetic church leader by that name in the Book of Acts. Renske shopped for maternity clothes, and we both spent a Saturday afternoon looking at all the paraphernalia one needs to welcome a newborn into the household. By then four months had passed and all appeared well, so we sent a letter to our forty-two RCA supporting churches announcing the glad news.

The very next day, I was called out of a broadcast session to answer an urgent phone call. It was Renske, and she was sobbing. She had been to the doctor for a routine check-up, and the doctor announced sadly that little Priscilla had inexplicably died in the womb. I raced home to try and console a shattered Renske, and then we went to the hospital where the fetus was induced. The whiplash effect of anticipating a birth but experiencing a death was traumatic. Ironically, the day was Good Friday.

Weakened but determined, my dedicated wife insisted on going through with a liturgical dance at Union Church Hong Kong on Easter Sunday for a service that was to be televised. Knowing the difficult circumstances under which she was dancing, she was a great inspiration of faith and courage to me and many others on that day. Then it was

---

[12]   Ibid., 216.

our sad duty to write an addendum to the letter we had just sent out to the churches telling of this sorrowful turn of events. As with so many others who suffer miscarriages, we will always wonder what little Priscilla might have been like had she seen the light of day.

Cracks in the Christian Coalition

Throughout the roller coaster events of the Patten years, cracks had appeared in the unity of the Hong Kong church as it responded to public events. For the most part, the Evangelical churches and the Chinese Christian Churches Union took the conservative view that the churches should expend their energy preparing local Christians to survive life under the Communists, and that they should leave the political arena to others. As Philip Lam wrote,

> Among evangelical churches, the emphasis is on church growth and evangelism, both in the number of churches and in the number of individual Christians. The goal is to have 2000 [Protestant] churches in Hong Kong by the year 2000....The basic unit is a cell group of about 15 people who meet together for Bible study and fellowship in different locations. New cell groups are started with three people who invite friends and newcomers until the group grows to 15.[13]

Dr. Philemon Choi, director of the evangelical Breakthrough parachurch organization, outlined the three major issues that, in his opinion, should dominate evangelical mission thinking.

> 1. Hong Kong is facing the crisis of [its people] becoming a rootless generation....Half a million will emigrate by 1997....The Roman Catholic Church has made a public pledge to stay, but the Protestant churches have spoken with a confused voice....2. Hong Kong is now facing a crisis of the family. Many families of our businessmen are becoming a fatherless generation....They are "astronauts" who fly back and forth to visit absentee families....How will our churches fill the breech?...3. Hong Kong is now facing the crisis of being over-saturated with information. This is resulting in the pluralization of our society. Our churches do not have a serious commitment to offer a "voice in the wilderness."[14]

[13] Lam, Philip, "Current Trends in Theological Thought Regarding Hong Kong and 1997," *News & Views*, Dec. 1994, 17.

[14] Choi, Philemon, "Quotable Quotes: Mission in Hong Kong in the 90s," *News & Views*, March 1993, 26–27.

The Hong Kong Christian Institute, the Hong Kong Christian Women's Council, and other such organizations and groups took the activist view that the churches should confront those who would deny democracy and human rights to the people of Hong Kong as an integral part of their participation in the redemptive mission of God. Reflecting this view, the institute's director, Kwok Nai-wang, in a major policy paper entitled, "The Response of Hong Kong's Churches to 1997," wrote,

> Both the evangelical and the mainline churches have become more and more conservative. There is an eleventh commandment that dominates their minds: "Do not rock the boat; play it safe."...Fortunately, the Church of Jesus Christ is not just made up of denominations and congregations. It also includes those Christians who gather together and try to witness to God's love and justice. There have been Christian groups formed in recent years whose major aim is to address the 1997 needs by trying to make some contribution towards the further development of Hong Kong....They constantly provide a much needed forum for concerned Christians. Because of their efforts, a Christian voice is often heard on important socio-political issues, and a Christian presence is felt in the citizens' struggle for justice, democracy and human rights.[15]

In another policy paper, entitled "The Political Future of Hong Kong," he wrote,

> Since Hong Kong's Governor, Chris Patten, put forth his constitutional reform proposals in October 1992, China and Britain have both been using microphone diplomacy in attempting to force the other party to accept their position. At this moment, they have come to an impasse....Nevertheless, I want to argue that yes, Hong Kong's political future is at the mercy of China, but there is still a role that the citizens of Hong Kong can play....I personally think that Chris Patten is going in the right direction. What he is trying to do is to build a stronger government by making it more representative and more accountable to the citizens. In this way, he is setting standards for the future government of Hong Kong. The British Government should continue to give Patten its full backing.[16]

---

[15] *News & Views*, Dec. 1992, 16.
[16] *News & Views*, March 1994, 14, 16.

HKCC general secretary
Tso Man-king (left) with
staff member Philip Lam

By and large, the mainline churches, represented by the Hong Kong Christian Council, took the mediating view that the churches should neither retreat from involvement in public issues nor antagonize the participants in the political struggle through confrontation. Instead, it should seek to find a middle way that would bring reconciliation and meet everyone's needs. For example, after the breakdown in relations between Britain and China in 1992, the council's alarmed general secretary wrote,

> The dispute between Britain and China over the Governor's political reform plan has drawn a mixed reaction from the people of Hong Kong. Unfortunately, most of these reactions, whether "pro" or "con," have not been helpful to the situation, but have rather polarized and intensified the confrontation. During this time of conflict, it is crucial to maintain calmness and a proper posture. I believe that the church in Hong Kong can play a mediating role in this situation.[17]

A "Pastoral Letter to All Christians in Hong Kong" issued by the 120 participants in a November 1–5, 1995, council-sponsored Mid-Decade Church Mission Consultation reiterated Tso's line. The theme of the consultation, "Towards the 21st Century—Strong and Courageous in the Work of the Lord," was deliberately upbeat.

> We deeply hope that the citizens of Hong Kong do not feel powerless. We hope that you can have an attitude of trust and faith in China to participate in building a Hong Kong that is highly autonomous, prosperous, stable and just. Only on the basis of mutual trust can we have the right to petition the Chinese Government, to oversee the forthcoming SAR Government and

[17]   Tso Man-king, "A Response to Gov. Patten's Political Reforms," *News & Views*, Dec. 1992, 12.

to actualize the promises made in the Sino-British Declaration. Herein, we hope the Chinese and British Governments can truly cooperate with each other to build up the confidence of Hong Kong People for the future. Because of the many disputes between the British and Chinese Governments over the past few years, Hong Kong citizens are very conscious that their desires and wishes have been ignored and not respected. Therefore, they are anxious about the future. In the interest of Hong Kong's citizens, we want the Chinese and British Governments to replace suspicion with trust, engage in dialogue instead of disputes and seek cooperation rather than confrontation."[18]

Freedom, Democracy, and Human Rights

Meanwhile, Martin Lee's United Democrats continued to campaign actively for democratic reforms in Hong Kong, while Szeto Wah's Alliance in Support of the Patriotic and Democratic Movement in China continued to rally the people of Hong Kong to encourage the people of China to do the same. Each June 4 saw massive candlelight demonstrations, in which many Christians and their activist leaders participated, to commemorate those who had been massacred in Beijing in the struggle for democracy. China, of course, was not amused. It branded Lee and Wah as subversives, condemned their movements as efforts to turn Hong Kong into a subversive base from which to undermine the Chinese Communist Party, and banned the two men from visiting China. However, the louder the PRC complained, the more Hong Kongers rallied to Lee and Wah's cause. In the end, each passing year saw greater and greater percentages of Hong Kong's people leaving their apathetic attitudes behind and becoming more vocal in their determination not to allow China and Britain to simply supplant one colonial master with another.[19]

---

[18]   "Hong Kong Mid-Decade Church Mission Consultation: A Pastoral Letter to All Christians in Hong Kong," *News & Views*, Dec. 1994, 15.

[19]   Tsang, *Hong Kong*, 177. This state of affairs lasted until September 2005, when the chief executive, Donald Tsang Yam-kuen, initiated an offer for leading democrats to tour cities in the Pearl River Delta under the Legislative Council banner. This signaled a change in Beijing's policy, and henceforth the PRC pursued a strategy of "reconciliation" with the democrats in an effort to neutralize them and erode their support among the people of Hong Kong. Wu, Rose, "Democrats at the Crossroads," *Hong Kong Women Christian Council Newsletter*, July 2006, 1-2.

Lau Chin-shek and
the author at 2003 reunion

Protestant Christian voices were also prominent in rallying the people to the cause of democracy and human rights. Lau Chin-shek, director of the Christian Industrial Committee, was a vocal proponent who eventually gained a seat on the Legislative Council. Methodist pastor Lo Lung-kwong was active in organizing public rallies and demonstrations. Kwok Nai-wang, director of the Hong Kong Christian Institute, participated in demonstrations and wielded a powerful pen in publications that were widely read locally and around the world. For example, in an essay entitled "Hong Kong: A Modern City at Risk," he wrote,

> Hong Kong's future has been put in great danger because many of the ingredients for its success may not be present after 1997. We can blame China. But it is also true that as the sovereign state, Britain did not take time to explain the Hong Kong system to the Chinese side, and in crucial moments, failed to stand up to China and fight to have Hong Kong's system remain in force for 50 years after 1997 as promised by China and as enshrined in the Joint Declaration. Invariably, Britain caved in to China's demands.... Democracy is the only long-term solution for Hong Kong. Democracy is synonymous with the people's awareness of their responsibility for public affairs. As Hong Kong moves forward, it needs the full participation of all its citizens. Only a government elected directly by its citizens enjoys full support. In return, only such a government is duty bound to safeguard citizens' basic rights and freedoms. Hong Kong must have a government that authoritatively represents its citizens' views and is accountable to its citizens, rather than to Beijing, after 1997....Hong Kong's citizens must demand that China and Britain jointly implement the Sino-British Joint Declaration in both letter and spirit....To stand up to China, one of the biggest military powers in the world, whose population is 200 times greater than Hong Kong's,

is an awesome task. It requires a great deal of courage and even self-sacrifice. Hong Kong deserves the support of all those who are concerned about building civil societies in this world.[20]

During the two years leading up to the handover, the local newspapers were filled with articles ranging from in-depth analyses of every angle of the projected new arrangements in Hong Kong to sheer speculation. Every word any Chinese, British, or Hong Kong official said was put under the microscope, and the public hung on every syllable, Renske and I included. The pages of church publications were no different. Tso Man-king, Kwok Nai-wang, Lo Lung-kong, Joseph Kuang, Luk Fai, Hans Lutz, Peter Lee, and their evangelical and Roman Catholic counterparts continued to pour out a steady stream of articles that not only dealt with the ramifications of the handover for the church, but that also addressed the wider issues faced by the people of Hong Kong. These articles reflected the differences in opinion among the three "camps" when it came to strategy. However, all were agreed that the terms of the joint declaration and the Basic Law should be fully implemented with regard not only to religious freedom, but also to human rights and the democratization process. They differed in how they viewed Patten's attempted reforms, and the consequent row with China, but they were united in their distaste for China's disregard of the Basic Law that had resulted in the derailing of the "through train" and the establishment of an extra-legal Provisional Legislature. Meanwhile, fifty thousand Hong Kong people per year continued to emigrate, many of them Chinese Christians who, they said, had "been through this before."

The Last Lap to 1997

To rally Christian and community confidence in the final run-up to 1997, the Hong Kong Christian Council deliberately took a positive approach towards a rapidly modernizing China, the church in China, and the future of Hong Kong. On September 25, 1996, as a member of Hong Kong's Colloquium of Six Religious Leaders, it jointly hosted a first-ever China National Day Celebration at the Furama Hotel to celebrate China's national day October 1. Fifty members of the "Christian sector," including myself, were invited to meet and mix with over 350 PRC local officials and other guests.[21] In June 1996, the Hong Kong Christian Council joined others in welcoming an eleven-

---

[20]   *News & Views*, Sept. 1994, 16–17.
[21]   The Christian activist camp boycotted the ceremony. They believed strongly

member delegation from the PRC State Council's Religious Affairs Bureau to Hong Kong. At a Protestant reception hosted by the council, the director-general of the Religious Affairs Bureau, Ye Xiao-wen, gave a highly reassuring address concerning China's commitment to freedom of religion in the future SAR, and to the continued independence of Hong Kong's Christian churches and other faiths vis-à-vis the RAB and its counterparts in China.[22]

The council called on the churches to leave their colonial mentality behind, to celebrate their Chinese heritage, and to develop a more indigenized theology and practice. It further encouraged its member churches, rather than fearing and fleeing China, to create an intentional vision of their participation in the modernization and liberalization of China as part of their mission. As Tso Man-king put it, "Ask not what China can do for Hong Kong, but what Hong Kong can do for China."[23] As a practical demonstration of this principle, in the spring of 1995 the council, in cooperation with the China Christian Council, had launched "Project Nehemiah"—a fund-raising program to provide aid to rural Chinese churches for the reconstruction of crumbling church buildings. This was eventually expanded to include school buildings, disaster relief, and community development projects.[24]

What had been a steadily increasing stream of contacts between Hong Kong Christian groups and China Christian Council delegations and church groups since 1980 turned into a flurry of visits and exchanges. Hong Kong Christians saw firsthand how the churches in China were faring, and Chinese church leaders came to a better understanding of how Hong Kong's churches operated in both the spiritual and social realms. These exchanges also served to reassure Hong Kong's Christians that Christians in China were indeed experiencing a new day in terms of religious freedom and that the China Christian Council had no designs on gaining control over Hong Kong's churches.[25]

---

that until the PRC admitted responsibility for the Beijing massacre and showed a greater inclination towards encouraging the development of democracy and human rights in Hong Kong and China, the Hong Kong church should avoid any action that would give the slightest appearance of endorsing that regime.

22   "HKCC News," *News & Views*, Sept. 1996, 8–9 and Dec. 1996, 7.
23   Tso Man-king, "What Hong Kong Can Do for China," *News & Views*, Dec. 1995, 9.
24   It was our privilege to have the unforgettable experience of being part of several HKCC delegations to visit Christians in remote areas of China to help implement this project.
25   See my editorial, "China 1993: Impressions," in *News & Views*, Sept. 1993, 4.

CCC delegation in Hong Kong. CCC Gen. Sec. Shen Yi-fan (center); HKCC Gen. Sec. Tso Man-king (right)

To generate a spirit of hope, the council organized a yearlong series of upbeat events leading up to the handover. From December 6–8, a mock election for the first SAR chief executive was held in 130 voting stations around Hong Kong. The exercise was intended as a civic education program for Hong Kong people concerning their future right to directly elect the chief executive. Four fall seminars on various aspects of the Christian faith in the context of 1997 were organized. A "1997 Hong Kong Global Prayer Chain" among international ecumenical partners and overseas Chinese churches was launched. "The Hong Kong Christians Prayer Convention" for "Christians across denominational lines" was held June 1, 1997, in the Hong Kong Coliseum with ten thousand people in attendance.[26] The purpose of the gathering was "to give thanks for what God has done through the church in the past 150 years, and to pray for the future of Hong Kong on the eve of the change of sovereignty." An equally impressive and well-attended Christian music night was also conducted at the Coliseum. Massed church choirs sang anthems and led the audience in hymns and songs.

The evangelical churches had also been gearing up for 1997. The Hong Kong Church Renewal Movement organized a series of rallies at the Hong Kong Coliseum from November 29–December 1, 1996, with the theme, "Walking Together in Harmony." It also published the results of an exhaustive survey that showed that in the run-up to 1997, there were 1,056 Protestant churches with 380,000 members (of which 250,000 were currently in Hong Kong) and 300 Roman Catholic parishes with 250,000 members. The noted Taiwan evangelist, Christopher Sun, held a crusade in the Hong Kong Stadium December 7–8 of that year around the theme, "Hope of Tomorrow." A Luis Palau Crusade was conducted at the Hong Kong Stadium from April 10–13, 1997, with the theme, "The Eternal Hope." Popular Christian speaker

---

[26] "HKCC News," *News & Views*, March 1997, 7, and June 1997, 7.

and author, Dr. Tony Campolo, was featured during twelve days of events aimed especially at young people and youth workers. Dr. Stephen Tong, a world-famous speaker on mission to the Chinese people, held a series of meetings June 13–14. Most of these events stressed personal salvation in a context of crisis and potential suffering but did not deal with the wider practical concerns that the community as a whole was facing in terms of human rights, democratic values, and Christian social responsibilities.[27]

Meanwhile, the Christian activist groups had not been idle. Nine Christian organizations organized a forum, "Crisis and Opportunities of Religious Freedom in Hong Kong after 1997," in May 1996. The Hong Kong Christian Democratic Movement organized a memorial prayer gathering on May 31 and a "Special China Sunday" on June 2.[28] The Hong Kong Christian Institute organized a three-month study workshop based on books written by its director, Kwok Nai Wang, with topics like "Hong Kong—on the Verge of Re-colonization."[29] These groups energetically supported what had become an annual commemoration of the June 4th massacre and a rally for democracy in Hong Kong. On June 4, 1997, over twenty-five thousand people gathered in Victoria Park for what some feared might be the last such candlelight vigil that would be allowed.[30]

For months, visible preparations for the handover had been going on. The Royal Hong Kong Post dropped its "royal," retired the old red pillar QE II post boxes, and adopted a new logo and color scheme. For the first time in 156 years, as of July 1, Hong Kong stamps would appear without the royal visage on them and would read, "Hong Kong, China." The monarch would also disappear from the newly designed currency and from public buildings. A new pinkish flag, with Hong Kong's native Bauhinia blossom on it, would replace the old Hong Kong flag, with its British Union Jack and colonial logo. The PRC flag would, of course, replace the British Union Jack on all government buildings. All government branches and public organizations would have the word "royal" deleted from their names. They would also remove all vestiges of the colonial era from their premises—even the Royal Hong Kong Jockey Club.[31] British logos on Hong Kong & Shanghai Bank buildings

---

[27] "Local Church News," *News & Views,* Sept. 1996, 5; Dec. 1996, 6–7; and March 1997, 7.

[28] "Local Church News," *News & Views,* June 1996, 8.

[29] "Local Church News," *News & Views,* Sept. 1996, 7.

[30] Ibid., 11.

[31] The lone holdout was the Royal Hong Kong Yacht Club, which refused to follow suit.

Flag of the Hong Kong Special
Administrative Region

and other buildings began to disappear. An impressive Chinese foreign affairs building was erected just down the street from Union Church Hong Kong, while the British built a beautiful new consulate on the edge of Hong Kong Park. The most impressive structure of all was a huge new extension of the Hong Kong Exhibition and Convention Centre jutting out into Hong Kong harbor, built especially for the handover ceremonies.

Some things, however, would not be changed. Traffic would continue to move on the left. English street names, even royal ones, would be allowed to remain, along with the statues of Queen Victoria in Victoria Park and King George VI in the Botanical Garden. "Government House," the impressive mansion of Hong Kong's governors, would be preserved as well, but would be turned into a venue for chamber music concerts and other community events. The historic commander in chief's residence had already been converted into a Chinese teapot museum; the admiral of the fleet's residence was turned into an orphanage; and the old military barracks in what were now Kowloon Park and Hong Kong Park became history and art museums. The new SAR would remain a separate jurisdiction, continuing to use English common law. The border between the SAR and the PRC would continue to be patrolled as before, and only authorized immigrants and tourists would be able to cross it. Hong Kong would remain a free port with its own customs and retain its own immigration controls.

The week of the handover finally arrived. What had seemed like a long way off upon our arrival in Hong Kong in 1974 was now upon us. In another week's time, we and our colleagues and compatriots would be living under a Communist regime. Spurred on by the speculative foreign press (who sent some six thousand media people to cover the event), there were those who looked with trepidation at the columns of People's Liberation Army troops who were poised just north of the

The Rev. Lee Ching-chee

border, ready to occupy agreed-upon British military installations. Would there be protests by the Democrats? Would there be shooting in the streets?

My close colleague and prominent Church of Christ in China leader, Lee Ching-chee, best summed up the feelings of the majority of Christians in Hong Kong immediately before the handover in an interview with *News & Views*.

Some people say that things will just continue more or less the same. Now if that is true, if things continue and we carry on as usual, why do we get so excited or get so frightened? Feeling-wise, though, things will be different because we feel that we will be real Chinese, that we are in China, not a colony, so emotionally Chinese would naturally feel happy. But we have our reservations and hesitations. We know the record of human rights in China, the way they treat their people, the way they do things—it's another standard. It really seems like a different world.

Hong Kong people have to try to live in this different world, we have to try to get used to it. For those of us who don't want to leave or can't leave, we have to face the facts and make the best of it. Hong Kong people are good at that. We didn't have smooth sailing all these past 150 years. There were times when people thought it was the end of the world too. I remember the riots in the '60s...I have mixed feelings—I am not for, I am not against the Hand-over. There is no choice. There are bound to be some "inconveniences," such as traveling to other countries or dealing with government officials, etc. We must be prepared for it. Don't expect that everything will be the same as now. It can't be the same. We have to get ourselves ready. Many of our partner churches are so nervous about the Hand-over. But if you look at changes of governments in other places, there is usually bloodshed, violence, and unrest. In Hong Kong, it is very smooth. We don't expect rioting and violence. Except what is not smooth are the feelings of people's hearts. On the surface there is nothing, all very calm, but deep down there are storms of the heart. There are many different feelings about China, about the future.[32]

My friend Ng Shan-ho, head pastor of the fastest growing church in Hong Kong, the four-thousand-member Wing Kwong Pentecostal Holiness Church, put it this way.

> Quite a lot of local pastors, like me, are very positive about seeing Hong Kong return to our motherland. We recognize the Church may encounter a lot of difficulties and hindrances in the future, but 1997 has brought a lot of fresh air and good changes to the Church. The 1997 issue in the early 1980s came like a bomb and shocked most of our pastors. But eventually it did a lot of good things to the Church. It helped the Church to revive...1997 has helped the pastors as well as the churches to cope with a different environment. In the past, pastors always preached they really trusted in the Lord. But in reality, no—they trusted in the environment, they trusted in the peaceful situation in Hong Kong. But now when the pastors say they trust in the Lord, they are really trusting in the Lord."[33]

The council's Tso Man-king summed it up this way:

> The church in Hong Kong should give a positive and constructive interpretation of the 1997 reality by bringing hope to the people and serving as a bridge between the two systems....The churches in Hong Kong have a very important role to play by encouraging the people to accept the reality of "One Country, Two Systems," which does not mean that Hong Kong will be an "independent" entity, but rather under the sovereignty of China striving forward to a self-governing capitalist system with a high level of autonomy. It will take the wisdom of discernment to strike a balance in order to maintain prosperity and stability as well as full cooperation from the China counterpart. The churches need to stand in solidarity with the people and to take into serious consideration the majority of the people, their concerns and their total well being. Most of all, the churches need to be united in

---

[32] Lee, Ching-chee, "Lift Up Thy Voice," *News & Views*, June 1997, 3.
[33] "HKCC News," *News & Views*, Sept. 1996, 3.

faith, hope and love, especially on issues of peace, justice and the integrity of God's creation.[34]

I expressed my own view in an article for the *Church Herald*, in which I surveyed the reactions of various Christian groups in Hong Kong to the advent of 1997 and suggested six areas of ministry and mission that were crucial for the survival and growth of the Hong Kong church: involvement in the democratic process, communicating hope rather than fear, investing in young people, improving theological education, reaching the grassroots, and building bridges of understanding with China's churches. I summed it up by saying,

> The majority of Hong Kong's Christians have been involved in seeking a middle way: communication, negotiation, and accommodation. They believe that Christians need to live by faith and hope, not by fear and despair. They have been at work for years trying to build bridges of understanding and cooperation between churches in China and Chinese government officials. These efforts have resulted in a number of "understandings" with Beijing that rest on the basic principles of religious freedom as enshrined in the Basic Law....The key question, of course, is whether a leopard can ever fundamentally change its spots, and whether to trust the word of the present regime is naiveté. Speaking as a Christian minister in Hong Kong, this approach needs to be given a fair chance as long as no basic element of the gospel or no essential ingredient in the recipe for religious freedom is compromised.[35]

In November 1995, I accepted a call to be the pastor of the historic Union Church Hong Kong. Founded by British missionary scholar James Legge in 1854, it had subsequently birthed four congregations—one English-speaking and one Chinese-speaking on each side of the harbor. The congregation I pastored was multicultural, multidenominational, and ecumenical. It included people from twenty-two nations, including many local bilingual Chinese. On the Sunday before the handover, I knew that my people were expecting me to address their fears and bolster their hopes. I preached on Paul's instructions in Romans 13:1-7 concerning the duties of a just government and the

---

[34] Tso, Man-king, "General Secretary's Column," *News & Views*, Sept. 1996, 2.
[35] Karsen, Wendell, "Handing Over Hong Kong," *Church Herald*, July/Aug. 1997, 8–11.

Ecumenical participants
in author's induction service
at Union Church

duties of loyal citizens. I expressed the hope that China would not only keep its promises regarding religious freedom and the legal provisions outlined in the Basic Law, but that it would also allow the development of human rights and the democratic process as outlined in the joint declaration. Christians are called on to obey the authorities, I said, but only insofar as those authorities promote the good of the society they govern and oppose evil. When they do not, like Jeremiah, it is a Christian's patriotic responsibility to expose, oppose, and sometimes even depose whatever is harmful to that society. I cited devout Roman Catholic and ardent democrat Martin Lee as a courageous example of such a patriot in our own time. After the service, a concerned member said to me, "If you keep preaching like that, you could land in jail."

Five Stars over Hong Kong

Prince Charles steamed into the harbor aboard the Royal Yacht. The departing British staged a number of celebrative events, including an outdoor concert and a spectacular fireworks display over the harbor. On June 30, the day of the historic Hand-over, I rushed around the territory, camera in hand, to record the removal of the last vestiges of British power on buildings, flag poles, and vehicles. Like everyone else, Renske and I watched on television as the British flag over Government House was lowered for the last time and presented to Chris Patten, the last governor, who struggled to control his emotions. That evening, in a gala outdoor ceremony marred by pouring rain, Patten addressed the people of Hong Kong for the last time, and Prince Charles bid Great Britain's farewell to a place and a people over whom it had ruled for 156 years. Precisely at midnight, in the special hall built for the occasion, we watched as the transfer of power took place. Both the prince and the president of the PRC, Jiang Ze-min, addressed the gathering of dignitaries, followed by a flag ceremony and the swearing in of the new Hong Kong administration. The new chief executive, Tung Chee-hwa, then addressed the people of Hong Kong. Meanwhile, we had become the first Reformed Church missionaries to serve in China since the last one had been expelled by the Chinese Communists in 1951.[36]

Following the Hand-over ceremony, the prince, the governor and other British dignitaries boarded the royal yacht and, with a naval escort bearing the rest of the British administration who had not flown out, sailed away into the night. At the same time, People's Liberation Army units crossed the border and proceeded through the streets to former British military installations without incident. Next, we watched Martin Lee and his United Democrats colleagues mount a demonstration on the balcony of the Legislative Council building. They were protesting the illegal formation of a Provisional Legislature and the expulsion of the duly elected 1995 Legislative Council before its term was due to expire in 1999. There was concern that they might be arrested. We, like our compatriots, had mixed feelings. Nostalgia, joy, foreboding, relief, anger, pride, uncertainty, and hope all swirled inside us.

The next morning, it felt strange to walk to my study at Union Church and see the PRC's red flags, with their five yellow stars, flying above Government House and other government buildings. It was even more ironic to see the flag flying over the downtown military headquarters that had a Christian chapel with a prominent cross built into the side of it. I had once visited that chapel, but now it would be used for other purposes. However, I found myself praying that, like the miracle of the resurrection of the Christian Church in China over the previous eighteen years, some day the people who now occupied that building would also find salvation in the Christ of that cross.

No sooner had the British left than the celebrations sponsored by the new government began. In an omen that was not lost on the superstitious Chinese, the weather cleared up, the sun came out, and all enjoyed the show. Official receptions and gala events were capped with an even more spectacular fireworks show over the harbor. One could almost sense a huge collective sigh of relief going up from the people of Hong Kong that the Hand-over had gone so smoothly. There was caution in the air, but there was also a palpable sense of Chinese pride welling up in people's breasts. They were no longer colonial subjects but had returned to the motherland. In that vein, there was an aura of genuine celebration. The foreign press was baffled. Many had been making dire predictions about the Hand-over and its aftermath, and

---

[36] Dr. Ted Oltman, who served as a physician at the Hope-Wilhelmina Hospital in Amoy from 1930–1943 and 1947–1951.

here was a citywide celebration going on! At a large press assembly, one reporter remarked, "There is no story here," meaning that good news was not really news.

As for the churches, prayer services, candle light vigils, fasts, thanksgiving services, and other events were held by Christian groups all over the territory. Most of them took place during the actual Hand-over ceremonies marking the transfer of power from the United Kingdom to the People's Republic of China. The Salvation Army, the Methodist Church Hong Kong, an ecumenical coalition of eight Christian activist groups, the Roman Catholic Church, the Hong Kong Chinese Christian Churches Union, the Anglican Diocese of Hong Kong and Macao, the Hong Kong Christian Renewal Movement, and others urged people to be steadfast in their faith and hopeful about their future as Hong Kong entered a new era. The people of Hong Kong had not gotten all that they had hoped for in the Basic Law, but they had gotten more than they had expected. They were at last free of the cross of colonialism. They could only hope that another cross would not be thrust upon them.

Changes and Challenges

There were a number of immediate changes. Public holidays for the Queen's birthday and Liberation Day were replaced with the Chinese National Day and Hong Kong SAR Establishment Day. It was announced that in 1999, one of the Christian holidays (of which there were four) would be replaced with a holiday to commemorate Buddha's birthday. Beginning in 1998, all secondary schools would be required to use Chinese as the chief language of instruction. On October 10, Taiwan's national day, police tore down Taiwanese flags and banners hung from their traditional places. The "flag wars" were over. A government representative said such displays were "against the one country principle," and permission had not been given to display them. On November 9, flags were raised as usual at the downtown Cenotaph to mark Remembrance Day, which commemorated soldiers of all nationalities who had died during the two World Wars, including those who had died defending Hong Kong. However, this time the event was privately sponsored. There was no governor, there were no military officers, and there was no official pomp. Even though Chinese flags were substituted for British flags, no SAR official made an appearance.

During the first year after the Hand-over, the churches, and indeed the whole community, breathed a lot easier. It became apparent that China by and large was making a great effort to abide by the terms of the Basic Law and not meddle in Hong Kong's local affairs, particularly its religious affairs. However, Christians were soon called upon to make some hard decisions about which they had differences of opinion. The SAR government invited the "religious sector" to participate in an eight hundred-member SAR Election Committee, which would be responsible for the "election" of ten members of the new Legislative Council to replace the Provisional Legislative Council in 1998. Forty seats on the committee were reserved for this sector, seven of which were to be filled by the Hong Kong Christian Council to represent the Protestant subsector.

The Christian activist camp encouraged the churches to boycott the process. They argued that this "Election Committee" was not provided for in the Basic Law and was therefore an illegal move by the PRC to weaken further Hong Kong's progress towards democracy. Patten's reforms had provided for ten legislators to be directly elected by the people of Hong Kong on a "one person, one vote" basis, along with the twenty others that had already been agreed upon by China and Britain before the Hand-over. In other words, half of the sixty-seat legislature should have been elected by universal suffrage. Now ten would be indirectly "elected" by the Election Committee, while the other twenty would be elected by geographical constituencies.

As with the previous election controversy, the HKCC sought a middle way. The council had two concerns. It did not want to be seen as endorsing the undemocratic "election" process engineered by the PRC. It also did not want to violate the principle of separation of church and state by appointing representatives to participate directly in the political process. After two broad public consultations, the HKCC decided that instead of simply nominating seven candidates to the Election Committee, it would spend thousands of staff hours and HK$85,000 organizing a public election process among Protestant Christians to *elect* the candidates. This would in effect enable the council to avoid direct participation in the "election'" process and at the same time provide an excellent educational exercise in public democracy for Hong Kong's Protestant Christians. The church leaders reasoned that in this way they were setting an example for the authorities, rather than endorsing the limitations that had been illegally placed on the selection process for the new 1998 legislature.

The council conducted a mass advertising campaign, held a series of training events for poll workers, and organized a public forum where voters could meet and question candidates. March 15, 1998, was proclaimed "Democracy Sunday," and the election was conducted through voting stations set up in more than 150 ecumenical, evangelical, and Pentecostal churches, including Union Church. The slogan was, "We need to pay a price to enhance democracy in an undemocratic world." The public media gave the election wide coverage. Tso Man-king summed up the exercise by saying, "Although the council had only two months to promote the public election among the churches, the council has created an unprecedented event by maximizing democracy to its best in a not yet fully democratic SAR context. Hopefully by doing so, we may speed up the process of the full realization of democracy in Hong Kong!"[37]

In the end, three main political parties contended for seats in the Legislative Council elections—the prodemocracy Democratic Party, the probusiness Liberal party, and the Beijing-oriented Democratic Alliance for the Betterment of Hong Kong. Fifty-three percent of the electorate turned out in torrential rains for the May 23 elections. Even though the political deck was stacked against them, the prodemocracy candidates, many of whom had been "de-elected" by the PRC in 1997, won more than 60 percent of the popular vote and took sixteen of twenty directly elected seats. However, thanks to the PRC-arranged system of functional constituencies, which it could more easily influence, the remaining two-thirds of the assembly was chosen by fewer than a hundred thousand voters of various "professions." Therefore, despite their victory in the public polls, prodemocracy candidates won only twenty of the Legislative Council's sixty seats. Nevertheless, we all rejoiced. Fresh from victory, Martin Lee vowed that the Democrats would do their best to push for full democracy in the next elections in the year 2000.[38]

The Calm before the Storm

By the first anniversary of the Hand-over in July 1998, the atmosphere in Hong Kong was quite positive, and confidence had been dramatically restored. Although it maneuvered behind the scenes to make sure its vital interests were not compromised, the PRC by and large had acted responsibly in keeping its commitments. The steady flow of emigrants out of Hong Kong had dropped by half, and many that had fled abroad began making plans to return. The HKCC's Tso Man-king summed up the mood of the majority of Hong Kong's Christians:

[37] Tso, Man-king, "Maximizing Democracy in An Undemocratic World," *News & Views*, March 1998, 1–2.

[38] "Freedom in the World—Hong Kong," [China] (2008) *Freedom House*, http://www.freedomhouse.org/inc/content/pubs/fiw/inc_country_detail.cfm?year=2008&country=7527&pf, October 22, 2009.

HKCC general secretary Tso Man-king

One year ago before the Hand-over from British sovereignty, Hong Kong was overcast by the shadow of uncertainty. Many foreign journalists and reporters painted a bleak picture of Hong Kong, as if the 1st of July, 1997, would be the doomsday for Hong Kong....Some democratic leaders and church groups who vowed to take a "prophetic role" echoed the outsiders' opinions by proclaiming the "gospel of despair"....Thank God the Hand-over did not happen the way the outsiders and so-called prophets had speculated. The Hand-over process actually was too good to be true. It was the most peaceful transfer of power and sovereignty in the history of the world. Not only was there no violence, no bloodshed or military coup, the whole process was filled with glamorous events and grandiosity. During the past year, the top leadership of China...repeatedly affirmed the Government's commitment to the "One Country, Two Systems" policy for Hong Kong people to govern Hong Kong with a high degree of autonomy. [President] Jiang also reminded the high officials not to interfere in the internal affairs of Hong Kong....There is still freedom of speech, freedom of the press, and nothing much has changed....During the past year in Hong Kong, there were 1,200 requests for rallies and all were approved. Even when about 40,000 people gathered together to commemorate the June 4th incident this year in Victoria Park, it was a peaceful gathering with honor and dignity, regardless of the heavy downpour of rain. There were no comments from either the Chinese authority or the Hong Kong SAR Government....Religiously speaking, Hong Kong still enjoys its religious freedom....I have never heard of any mention of religious interference from China. As far as the churches are concerned, not only are activities going on as usual, there are more and more churches in Hong Kong building rapport and relationships with the Church in China....This is being carried out through mutual visits and the implementation of different projects in China, including evangelism and lay leadership training....I have no intention to paint a simple picture, but rather to point out that it is a very crucial moment for Hong Kong. We are shaping our own destiny and direction based on "One Country, Two Systems," maintaining the capitalistic identity and way of life for another 50 years unchanged. On the one hand, the people of Hong Kong are rediscovering their identity as Chinese and becoming proud of it; on the other hand we are also building the future of Hong Kong to be a more democratic, prosperous and caring society with freedom for all.[39]

Significantly, beginning in September 1998, the issues raised by the lead-up to the Hand-over that had dominated the church's agenda for over a decade, and indeed reference to any political and human rights concerns, all but disappeared from the pages of the council's publication, *News & Views*. Unlike previous consultations, the statement issued by the Mission Consultation of the Hong Kong Churches in the 21st Century in November 1999, contains *no mention* of such issues.[40] However, there were those, like veteran missionary activist Hans Lutz, who had joined the council staff in 1997, who were uneasy about emerging signs that pointed to the deterioration of Hong Kong's human rights guarantees.[41] Before its demise, the Provisional Legislature had repealed labor laws on collective bargaining, antiunion discrimination, the right to associate internationally without notification, and the use of union funds for political purposes. It had also repealed or amended twenty-four Hong Kong laws that allegedly contravened the Basic Law in a way that strengthened the hand of the governing authorities. These included one law that had placed the Bill of Rights above other laws and two laws (the Societies Ordinance and the Public Order Ordinance) that had taken some of the teeth out of the previous colonial security laws.

Christian activist groups like the Hong Kong Christian Institute and their allies continued to support the Democrats' push for the

---

39 Tso Man-king, "One Year After the Handover," *News & Views*, June 1998, 1–2.
40 See "Mission Consultation of the Hong Kong Churches in the 21st Century: The Consultation Statement," *News & Views*, Dec. 1999, 4.
41 See Lutz, Hans, "Human Rights in Hong Kong after July 1, 1997," *News & Views*, June 1998, 9–11.

St. Andrew's
Anglican Church

development of full democracy in Hong Kong. The Basic Law allowed for all legislators as well as the chief executive to be elected by universal suffrage after 2007, but the British had never gotten the PRC to agree to a definite timeline to achieve this. In addition, such developments would have to be approved by two-thirds of the legislature (only half of which would be directly elected by then), the chief executive, and China's National People's Congress. Nevertheless, the activists believed that "people power" would eventually prevail.

The basic mood in 1998 was one of renewed hope. By and large, a relieved calm descended on the SAR as a whole and on the Christian church in particular. The church had struggled to remove the colonial cross and to avoid replacing it with a Communist cross, and it had been strengthened in the process. Despite the attrition of more than a decade of emigration, Protestants numbered 280,000 and Roman Catholics 250,000 (or a combined 7.7 percent of a population of 7 million), worshiping in 1,100 congregations and 58 parishes respectively. Christians were sponsoring 40 percent of the schools in Hong Kong, 60 percent of the social service agencies, and running 12 hospitals and 19 theological seminaries.[42] However, more important than statistics, congregations had been strengthened and faith deepened among those who had stayed through those uncertain years that had spanned the transition of Hong Kong from a British colony to a Chinese Special Administrative Region.

[42] "Hong Kong Churches (1999 Statistics)," *News & Views*, Fall 2000, 3.

Karsens with HKCCC staff

With the crisis generated by the transition to Chinese rule abated, it was time for us to bid farewell to a place that we had come to call home and a people that we had come to know as friends. The church in strife-torn and needy Indonesia beckoned us to "come over and help us," and we responded to what would be our last mission challenge abroad. The outpouring of gratitude from our congregation, our former colleagues at the Church of Christ in China and the Hong Kong Christian Council, the Wai Ji Centre Board, the Bible Society Board, and the many friends we had made in the community at large was humbling. As we "ate our way out of Hong Kong," we gained weight but shed tears. God had given us so many opportunities for challenging service in solidarity with a people who had faced and then weathered a major crisis. We left with grateful hearts.

Fast Forward

Return and Reunion

Renske and I had the privilege of visiting Hong Kong again in 2001, 2006, and 2007. We had, of course, kept up with events through various publications and through our contacts with friends and colleagues. However, it was helpful to have these three opportunities to see for ourselves what we had been hearing. We also enjoyed reunions with our colleagues at the Hong Kong Christian Council, Union Church and elsewhere, and with dear friends like Hudson and Amy Soo, Judy Butler, Kwok Nai-wang, Lee Ching-chee, Silva Yeung, and many others.

Despite an economic setback, Hong Kong had continued to develop physically and to generate wealth at a breathtaking pace. The Pearl of the Orient was even more spectacular than we remembered it, except for an increase in air pollution. It had welcomed the new millennium with optimistic hoopla like the rest of the world. It had also weathered the Asian economic crisis of 1999, the SARS epidemic of 2003, and the bird flu epidemic of 2004.

However, after the first euphoria of the peaceful Hand-over had worn off, considerable tension had developed in the areas of democracy and human rights. There had been an uproar in 1999 when the supposedly independent High Court ruled in favor of the children of refugees who were now Hong Kong citizens having the right of abode in Hong Kong. The chief executive, backed by the PRC, opposed the ruling because it would open the floodgates for thousands of children in China to legally come to Hong Kong and put a huge strain on the SAR's resources. When the SAR government lost the case, the chief executive asked for a ruling from China's National People's Congress as to whether the High Court decision could be overturned on the basis of the NPC's right to interpret the Basic Law. The NPC said yes and, in effect, undermined the independence of Hong Kong's judiciary. A large public outcry, including the voices of the Hong Kong Christian Council and other Christian groups, produced a promise from Tung Chee-hwa that he would only resort to such an appeal in the future in a rare instance. But a precedent had been set, and the damage had been done. A council statement declared, "The resolution to ask the National People's Congress for interpretation of the Basic Law is contrary to the spirit of a high degree of autonomy in Hong Kong."[43]

---

[43] "Uniting Together for a Future with Love," *News & Views*, June 1999, 5. This

Hong Kong Island in 2007

The September 2000 Legislative Council elections saw 43 percent of the registered voters elect a second Legislative Council for a four-year term. Twenty-four seats were elected on a geographic basis through universal suffrage, 30 seats through functional (occupational) constituencies, and 6 seats through indirect election by an Election Committee. Democracy advocates complained that the elections for functional constituency and Election Committee seats were undemocratic. Only 180,000 voters were eligible to elect the 36 legislators elected by the functional constituencies and the Election Committee, while over 3 *million* voters were eligible to vote for the 24 legislators elected by geographical constituencies. Prodemocracy candidates won 17 of the 24 seats elected on a geographic basis and 22 seats overall. However, as in 1998, they won a pyrrhic victory since, although they had garnered a majority of the popular vote, they constituted a minority on a council whose Byzantine rules further restricted their access to actual power.[44]

One of the biggest controversies of this period was over the SAR government's bid, at the behest of Beijing, to have the legislature pass a stiffened set of "antisubversion laws" under Article 23 of the Basic Law. This move really set the people of Hong Kong, including its Christians, on edge. The controversy raged from the winter of 2002 through the fall of 2003. Political issues were suddenly once again splashed across the pages of Christian publications, including *News & Views*, and brought Christians together in a way that they had not been together since the

statement was endorsed by twenty-three Christian organizations. See also Lutz, Hans, "The Right of Abode Issue and the Churches," *News & Views*, Sept. 1999, 5–7.

44 "Hong Kong Legislative Election 2000," *Wikipedia*, 20 October, 2009, http://en.wikipedia.org/wiki/Hong_Kong_legislative_election,_2000, October 22, 2009.

days after the Tiananmen massacre. People sensed that this issue could make or break the protection of their basic rights.

The council issued a paper, "Response to the Consultation Paper Regarding Implementation of Article 23 of the Basic Law." It read,

> For many Hong Kong people the implementation of Article 23 of the Basic Law is a very sensitive and emotionally charged issue. Many Hong Kong people do not yet have a concept of what it means to belong to a country. Legislation on Article 23 brings them face to face with the Central People's Government. There are fears that in this context "one country" may over-ride "two systems." We also note that there is a fear that the local judiciary may not stand up to political pressure....The consultation on implementing Article 23 of the Basic Law has reminded us that many of the laws left from colonial times give the authorities far-reaching powers to restrict activities by citizens. They lend themselves easily to abuse. Both authorities and the community must remain vigilant and strive to eliminate or amend laws which threaten the freedoms guaranteed in the Basic Law.[45]

The statement goes on to discuss the negative implications of the suggested changes in laws governing misprision of treason, freedom of expression, freedom of information, proscription of organizations, emergency search and seizure powers, and time limits for bringing prosecutions. It concludes, "Security of the state cannot be achieved at the expense of people's security. We put the highest value on the respect for human rights, including freedom of information, expression and religion."[46] This statement was followed by "An Open Letter on the Legislation of Article 23 of the Basic Law," addressed to the members of the Legislative Council,[47] and an article by the council's new general secretary, the Reverend Eric So,[48] entitled, "In Christ There is No Boundary."[49]

---

[45]   "Hong Kong Christian Council: Response to the Consultation Paper Regarding Implementation of Article 23 of the Basic Law," *News & Views*, Dec. 2002, 3.

[46]   Ibid., 4.

[47]   *News & Views*, Summer 2003, 5.

[48]   Tso Man-king had retired in August 1999, and Eric So, publisher of the Chinese Christian Literature Council, had replaced him in September of that same year.

[49]   *News & Views*, Hong Kong Christian Council, Sept. 2003, 3.

To the Streets!

The people of Hong Kong were aroused. Beginning on July 1, 2003, the sixth anniversary of the Hand-over, a half million people, including thousands of Christians and many of their leaders, turned out to participate in a series of mass protests against the adoption of these measures. The protests were peaceful, but the message was not lost on the chief executive and his administration. In September, surprisingly, and in the face of PRC pressure, Tung Chee-hwa scrapped the proposals "for the immediate future."

It was in this context that the run-up to the September 2004 Legislative Council elections began. Since, as per agreement with the British, the number of directly elected seats was to be increased to thirty, the Democrats and their allies, despite formidable odds, were hoping to gain an outright majority. Their platform called for direct elections for the chief executive in 2007 and for all of the Legislative Council in 2008, as well as rapid political reform. The combination of the Article 23 reversal, plus the very real possibility that the Democrats might actually pull off what they were aiming at, was too much for the PRC. If there was one thing that the regime detested, it was any suggestion of knuckling under to "people power." The reaction was predictable. In order to "remove doubts" and "minimize disputes," in April the Standing Committee of the National People's Congress, upon receiving Tung Chee-hwa's report, gave an "interpretation" of parts of the Basic Law that relate to the constitutional development of Hong Kong. In essence, contrary to the Basic Law, the committee postponed indefinitely the direct election of the chief executive that had been scheduled for 2007 and any expansion of the number of directly elected legislators. It also made prior NPC consent yet another hurdle to be jumped if democratic reforms were to be initiated in the SAR. In effect, the "one country, two systems" formula had been replaced by "one country, one system," and the political rug had been pulled out from under the Democrats.[50]

The reaction in Hong Kong was also predictable. The people were now more than aroused; they were angry. The council issued a response that stated:

[This action] has caused Hong Kong people to worry whether the Central Government will continue to implement the policy

[50] Wu, Rose, "The Beginning of Beijing's Rule of Hong Kong," *Hong Kong Christian Institute Newsletter*, Issue 188, May, 2004.

of "One Country, Two Systems"....We deeply regret that the NPCSC...set unnecessary restrictions on universal suffrage which seriously hinder the progress of the constitutional development of Hong Kong....In our opinion, the discussions on the constitutional development are not finished but have entered into another more important stage. Thus, Hong Kong citizens should take hold of their rights and duties and continue to express their views actively. We pledge with the HK churches to promote the social concerns among the believers, and to work together to create a more democratic, just and compassionate society....The comprehensive discussions on the constitutional development should include other issues such as the relationship between the Executive and the Legislature, the evaluation of the Principal Officials Accountability System, Advisory and Statutory Bodies and the increasing power of the District Boards.[51]

Many churches and Christian bodies not only voiced the same objections, they participated in organizing the largest protests in Hong Kong's history. On June 4, 2004, the fifteenth anniversary of the Beijing massacre, 82,000 people gathered in Victoria Park to honor the memory of the dead and to demand democracy. A monument was set up that read, "Democracy's heroes stand forever." The crowd bowed three times in a traditional Chinese funeral gesture, then chanted slogans including "Demand accountability for the massacre!" One woman commented, "The People's Republic should be *for* the people, not for *killing* the people."[52]

Just one month later, on July 1, the seventh anniversary of the Hand-over, over half a *million* people gathered in and around Victoria Park. They gathered, in the words of Roman Catholic Bishop Joseph Zen Ze-kiun of Hong Kong, "to tell the central Chinese Government about the sufferings people have experienced in Hong Kong and their demand for justice."[53] It was the largest demonstration in the history

---

[51] "HKCC's Response to the Constitutional Development of Hong Kong and the Interpretation of the Basic Law by the NPCSC," *News & Views*, Summer 2004, 3.

[52] *The (London) Independent*, June 5, 2004, 2.

[53] *National Catholic Reporter*, July 16, 2004, 6. Five years later, on June 4, 2009, the twentieth anniversary of the massacre, 150,000 people gathered for another candlelight vigil in the same park. Bradsher, Keith, "Thousands Gather in Hong Kong for Tiananmen Vigil," June 4, 2009, *New York Times*, http://www.nytimes.com/2009/06/05/world/asia/05hong.html, October 25, 2009.

Hong Kong people march for democracy

of Hong Kong. The march was preceded by an ecumenical prayer rally attended by more than fifteen thousand Christians. During the march to the downtown area, people shouted slogans and sang songs demanding freedom and democracy. Martin Lee was quoted as saying, "Even though Beijing has rejected direct elections in 2007 and 2008, it is worth protesting with a hope to fight for it in the future."[54]

In a September 2004 article entitled, "The Role of the Church in Constitutional Development," the HKCC's Eric So wrote:

> Through the Council's initiative, we are involved in social and political issues for the Churches in Hong Kong....The Hong Kong Christian Council has been playing an active role in social and political agendas because we are following God's word....Hong Kong has been developing the one country, two systems model since 1997. All the people living in this city have been given rights and the obligation to manage themselves. Now is an important moment for Hong Kong people to express their expectation and ideal on the future constitution, while Christians also need to assess our mission and ministry as well as the role and the participation of the Church in the constitutional development.[55]

On September 12, the people of Hong Kong went to the polls in record numbers. More than 3.2 million voters registered for the election, and the turnout rate was a historic high of 55.6 percent. The prodemocratic camp won eighteen out of thirty seats and 62 percent of the popular vote in the direct elections in the geographical constituencies, while picking up seven seats in the functional constituencies, for an overall total of twenty-five seats in the sixty-seat

[54] Ibid.
[55] *News & Views*, Fall 2004, 1–2.

legislature. Although it would still be in the minority, the prodemocracy camp had maintained the necessary threshold to block changes to the Basic Law if necessary.[56]

The last act in the drama before our June 2006 visit was the apparent sacking of Tung Chee-hwa as chief executive. In 2002, Tung had been "re-elected" unopposed by an eight-hundred-member "committee" loyal to Bejing for a second five-year term. In December 2004, China's new president, Hu Jin-tao, had humiliated Tung by reprimanding him on public television and instructing him to do a better job of governing Hong Kong. Two months later, Hong Kong's first chief executive, pleading ill health, handed in his resignation. Without any consultation with the people of Hong Kong, Beijing immediately and surprisingly replaced him with the popular former finance secretary, Donald Yam-kuen Tsang, as "acting chief executive"— surprisingly because Tsang was an ardent Roman Catholic and because his bishop, Joseph Zen, had been a key activist in the democracy and human rights movement in Hong Kong. In July, the Beijing-controlled eight-hundred-member elite Election Committee went through the motions of "electing" the unopposed Tsang to serve out Tung's remaining term until mid-2007.[57]

What Hong Kong's people would say and do about that had yet to be seen. The Beijing regime would need to be careful. Hong Kong was still the goose that laid golden eggs for the motherland, but the people of Hong Kong could only be pushed so far without killing the goose. Then, too, there was Taiwan. If the PRC were to kill the Hong Kong chicken to teach the Taiwan monkey a lesson, the Taiwan monkey would simply run away.

What would the future hold for Hong Kong? Would the people and the churches eventually be made to exchange the cross of colonialism for the cross of communism after all? Or would "people power" ultimately prevail and China change its ways and give Hong Kong's people the blessing they sought—the blessing of living as a patriotic but free people with a direct say in the decisions that affected their lives. Only time would tell. But somewhere in the background, people were already beginning to hear another clock ticking towards another deadline—2047, the year when China's fifty-year commitment to the "one country, two systems" formula would run out.

[56] "Hong Kong legislative election, 2004," Wikipedia, 20 October, 2009, http://en.wikipedia.org/wiki/Hong_Kong_Legislative_Council_elections,_2004, 22 October, 2009.

[57] Ibid.

As we left Hong Kong at the end of our 2007 visit, we encouraged our dear friends and colleagues at the Hong Kong Christian Council and elsewhere. We promised to pray for them as they continued their pilgrimage and faithfully carried out the mission of Christ, with all of its ramifications, in that strategic place that we had called home for so long.

Keeping in Touch

After our return to the United States, we kept in touch with events in Hong Kong and the church in Hong Kong through correspondence with our friends there, through new publications, and through the media. Overall, the year 2008 was fairly routine, except for the global financial tsunami that hit near its end. Suddenly the majority of Hong Kong's people, many of whom were just managing to make ends meet in the first place, had to tighten their belts. The widening gap between the wealthy and the poor got even wider. At the end of 2007, the unemployment rate had averaged 4.1 percent, the fourth straight year of decline, but by the end of 2008, many more people had lost their jobs. This situation was exacerbated by Hong Kong's continued population growth, its inhabitants in that year numbering more than 7 million.[58]

On the political front, the struggle continued for democratic reform and universal suffrage, but during the remainder of the year, the outcome remained uncertain. On the whole, Hong Kong's relations with China continued on a fairly even keel, but the PRC was as determined as ever to keep control of the political situation behind the scenes while granting a relatively free hand in the social and economic spheres. The chief executive, Donald Tsang, had submitted a report to Beijing saying that a substantial majority of Hong Kong's people wanted the chief executive elected by universal suffrage by 2012. However, in December, the Standing Committee of the National People's Congress issued a ruling saying it would only allow direct elections for the chief executive in 2017. It added that if the chief executive was elected directly, it would then *consider* introducing universal suffrage for the Legislative Council election in 2020.[59] In other words, if the 2017 election turned out to

[58] http://www.bing.com/search?q=Hong%20Kong%20Chief%20Executive%2
0Elections%202005&mkt=en-us&FORM=TOOLBR&DI=6244&CE=14.0
&CM=SearchWeb, September 30, 2008.
[59] Nevertheless the democrats kept the pressure on, hoping the PRC would bow to public pressure and move the dates up. Prodemocracy marches continued to be held on every anniversary of the Hand-over. On July 1, 2009, for example, 150,000 people took part in the march. Bradsher,

Beijing's satisfaction, the NPC would then allow direct election of the legislature in 2020.

This additional delay was a bitter disappointment for the democrats, who were fearful that the longer the delay, the more maneuvering room China would have to engineer yet another way to keep control in the future while appearing to concede it. As Andrew Jacobs reported,

> Many democracy advocates and civil libertarians here are increasingly anxious about whether laissez-faire Hong Kong can maintain its independence from Beijing's authoritarian grip and its distinct identity as an amalgam of Western and Chinese sensibilities....A growing roster of overseas visitors whose politics irritate Beijing have been denied entry to Hong Kong, and pro-China legislators have blocked efforts to include an uncensored account of Tiananmen Square in high school textbooks. Longtime advocates of democracy like Martin Lee warn that China is chipping away at Hong Kong's autonomy by fiat or by co-opting business leaders and politicians.
>
> On Saturday, Mr. Lee, the founder of Hong Kong's Democratic Party, disclosed that he had been the target of an assassination plot that he said the authorities foiled last August. He said the men were arrested not long after he wrote an editorial accusing China of failing to live up to its pledge to improve human rights. "If you throw a frog into boiling water, it will jump out right away," Mr. Lee said,..."but if you put the frog in warm water and cook it slowly, it doesn't jump. We are being cooked in Hong Kong, but hardly anyone is noticing."[60]

The Hong Kong Christian Council continued to press for democratic reform, universal suffrage, and ministry to the poor, but a number of churches (and particularly some megachurches) had once again become more inward-looking. As Ralph Lee, honorary general secretary of the HKCC put it,

---

Keith, "Hong Kong's Pro-Democracy March Draws Thousands," *New York Times*, July 2, 2009, http://www.nytimes.com/2009/07/02/world/asia/02hongkong.html?_r=1, October 25, 2009.

[60] Jacobs, Andrew, "Civil Liberties Within Limits After 12 Years of Beijing Rule," Memo From Hong Kong, *New York Times*, June 9, 2009, http://www.nytimes.com/2009/06/01/world/asia/01hong.html.

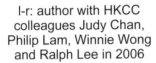

l-r: author with HKCC colleagues Judy Chan, Philip Lam, Winnie Wong and Ralph Lee in 2006

Paradoxically, as the world is getting larger and more complex, the church is shrinking and becoming more withdrawn....We tend only to find safety and satisfaction within the walls of the church. Even more so, faith and religion have become so personal that it is only "I and me" that matters. Sadly to say, ministers are not immune from the world values of a person in this present age. To be successful and powerful is to build up a personal power base in terms of numbers; that is, numbers of membership and the wealth of the church account. Even more frightening are some church ministers who would only target building up a congregation of young people and sidelining anybody over 30, much less the elderly, the vulnerable and the marginalized. Such is the peculiar, if not abnormal, church phenomenon in this city....We tend to mind our own "success" and care little about God's kingdom on earth.

To some, it's the pride of building one's own "kingdom" that matters, even to the point of separation from one's own denomination....Quite often now, a "healthy" church is measured by numerical growth and the age of the congregation....Does the society that we are now in push us to transform the church into an enterprise, and the ministers into CEOs, with offices that look like corporate suites? Or are the concerns and issues—whether social, economic or political—unrelated to the gospel, so that we only tend to find satisfaction in the so-called spiritual matters?...[Jesus] would never shy away from the social and religious issues of the people, much less purposely avoid getting into heated issues that affect the weak and powerless. In fact, the concerns and issues of our society and the general public in the post-1997 age are so enormous that people are crying out to church leaders for help. Yet, we continue to amuse ourselves within our own domains, tending to our own egos only.[61]

[61] "The Call to Unity That Will Prevail," *News & Views*, Summer 2008, 1–3.

This was quite a strong indictment, but my colleague Ralph had always been a person who spoke his mind plainly. Renske and I hoped and prayed that, with the new realities of the delayed democratization of Hong Kong and the new economic crisis, these Christians would heed Ralph's call, re-examine their churches, their lifestyle, and their mission and once again join their colleagues in rising to meet the critical needs of their people in the name of Christ.

Bibliography

Books

Arrigo, Linda, and Lynn Miles. *A Borrowed Voice: Taiwan Human Rights through International Networks, 1960-80*. Taipei: Hanyao Color Printing, 2008.

Cameron, Nigel. *An Illustrated History of Hong Kong*. Hong Kong: Oxford, 1991.

Chai, Chen Kang. *Taiwan Aborigines: A Genetic Study of Tribal Variations*. Cambridge: Harvard University Press, 1967.

Chen, Lung-Chu, and Harold D. Lasswell. *Formosa, China, and the United Nations*. New York: St. Martin's Press, 1967.

Club, Edmond. *20th Century China*. New York: Columbia University Press, 1964.

Cradock, Percy. *Experiences of China*. London, 1994.

De Jong, Gerald. *The Reformed Church in China 1842-1951*. Historical Series of the Reformed Church in America, no. 22. Grand Rapids: Eerdmans, 1992.

Dimbleby, Jonathan. *The Last Governor*. New York: Warner Books, 1997.

Embree, Bernard L.M. *A Dictionary of Southern Min*. Hong Kong: Hong Kong Language Institute, 1973.

Fenby, Johathan. *Chiang Kai-Shek: China's Generalissimo and the Nation He Lost*. New York: Carroll & Graf, 2003.

Goldsmith, Sydney. *The Jade Phoenix*. Lincoln, Nebraska: Universe Books, 2006.

Grichting, Wolfgang. *The Value System in Taiwan 1970*. Taipei: 1970.

History of Taiwan's Democratic Movement, The. Taipei: Tsunah Foundation, 2003.

Hsieh, Chiao-min. *Taiwan—Ilha Formosa, a Geography in Perspective*. Washington, D.C.: Catholic University Press, 1964.

Hughes, Richard. *Borrowed Place—Borrowed Time*. London: Andre Deutsch, 1968.

Karsen, Wendell. *A Book, A People, A Mission*. Hong Kong: Federal Publications, 1980.

———. *Christianity under the Microscope*. Hong Kong: Federal Publications, 1982.

———. "The Church and Education in Hong Kong," in Evans, Rob, and Tosh Arai, *The Church and Education in Asia*. Singapore: Christian Conference of Asia, 1980.

———. "The Concern of the Church for the Children of Hong Kong," in *The Child in Hong Kong*. Hong Kong: International Year of the Child Commission, 1980.

———. *The Lifestyle of Jesus*. Hong Kong, Federal Publications, 1981.

———. *Living Life Fully*. Hong Kong: Chinese Christian Literature Council, 1994.

———. *Man on a Mission*. Hong Kong: Chinese Christian Literature Council, 1994.

———. *Me and My World*. Hong Kong: Federal Publications, 1981.

———. *People of Faith*. Hong Kong: Federal Publications, 1982.

———. *People Who Knew God*. Hong Kong: Chinese Christian Literature Council, 1996.

Kerr, George H. *Formosa Betrayed*. Boston: Houghton Mifflin, 1965.

Koen, Ross Y. *The China Lobby in American Politics*. New York: Harper & Row, 1974.

Lederer, William. *A Nation of Sheep*. New York: Norton, 1961.

Lee, Martin and Wah, Szeto. *The Basic Law: Some Basic Flaws*. Hong Kong: Kasper, 1988.

Liu Xiaoyun. *A Partnership for Disorder: China, the United States, and Their Policies for the Postwar Disposition of the Japanese Empire, 1941-1945*. Cambridge: Cambridge University Press, 2002.

MacKay, George L. *From Far Formosa: The Island, its People and Missions.* Toronto: Revell, 1895.

Mendel, Douglas. *The Politics of Formosan Nationalism.* Los Angeles: Univ. of California Press, 1970.

Merwin, Wallace. *Adventure in Unity.* Grand Rapids: Eerdmans, 1974.

Patten, Christopher. *East and West: China, Power and the Future of Asia.* New York: Times Books, Random House, 1998.

Payne, Robert. *Chiang Kai-Shek.* New York: Weybright and Talley, 1969.

Ratmeyer, Una, ed. "Joyce Hughes Karsen," in *Hands, Hearts and Voices: Women who Followed God's Call.* New York: Reformed Church Press, 1995.

Report for the Year 1974, Hong Kong 1975: Hong Kong: Government Information Service, 1975.

Report for the Year 1984, Hong Kong 1985: Hong Kong: Government Information Service, 1985.

Riggs, Fred W. *Formosa under Chinese Nationalist Rule.* New York: Macmillan, 1952.

Seagrave, Sterling. *The Soong Dynasty.* New York: Harper & Row, 1986.

Segal, Gerald. *The Fate of Hong Kong.* London: Simon & Schuster, 1993.

Snow, Edgar. *Red Star over China.* Middlesex, England: Harmondsworth.

Stamps, Famous Paintings and the Good News. Hong Kong: Hong Kong Bible Society, 1982.

Swanson, Allen J. *Taiwan: Mainline versus Independent Church Growth, A Study in Contrasts.* Pasadena: Carey, 1970.

Taiwan Christian Year Book Statistics 1972. Taipei: Dixon Press, 1973.

Tong, Hollington K. *Christianity in Taiwan: A History.* Taipei: China Post, 1961.

Tsang, Steve. *Hong Kong: An Appointment with China.* London: I.B. Tauris, 1997.

Periodicals

Armbruster, William. "Jailings: A Warning to Dissidents." *Journal of Commerce*, June 11, 1976.

Bailey, J. Martin. "Taiwan: the Church, the Government and American Reality." *A.D.*, January 26, 1979.

Benes, Louis. "Are We for Righteousness, Freedom, and Peace?" *Church Herald*, January 28, 1972.

"Bush Confers Medal on Dalai Lama," *Seattle Times*, October 18, 2007.

Choi, Philemon. "Quotable Quotes: Mission in Hong Kong in the 90s." *News & Views* (Hong Kong Christian Council), December 1984.

Chou, Timothy. "Comments on the Position Paper." *News & Views* (Hong Kong Christian Council), March 1993.

"Cross of Courage in Taiwan." *Disciple*, September 19, 1982.

"Daya Bay Fiasco, The." *News & Views* (Hong Kong Christian Council), September 1986.

Ding, L.K. "Chairman's Remarks." Christian Industrial Committee Report of Annual General Meeting, *News & Views* (Hong Kong Christian Council), December 1981.

———."The Hong Kong Christian Industrial Committee's Imperatives in the '80s." *News & Views* (Hong Kong Christian Council), 1980.

Fung, Raymond. "The Corporation and the Contractor." *News & Views* (Hong Kong Christian Council), March 1980.

———. "Opinion Page." *News & Views* (Hong Kong Christian Council), December 1978.

Goldsmith, Sydney. "For China and Taiwan, a Welcome Thaw." *Christian Science Monitor*, November 25, 2008.

"HKCC's Response to the Constitutional Development of Hong Kong and the Interpretation of the Basic Law by the NPCSC." *News & Views* (Hong Kong Christian Council), Summer 2004.

"Hong Kong Christian Council: Response to the Consultation Paper Regarding Implementation of Article 23 of the Basic Law." *News & Views* (Hong Kong Christian Council), December 2002.

"Hong Kong Churches (1999 Statistics)." *News & Views* (Hong Kong Christian Council), Fall 2000.

"Hong Kong Mid-Decade Church Mission Consultation: A Pastoral Letter to All Christians in Hong Kong." *News & Views* (Hong Kong Christian Council), December 1994.

"Joint Conference of Christians on the Response to the Basic Law Position Paper." *News & Views* (Hong Kong Christian Council), September 1988.

Karsen, Wendell. "Beat Goes On, The" *Church Herald*, January 4, 1985.

———. "Boat Opportunities." Hong Kong: *YMCA Bulletin*, August 1979.

———. "Borrowed Place, Borrowed Time." *Church Herald*, December 1989.

———. "Child in Hong Kong, The." *Yu Chun Keung Memorial College Magazine*, No. 4, 1978-1979.

———. "China 1993: Impressions." *News & Views* (Hong Kong Christian Council), September 1993.

———. "Christian Schools in Hong Kong; Why Have Them?" *Happy Children Magazine*, January 1977.

———. "Christmas and the Consultation." *News & Views* (Hong Kong Christian Council), December 1980.

———. "Church Must Heed Wind of Change." *South China Morning Post,* March 31, 1980.

———. "Church, the Schools and 1997, The." *News & Views* (Hong Kong Christian Council), March 1983.

———. "Dawn of a New Day The." *Church Herald,* September 5, 1986.

———. "Dreams and Nightmares." *News & Views* (Hong Kong Christian Council), June 1993.

———. "Experience Overseas, An." September 1972 (unpub. ms.).

———. "First Impressions." *News & Views* (Hong Kong Christian Council), December 1990.

———. "Interns in Mission." *Church Herald,* August 8, 1980.

———. "Lest We Forget." Hong Kong: *South China Morning Post,* December 15, 1979.

———. "Let Them Eat Congee!" *News & Views* (Hong Kong Christian Council), March 1993.

———. "Lighting a Candle at Both Ends." *Church Herald,* December 1, 1972.

———. "Ministry to Vietnamese Refugees, A." *News & Views* (Hong Kong Christian Council), December 1979.

———. "Miracle of Mackay, The." *Church Herald,* February 2003.

———. "New Chapter in Acts, A." *Church Herald,* October 31, 1980.

———. "New Cry from Barmen! A." *Church Herald,* June 14, 1974.

———. "Nineteen Ninety-Seven...Again." *News & Views* (Hong Kong Christian Council), March 1983.

———. "No Room in the Inn." *News & Views* (Hong Kong Christian Council), December 1991.

———. "Rags and Riches." *News & Views* (Hong Kong Christian Council), September 1995.

———. "Rationale for a New Religious Studies Series for Senior Secondary Students, A." *Hong Kong Journal of Religious Education,* vol. 6, December 1994.

———. "Religious Broadcasting in Hong Kong." *RTHK Magazine: FM Fine Music,* October 1996.

———. "Sharing the Word in Hong Kong." *Church Herald,* July/August 1991.

———. "Summer with a Purpose." *Church Herald,* October 15, 1971.

———. "Summer with a Purpose." *News & Views* (Hong Kong Christian Council), June 1980.

———. "Taiwan after Nineteen Years." *News & Views* (Hong Kong Christian Council), June 1992.

———. "Thoughts on a Philosophy of Education from a Christian Perspective." *Christian Conference of Asia Christian Education Newsletter*, July 1978.

———. "Tourists or Pilgrims?" *St. John's Review*, vol. 50, no. 9, September, 1983.

———. "Vietnamese Refuge Situation in Hong Kong, The." *News & Views* (Hong Kong Christian Council), June 1983.

———. "Vietnamese Refugee Update." *News & Views* (Hong Kong Christian Council), March 1979.

———. "Vietnamese Refugee Update." *News & Views* (Hong Kong Christian Council), March 1991.

———. "Whither the Church in Hong Kong?" *News & Views* (Hong Kong Christian Council), March 1980.

King, Bob. "The Church under Fire." *Far Eastern Economic Review*, May 23, 1980.

Kurata, Phil. "The Sound of Silence." *Far Eastern Economic Review*, June 13, 1980.

Kwok, Nai-wang. "The Church and the Joint Declaration." *News & Views* (Hong Kong Christian Council), December 1984.

———. "Employment of a Lawyer, The." *News & Views* (Hong Kong Christian Council), June 1985.

———. "Hong Kong: A Modern City at Risk." *News & Views* (Hong Kong Christian Council), September 1994.

———. "Political Future of Hong Kong, The." *News & Views* (Hong Kong Christian Council), March 1994.

———. "Reflections on Ten Years as HKCC's General Secretary." *News & Views* (Hong Kong Christian Council), September 1988.

———. "Response of Hong Kong's Churches to 1997, The." *News & Views* (Hong Kong Christian Council), December 1992.

———. "Some Thoughts on the Future Prospect of Education in Hong Kong." *News & Views* (Hong Kong Christian Council), June 1984.

Lam, Philip. "Common Ground." *News & Views* (Hong Kong Christian Council), June 1984.

———. "Current Trends in Theological Thought Regarding Hong Kong and 1997." *News & Views* (Hong Kong Christian Council), December 1994.

Lee, Ching-chee. "Lift Up Thy Voice." *News & Views* (Hong Kong Christian Council), June 1997.

Lee, Peter. "The Limit Set by 1997." *News & Views* (Hong Kong Christian Council), March 1983.

Lee, Ralph. "The Call to Unity That Will Prevail." *News & Views* (Hong Kong Christian Council), Summer 2008.

Lo, Lung-kwong. "Christian Concerns." *News & Views* (Hong Kong Christian Council), December 1990.

———. "Tentative Search for a Standpoint in Envisaging the Future of Hong Kong, A." *News & Views* (Hong Kong Christian Council), March 1984.

Lutz, Hans. "Human Rights in Hong Kong after July 1, 1997." *News & Views* (Hong Kong Christian Council), June 1998.

———. "Hong Kong People's Council on Public Housing Policy, The." *News & Views* (Hong Kong Christian Council), June 1983.

———. "Justice in Yaumatei." *News & Views* (Hong Kong Christian Council), June 1979.

———. "Right of Abode Issue and the Churches, The." *News & Views* (Hong Kong Christian Council,) September 1999.

———. "White Paper Reforms—'Far too Late, Far too Few.'" *News & Views* (Hong Kong Christian Council), March 1988.

"Manifesto of the Protestant Churches in Hong Kong on Religious Freedom." *News & Views* (Hong Kong Christian Council), October 1984.

"Manifesto on the Mission of the Church in Hong Kong in the Nineties, A." *News & Views*, (Hong Kong Christian Council), December 1990.

"Mission Consultation of the Hong Kong Churches in the 21st Century: The Consultation Statement." *News & Views* (Hong Kong Christian Council), December 1999.

"Missionary Honored for Human Rights Work in Taiwan." *RCA Today*, February 2004.

Mortenson, Pete. "Mission Possible." *Holland Sentinel*, January 3, 2004.

Phipps, Gavin. "Turbulent Times Recalled." *Taipei Times*, December 13, 2003.

"Position Paper on the Future of Hong Kong." *News & Views* (Hong Kong Christian Council), December 1984.

Presbyterian Church in Taiwan. "Public Statement on Our National Fate." (December 29, 1971). *Hotline* (Reformed Church in America), April 10, 1974.

"Reaffirmation of the Role of the Hong Kong Church: a Position Paper of the 1991 Hong Kong Church Delegation to China, A." *News & Views* (Hong Kong Christian Council), December 1991.

So, Eric. "In Christ There Is No Boundary." *News & Views* (Hong Kong Christian Council), September 2003.

———. "Role of the Church in Constitutional Development, The." *News & Views* (Hong Kong Christian Council), Fall 2004.

"Statement of Opposition to the Selection Committee." *News & Views* (Hong Kong Christian Council), June 1996.

Thornberry, Milo and Judith. "Our Human Rights Activities in Taiwan." *International Friends and Taiwan's Democracy and Human Rights*, 2003.

Tsang, Iris Y.L. "The Ko Shan Mass Rally." *News & Views* (Hong Kong Christian Council), September 1986.

Tso Man-king. "A Response to Gov. Patten's Political Reforms." *News & Views* (Hong Kong Christian Council), December 1992.

———. "General Secretary's Column." *News & Views* (Hong Kong Christian Council), December 1990.

———. "General Secretary's Column." *News & Views* (Hong Kong Christian Council), September 1996.

———. "Maximizing Democracy in an Undemocratic World." *News & Views* (Hong Kong Christian Council), March 1998.

———. "One Year after the Handover," *News & Views* (Hong Kong Christian Council), June 1998.

———. "What Hong Kong Can Do for China." *News & Views* (Hong Kong Christian Council), December 1995.

"Uniting Together for a Future with Love." *News & Views* (Hong Kong Christian Council), June 1999.

"Universal Declaration of Human Rights' 60th Anniversary Makes 2008 an Opportunity for Passionate Church Advocacy, The." *Oikoumene*, December 7, 2007.

Van der Wees, Gerrit, and Mei-chin, eds. "A Journey of Remembrance and Appreciation: International Friends Return to Taiwan." *Taiwan Communique*, January 2004.

Wong, K.C. "What Does the Church Want in 1997?" *News & Views* (Hong Kong Christian Council), March 1983.

Worssam, Richard. "Church and State Debate, The." *News & Views* (Hong Kong Christian Council), December 1986.

———. "Reflections on the White Paper Reforms." *News & Views* (Hong Kong Christian Council), March 1988.

———. "To Vote or Not to Vote." *News & Views* (Hong Kong Christian Council), July 1987.

Wu, Rose. "Beginning of Beijing's Rule of Hong Kong, The." *Hong Kong Christian Institute Newsletter*, May, 2004.

———. "Democrats at the Crossroads." *Hong Kong Women Christian*

Council Newsletter, July 2006.
"'Yeh Sik-yin' Fights On," *Asiaweek*, no. 36, 1976.

Internet

"Cross-straits Relations" and "Direct Links." "Ma Jing-jeou." *Wikipedia*, September 9, 2009, http://en.wikipedia.org/wiki/Ma_Ying-jeou, September 10, 2009.

Enav, Peter. "Opposition wins Taiwan presidential vote." *Democratic Underground.com*, January 12, 2008, http://www.democraticu nderground.com/discuss/duboard.php?az=view_all&address =389x3046736, September 9, 2009.

"Freedom in the World—Hong Kong [China] (2008). *Freedom House*, http://www.freedomhouse.org/inc/content/pubs/fiw/inc_country_ detail.cfm?year=2008&country=75 27&pf, October 22, 2009.

"Hong Kong Legislative Election, 2000." *Wikipedia*, 20 October, 2009, http://en.wikipedia.org/wiki/Hong_Kong_legislative_election,_ 2000, October 22, 2009.

Keating, Jerome. "Freedom, Taiwan's Presbyterian Church, China, and Religion." *Jerome F. Keating's Writings*, December 5, 2007, http://zen.sandiego.edu:8080/Jerome/1196920787/index_html, September 9, 2009.

———. "The Presbyterian Church of Taiwan Goes on Record for Taiwan and the UN." *Jerome F. Keating's Writings*, Friday, December 28, 2007, http://zen.sandiego.edu:8080/Jerome/1196920787/index_html., September 10, 2009.

Lai, Jonathan. "Opposition sweep to victory in Taiwan." *CNN. Com*, January 12, 2008, http://www.cnn.com/2008/WORLD/asiapcf/01/ 12/taiwan.election/index.html, September 9, 2009.

"Politics of Hong Kong: Universal Suffrage." *Wikepedia*, 25 October, 2009, http://en.wikipedia.org/wiki/Politics_of_Hong_Kong, 25 October, 2009.

"Table—Taiwan 2007 Investments in China." *Reuters: India*, January 21, 2008, http://in.reuters.com/ article/idINTP26278020080121, September 10, 2009.

"Taiwan." *Wikipedia*, 10 September, 2008, http://en.wikipedia.org/wiki/ Taiwan, 10 September, 2009.

Documents

1983 Report by a Visiting Panel on the Hong Kong Education System. Hong

Kong: Hong Kong Government Press.

Annual Report, 25th Anniversary Commemorative Issue. Hong Kong: Wai Ji Christian Service, December, 2004.

"Appendix 12" *Hong Kong 1972.* Hong Kong: Government Information Office, 1972.

"Declaration on Human Rights by the Presbyterian Church in Taiwan." Taipei: Presbyterian Church in Taiwan, August 16, 1977.

Holkeboer, Tina. *Comments on a Study Document on the China Issue.* New York: Christian Action Commission, Reformed Church in America, 1961.

International Conference Program Manuel, Taipei: Presbyterian Church in Taiwan, 2007.

Introduction to Hong Kong Bill of Rights Ordinance, An. Hong Kong: Hong Kong Government, 1991.

Journey of Remembrance and Appreciation: International Friends and Taiwan's Democracy and Human Rights, A. Taipei: Taiwan Foundation for Democracy, Dec. 2003.

Karsen, Wendell. "Bringing People Together." (unpub. ms.) 1973.

———. "From Hudsonville to Hong Kong." (unpub. ms.) 1982.

———. "Where Have All the Revolutionaries Gone?" (unpub. ms.) 1975.

Lai, David. "The Christian Church in Taiwan: Past, Present and Future." (unpub. ms.).

"Our Appeal Concerning the Bible, the Church and the Nation," Taipei: Presbyterian Church in Taiwan, November 18, 1975.

"Report on a Consultation on the Mission of the Church in Asia Today." Taipei: Presbyterian Church in Taiwan, December 1978.

"Sino-British Joint Declaration on the Future of Hong Kong, The." *Hong Kong 1985*, Government Information Services.

Index

413

HISTORICAL SERIES
OF THE
REFORMED CHURCH IN AMERICA
Selected Books in Print
www.rca.org/series

This series was inaugurated by the General Synod of the Reformed Church in America acting through its Commission on History for the purpose of encouraging historical research and providing a medium wherein this knowledge may be shared both with the academic community and with the members of the denomination in order that a knowledge of the past may contribute to right action in the present. All have been published by the Wm. B. Eerdmans Publishing Company under the general editorship of Donald J. Bruggink.

The publication of a memoir creates a readily available primary source. It is important to let the voice of this source speak with all of its conviction, passion, and understanding of the events, dynamics, and the people of its time.

Gerald F. De Jong. *THE REFORMED CHURCH IN CHINA, 1842-1951.*

Beginning with an overview of the political context in which mission took place within the period, De Jong traces the efforts of the Reformed Church in America from its fi rst missionary, David Abeel, to the expulsion of American missionaries as the United States entered the Korean War. Sensitive to the cultural context, the missionaries hastened to train indigenous leadership. They also offered a Romanized script so that common people could become literate. In their determination to create one indigenous church in common with Presbyterians and the London Mission they offered to resign rather than organize a separate denomination. By the fourth decade of the twentieth century women were included in ordained church offices. Pp. xiii, 385, illustrations, index, 5½ x 8", 1992. $28.

Morrell F. Swart. *THE CALL OF AFRICA, The Reformed Church in America Mission in the Sub-Sahara, 1948-1998.*

Missionary biography and autobiography of Robert and Morrell Swart beginning with their service in the last days of the Anglo-Egyptian Sudan, then in the independent Sudan; their removal to Ethiopia when civil war broke out; and yet a third period of mission in Kenya. The mission in the Sudan took place primarily in Akobo and Pibor, in Ethiopia in Omo, and later in Alale,

Zambia, Nairobi, and Malawi. Told with vivacity and intimate personal insight into mission life. Pp. xvi, 536, illustrations, maps, glossary, index, 5½ x 8", 1998. $35.

Lewis R. Scudder III. *THE ARABIAN MISSION'S STORY: In Search of Abraham's Other Son.*

A scholarly history of the Arabian mission of the Reformed Church in America by a missionary to the Mideast, born of missionary parents who served that mission. Scudder presents a background of Middle Eastern mission, a history of the development of the Arab nations, and a history of the missions of the Reformed Church. The main areas of mission in education, evangelism, and medical work are chronicled, together with the areas of mission in Basrah, Bahrain, Kuwait, and Oman. Also included is a history and analysis of the varying relationship of the mission to the denomination and home churches. A magisterial history. Appendices include a timeline of the Arabian mission and missionary appointments and distribution by station. Pp. xxvii, 578, bibliography, index, 6 x 9". 1998. $39.

Eugene P. Heideman. *FROM MISSION TO CHURCH, The Reformed Church in America Mission to India.*

The story chronicles the period from the beginning of the mission under John Scudder in 1819 to 1987. Beginning with a focus on evangelism with the initiative in the hands of missionaries and mission societies, the organization of the Classis of Arcot puts the churches into relationship with the church in America. At the same time there is a growth of institutions in education and medicine. With the independence of India and the formation of the Church of South India in 1947, mission is seen as partnership, with the mission playing a supporting role to a self-determining church. The history is an honest portrayal of both failure and success. Pp. xix, 748, illustrations, maps, bibliography, index, 6 x9", 2001. $50.

Paul L. Armerding. *DOCTORS FOR THE KINGDOM, the work of the American Mission Hospital in the Kingdom of Saudi Arabia.*

Drawing upon original source materials from the missionary doctors and nurses involved, Armerding creates a compelling narrative of these men and women who witnessed to the love of Christ through the words and deeds of their medical mission. The book has been translated into Arabic and published by the King Abdulaziz Foundation in Riyadh, Saudi Arabia. The principal doctors cited in the book were featured in Saudi Aramco World, May/June 2004. Lavishly produced. Pp. 182, illustrations, glossary, gazetteer, maps, bibliography, 8½ x 10¼", hardcover, dust jacket. 2003. $39.

Donald J. Bruggink & Kim N. Baker. *BY GRACE ALONE, Stories of the Reformed Church in America Intended for the whole church.*

After a consideration of its European background in an introductory chapter "Reformed from What?," the story of the Dutch and their church in the New World from the early seventeenth century to the present is told with attention paid to relationships to Native and African Americans at home and missions abroad. The movement of the church across the continent and immigration to Canada, as well as its ecumenical involvement, leads to a challenge for the future. Additional personal interest stories in sidebars, as well as time lines and resources, accompany each chapter. Pp. ix, 222, illustrations, index, 8 1/2 x 11", 2004. $29.

LeRoy Koopman. *TAKING THE JESUS ROAD, The Ministry of the Reformed Church in America among Native Americans.*

The ministry began in the seventeenth century, carried on by pastors who ministered to their Dutch congregants and native Americans. After the Revolutionary War, ministry moved from pastors to missionaries, increasing in activity following the Civil War. Koopman does not shy away from multiple failed government policies in which the church was often complicit, but he also records the steadfast devotion of both missionaries and lay workers who sought to bring assistance, love, and the gospel to native Americans. Pp. xiv, 512, illustrations, appendices including pastors, administrators, other personnel, and native American pastors, index, 6 x 9", hardcover, dust jacket, 2005. $49.

Mary L. Kansfield. *LETTERS TO HAZEL, Ministry within the Woman's Board of Foreign Missions of the Reformed Church in America.*

A collection of letters, written by overseas missionaries in appreciation of Hazel Gnade, who shepherded them through New York on their departures and returns, inspired this history of the Woman's Board. Kansfield chronicles how a concern for women abroad precipitated a nineteenth century "feminism" that, in the cause of missions, took women out of their homes, gave them experience in organizational skills, fundraising and administration. Pp. xiii, 257, illustrations, appendices, bibliography, name index, subject index, 8½ x 11", 2004. $29.

Johan Stellingwerff and Robert P. Swierenga, editors. *IOWA LETTERS, Dutch Immigrants on the American Frontier.*

A collection of two hundred fifteen letters between settlers in Iowa and their family and friends in the Netherlands. Remarkable is the fact that the collection contains reciprocal letters covering a period of years. While few have heard of the Buddes and Wormsers, there are also letters between Hendrik Hospers, mayor of Pella and founder of Hospers, Iowa, and his father. Also unusual is that in contrast to the optimism of Hospers, there are the pessimistic letters of Andries N. Wormser, who complained that to succeed in America you had to "work like a German." Pp. xxvii, 701, illustrations, list of letters, bibliography, index, 6 x 9", hardcover, dust jacket. 2005. $49.

Karel Blei (translated by Allan J. Janssen). *THE NETHERLANDS REFORMED CHURCH, 1571-2005.*

Beginning with the church's formation in 1571 during the upheavals of the Reformation, Karel Blei's Netherlands Reformed Church follows a dynamic path through over 400 years of history, culminating in the landmark ecumenical union of 2004. Blei explores the many dimensions of the Netherlands Reformed Church's story including the famous splits of 1834 and 1886, the colorful and divisive theological camps, and the hopeful renewal of the church in the mid-twentieth century. Also included are incisive explorations of new confessions, church order, and liturgical renewal. Pp. xvi, 176, index, 6 x 9", 2006. $25.

Jacob E. Nyenhuis, ed. *A GOODLY HERITAGE, Essays in Honor of the Reverend Dr. Elton J. Bruins at Eighty.*

The festschrift honors Bruins for his career as pastor, college professor and administrator, and founder of the Van Raalte Institute. There is a biography of Bruins as well as a bibliography of his writings by Jacob Nyenhuis. The fifteen contributors are colleagues and former students, now professors and presidents. Essays, under three sections representing the primary areas of interests in Bruins career, include: "Singing God's Songs in a New Land: Congregational Song in the RCA and CRC" by Harry Boonstra; "Ancient Wisdom for Post-Modern Preaching: The Preacher as Pastor, Theologian, and Evangelist" by Timothy L. Brown; "Extra-Canonical Tests for Church Membership and Ministry" by Donald J. Bruggink; "Dr. Albertus Pieters, V.D.M.: Biblical Theologian" by Eugene Heideman;"Scripture and Tradition—A Reformed Perspective: Unity in Diversity—Continuity, Conflict, and Development" by I. John Hesselink; "'No One Has Ever Asked Me This Before': The Use of Oral History in Denominational History" by Lynn Winkels Japinga; "Richard Baxter: An English Fox in a Dutch Chicken Coop?" by Earl Wm. Kennedy; "A Decade of Hope and Despair: Mercersburg Theology's Impact on Two Reformed Denominations" by Gregg Mast; "A Century of Change and Adaptation in the First English-Speaking Congregation of the Christian Reformed Church in Holland, Michigan" by Jacob E. Nyenhuis; "What Happened to the Reformation? The Contentious Relationship between History and Religion" by J. Jeffery Tyler; "Civil War Correspondence of Benjamin Van Raalte during the Atlanta Campaign" by Jeanne M. Jacobson; "Albertus C. Van Raalte as a Businessman" by Robert P. Swierenga; "Will the

Circle Be Unbroken?: Essay on Hope College's Four Presidential Eras" by James C. Kennedy; "The Vexed Question: Hope College and Theological Education in the West" by Dennis N. Voskuil; "The Joint Archives of Holland: An Experiment in Cooperative Archival Preservation and Access" by Larry J. Wagenaar. Pp. lii, 412, illustrations, index, 6 x 9″, hardcover, dust jacket. 2007. $49.

Marvin D. Hoff. *CHINESE THEOLOGICAL EDUCATION.*

This book offers insight into the emergence of the Christian church after Mao's Cultural Revolution. Hoff's reports of his encounters with Chinese Christians, especially those involved in theological education, are a historic record of the church's growth--and growing freedom. Pp. xxii, 442, index, 6 x 9", hardcover, dustjacket, 6 x 9″, 2009. $49.

Jacob A. Nyenhuis, Robert P. Swierenga, and Lauren M. Berka, eds. *AUNT TENA, CALLED TO SERVE: Journals and Letters of Tena A. Huizenga, Missionary Nurse to Nigeria* (with essays by Harry Boonstra).

As Huizenga ministered to the people of Lupwe, Nigeria, she recorded her thoughts and feelings in a diary and in countless letters to family and friends. The extensive letters from Tena's brother Pete (Waste Management Inc.) offer insights into the Dutch Reformed subculture of Chicago's West Side. Pp. xxxii, 944, illustrations, bibliography, index, 6 x 9″, 2009. $49.

James Hart Brumm, ed. *TOOLS FOR UNDERSTANDING: Essays in Honor of Donald J. Bruggink*

The festschrift honors Bruggink for his career as pastor, seminary professor, liturgist, and general editor of the Historical Series. In Bruggink's words, "History as a tool for understanding" helps us understand who we are and where we are today. This volume celebrates his fifty-five years in ministry with the following essays: "From Dosker to Bruggink: Teaching Historical Theology at Western Theological Seminary," by Eugene P. Heideman; "Finding a Place at the Table," by George Brown, Jr.; "Francis Davis Beardlsee and the Leading Ladies of Holland, Michigan, 1912-1917," by Mary Kansfield; "The Story of the Archives of the Reformed Church in America," by Russell L. Gasero; "Bottoms Up—A Copy Editor's Perspective on the Historical Series of the Reformed Church in America," by Laurie Z. Baron; "Teacher of the Church: The Office of Professor of Theology in the Reformed Church in America," by Norman J. Kansfield; "John Henry Livingston as Professor of Theology," by John W. Coakley; "When East Meets West: Theological Education and the Unity of the Reformed Church in America," by Dennis N. Voskuil; "Human Diversity and Christianity Imagined: Past, Present, Eternal," by J. Jeffery Tyler; "The Ministry of the State: A Reformed Approach to Public Theology," by Allan J. Janssen; "Not Only for Necessity: The Problem of Aesthetics in Reformed Worship," by James Hart Brumm; and, "Calvin on the Atonement: A Reexamination," by

I. John Hesselink. Pp. 404, bibliography, index, hardcover, dust jacket, 6 x9", 2009. $32.50.

Eugene P. Heideman. THE PRACTICE OF PIETY: *The Theology of the Midwestern Reformed Church in America, 1866-1966.*

The title of this book reflects the concern of Dutch pietists to live a holy life. Attention is given to the nature of the piety that the immigrant members of the midwestern Reformed Church in America practiced *after* arriving in America. Reformed piety has its focus on God rather than on the development of one's self. The practice of piety among the Dutch Reformed immigrants was as concerned for theological integrity as for personal devotion to God. Thus, this book sets forth a history of theological thought in the midwestern RCA. That history provides insight into the ways in which the leaders sought to remain faithful to their theological and ethnic heritage while adjusting to the new demands of modernity and American culture. It was a time when the immigrants were coming to terms with their calling to live a life to the glory of God in the New World. Pp. 286, illustrations, bibliography, index, 6 x 9", 2009. $28.

Hans Krabbendam. *FREEDOM ON THE HORIZON: Dutch Immigration to America, 1840 to 1940.*

This book seeks to understand the settlement process of an unproblematic and relatively small immigrant group during the century when the door to America was wide open and Dutch emigration reached its apex. It takes a closer look at the transatlantic ties to explain the formation of a new Dutch-American identity. This is the English translation of Krabbendam's Dutch book, *Vrijheid in het verschiet. Nederlandse emigratie naar Amerika, 1840-1940,* adapted for an American audience. Pp. 432, illustrations, bibliography, index, 6 x 9", 2009. $32